P9-DMO-557

Women at Work

Leadership for the Next Century

Dayle M. Smith, Ph.D.

McLaren School of Business
University of San Francisco

Prentice Hall, Upper Saddle River, New Jersey 07458

VP/Editorial Director: James Boyd
Editor-in-Chief: Natalie Anderson
Managing Editor: Jennifer Glennon
Managing Editor: Melissa Steffens
Assistant Editor: Hersch Doby
Executive Marketing Manager: Michael Campbell
Director of Production: Michael Weinstein
Production Manager: Gail Steier de Acevedo
Production Coordinator: Maureen Wilson
Permissions Coordinator: Monica Stipanov
Manufacturing Buyer: Natacha St. Hill Moore
Senior Manufacturing Manager: Vincent Scelta
Cover Design: Bruce Kenselaar
Cover Art/Photo: Shoji Sato/Amana America, Inc.
Full Service Composition: Carlisle Publishers Services

Copyright © 2000 by Prentice-Hall, Inc.
Upper Saddle River, New Jersey 07458

All rights reserved. No part of this book may be reproduced, in any form or by any means, without written permission from the Publisher.

Library of Congress Cataloging-in-Publication Data
Smith, Dayle M.
    Women at work : leadership for the next century / by Dayle M. Smith
      p. cm.
    Includes bibliographical references and index.
    ISBN 0-13-095544-2
    1. Women—Employment—Case studies.   2. Women—Employment—Interviews.   I. Title.

  HD6052 .S63 2000
  331.4—dc21

                                  99-048926

Prentice-Hall International (UK) Limited, London
Prentice-Hall of Australia Pty. Limited, Sydney
Prentice-Hall Canada, Inc., Toronto
Prentice-Hall Hispanoamericana, S.A., Mexico
Prentice-Hall of India Private Limited, New Delhi
Prentice-Hall of Japan, Inc., Tokyo
Prentice-Hall (Singapore) Pte Ltd.
Editora Prentice-Hall do Brasil, Ltda., Rio de Janeiro

Printed in the United States of America

10 9 8 7 6 5 4

Dedicated with love to two future leaders — my beautiful daughters

Lauren Elizabeth and Madeleine Alexis Bell

Contents

Preface

Demographic reports, Labor Department projections, and glowing reports of women breaking into the top echelons of business paint a rosy picture for women and work. Women aiming for senior management positions will account for more than one-third of all net additions to the nation's workforce by the year 2005. Success stories and other anecdotal data suggest women are making significant inroads where once significant barriers prevented them from reaching their objectives. Organizations have jumped onto the diversity bandwagon, celebrating cultural, racial, and gender differences and valuing the efforts of the once disenfranchised. The twenty-first century, it has been argued, will focus on what a person can contribute, not what they look like, their gender, or their ethnic background.

So, why another book on women and barriers? Why another text offering advice and new perspectives? As organizations compete for the best and brightest of the workforce, women should be welcomed into a workplace of opportunity. Yet the reality is that the workplace still does not meet the needs of women at work. Although we can applaud the efforts that have been made, we still have a long way to go in decreasing the inequity that characterizes many work environments. This book looks ahead as we enter the twenty-first century, highlighting the challenges organizations and their employees face as well as offering new directions women can look to in managing their success. The text provides the reader with a foundation for exploring the glass ceiling, analyzing women's experiences in the workplace, identifying strategies for managing successful careers, and taking a look at the future. Women leaders from a variety of industries speak to these issues, offering a number of perspectives on how they "broke through" and found success. Their stories are varied; the lessons, often conflicting. Their impressions and perspectives are presented in all four sections of the book, culminating in a summary of lessons they want to share with readers.

The book is comprised of chapters written by a number of my colleagues around the country. Each of the contributing authors has developed an expertise in her particular area, and together we have formatted our respective chapters to provide, you, the reader, with an overview of the issue, an outline of relevant aspects to the topic, and a summary culminating with cases to explore and issues to debate. As colleagues, we mutually agreed not to strive for a monolithic single voice for the sake of an authorial consistency. Women have contributed the important insight to leadership theory that multiple voices should be heard and valued. That insight deserves to be practiced, not merely preached, in these pages. Therefore, some chapter authors take a more traditional scholarly tone; others are more journalistic in style; and still others use a managerial coaching voice. These alternative voices reflect who the authors are and what they want to communicate.

We believe that many of the topics covered in this book will give you a chance to reflect on your own experiences and critically evaluate the conclusions we draw. Oftentimes, we mean to provoke you and have you challenge basic assumptions as you think about the kind of leader you want to become and the type of work environment you can create.

The book is divided into four major sections. Part I provides readers with a foundation for exploring the issues outlined in the text. Chapter 1 explores the glass ceiling, analyzing how gender and equity issues have characterized the landscape. Chapters 2 and 3, coauthored by both genders, ask the central question: Does gender matter? They analyze real and perceived differences in communication and leadership style between men and women. Part II presents the challenges inherent in the workplace, describing men's and women's experiences in the work environment. Chapter 4 examines how gender roles develop and play out in the workplace. Chapter 5 looks beyond gender to see how race and ethnic background affect experiences at work. Chapter 6 explores the concept of dysempowerment, introducing readers to a chapter-long case that affords an understanding of a common experience of the "disenfranchised." Chapter 7 provides an analysis of common experiences related to gender and the law such as discrimination, affirmative action, and sexual harassment. Part III of the text, although it captures workplace experience, shifts focus a bit, to provide readers with a strategic orientation on how they can manage their career from different perspectives. Chapter 8 analyzes career paths and identifies effective ways of using networking and mentoring to manage the career path. Chapter 9 explores the challenges inherent in balancing work and family, offering perspectives in creating family-friendly environments and suggesting methods for balancing work/life. Chapter 10 examines the international dimension, exploring what happens to women working abroad. Chapter 11 captures another alternative path—entrepreneurial endeavors. In the last section of the book, Part IV, future directions for women at work are explored. Chapter 12 offers the reader a unique framework for considering the role of women as change agents in the organization. Chapter 13 concludes with a summary of new directions and explication of themes emerging from the many women leaders who were interviewed for this book.

Although the title of the book would suggest that women will lead organizations in the twenty-first century, the argument we are developing is that women can lead organizations. Their abilities and experiences add uniquely to the organizations of the year 2000 and beyond. The key to using this book is not to articulate a new gender for leadership, but rather to explore potential synergy in an equitable work environment. This book is not just for women, however. *Business Week,* in a classic cover story headlined with "White, Male and Worried," outlined the concerns men have in protecting their opportunities as awareness of gender and racial discrimination grows in corporate boardrooms. Yes, the playing field is more crowded now. Both men and women will have to compete for the opportunities. Yet, an equitable workplace will increase the skill set and expertise level of all those competing for jobs. And that competition will serve the organization and its members best. As we learn from each other, and bring the best from both genders to our organizations, we can create the kind of change that makes an organization exciting, competitive, and able to meet the needs of all of us—our businesses, our society, our families, and ourselves.

Dayle M. Smith
McLaren School of Business
University of San Francisco

About the Contributors

Gayle Baugh, Ph.D., received her doctorate in management from the University of Cincinnati in 1992. She taught for six years at Russell Sage College, a small women's college, and is currently assistant professor of management at the University of West Florida. Her research interests include career development and mentoring, as well as gender issues in the workplace. Her work has appeared in *Group and Organization Management, Journal of Business Ethics,* and the *Journal of Social Behavior and Personality.* She is a member of both the careers division and the gender and diversity in organizations division of the Academy of Management.

Laura L. Beauvais is associate professor of management at the University of Rhode Island. She is also an adjunct faculty member of the Labor Research Center and an affiliate member of the Women's Studies Advisory Committee. She received her doctorate from the University of Tennessee in industrial/organizational psychology. Beauvais teaches courses at the undergraduate, MBA, EMBA, and doctoral level in general management, organization behavior and theory, human resources management, leadership and motivation, and women in business and management. Her research interests include the study of work/professional/family roles among employees, self-concept–based motivation processes, union and organization commitment, and labor management cooperation. Her work has been published in the *Journal of Applied Psychology, Industrial and Labor Relations Review, Human Relations,* and the *Journal of Business and Psychology.*

Arthur H. Bell, Ph.D., holds his doctorate from Harvard University and teaches business communication at the University of San Francisco in the McLaren School of Business. He has worked extensively with the executive MBA program on communication needs including gender communication, managing crisis communication, and working with the media. Bell has authored more than 37 books and a number of articles in the area of communication particularly in business applications. Recent publications include *Management Communication* (Wiley, 1999), *Intercultural Business* (Barron's, 1999), *Effective Letters and Memos* (Barron's, 1997), *Extraviewing: The Art of Hiring* (Irwin, 1992), *Mastering the Meeting Maze* (Addison Wesley, 1992), and *Business Communication: Toward 2000* (Southwestern, 1996). His new research interests are taking him into the areas of communication architecture and knowledge management. He has a book forthcoming with McGraw-Hill, *A Framework for Knowledge Management.* In addition to teaching and writing, Bell is an active consultant with Fortune 500 companies, providing general consulting, organizational development assistance, and training on a variety of management communication needs.

Deborah Carr is assistant professor of sociology at The University of Michigan (Ann Arbor), and is a faculty associate at the Survey Research Center and Population Studies Center, both at the Institute for Social Research. Her interests span the areas of social stratification, aging and the life course, social psychology, and gender. Her research focuses on women's entrepreneurship, the causes and consequences of midlife career change, and the relationship between socioeconomic status and both physical and mental health across recent cohorts of men and women.

Ellen A. Fagenson-Eland is associate professor at George Mason University in the School of Management. She has presented more than 60 papers in academic journals and books and at national and international conferences, including the *Journal of Applied Psychology, Journal of Applied Behavioral Science, Journal of Organizational Behavior, Journal of Vocational Behavior, Journal of Business Venturing, Journal of Business Ethics, Journal of Management Development,* and *Organizational Dynamics,* among many others. She published *Women in Management: Trends, Issues and Challenges in Managerial Diversity* (Sage, 1993). Her work has received many honors and awards and been recognized in a number of media outlets including the *New York Times, Washington Post, USA Today, US News & World Report,* and *National Public Radio.* Her research and consulting are in the areas of organization development and change, mentoring, women in management, and career success. She has served as a reviewer for more than two dozen journals and is a multiterm member of the editorial review boards for the *Academy of Management Journal, Academy of Management Executive,* the *International Review of Women and Leadership,* and the *Journal of Occupational Behavior.* She is former chairperson of the Women in Management Division and the Careers Division Steering Committee of the Academy of Management. Fagenson-Eland received her Ph.D. from Princeton and was a post doctoral fellow at Columbia University.

Alissa Hauser, is the director of Resourceful Women, a San Francisco-based nonprofit, serving socially progressive women with wealth. In addition to managing marketing and development efforts at Resourceful Women, Hauser is actively involved in leading this organization in new directions that help empower women in their financial independence and in the choices they make for improving society. She holds an MBA in management and nonprofit administration and is on the board of a nonprofit arts organization. Hauser considers herself a fervent community activist and advocate, especially on behalf of women and girls.

Kathleen Kane, Ph.D., is associate professor at the McLaren School of Business at the University of San Francisco. Receiving her doctorate at Claremont in organizational behavior, Kane studied with Peter Drucker at the Drucker School of Management. Kane teaches courses in leadership, organizational dynamics, management, and cross-cultural awareness. She consults in the areas of organizational culture, vision and values, workforce empowerment, self-organizing systems, and diversity. Her research interests include Chinese management practices, dysempowerment in the workplace, feminine approaches to consulting, and traditional healing practices as tools for change in organizations. She is currently interested in promoting integration of people with disabilities into the mainstream workforce through both her research and consulting. Kane is the recipient of a number of honors and awards including best paper at conferences, and the very prestigious Ignation Faculty Award given to an outstanding faculty member each year by the University of San Francisco.

Marilyn Kern-Foxworth, Ph.D., is the Garth C. Reeves Sr. Endowed Chair in the department of journalism at Florida A&M University. She is the first African American to receive a Ph.D. with a concentration in advertising. In 1994, she penned the first book chronicling the history of blacks in advertising, *Aunt Jemima, Uncle Ben and Rastus: Blacks in Advertising, Yesterday, Today and Tomorrow* (Greenwood Press). She coedited with Shirley Biagi *Facing Difference: Race, Gender and Mass Media* (Pine Forge Press, 1997). She has contributed more than 65 publications in books, newspapers, academia, and trade and popular periodicals. In 1997, she was the only African American female of 12 selected as a Leadership Foundation Fellow—a program operated under the auspices of the International Women's Forum, an organization comprised of 3,000 of the most influential women in the world. Kern-Foxworth serves as president of the Association of Education for Journalism and Mass Communication. She lectures and presents seminars throughout the world on topics ranging from diversity, gender, mass media, and advertising to leadership.

Anne C. Levy, J.D., is an associate professor of law, public policy and business in the Eli Broad College of Business and Graduate School of Management at Michigan State University. She teaches courses in the legal environment of business for undergraduates and graduates in the MBA on-campus, the Program in Integrative Management, and the Executive MBA programs. Professor Levy received her B.A. and M.A. in English from Oakland University and her J.D. *cum laude* from Wayne State Law School. Before joining the faculty at Michigan State University, Professor Levy served as Judicial Law Clerk to The Honorable Patricia J. Boyle, Associate Justice of the Michigan Supreme Court. Prior to attending law school, she spent many years in the field of public relations. Professor Levy is the co-author of the book *Workplace Sexual Harassment* (Prentice Hall, 1996). She has also published a variety of articles on the subjects of employment discrimination in such publications as the *Albany Law Review,* the *Kansas Law Review,* and the *Wisconsin Law Review.* In addition, she is involved in a variety of legal seminars and training sessions for employees, managers, students, faculty, and administrators. As a consultant, Professor Levy aids attorneys and clients involved in employment discrimination cases in understanding the law and preparing evidence. She is also involved in the training and preparation of expert witnesses.

Kathleen M. Merrill received a J.D. and an MBA from the University of Michigan in 1998 and a B.S. from Cornell University in 1995. She is an associate at the law firm of Skadden, Arps, Slate, Meagher & Flom in Chicago, Illinois.

Debra E. Meyerson is professor of management at the Center for Gender in Organizations at the Graduate School of Management, Simmons College, and visiting associate professor in the department of industrial engineering, Stanford University. She received her Ph.D. in organizational behavioral from Stanford after receiving her BS and MS degrees from MIT. Meyerson has been on the faculty of the University of Michigan Business School, a visiting faculty member at Stanford and Berkeley Business Schools, and a visiting scholar at Stanford's Institute for Research on Women and Gender. She is currently writing a book, *Standing Out and Standing Up: How Being Different Can Make a Difference in Organizations,* to be published by Harvard Business School Press. For the past three years, she has been principle investigator of a cross-cultural research project sponsored by the Ford Foundation that has developed methods of change aimed at eradicating culturally based gender inequities in organizations. She has published several articles and book chapters related to the topics of organizational change and gender and race inequities and has written extensively about organizational culture and its impact on everyday life. Some of her most recent work examines experiences of silence and voice among black and white professional women. Meyerson has taught classes on gender and race in organizations, organizational change, cultural diversity, leadership, organizational behavior, and human resources. She currently serves on the advisory boards of Pacific Crest Outward Bound School and Aspen Institute's Initiative on Social Innovation through Business.

Kathleen Montgomery, Ph.D., is associate professor of organizations and management in the Anderson Graduate School of management at the University of California, Riverside. She received her Ph.D. in sociology from New York University. Montgomery teaches and conducts research on issues of workplace diversity and trust among organization members. Her current research projects include a study of the dynamics of the trust relationship between physician executives and lay executives in managed health care; and a related project examines ethical issues generated by new approaches to health care delivery. Her publications have appeared in *Organization Studies, Labor Law Journal, Human Resources Management Journal, Current Research on Occupations and Professions, Health Services Research, Social Science and Medicine,* the Academy of Management's Best Paper's Proceedings, and elsewhere.

Dayle M. Smith, Ph.D., is professor of management and organizational behavior at the McLaren School of Business at the University of San Francisco where she teaches leadership in the executive and MBA programs as well as undergraduate classes in global management, organizational behavior, and women in management. She holds her doctorate in organizational communication and organizational behavior from the University of Southern California. Smith has authored a number of articles and books on these topics including *Leadership* (NTC, 1997), *Corporate Teams* (NTC, 1997), *Motivating People* (Barron's, 1992; 1997), *Winning with Difficult People* (Barron's, 1992; 1996), and *Kincare and the American Corporation: Solving the Work-Family Dilemma* (Irwin, 1991). In addition to writing and teaching, Smith consults regularly for a number of organizations around the country in the areas of leadership, team development, and other human resource management related areas.

Peggy Takahashi was born in Los Angeles. She has an M.A. in Asian Studies, an M.B.A. and her Ph.D. in organizational behavior industrial relations from the University of California at Berkeley. Her research interests include spin-off formation in Japanese industry. She has thrived in a variety of cross-cultural work environments from managing Mexican farm labor to assisting a Tokyo art gallery owner with cross-cultural communications. She currently enjoys teaching comparative management and organizational dynamics at the University of San Francisco as an assistant professor of management.

Cynthia A. Thompson, Ph.D., is a professor in the management department at the Zicklin School of Business at Baruch College, City University of New York, where she teaches undergraduate, MBA, and honors MBA courses in organizational behavior and human resource management. In addition, she recently developed and taught a graduate-level seminar on work/family issues entitled Balancing Work, Family, and Life: Individual and Organization Perspectives. Her syllabus for the course has been published in *Integrating Work and Life: The Wharton Resource Guide* (1998). Thompson has been studying work/family issues since 1993 and has published her work in numerous scholarly and practitioner journals. For the past three years, she has been a member of the Wharton-Merck Work/Life Roundtable, a group of academics and practitioners devoted to developing ways to incorporate work/life issues into business school curricula and industry training programs. In addition, she has also worked as a senior consultant at Learn Tech Associates, a management training and executive development consulting firm. Thompson received her doctorate in industrial/organizational psychology from the University of Tennessee.

Emily Zaslow is a doctoral student in New York University's media ecology program. She received her MA in American studies from SUNY Buffalo and her BA from Oberlin College. Her current research interests include how girls find meaning and form subject-identities through the consumption of popular media designed for girls and through the production of alternative, girl-created media.

Acknowledgments

I am genuinely indebted to the many people who helped me in the development of this book. Their ideas, thoughts, comments, and critiques significantly contributed to the overall quality of the project.

For those who diligently reviewed the manuscript at different stages, thanks for your thoughtful commentary and suggestions: Afsaneh Nahavandi, Arizona State University West; Laura L. Beauvais, University of Rhode Island; Cynthia A. Thompson, Baruch University; Judith R. Gordon, Boston College; Jean Renshaw, Pepperdine University; Erika L. Hayes, Emory University; Audrey J. Murrell, University of Pittsburgh.

Thanks also go to Dean Gary Williams and Associate Dean Denis Neilson for their ongoing support for this project along with the many faculty colleagues and friends at the University of San Francisco and the McLaren School of Business.

The contributors from USF as well as institutions around the country helped make this book a reality. Their unique perspectives and areas of expertise enhanced the project significantly: Gayle Baugh, University of West Florida; Arthur Bell, University of San Francisco; Laura Beauvais, University of Rhode Island; Deborah Carr, University of Michigan; Ellen Fagenson-Eland, George Mason University; Alyssa Hauser, Resourceful Women; Kathleen Kane, University of San Francisco; Marilyn Kern-Foxworth, Florida A&M University; Anne Levy, Michigan State University; Kathleen Merrill, Skadden, Arps, Slate, Meagher & Flom Law Firm, Chicago, IL; Debra Myerson, Stanford University; Kathleen Montgomery, University of California, Irvine; Peggy Takahashi, University of San Francisco; Cynthia Thompson, CUNY; and Emily Zaslow, New York University.

I'd also like to acknowledge the contributions made by my Executive MBA students whose companies represent a cross section of "Who's Who" in Corporate America, along with the MBA and undergraduate students who, over the past couple of years, shared their experiences, hopes, and concerns related to gender and work issues. Their insights and questions were instrumental in the development of this book and the issues the book addresses.

Women at work in organizations throughout the country influenced me in too many ways to count. Their experiences, insights, progress, and challenges shaped my thinking, and their stories are well represented in the pages that follow. My friends and family, who provided so much support, also merit acknowledgment here. In particular, I want to thank the women I interviewed formally and informally for their many contributions: Lucy Alexander; Monica Blaizgis and Debbie Zarlin, Catalyst; Carol Atwood, TMG; Sara Barnes, IDG; Carol Bartz, Autodesk; Naima Beykpour, Meadow Daycare; Aviva Schiff Boedecker, Marin Community Foundation; Christy Burrell and Pamela McDougal, Belvedere-Tiburon Children's Center; Margaret Chan, Kaiser

Permanente; Betsy Z. Cohen, Jeffbanks; Heather Cowen-Speigle, Charles Schwab; Marian Fitzgerald; Margot Fraser, Birkenstock; Joan Fujii, Cost Plus World Markets, Inc.; Linda Glick, Levi Strauss & Co.; Dale Hardin, Charlotte Pepsi-Cola Bottlers; JoAnn Heffernan Heisen, Johnson & Johnson, Inc.; Cathy Hughes, Landmark Systems; Simone Jordan, Howlin' Pictures, Inc.; Gail Koff, Jacoby & Meyers; Nancy Keprtra, Lucky/ Sav-On, Inc.; Nori Kricensky, Lucas Learning, Limited; Ann Spector Lief, Spec's Music; Pamela Lopkar, QAD, Inc.; Laurie MacPherson; Bettye Martin Musham, Gear Holdings; Roberta Masson; Chris Miller, University of the Pacific Dental School; Christina Morgan, Hambrecht & Quist; Roberta Natelsen, Companion Health; Kim Polese, Marimba Inc.; Gail Omahana, Landau, Omahana & Tucker; Teri Randall; Rebecca Ravizza; Judy Rose, University of North Carolina, Charlotte; Allison Ross, Charles Schwab; Rhoda Schwartz; Hinda M. Smith, Johnson & Johnson Medical Inc.; Richard and Kathy Smith, Electroventure; Marci Syms, Syms Inc.; Mary Vella, Belvedere-Tiburon Library; Ellen Warren, Levy Warren Marketing Media; Suzanne Whittaker, New Iberia School District; and Lyn Zanville.

The editorial and production staff at Prentice Hall deserve a very special thanks for all their help, direction, and patience. A very grateful thanks go to Stephanie Johnson, who believed in the project and nurtured me through the stages from idea to manuscript. Others at Prentice Hall who helped in all the stages include the following: Natalie Anderson, Hersch Doby, Paul Feyen, Jennifer Glennon, Melissa Steffens, and Maureen Wilson; and at Carlisle Publishers Service: Terry Routley and the production team.

Special thanks also go to my wonderful research assistants, who, over the past two years, provided outstanding research assistance in the development and production stages of the book: Alyssa Hauser, Chris DeCaria, Vinita Natawijaya, and Christina Masson.

And last, but not least, thanks to my family for their patience, support, and unconditional love: my husband and best friend Art, our children Arthur, Lauren, and Madeleine.

PART

Foundations

This first part of the book is introductory in nature. Chapter 1, "The Glass Ceiling," reviews and surveys women's history and progress in the workplace. It is designed to introduce readers to the concept of the glass ceiling and begins with a brief history of women at work, discussing initial entry into the workplace providing a historical perspective. The concept of the glass ceiling is introduced along with an explication of the barriers women face charging ahead in their organizations. Studies and reports indicate how women have fared in terms of mobility and advancement over the past few decades. Issues of gender inequity are presented to introduce readers to many of the topics that will be developed in later chapters of the book, thereby laying a foundation from which to explore the experience of women at work. Chapters 2 and 3 examine the underlying causes for perceived gender differences. By focusing on men's and women's differing styles of communication and leadership, these two chapters address questions of appropriate behaviors to model, relevant paradigms to consider in choosing a leadership style, and the overall management of real and/or perceived gender differences. Taken together, these first three chapters provide the building blocks for understanding the landscape, developing a personal communication and leadership style, and making the day-to-day choices regarding how to present yourself and manage others in the organization.

Before reading ahead, we invite you to meet two women leaders who have given considerable thought to the issues outlined in these first three chapters.

Meet Betsy Z. Cohen

Betsy Z. Cohen, Chair and CEO, Jeff-Banks, Inc., Jefferson Bank and Jefferson Bank New Jersey

Corporate Headquarters, Philadelphia, PA

BACKGROUND

Betsy graduated from Bryn Mawr College with high honors; she received her J.D. from the University of Pennsylvania Law School. At age 25, she was law clerk to the Honorable John Biggs, chief judge of the U.S. Court of Appeals for the Third Circuit. One year later, she became the second female law professor on the East Coast (Supreme Court Justice Ruth Bader Ginsberg was the first) at Rutgers University Law School. Newly married, Betsy Zubrow Cohen began, with her husband, the first of the many entrepreneurial enterprises that would mark her career.

In her late 20s, with two preschoolers in tow, Betsy founded a shipping business in Hong Kong, a leasing company in Brazil, and a joint venture with a bank in Spain. At the same time, she and her husband cofounded Spector, Cohen, Gadon & Rosen, a Philadelphia law firm specializing in the representation of financial institutions and industry clients in complex real estate and financial matters. Although Betsy stopped practicing law in 1984, the firm now employs 75 people. In 1971, following the passage of the Bank Holding Act, Betsy translated her expertise in debt restructuring, recapitalization, and regulatory issues into a business where she provided consulting to national small and midsize banks and bank holding companies.

Her great love is building businesses. While she was still practicing law, just three weeks after her third child was born, Betsy went to Harrisburg to apply for a charter to found a new bank.

Harrisburg had not granted a new bank charter in 11 years, and did not have any applications. "I went home, wrote an application, raised $2 million in capital and went back to Harrisburg. The Undersecretary of Banking believed that, since a new bank had not been opened in Downingtown in 110 years, the area was overlooked and needed a bank. Nine months later, in August of 1974, Jefferson Bank was born in the basement of a local Downingtown hotel. I had a staff of two . . . one assistant and myself."

At age 32, Betsy Cohen was the only female bank CEO in the state of Pennsylvania. The bank grew. In October of 1974, the fledgling bank moved to a trailer in the parking lot of what was then Downingtown Center. Nearly 25 years later, the trailer is now Two Jefferson Bank Center—home of a branch office and the Bank's operations center, and the largest employer in Downingtown. Jefferson has grown to become the largest financial institution headquartered in Philadelphia: an $865-million-total-asset, FDIC-insured commercial bank with more than 30 locations in Chester, Delaware, Philadelphia, and Montgomery Counties. In 1992, Betsy founded its sister institution, Jefferson Bank New Jersey, which has six locations in southern New Jersey. In November of 1993, Betsy successfully orchestrated an initial public offering (IPO) of stock in

State Bancshares, Inc. (SBI), the holding company of both banks. The holding company name was later changed to JeffBanks, Inc. (JBI). Both banks are now wholly-owned subsidiaries of JBI, which is traded on the NASDAQ. Total assets approximate $1.6 billion. Betsy serves as Chair and CEO of the holding company and both subsidiary banks.

WHAT IS LEADERSHIP ABOUT?

"The essence of leadership is what I think of as 'empathetic enabling.' To take that apart, it means unlocking the potential in your employees—enabling them to perform leadership in other tasks, with an understanding both of their needs and needs relative to the vision of the corporation. I view leadership as a process, as opposed to a product, in an age in which knowledge is all that really counts in most organizations. Leadership is inspiring people to obtain the knowledge they need in their quest for better performance, but at the same time, giving them the process tools to carry on leadership at their own level. Leadership is also problem-solving: part of the process of teaching people to actualize their potential is teaching them to solve problems, and instilling in them the confidence that they can come to you for help in solving problems."

CHALLENGES TO WOMEN IN LEADERSHIP

"As a general principle, one should think perversely—which really means to take the problem or obstacle and pull out of the situation the things that can be of use to you, and discard the rest. Perhaps because I practice this principle, I don't remember situations

as challenges or obstacles, and as such have no recall for them. What others might consider barriers are, I hope, for me merely turning points."

BREAKING THE GLASS CEILING

"When people talk about glass ceilings, my belief is that glass ceilings arise from stereotypical perceptions that take time to erode. There are two elements or dynamics that are helping to break the glass ceiling. The first is the presence of more women in the corporate pipeline and on corporate boards. These people—women—are now in decision-making positions, and so their decisions may include the elevation of women within their organizations. The second dynamic is the strong influence being exerted by the adult and working daughters of men who are in top corporate positions. As a result of this familial pressure, the way these men view women is changing. Over time, I believe, these two factors will lead to great cracks in the glass."

COMMUNICATION AND MANAGEMENT STYLE

"Find your own voice. Really understand what it is that is motivating you to have a particular style. It is not always easy to identify that, but if you find it, you'll also find that even if it is not the most effective way, it will be your way. Having and exercising your own personal style helps to define your personality in other people's minds—it gives them a clearer picture of how to think about and remember you.

"It's important to find a particular management style that is a comfortable fit for you. If you are not by nature a warm and fuzzy person, then you'll need to have a more formal style of management. As a manager, I teach people to solve problems by doing problem solving with them. It's important to me to have a corporate culture that does not punish people for thinking creatively—even if the end result is less productive than for what we might have hoped. I also practice positive reinforcement and inclusiveness. I place real value on listening as well as talking.

"Once, when I was touring a major national company, a division head approached me as I was leaving. 'I know I shouldn't say this,' she said, 'but we were all so surprised to see that your style is so feminine.' They had apparently heard something about me prior to my visit—perhaps that I was a female CEO of a bank—and I wondered what she was expecting. A dark, pinstriped suit? (I tend to like soft, unconstructed fabrics.) No jewelry, or a string of pearls? (I enjoy wearing one-of-a-kind handcrafted brooches and necklaces.) A more serious demeanor? (I love to laugh.) The male model of a manager? (It's just not me!)

"That's my style. It might not be right for other people, but it's how I find I'm most comfortable and how I work best. But, as manager, you also have to recognize that there are appropriate responses to certain situations, and not confuse those necessary responses with your personal management style."

INTERVIEW WITH A LEADER

Meet Carol Bartz

Carol Bartz, CEO, Autodesk Corporate Headquarters, Marin County, California

Carol Bartz, heads up the fourth largest PC software company in the world. She was one of three women named to last year's Fortune 500, and at 49 years old is considered as noted by media reports, to be one of the "toughest, smartest and most decisive female bosses anywhere." In 1971, Bartz graduated from the University of Wisconsin, degree in computer science in hand. She spent her early days in banking to put herself through school, then sold computerized systems to banks, moving on to 3M, Digital Equipment, and then Sun Microsystems. Starting as a technical analyst, Carol moved around the organizations she worked in with stints in sales, marketing, and general management. Learning from these different areas was key. At a Women in Technology Conference, held in Santa Clara in 1998, Bartz shared her experience, telling the audience, "Pack your bags for a long trip. You never know where you are going. Take a variety of jobs and build a pyramid of knowledge. Don't be afraid to take lateral assignments if they will teach you something." As an example, Bartz left a high-paying field job at 3M for a lower paying assignment at 3M headquarters "to understand *corporate.*" She held a Senior level position at Sun when Autodesk called. "I wanted to explore the dynamics . . . the opportunity made me jump." Since taking over Autodesk in 1992, the company's net revenues have increased from $285 million to more than $618 million in

1998. The company employs more than 550 employees with research centers in 13 cities. Customers are found all over the world—Autodesk is the standard by which all CAD/CAM products are measured.

THOUGHTS ON LEADERSHIP

"Either you have it or you don't," says Carol. "You can fine tune it, grow it, expand it, but you need to be a person people naturally want to follow.... I've promoted several people who ended up ill suited to take leadership positions. Leaders have to create interest, excitement, vision, and the atmosphere so that people will want to follow. Vision and excitement is key even without the other stuff. You've not really tested your mettle as a leader until you have been through tough times, started making the tough choices, telling the bad news, and then getting an organization excited and moving again after bad times." Bartz points to the difficult times Autodesk went through with Release 13. The company had to hear from unhappy customers and critics. "Performance wasn't great.... it was a big blow to the company. ... I had to lead us through that cycle and get the company motivated again. Getting down to business, analyzing what we did wrong and having the confidence to know what was right. You can't get up if everybody is pointing fingers at sales and marketing or engineering. You have to step in and manage the situation. Release 14 is out and doing great."

CHALLENGES TO LEADERSHIP

When asked about challenges or barriers that women leaders face, Carol argues that "gender doesn't matter in

technology—ability and knowledge is key," but then admits "once you are there." Getting there is something Bartz focuses on, especially when it comes to mentoring young women. Programs at the company focus on high school kids and girls programs. For example, an Autodesk initiative developed to encourage women in math, science, and technology is a case in point. Called "Design Your Future," this program brings girls to headquarters and involves them in a demonstration worksite where they are creating model vehicles using Autodesk Lego-CAD design software. "Given a little attention, these young women just blossom," says Bartz. "There's so much talent sitting on our side of the gender. . . . but girls still shy away from such courses, victimized by the cultural message that science and math are boys-only courses and too tough for girls."

Facing challenges is a function of the career choices women make. "Draw your own road map, for yours is a unique journey. Nobody cares about your career the way you do. . . . Take chances. Jump out of your comfort zone. A little insecurity keeps you on your toes. . . . High tech has the challenge of pace. Technology waits for no one. . . . velocity is the word inside. . . . You don't have the luxury of certainty so [leadership] is about making 80 percent decisions."

BREAKING THE GLASS CEILING

"The glass ceiling does exist in technology but the greater barrier is the glass walls. Glass walls tend to put women in marketing and human resources. They have a hard time breaking through to the top. There are more start-ups by women because of this frustration, but also because of flexibility. And, pay equity means sometimes you have to go." To break through within the organization requires specific strategies. "I'm a fan of moving people through the organization, not a fan of one-to-one mentoring. People are responsible for learning from a variety of others; remembering bad bosses and good ones and what can be learned from each. We pay attention to our up and coming [women] and try to get them visibility and move them around the organization. Get them on task forces, where they will work with executives."

The key, she says, is to recognize that "we all have 40 years of work life. . . . Everything doesn't happen in the first 5 years. New MBAs can get so pumped up and then spend time being disappointed [when the jobs up the ladder don't come immediately]. Be patient. Take a couple of years with time for reflection."

MANAGEMENT AND COMMUNICATION STYLE

Carol gives the distinct sense that she is a no-nonsense get-to-the-bottom-line kind of person. She likened being a leader to dimensions of parenting. "Like being a mother, the skills of parents are skills of managing and then learning from the 'kids.'" Diverting from the parenting analogy, she does indicate that you need to be tough. "It is somewhat like 'eat your broccoli.' You need to do the things that the organization may not think is good for the process. It's not about winning popularity contests. No one style is good at any one time. Communication and control means the person does not have to be right all of the time. In our business, I give orders, but I do not have all the answers so I have to have an empowered organization to solve problems. At times, to blend is the key. 'Shared responsibility' at Autodesk makes the difference."

CHAPTER

The Glass Ceiling: An Introduction

Dayle M. Smith

[G]lass ceilings arise from stereotypical perceptions that take time to erode. There are two dynamics that are helping to break the glass ceiling. The first is the presence of more women in the corporate pipeline and on corporate boards ... women now in decision-making positions, may make decisions that include the elevation of women within their organizations. ... The second dynamic is the strong influence being exerted by the adult and working daughters of men who are in top corporate positions. As a result of this familial pressure, the way these men view women is changing. Over time, I believe, these two factors will lead to great cracks in the glass.

—BETSY Z. COHEN
CEO, Jefferson Bank

Chapter Overview

The topic of gender and the workplace has fascinated the popular press in the past decades. Hundreds of recent magazine and newspaper articles discuss breaking the glass ceiling, women and the 50-cent dollar, the queen bee syndrome, and how-to books by the dozen. This chapter establishes a foundation for exploring the many issues in the book related to gender, the workplace, leadership, and career management. A survey of women's history and progress in the workplace suggests that the perception of a glass ceiling, whether real or imagined, is impeding women at work. Other inequities plague their progress as well. Yet, as Betsy Cohen points out, breaking down these barriers is quite plausible. By creating awareness, identifying specific strategies, and changing the cultures of the organizations in which women work, we can inaugurate a new kind of leadership for the future—leadership in which talent and skill rather than gender, ethnicity, age, or other traditional factors determine success.

Learning Objectives

■ To understand the historical perspective of women in the workplace

■ To assess the impact of glass ceilings and other real or imagined barriers that affect women at work

■ To identify causes for gender inequity

Although the book will develop a number of the issues outlined in this chapter, we will begin with foundation questions: How far have women advanced into business leadership roles in the latter part of the twentieth century? What lies in store for women in the next century? Does a glass ceiling still exist, if it ever did? Do men and women have different leadership styles? Are there specific strategies that help women become leaders? While the chapter focuses on women in general, it should be acknowledged that the issues surrounding the study of women and leadership can be viewed in several subsets. Women of color, women with disabilities, and other diverse populations continue to experience their own versions of breaking the glass ceiling on their way to assuming leadership roles. Their story is told in detail in chapter 5.

A HISTORICAL PERSPECTIVE

Highly charged political filters often have obscured the precise facts of women's leadership roles throughout history. Too often, the true status of women leaders in former decades has either been exaggerated or downplayed to serve the needs of a rhetorical argument for women's place in society. In truth, women throughout the twentieth century have worked in virtually all sectors of government, business, the nonprofit community, and social movements. Many women have risen to leadership positions, although, their numbers were generally far lower than their percentage in the population.

The War Years

During the decades of World War I and World War II, women were drawn into business and government positions by circumstance as much as by choice. The early draft in World War I conscripted white American males into service; women and African Americans were left to make up the workforce.[1] Women proved essential in running businesses, working in the manufacturing and service sectors, and in keeping American business alive. However, when World War II ended and men returned to their jobs, women found themselves displaced from business and government positions. With many exceptions, of course, women tended to return to their more traditional roles: mothers, homemakers, schoolteachers, nurses, and secretaries.

From the 1950s to 1960s

The 1950s saw a surge in marriage and a renewed search, in earnest, for the suburban American dream. House, family, cars, vacations, and domestic luxuries were the dreams of the booming population. But the healthy economy during these years meant that a family could survive and even prosper on one income. The business boom ironically consigned many women to another kind of boom antithetical to business leadership roles—the baby boom that kept millions of women in the nursery rather than in the boardroom.

By the early 1960s, however, more severe economic conditions and the growing popularity of birth control measures sent women once more into the workforce. Family planning allowed women to exercise career choices and make decisions regarding

---

[1]Small units of African-American men served in the military but widespread segregation of units characterized the armed services during the first two world wars.

the types of contributions they might make to work and community. Many women found support, or at least less criticism, for opting not to marry or for postponing marriage and childbearing in pursuit of careers. The old maid and spinster stigma of earlier decades began to lose its currency. In the mid-1960s there was also an increase in the divorce rate. As single parents with few resources and/or skills to enter the workforce, women found what work they could, often at low levels and on part-time schedules.

The Women's Movement and Workforce Change

Largely in response to women's frustrations in their professional and domestic situations, the Women's Movement took powerful hold on the popular imagination and, eventually, on public policy beginning in the late 1960s. The Women's Movement in the United States was comprised of two groups (Carden, 1974; Freeman, 1975; Hole and Levine, 1971).[2] One group emerged from President Kennedy's establishment in 1961 of the Commission on the Status of Women. Later, a second more radical group, often referred to as the "women's liberation" segment, emerged in 1967 from civil rights activism and peace movements. Although their methods and political theories may have differed, both groups were significant in bringing attention to women's rights and increased opportunities for women in the workforce.

The Commission's 1963 report and committee publications documented discrimination against women in a way that legislators ignored only at their political peril. The Equal Employment Opportunity Commission (EEOC), whose task it was to enforce antidiscrimination law (primarily the 1964 Civil Rights Act), failed miserably at first in taking action against women's discrimination claims. This inaction galvanized women in their resolve to have sex discrimination complaints and other violations of the law taken seriously by the EEOC. The National Organization for Women (NOW) formed to put political and legal pressure on government agencies to eliminate legal and economic discrimination in the workplace (Carden, 1974; Freeman, 1975). These early feminists believed that (1) individuals should have equal opportunities regardless of gender; (2) the criteria used to evaluate job performance should be gender-blind; and (3) perceived differences in abilities and interests between genders is not innate but rather is the result of socialization and the general lack of equal opportunity for women (Jaegger, 1983).

The 1970s saw widespread public recognition of women's rights and their abilities to make significant contributions to the workplace and to society in general. As in earlier decades, economic necessity continued to change the make-up of the family and the work environment—and hence the professional options of women. Rising inflation and interest rates in the 1970s enforced the reality that living the American dream required dual incomes, especially in major urban centers. More and more women entered the workforce, this time in search not only of a job but of a career that paid well. Although

[2]The popular Women's Movement of the 1960s and 1970s was primarily engineered by and focused on white women. In 1974, the Combahee River Collective, a group of African American women, began talking about women of colors' place within feminism. By the late 1970s, popular feminist discourse began to discuss women of color and their glaring absence from the earlier feminist movement. For more information and perspectives on women of color and feminism, refer to Combahee River Collective, "A Black Feminist Statement"; Yamada, Mitsuye, "Asian Pacific American Women and Feminism;" and Moraga, Cherrie, "La Guera;" all reprinted in Moraga and Anzaldua (Eds.), *This Bridge Called My Back: Writings by Radical Women of Color* (New York: Kitchen Table Press, 1993).

women made up an increasing percentage of the workforce during the 1980s, they continued to be excluded from most leadership positions (as documented by Morrison et al., 1992). Even in occupations such as school teaching where women dominated the workforce, leadership roles (principal, headmaster, and department chair) were still given almost exclusively to men. Although women in increasing numbers were receiving university training as doctors and engineers, practitioners and companies in these fields were reluctant to hire even the most qualified women, especially to positions of authority and leadership. Business was particularly slow in opening doors for women. Harvard Business School, for example, did not admit the first woman to an entering class until 1974. The Air Force Academy, West Point, and other service academies did not admit women until 1976. More recently, the Virginia Military Institute and the Citadel continue their active and passive resistance to accepting women into their programs, even in the face of a U.S. Supreme Court mandate. In sum, opportunities for women in the workforce lagged far behind those for men throughout the past several decades of the twentieth century, at first by law (or lack of law) and later by convention and practice.

The Women's Movement, which spawned so many groups and professional organizations, continued to apply pressure to place laws on the books that prohibited discrimination against women and other protected groups (e.g., Title VII, which prohibits sex discrimination in employment). At the same time, the attitudes of the country were changing with regard to a woman's place. The baby boomers were growing up. They had lived the reality of dad-at-work and mom-at-home; they had a different set of expectations for themselves and their own children. Men and women by 1985 were going to college in approximately equal numbers. Women felt free to put off marriage and childbearing if they chose, with only an occasional grumble from parents expecting grandchildren. But even the most traditional parents recognized that security for their daughters lay more in defining a career and obtaining an education than in finding the right marriage partner.

Present Trends

This trend has accelerated to the present. Whether motivated by economic necessity or by choice, women are competing in the workforce for the same jobs and opportunities as men. The workforce of the twenty-first century not only accepts but depends on these contributions. In short, competitive businesses cannot afford to discriminate against women in the workplace. Finding and using talent in an era of global competition requires companies to seek the best workers, no matter what their demographic group. The costs to businesses that follow only traditional habits of "male-and-white" hiring include the following:

1. *Recruitment problems.* Companies who insist on fishing in a small pond inevitably come up short; the shrinking percentage of available white males should discourage companies from this narrow range of hiring. In addition, companies who hire too narrowly acquire a reputation among underrepresented groups for bias in the hiring process. When those companies need to reach out to a broader job candidate pool, they meet resistance and suspicion among the very workers they seek to attract.

2. ***Productivity loss.*** If the organization's culture is one in which opportunities for advancement for women and others are never realized, the understandable result is low morale, absenteeism, and a marked decline in productivity.
3. ***Opportunity cost losses.*** Failing to capitalize on diverse representation often has serious consequences for companies in terms of marketing to a variety of demographic groups, teamwork, workforce quality, overall employee commitment, and relations with clients and other stakeholders.

Thus, recognizing the inherent gains captured in the changing workforce is critical for business. As the baby bust generation enters the workforce, help-wanted opportunities will open to women as never before because of a shrinking labor pool. Department of Labor statistics for Workforce 2000 suggest that 80 percent of all new entrants to the workforce will be women and other minorities. But this dramatic increase in numbers for women does not ensure a concomitant rise in their status at work. Even in those organizations where women workers exceed the number of male workers, it is likely that women will still lag far behind men in obtaining leadership positions.[3]

Quantity of Labor versus Quality of Labor

This gap between the quantity of female labor versus the hierarchical quality of those positions has been explained by the fact that women have had a later start in making inroads into corporate and governmental levels of power. Only during the 1990s have the number of women at work approached the number of male workers; by 1991, almost half of the American workforce was composed of women (Morrison et al., 1992). However, they were not typically found at parity with male workers in leadership roles. Career development and climbing a corporate ladder takes time, often as much as 20 years according to some studies (Kotter, 1990). The questions for women and for American business at the end of the twentieth century are apparent: Is it just a question of time for women to rise naturally in organizations? Or does a woman's style of leadership explain the gap? Are there organizational barriers to women becoming leaders— in effect, a glass ceiling?

THE GLASS CEILING

The *glass ceiling* is the phrase used to describe phenomena that occur when invisible, artificial barriers prevent individuals from advancing within their own organizations despite their qualifications. Although the term originally was used to describe the point above which women managers were not allowed to rise, the term is used today in a broader sense to describe both obvious and subtle barriers, which prevent advancement opportunities for men and women from a wide variety of underrepresented groups. Qualified individuals hit the ceiling when they find they can't seem to rise any further

[3]For a more comprehensive discussion of the history of women in the workforce, see Householder Vanhorn, Susan, *Women, Work and Fertility, 1900–1986* (New York: New York University Press, 1988); Kessler-Harris, Alice, *Out to Work: A History of Wage Earning Women in the U.S.* (New York: Oxford University Press, 1982); Kessler-Harris, Alice, *Women Have Always Worked: A Historical Overview* (New York: The Feminist Press, 1981).

in the organization. The ceiling is painfully apparent to them—yet often invisible to executives at the top of the organization. Even when company executives recognize that there may indeed be unwritten or unspoken barriers for women and others, these leaders look to external or personal reasons to explain the dearth of women at the top (for example, "she just wouldn't be a good fit with our clientele" or "she had family responsibilities that would have interfered with the demands of the job").

In 1991, the president and Congress appointed 21 members to a Glass Ceiling Commission (as part of the Civil Rights Act of 1991). At this time, the Commission was charged with identifying barriers to advancement and identifying the strategies that would help propel women and minorities into the upper ranks of management in the private sector. Chair of the Commission, then, Secretary of Labor Lynn Martin wrote in *A Report on the Glass Ceiling Initiative*

> . . . Ample evidence has been gathered to show that minorities and women have made significant gains in entering the workforce. But there is also significant evidence from research conducted by universities, non-profit organizations, executive recruiters, and the Department of Labor that documents a dearth of minorities and women at management levels—the so-called "glass ceiling." (U.S. Department of Labor, 1991, pp. 1–2)

Glass Ceiling Commission: Final Recommendations

The Glass Ceiling Commission completed its work in January 1996. Secretary of Labor at the time, Robert Reich, noted the pervasiveness of the glass ceiling problem:

> The Glass Ceiling is not only a setback that affects two-thirds of the population, but a serious economic problem that takes a huge financial toll on American Business. Equity demands that we destroy the glass ceiling. Smart business demands it as well. . . . If America's businesses fully utilized the nation's human capital, they would be making a solid investment. . . . For real change to occur, bias and discrimination must be banished from the boardrooms and executive suites of corporate America. (U.S. Department of Labor, Office of Public Affairs, Glass Ceiling Commission, May 1995)

In the conclusion of the final report, the Commission issued 12 recommendations to businesses and government. These recommendations identified general strategies for eliminating the barriers that were keeping women and minorities from reaching their full potential in business, government, and society (see Figure 1-1).

What has been the result of these recommendations? Based on Department of Labor demographic and workforce predictions, the status of the glass ceiling in all its forms is cloudy. It seems certain that by the year 2005 women will make up at least 47 percent of the U.S. workforce. But will their percentage of leadership roles in business come anywhere close to their percentage in the workforce? Consider women as corporate officers in Fortune 500 companies.

Progress in the Fortune 500

Women's progress on corporate boards has been inconsistent. Catalyst, a nonprofit research and advisory organization for advancing women in business, reported a slowing

FIGURE 1-1 Summary of Glass Ceiling Commission Recommendations

BUSINESS INITIATIVES

Demonstrate CEO commitment

Eliminating the glass ceiling requires that the CEO communicate visible and continuing commitment to workforce diversity throughout the organization. The Commission recommends that all CEOs and boards of directors set companywide policies that actively promote diversity programs and policies that remove artificial barriers at every level.

Include diversity in all strategic business plans and hold line managers accountable for progress

Businesses customarily establish short- and long-term objectives and measure progress in key business areas. The Commission recommends that all corporations include in their strategic business plans efforts to achieve diversity both at the senior management level and throughout the workforce. Additionally, performance appraisals, compensation incentives and other evaluation measures must reflect a line manager's ability to set a high standard *and* demonstrate progress toward breaking the glass ceiling.

Use affirmative action as a tool

Affirmative action is the deliberate undertaking of positive steps to design and implement employment procedures that ensure the employment system provides equal opportunity to all. The Commission recommends that corporate America use affirmative action as a tool ensuring that all *qualified* individuals have equal access and opportunity to compete based on ability and merit.

Select, promote and retain qualified individuals

Traditional prerequisites and qualifications for senior management and board of director positions focus too narrowly on conventional sources and experiences. The Commission recommends that organizations expand their vision and seek candidates from noncustomary sources, backgrounds and experiences, and that the executive recruiting industry work with businesses to explore ways to expand the universe of qualified candidates.

Prepare minorities and women for senior positions

Too often, minorities and women find themselves channeled into staff positions that provide little access and visibility to corporate decision makers, and removed from strategic business decisions. The Commission recommends that organizations expand access to core areas of the business and to various developmental experiences, and establish formal mentoring programs that provide career guidance and support to prepare minorities and women for senior positions.

Educate the corporate ranks

Organizations cannot make members of society blind to differences in color, culture or gender, but they can demand and enforce merit-based practice and behavior internally. The Commission recommends that companies provide formal training at regular intervals on company time to sensitize and familiarize all employees about the strengths and challenges of gender, racial, ethnic and cultural differences.

Initiate work/life and family-friendly policies

Work/life and family-friendly policies, although they benefit all employees, are an important step in an organization's commitment to hiring, retaining and promoting both men and women. The Commission recommends that organizations adopt policies that recognize

FIGURE 1-1 Summary of Glass Ceiling Commission Recommendations—*continued*

and accommodate the balance between work and family responsibilities that impact the lifelong career paths of all employees.

Adopt high performance workplace practices

There is a positive relationship between corporate financial performance, productivity and the use of high performance workplace practices. The Commission recommends that all companies adopt high performance workplace practices, which fall under the categories of skills and information; participation, organization and partnership; and compensation, security and work environment.

GOVERNMENT INITIATIVES

Lead by example

Government at all levels must be a leader in the quest to make equal opportunity a reality for minorities and women. The Commission recommends that all government agencies, as employers, increase their efforts to eliminate internal glass ceilings by examining their practices for promoting qualified minorities and women to senior management and decision making positions.

Strengthen enforcement of antidiscrimination laws

Workplace discrimination presents a significant glass ceiling barrier for minorities and women. The Commission recommends that Federal enforcement agencies increase their efforts to enforce existing laws by expanding efforts to end

systemic discrimination and challenging multiple discrimination. The Commission also recommends evaluating effectiveness and efficiency and strengthening interagency coordination as a way of furthering the effort. Additionally, updating antidiscrimination regulations, strengthening and expanding corporate management reviews and improving the complaint processing system play major roles in ending discrimination. Finally, the Commission recommends making sure that enforcement agencies have adequate resources to enforce antidiscrimination laws.

Improve data collection

Accurate data on minorities and women can show where progress is or is not being made in breaking glass ceiling barriers. The Commission recommends that relevant government agencies revise the collection of data by refining existing data categories and improving the specificity of data collected. All government agencies that collect data must break it out by race and gender, and avoid double counting of minority women, in order to develop a clear picture of where minorities and women are in the workforce.

Increase disclosure of diversity data

Public disclosure of diversity data—specifically, data on the most senior positions—is an effective incentive to develop and maintain innovative, effective programs to break glass ceiling barriers. The Commission recommends that both the public and private sectors work toward increased public disclosure of diversity data.

Source: "A Solid Investment: Making Full Use of the Nation's Human Capital," Final Report of the Glass Ceiling Commission (November 1995).

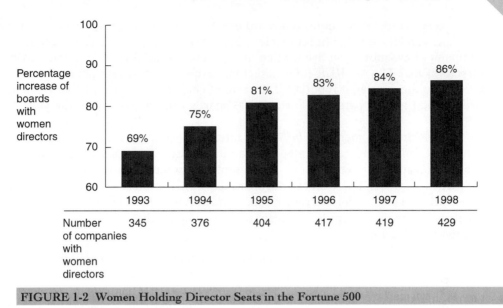

FIGURE 1-2 Women Holding Director Seats in the Fortune 500

Source: Catalyst (1998).

rate of increase in women's representation on corporate boards in their 1997 study (see Figure 1-2).

The 1998 Census of Women Board Directors of the Fortune 500 now demonstrates women are gaining ground. The report indicates that women hold 11.1 percent of board seats, 671 of the 6,064 board seats in the Fortune 500. In 1997 women represented 10.6 percent of total seats and only 8.3 percent in 1993, the year Catalyst began the census reports. Of the Fortune 500 companies, 429 report 1 or more women directors, and 188 of these have more than 1 woman director. No women are on the board for 71 companies.

In 1996, only 57 women held positions at the highest rank in these companies compared to 2,373 men. In this leadership group, the women represent just 2.4 percent of those who hold the title of chair, vice chair, president, chief executive officer, chief operating officer, or executive vice president. Sheila Wellington, president of Catalyst, notes that women tend to attain leadership roles and board positions in companies "that have looked to the women's market for a very long time." For example, the highest percentages of seats held by women tend to be in the soaps and/or cosmetics industries (29.9 percent in 1998), while the lowest percentage is found in the engineering and construction industries (6.7 percent) or mail, package, freight delivery (6.7 percent). When one assesses board committee leadership and membership, the findings do suggest some interesting results: "Women directors are least likely to chair executive committees (2 percent) and most likely to chair social/corporate responsibility committees (21 percent)" (Catalyst, 1998, p. 2). These results are consistent with 1997 reports regarding top management positions. When you consider corporate officers, only 20 percent of women in the Fortune 500 hold line positions (235 women in 1997), which are the positions that ultimately lead to the top executive positions. Of the almost 90 percent of corporate officers who are men, 41 percent (4,070) hold line positions. Thus, women represent just 5.3 percent of corporate officers.

The 1998 report does note an upward trend overall, given the number of seats held by women and the number of companies with one or more women directors. In fact, two companies have more than five women sitting on the board for the first time: Avon (six directors) and TIAA-CREF (nine directors). However, reaching gender parity may take some time. Catalyst reports, "If the rate of change over the past five years holds, [we predict] gender parity on Fortune 500 boards will be attained in the year 2064" (1998, p. 1).

Although all women may be underrepresented on corporate boards, women of color are even less well-represented compared to white women. Statistics from the 1998 census indicate that women of color represent 12.2 percent of women board directors (58), a little less than 1 percent of total board seats. Their representation in management may explain these findings. A recent report in *American Demographics* indicated that minority women represent 12.6 percent of women board directors, holding 1.4 percent of total board seats.

> Of the 57.8 million working women in the United States, 12 percent are African American. But this group only accounts for 7 percent of women managers. African American women who have made it into managerial positions make nearly as much as their white counterparts, but they may have had to work harder to get it. Thirty-nine percent of black women managers have college or advanced degrees, compared with 34 percent of white women managers. Twenty-two percent of African American women managers also have to contend with the difficulties of being a single mom, compared with 8 percent of their white counterparts (Klein, 1998).

Extending the Glass Ceiling Metaphor

Thus, the glass ceiling appears to be intact in the United States despite positive trends. The metaphor has even been elaborated and extended by some groups who experience its impact. In the case of people with disabilities, the glass ceiling may take the form of "cement steps" that literally and figuratively prevent wheelchair access. The question of advancement opportunity is secondary to just getting in the door. Lack of accommodation often prevents an organization from seeing the value a person with disabilities brings to the company. The barrier for others takes the form of "glass walls." Carol Bartz, CEO of Autodesk, in an interview with the author, described situations where the problem lies in not having the breadth of experience in a number of operations functions within the company. Before moving up, individuals must move horizontally within the organization, gathering operational or line responsibility. Ethnic minorities have described the ceiling, not of glass, but of "brick." In other words, not even the illusion of seeing through to the top is presented to these workers. Whatever the metaphor, the point here is that invisible and, in some cases, visible barriers impede the progress of women and others in many organizations.

WOMEN'S PERCEPTIONS OF BARRIERS

Women are crucially aware of the problem. In a survey of women managers, 90 percent felt that the glass ceiling is the most significant problem facing women managers. Eighty percent of these women said that women were underrepresented at the executive level. Women also know that pay inequities exist. In 1995, the U.S. Department of

Labor reported that women earned approximately 74 percent of what men earned for doing the same work. A report on salaries in *Working Woman* magazine (February, 1996) reported that women were earning 85 to 95 percent of what men earn in the same positions, depending on the profession. Although the ratio continues to increase (see, for example, Blau, Ferber, and Winkler, 1998), the barriers to pay equity may be attitudinally ingrained. Despite significant gains in reducing the wage gap over the past 25 years, the movement has slowed down during the 1990s.

The barriers to women's advancement, whether visible or invisible, represent the major issues that will be developed in this book. Viewed in a positive light, women seem to face fewer entry barriers today than ever before, thanks to educational gains, antidiscrimination practices, and a tight labor market. But viewed more closely, significant barriers to women's careers continue to arise as women workers drop out of corporate positions after a few years or fail to make the so-called "fast track" for future business leaders. The Catalyst organization, a nonprofit think tank, has studied the role of women in business for more than 30 years. The most significant barriers that may account for a lack of real mobility or a tendency for "fast trackers" to fall off the track are presented in Figure 1-3.

How have women responded when faced with these barriers? Some exit the corporation to begin their own businesses. More than 4.5 million women in America run

---

FIGURE 1-3 Barriers to Advancement and Mobility

- Preconceptions, stereotypes, and/or negative assumptions held by those in power about women and their abilities and/or commitment to careers.
- Perceptions regarding corporate culture and individual job fit.
- Lack of career and succession planning for women.
- Lack of line (revenue-generating) opportunities and other job experiences for women necessary to meet the needs of the organization.
- Assumptions regarding dual career couples.
- Assumptions regarding relocation/transfer decisions for women.
- Failure to hold managers accountable for giving challenging and visible assignments to women.
- Inadequate time in the pipeline for women.
- Lack of formal or informal mentoring for women; exclusion from networks where men have traditionally learned the ropes, and the unwritten rules for achieving success.
- Creation of ghettos where women tend to self-select into staff positions, or stay in areas traditionally made up of women.
- Inequitable appraisal and compensation systems for women.
- Failure to consider alternative ways to measure productivity for women (e.g., face time versus actual work produced).
- Limited support for work/family initiatives.
- Subtle and/or blatant discrimination and sexual harassment.

Source: Adapted from *Advancing Women in Business—A Catalyst Guide* (Jossey-Bass, 1998). San Francisco, CA.

their own businesses and it is predicted that nearly half of all small, entrepreneurial businesses will be owned by women by the year 2000 (Nelton, 1990). Although the flight of women to their own businesses may be heartening in some ways, it may tend to mask the precipitating problem within corporations of barriers to advancement, promotion, and pay equity. Entrepreneurial women may leave those problems behind—but they leave them behind to be faced by other women. Both internal and external barriers present obstacles to women who want to break the glass ceiling. Consider the following:

- Women managers tend to be clustered in the lower paying, entry levels of management, such as working supervisor and first-line supervisor.
- Women managers' pay lags behind men's at every level. When women move into an occupation in significant numbers, the occupation loses status and decreases in pay, and men tend to move out of it. Conversely, if an occupation loses status and reasons, women are more likely to be hired into it.
- Women are likely to hit the glass ceiling even at middle-level positions, according to a 1991 Labor Department study. (Carr-Ruffino, 1993, p. 12)

The Office of Federal Contract Compliance Programs yielded data, which showed other factors that blocked women's advancement. These factors included

1. A continued reliance on old-boy networks (relying on word-of-mouth referrals instead of recruiting and hiring from a diverse labor pool as legally required by Equal Employment Opportunity/Affirmative Action (EEO/AA) guidelines; using executive search firms without stressing the need for diversity in candidates).
2. Skewed appraisal and compensation systems (in which bonuses, perks, and favorable performance reviews were most frequently given to white men).
3. Lack of corporate responsibility or executive accountability (top executives made no effort to give high-visibility, career-enhancing assignments to women and minorities and failed to keep records of their informal hiring and promotion systems).

The executives, reportedly, were oblivious to the gender and racial disparities they were creating (cited in Maier, 1993, p. 289).

Stereotypes about women also hinder their ability to move ahead. A wealth of survey research and anecdotal data documents the negative preconceptions across industries of women's leadership skills (e.g., Cook, 1987; Fierman, 1990; McIntosh, 1988). Work and family conflicts may also contribute to career path halts for women. Many of those conflicts, of course, could have been eased by flexible organizations willing to help women (and men) better balance work/family issues and continue to pursue career advancement. Companies that espouse family-friendly policies in the form of corporate child care, flexible work arrangements, resource and referral support, vouchers, dependent care assistance plans, adherence to the Family and Medical Leave Act, and other programs may not in fact practice what they preach. Even in Working Mother's list of top family-friendly companies to work for, men and women in these organizations often indicate that a company is only as family friendly as an employee's immediate supervisor (Smith, 1991; 1992). Without company flexibility and support, it is often difficult for women (and men) to have both families and fast-track careers (see, for example Schwartz, 1989).

Breaking Through

Breaking the glass ceiling is a significant challenge for women, especially given that the gatekeepers and power brokers in companies tend to be white males. Mark Maier (1993), in his analysis of how to reduce sex stereotyping and promote egalitarian male–female relationships in management, indicates what must occur for women to advance: "Men . . . by virtue of their status as the gatekeepers and power brokers in organizations, possess, as a group, inherent structural advantages over women" (p. 290). Citing other research (Acker, 1990; Lorber, 1983; Schwartz and Rago, 1984) in the case, Maier continues, "And for women, as a group, to break the glass ceiling depends on the extent to which men are prepared to work with them as equals, offering them the same types of informal as well as formal supports that men have themselves historically relied on for advancement. For this to happen, men have to assume an active role as equal teammates and allies of women, which requires identifying compelling reasons to do so" (p. 290).

In other words, breaking the glass ceiling requires a major commitment on the part of organizations to take action in promoting and advancing people regardless of their gender or ethnicity—and for men to take an active role as partners in implementing this change. Some of this work has already begun with major corporate efforts in diversity training, recognition of the unique qualities of women's leadership styles, formal mentoring programs for women, and implementation of work/life human resource management strategies.

ORGANIZATIONAL GAINS AND LOSSES

The research on how women perceive the glass ceiling helps us identify how organizations lose talent as well as what can be gained by understanding the problems. Several studies exploring how women both succeed at and get derailed in their careers have been undertaken. These studies help identify factors that explain both gender inequity and contributors to success in breaking through. In *Breaking the Glass Ceiling,* researchers from the Center for Creative Leadership report on their three-year study of corporate executives and follow up studies on the Executive Women Project. In the Executive Women Project, researchers surveyed and interviewed 76 women at 25 Fortune 100 companies. Sixty-eight percent of the women were identified as general managers with line responsibility, and 25 were identified as one level below that of a general manager. In addition, 22 "savvy insiders" at 10 of these firms were also interviewed. These insiders were responsible for pinpointing managers for the top jobs within 10 of these same companies. Analysis of the data focused on what factors explained why these women were successful and, in cases where women were demoted, plateaued, fired, or forced to retire, the analysis focused on what caused career derailment. Although the study reports 22 factors, which could account for the success of women who were making inroads and moving up the corporate ladder, 6 key factors were highlighted as major reasons for this upward movement by women:

1. Help from above.
2. A track record of achievements.
3. Desire to succeed.
4. An ability to manage subordinates.

5. A willingness to take career risks.

6. An ability to be tough, decisive, and demanding.

In terms of the factors that led to derailment, the ones most often mentioned included (1) inability to adapt, (2) wanting too much (for oneself or for other women), and (3) performance problems (Morrison et al., 1992, pp. 24, 36). Interestingly, the researchers found that women had to have more advantages going for them in order to succeed than their male colleagues do.

In another landmark study, Deborah Swiss undertook a national survey of 325 professional women representing nearly every industry. Twenty-five percent of these women held senior management positions, whereas the other 75 percent were in middle or upper-middle management. Results indicated that, despite the success that most of these women experienced, the majority of them felt that gender inequity existed in their organizations. They identified such factors as rate of promotion, inequities in performance standards by which they were measured, inequity in compensation, lack of opportunity for taking risks, lack of access to business relationship-building, and lack of support from top management as the obstacles that held them back (Swiss, 1996). Inequity in compensation has, statistically, been improving with a narrowing of the wage gap. This reduction, however, has been felt primarily by the younger, well-educated entrants into the labor market where we would expect that it would be retained over time. For those women already in the middle of their career, the findings of the Swiss study are not surprising.

Despite the grim results, Swiss conducted in-depth interviews with 40 of these women and reported that the themes emerging from these interviews demonstrate "a new momentum among women to ensure themselves equal opportunity and career advancement" (p. 3). Women are becoming their own change agents and are instrumental in changing company cultures where barriers prevent movement up the ladder. Such cultural change can result in increased morale, job satisfaction, and respect for differences; synergy; and productivity.

Thus, although the glass ceiling lies intact, the potential for women to take an active role in change is clear. Those constituencies experiencing the fall out from glass ceiling barriers can partner with other men and women in recognizing the opportunity to change the workplace landscape. The reality just may be that the barriers are ready to come crashing down in the twenty-first century.

SUMMARY OF KEY POINTS

This chapter introduced a historical perspective on women's entry into the labor market. Political events, societal norms, economic necessity, and individual choice are among the reasons driving workforce decision making. Facing a number of barriers in getting ahead and achieving pay equity, women's concerns over discrimination in the workplace came to the forefront with the Commission on the Status of Women. Their 1963 report documenting this discrimination made clear how women were faring. Despite accomplishments stemming from Civil Rights Legislation, women continued to find themselves facing glass ceilings, glass walls, as well as brick ceilings or cement steps. Factors contributing to these invisible and visible barriers include stereotypes, work/family role conflict, lack of line opportunities and/or high visibility assignments, performance review standards, and others. The chapter also explored causes for the glass ceiling, areas of gender inequity, and the impact of felt barriers, whether real or perceived. Reports from women executives and upper level managers identify some of the factors contributing to breaking through the glass ceiling.

Discussion Questions

1. Do you feel that the glass ceiling is a thing of the past? Why or why not?
2. Why are high-visibility assignments and opportunities for taking career risks so essential to moving up the corporate ladder?
3. How do men experience barriers to advancement differently? Men and women of color? Younger versus older employees?
4. How can men be partners in changing the culture of organizations?

Issues to Debate

Two arguments clearly have been advanced regarding the glass ceiling debate. Discuss the following

- The existence of glass ceilings is perception not reality.
- Women bear the primary responsibility for advancing their own careers.

Case Analysis

Samantha Woods

Samantha Woods, a 26-year-old graduate of West Coast College, received an E-mail from her human resources director informing her of two openings in the marketing department of the firm. The firm was a mail-order retailer, offering gourmet foods and upscale kitchenware for cooks and professional chefs. E-mail messages, alerting others of job openings in the growing company, were a regular happening. No one really knew her all that well but she had done a good job in the customer service area of the firm and had experience managing five other people in her department.

Sam tended to be a bit quiet but had earned the respect of her supervisor and the five members of her team. They all worked hard creating new initiatives for improving customer service operations in the business. Sam liked working with her staff and had a friendly relationship with her boss. In fact, one of the reasons she liked her current job so well was that she could focus on providing others with helpful advice and training her team members on the value of excellent customer service. Sam did know that she eventually would want to move up in the organization and take on more responsibility. In spite of liking her current job and colleagues so well, she did realize that advancement opportunities in this position were somewhat limited.

She considered the two openings. One opening was for a support person to the marketing director. In some ways, the job sounded clerical in nature, although the position would offer a significant increase in her current salary and an opportunity to work with a number of people in the marketing area. This was clearly a side of the business in which she was interested. She had heard rumors that the company was having difficulty getting a person to stay in this job. Apparently this was the third time this year the marketing director was hiring for this staff position.

The other opening also was in marketing, although she would report to someone a bit lower on the organization chart. This position was a new one, created for the purpose of identifying other ways to expand the business. The base salary was lower than the other position but there was the possibility of a bonus should the person develop and implement an expansion strategy. It seemed that the company wasn't clear on how much effort they would put into supporting this new role. Sam asked her friend in the human resources department which position she should interview for. Her friend was surprised that she was even interested. "Why take a risk when you have a great job now. You are managing others and have a boss you get along with. Just keep working hard and you'll be rewarded; new openings come along all the time. I'd wait until someone recognizes what you can really do. Wait and see, Sam." ■

Questions

1. Would you take the friend's advice and wait and see? Why or why not?
2. If you were interested in one of the openings, which one would you choose and why? Which job offers more possibility for advancement?
3. If you choose to make a move, which position is more likely to experience a glass ceiling? Why?

References and Suggested Readings

Acker, J. (1990). Hierarchies, jobs, bodies: A theory of gendered organizations, *Gender and Society, 4*(2), 139–158.

Blau, F., Ferber, M., and Winkler, A. (1998). *The economics of women, men and work.* Upper Saddle River, NJ: Prentice Hall.

Carden, M. L. (1974). *The new feminist movement.* New York: Russell Sage.

Carr-Ruffino, N. (1993). *The promotable woman: Advancing through leadership skills.* Belmont, CA: Wadsworth.

Catalyst. (1998). *Advancing women in business: The Catalyst guide.* San Francisco: Jossey-Bass.

Catalyst. (1998). Census of Women Board Directors of the Fortune 500.

(www.catalystwomen.org/press/facts1998wbd.html.)

Catalyst. (1997). Census of women board directors of the Fortune 500. (http://www.ilr.cornell.edu/Glass Ceiling)

Catalyst. (1996). Census of Women Board Directors of the Fortune 500.

Cook, K. (1987, August 17). Why aren't women in top jobs? *USA Today,* 2D.

Fierman, J. (1990, July). Why women still don't hit the top. *Fortune,* 40.

Freeman, J. (1975). *The politics of women's liberation.* New York: David McCay.

Jaegger, A. (1983). *Feminist politics and human nature.* Brighton, Sussex, UK: Rowman & Allanheld.

Klein, M. (1998, February). Women's trip to the top. *American Demographics.*

Kotter, J. P. (1990). *A force for change: How leadership differs from management.* New York: Free Press.

Lorber, J. (1983). Trust, loyalty and the place of women in the informal organization of work. In J. Freeman (Ed.), *Women: A feminist perspective* (pp. 370–378). Palo Alto, CA: Mayfield.

Maier, M. (1993). The gender prism: Pedagogical foundations for reducing sex stereotyping and promoting egalitarian male–female relationships in management. *Journal of Management Education, 17*(3), 288–317.

McIntosh, P. (1988). White privilege and male privilege (working paper series #189). Wellesley, MA: Wellesley College, Center for Research on Women.

Morrison, A., et. al., and the Center for Creative Leadership. (1992). *Breaking the glass ceiling: Can women reach the top of America's largest corporations?* Reading, MA: Addison Wesley.

Nelton, S. (1990, July). A nearly fearless forecast. *Nations Business,* 45.

Schwartz, F. (1992). *Breaking with tradition: Women and work, the new facts of life.* New York: Warner Books.

Schwartz, F., and Rago, J. (1984). Beyond tokenism: Women as true corporate peers. In J. B. Ritchie and P. Thompson (Eds.), *Organization and people* (3rd ed., pp. 420–428). St. Paul, MN: West.

Smith, D. (1991). *Kincare and the American corporation: Solving the work–family dilemma.* Homewood, IL: Business-One, Irwin.

Smith, D. (1992, March). *Company benefits and policies only a start to becoming family friendly.* Employee Plan Benefit Review.

Swiss, D. (1996). *Women breaking through.* Princeton, NJ: Peterson's Pacesetter Books.

U.S. Department of Labor. (1991). A report on the Glass Ceiling Initiative. Washington, DC: Government Printing Office.

U.S. Department of Labor. (1995). The Glass Ceiling Commission, News Release. Washington, DC: Office of Public Affairs, USDL 95-483.

Working Woman, February 1996.

CHAPTER

Gender Communication

2

Dayle M. Smith and Arthur H. Bell

Patience and competence have proven insufficient to advance women to the top echelons of traditional business. More than two decades of research and study have convinced me that the problem lies not so much in discrimination (although it is part of the equation) but in the enduring nature of dysfunctional communication patterns and the stereotypes that accompany them.

—KATHLEEN REARDON
They Just Don't Get It, Do They?

Chapter Overview

In the 1990s, several influential books (including Deborah Tannen's *You Just Don't Understand Me* and *Talking from 9 to 5* and Kathleen Reardon's *They Just Don't Get It, Do They?*) have argued that many aspects of women's verbal and nonverbal communication in business are distinctly different from those of men. Moreover, these authors assert, women's communication habits sometimes put them at a disadvantage for leadership roles, promotion, recognition, and full participation in decision making in corporate life.

In an oversimplified view, these arguments have sometimes been reduced to a latter-day version of Henry Higgins' complaint of Eliza Doolittle in *My Fair Lady:* "If only a woman could be more like a man!" But Tannen, Reardon, and others are making a much more substantial and sophisticated point: Women's communication habits in business exist for *reasons;* to understand those reasons is to put ourselves, both men and women, in a better position to choose mutually advantageous communication behaviors. In short, women and men must learn to listen to themselves and to one another, then make adjustments in communication styles to achieve fairness, make the best use of human resources, and attain the organization's mission.

Some communication patterns used by women have been labeled "dysfunctional" (that is, disadvantageous to a woman's business welfare) because they apparently do not work well in a male-dominated, traditional, business environment. That judgment, however, must be qualified and even refuted in many sectors of the rapidly changing business world of the twenty-first century. In the following specific descriptions of language patterns used by women, we pause in each case to look forward to positive ways in which those patterns may be useful to emerging business environments of the present and future rather than simply dismissing them as dysfunctional for the business environments of the past.

Learning Objectives

■ To recognize differences in the ways men and women communicate in business

■ To evaluate reasons for these differences

■ To understand the present and potential contributions of women's communication patterns to emerging organizational realities

HOW WOMEN TEND TO COMMUNICATE IN BUSINESS

Let it be said at the outset that the following research observations are by no means applicable to all women in all business environments. No researcher of women's communication behaviors has claimed universality for results of quite limited studies. In the words of Deborah Tannen

> I do not imply that there is anything inherently male or female about particular ways of talking, nor to claim that every individual man or woman adheres to the pattern, but rather to observe that a larger percentage of women or men as a group talk in a particular way, or individual women and men are more likely to talk one way or the other.

At the same time, the science involved in this increasing body of research must be taken seriously. Studies have been carefully designed and critically analyzed. We draw from such work the conclusion that all business people, men and women, should reevaluate their own communication styles and habits in the light of tentative findings from dozens of prominent linguists and social scientists.

Simply put, women do appear to communicate differently than men. Most often, women have been judged negatively for this difference, and they have been instructed to "talk the talk" (i.e., the male talk) if they want to rise to positions of power in modern organizations. This effort to re-create women's communication patterns after men's image ignores the very real contributions women bring to the organization by their ways of communicating. As a counterbalance, then, to the pervasive argument that women should learn to speak more like men, we offer brief interpretations of the first 20 gender communication differences in the following pages. These interpretations are intended to point out the value of women's communication patterns without alteration or repair for progressive organizations. We leave the last 10 gender communication differences in this list for your own analysis, discussion, and interpretation.

CHARACTERISTICS ASSOCIATED WITH GENDER COMMUNICATION PATTERNS

1. Men are less likely to ask for information or directions in a public situation that would reveal their lack of knowledge.

> MAN: I don't need to stop at the gas station for directions. I can find the right street.
> WOMAN: Why not stop and ask? It will save us time.

This aspect of women's communication patterns can prove useful to what Peter Senge has called "the learning organization." The reluctance, out of pride or embarrassment, of independent men in organizations to seek assistance is counterproductive. The language habits of one gender can be extended throughout a company's culture as a way of encouraging openness to new information, reliance on team members as resources, and a constant readiness to ask questions and learn.

2. Women perceive the question "What would you like to do?" as an invitation for discussion and negotiation. Men perceive the same question as the stimulus to a direct answer.

> WOMAN: We have to arrange a holiday party. What would you like to do? [expecting conversation about past holiday parties, anecdotes, personal memories, and possibility thinking]
> MAN: We have to arrange a holiday party. What would you like to do? [expecting places and times to be named]

Women's willingness to delay decision making pending a multidimensional review of background information and influences is sometimes portrayed as a deficit, especially for would-be leaders in an organization. But that same communication tendency can be valued as an antidote to a company's tendency to rush to judgment or to ignore relevant input. In modern organizations, leaders are cast less and less in the role of quick-draw decision maker and more in the role of seer, with wisdom and patience implied. The gender communication approach of women in this case fits well with the requirements of leadership in complex organizations where instant answers and quick decisions are often impossible or foolhardy.

3. Women misunderstand men's ultimatums as serious threats rather than one more negotiation strategy.

> MAN: This is nonnegotiable. [a bluff]
> WOMAN: Fine, then. Have it your way. [doesn't recognize the bluff but accepts it as reality]

This may be a way of saying that women tend to attach meanings to words and assume that male speakers do as well. In the preceding example, the woman speaker believes that the man knows what *nonnegotiable* means and chooses the word to describe his position. If the man knows that his position is negotiable but chooses to dissemble by his choice of language, are we to praise his strategy and recommend it to both genders? In George Orwell's fine phrase, "The great enemy of language is insincerity." Women have much to teach about integrity in saying what you mean and meaning what you say.

4. In decision making, women are more likely to downplay their certainty; men are more likely to downplay their doubts.

WOMAN: In making this recommendation, I think I've covered every base—at least the ones I'm aware of.

MAN: I make this recommendation with complete confidence.

This language tendency on the part of women is sometimes portrayed as an inability to stand strong as a confident decision maker. It can just as easily be regarded, and valued, as a reluctance to bluff the audience or to assume a posture of confidence that is neither felt by the speaker nor supported by the facts. The world may be seeking totems in which to believe, and men, by certain communication styles, may play into and even manipulate that need to believe in the all-confident, single-minded leader. Women, by their language of qualification and demural as exemplified here, may be providing a necessary caution against the common need for simple answers and the attraction to overclaim and totemism in our leaders. In effect, women are telling it like it is: "I'm not entirely sure about my conclusions and I'm not going to pretend that I am, simply for the sake of your feelings of security. To do so would be to lie to you and, ultimately, to empower myself at your expense."

5. Women tend to lead by making suggestions and explaining those suggestions in terms of the good of the group. Men are more likely to lead by giving orders, with explanations (if any) based on rationales related to project goals.

WOMAN: Let's proceed by dividing into teams. I think we can make the most of our individual talents by working with one another in smaller groups.

MAN: We're going to break into teams to divide up the workload and meet our deadlines.

Modern organizations obviously require both approaches to planning and decision making as a way of dealing with rapidly changing business conditions. For every occasion when the team must be nourished and encouraged there is also a circumstance when someone has to make decisions without consensus (or relying on a trust bond that already exists with the group). The important point is that neither style is dysfunctional; both can be useful to serve different, but complementary goals within the organization.

6. Women tend to apologize even when they have done nothing wrong. Men tend to avoid apologies as signs of weakness or concession.

WOMAN: I'm sorry, but I have to read you this e-mail that just arrived from the boss.

MAN: Listen up. The boss just sent this E-mail....

In this case, only the most rigid literalist would interpret the phrase "I'm sorry" as an apology for a mistake of some kind. These words instead reveal a recognition that the listener's feelings may be bruised by the ensuing message and that the speaker is not unaware of or unresponsive to those probable feelings. In this way, the communication patterns of women tend to insert emotional buffers into sometimes turbulent business life. What may on the surface appear to be unjustified apologizing is at a deeper level an effort to humanize the organization and its processes.

7. Women tend to accept blame as a way of smoothing awkward situations. Men tend to ignore blame or place it elsewhere.

WOMAN: I probably didn't welcome our Japanese visitors exactly as I should have, but I tried to be gracious and sincere.

MAN: I met the Japanese visitors at the airport. Next time someone should tell me how and when to bow.

Business makes much of the need for accountability except when it comes to the language patterns illustrated here. The woman is clearly accepting responsibility both for what went right and what went wrong in her efforts to greet the Japanese visitors. The male, by contrast, seeks to avoid personal accountability and instead to pass it on to a vague someone in the organization. When less-than-ideal situations in business occur, the language habits of women in this case may be more likely to depict accurately the accountability involved rather than the language of denial more typically used by men.

8. Women tend to temper criticism with positive buffers. Men tend to give criticism directly.

WOMAN: You're doing a great job on this report, but you may want to look at page eight one more time. At least see what you think.

MAN: Fix page eight, then let me reread your report one final time before we send it upstairs.

As remarked earlier in item 6, an awareness of the listener's feelings is not a bad thing in business relationships. In the preceding woman's example, the speaker tries to preserve the relationship while changing the behavior. The man seems more willing to sacrifice relationship for the sake of behavior. That choice leads directly in many organizations to low morale and excessive turnover.

9. Women tend to insert unnecessary and unwarranted "thank-you's" in conversations. Men may avoid thanks altogether as a sign of weakness.

WOMAN: Thanks anyway, but I don't think I want to trade my parking place with Jack.

MAN: No, I don't want to trade for Jack's spot.

The facade of thanks is only part of a complex architecture of courtesy and civility that women may tend to prefer in their work environment. By contrast, the apparent tone of the male response portrays the workplace as an arena for confrontation, victory, and defeat.

10. Women tend to ask "What do you think?" to build consensus. Men often perceive that question to be a sign of incompetence and lack of confidence.

WOMAN: What do you think about dividing my office into a work area and a waiting room?

MAN (thinks): It's her office. Can't she decide what she wants to do?

Let's asssume that the woman in the example knows full well what she wants to do with her office. Her question is not a solicitation of permission (although the man takes it as such) nor a sign that she cannot make her own decisions. Instead, it is another demonstration of the tendency we have already observed in women's language patterns to gather input and weigh opinions before acting.

11. Women tend to mix business talk with talk about their personal lives, and expect other women to do so as well. Men mix business talk with banter about sports, politics, or jokes (many of them sexually oriented).

WOMAN: I don't mind traveling to Cincinnati, but it will mean finding overnight care for our baby.

MAN: If I do go to Cincinnati, I'm taking an afternoon off to see a ball game. That's the least they can do!

This question is worth asking: Which gender is expressing most truthfully and accurately the impact business responsibilities have on personal life? Let's assume that the man in this case is a father and that he, no less than the working woman, has family matters to consider in arranging his business trip. He too must make provision for children, pets, and so forth. The point is that the woman tends to discuss with others how business duties influence her personal life. The man is reluctant to do so. Businesses probably operate best knowing what problems, obstacles, and burdens their employees face. By knowing an employee's circumstances, the business can often adapt for win–win solutions.

12. Women feel that men aren't direct enough in telling them what they (women) are doing right. Men feel that women aren't direct enough in telling them what they (men) are doing wrong.

WOMAN: I don't know how you feel about my work. [a request for more feedback]

MAN: Just tell me right out if you don't like what I'm doing. [a request to avoid mixed signals]

Feedback is a business buzzword that refuses to fade, perhaps because of its importance to employee motivation and quality management. Both genders in the previous examples are asking for feedback, but the woman's way of asking is more in line with the 360-degree-feedback systems currently used for performance evaluations at all levels of organizations. The woman's communication pattern allows for the possibility that feedback may include both positive and negative aspects—that is, the full range of evaluation. The man's communication pattern closes the door to praise almost entirely and solicits only negative feedback.

13. Women bring up complaints and troubles with one another as a means of arousing sympathy and building rapport. Men bring up problems only when they want to hear solutions.

WOMAN: Our problem at home is just not enough time with each other. I get home just as Bob is leaving for his job.

MAN: We haven't been out to a show for months. Where do you find babysitters?

Sharing problems is not just an effort to build rapport and arouse sympathy. In addition, and perhaps more crucially, it is an effort to understand pain and thereby alleviate it. The woman's communication pattern assumes that the group may have insights and experiences that will enlighten the nature of the pain or frustration at hand. The man's communication pattern is cynical about the ability of the surrounding group to provide in-depth perspectives or resonant ideas. The woman wants help in understanding the problem; the man wants help in postponing the problem.

14. Women's humor tends to be self-mocking. Men's humor tends to be razzing, teasing, and mock-hostile attacking.

WOMAN: So I said in my charming way, "You forgot to plug it in."
MAN: So I said, "Do you notice anything strange about that cord lying on the floor?"

Freud wrote at length about "tendency humor"—our effort to disguise in humor what we really want to communicate. The tendency of the preceding male communication pattern is to emphasize the person's stupidity or foolishness. By contrast, the speaker is seen as smarter, less foolish, and more powerful. The woman defuses this potential powerplay in her softened version of the verbal transaction. She recognizes that the person may feel insecure about the incident, and so consciously lowers her own status by self-mocking humor to avoid a breakdown in the relationship.

15. Women tend to give directions in indirect ways, a technique that may be perceived as confusing, less confident, or manipulative by men.

WOMAN: You can handle this account any way you want, but taking him out to lunch might be a possibility. Or meet in his office. Whatever you think. Lunch, though, might be the way to go.
MAN (thinks): Is she telling me to take him to lunch or not? Is she setting me up for an "I-told-you-so" if I don't do it her way?

Organizations make much of empowerment, which can only take place when the decision maker-in-training has options. In the previous example, the woman's communication pattern is conducive to empowerment because it leaves the decision maker free to choose, learn, and grow within a range of options. The man's apparent preference for a command style of management may allow short-term efficiencies but does not encourage empowerment, with its allied benefits of creativity, motivation, and loyalty.

16. When women and men gather in a group, women tend to change their communication styles to adapt to the presence of the men. Women also practice "silent applause" by smiling often, agreeing with others often, and giving more nonverbal signals of attentiveness than do men.

Audience adaptation is highly recommended in virtually all communication guides and textbooks, including this one. The apparent fact that women change their communication behaviors based on their audience is not a sign of uncertainty, deceit, or weakness. Instead, it is an effort to relate successfully.

17. Women in positions of authority tend to be less accustomed to dealing with conflict and attack than are men.

WOMAN: Why is everyone mad at me?
MAN: This is an unpopular decision, but I've got to make it.

As consensus builders, women respond quickly and vocally to signs that consensus is failing and that relationships are threatened. For generations, this behavior has been interpreted negatively— "If you can't stand the heat, get out of the kitchen." It can just as well be interpreted positively for the purposes of modern organizations. Women are no less tough for recognizing and responding to conflict and attack. It can be argued that they are all the more tough for their willingness to confront and deal with those forces rather than stoically ignoring them.

18. Women tend to be referred to more often by their first name than are men, sometimes as a sign of less respect for women and sometimes as a sign of presumed familiarity or intimacy.

MAN: Get Smith, Underwood, Connors, and Jill to go along with you on the sales call.

The use of the woman's first name in the example can also be interpreted as recognition on the part of the male speaker that Jill is different from the gray functionaries Smith, Underwood, and Connors. Perhaps because Jill has expressed herself in more disclosing and honest communication patterns, she has risen to personhood and personality in the eyes of the speaker. He works with Smith, Underwood, and Connors, but he feels that he knows Jill. This is all said not to justify the unwarranted use of women's first names in an otherwise formal business environment, but instead to point out one additional reason why men so frequently opt to use women's first names and men's last names.

19. Men tend to be uncomfortable with female peers, particularly those who may threaten their power.
     Working for a woman is uncomfortable for many men primarily because they misunderstand the communication patterns explained throughout this chapter. The male employee may complain about the woman boss's seeming lack of direct supervision and mixed messages, whereas the woman boss may simultaneously complain about the male employee's unwillingness to discuss problems openly, to work well with others, and to share ideas.

20. Men tend to perceive a group of women in conversation as wasting time or hatching a plot of some kind. Women tend to perceive a group of men in conversation as doing business or working out power relations through bonding and joking.
     These impressions from a distance of gender-exclusive groups tell volumes about the core misunderstandings between male and female co-workers. Interestingly, women credit men with more positive activities (doing business, working out relations even in the midst of joking) than is the reverse case (wasting time, hatching a plot). Are women more sanguine about their co-workers generally than are men? Do women tend to see the corporate glass half full and men to see it as half empty? These questions grow directly out of research into women's communication patterns but cannot be answered by such linguistic research alone.
     We offer the remaining 10 gender communication patterns without interpretative commentary to allow for your own analysis, discussion, and insight.

21. Women tend to avoid direct confrontation about offensive behavior. Men tend to take stronger, more immediate stands in relation to stimuli they dislike.

WOMAN (shocked): I . . . I guess that's one way to look at it.
     MAN (shocked): Wait a minute. You're way off base.

22. Women tend to react to disappointment by describing personal feelings. Men tend to react to disappointment by appealing to standards of fair play or by placing blame.

WOMAN: I felt absolutely sick when I found out I wasn't promoted.
     MAN: It's a raw deal. I deserved that promotion.

23. Women tend to express self-doubt and to seek affirmation after exhibiting assertive behavior. Men tend to repeat and reinforce their assertive behavior.

WOMAN: I don't want to make a big deal out of this, but you've got to get here right when the office opens. Are we OK on this?
MAN: We open at 8:30 and that's when you have to arrive. Not 8:35 or 8:40. I don't want to have this conversation again.

24. Men tend to interrupt women much more often than women interrupt men.

25. Men tend to usurp ideas stated by women and claim them as their own. Women tend to allow this process to take place without protest.

26. Men tend to be more fearful of losing to a woman than to another man. Women tend to be more fearful of losing to another woman than to a man.

WOMAN: I was up against Frank and Barbara for the two new job openings. I half expected to lose to Frank, but it killed me when they chose Barbara over me!
MAN: I was up against Frank and Barbara for the two new job openings. I understand why they chose Frank, but Barbara? What an insult to me!

27. Men tend to adopt patronizing behaviors in the presence of women. Women, in turn, may respond by finding father figures, knights, big brothers, and confessors in men.

MAN: I appreciate your interest in this project, Susan, but you've got enough on your plate. We'll let you know if we need more input.
WOMAN (as if to a father): If that's the way you want it, it's fine with me. I've really enjoyed the times we've worked together.

28. Men value conversation primarily for information. Women value talk primarily for interaction.

MAN: What do you have going tomorrow? [seeks a point by point list of items]
WOMAN: What do you have going tomorrow? [seeks conversation about job pressures, personalities, exciting or problematic situations]

29. Women appear to seek permission or validation by the addition of tag questions to their assertions. Men omit such tag questions or rephrase them as assertive challenges.

WOMAN: Let's hold the executive committee meeting in Conference Room A, OK?
MAN: Conference Room C is obviously the best place for the executive committee meeting.

30. Women use softer voice volume to encourage persuasion and approval. Men use louder voice volume to attract attention and maintain control.

WOMAN (softly): I've read the files on the Henderson account and I'm wondering if....
MAN (loudly): But have you read the files? I have! Here's what we need to do....

Kathleen Reardon sums up the conclusions of many researchers and social observers in the area of gender communication: "Patience and competence have proven insufficient to advance women to the top echelons of traditional business. More than two decades of research and study have convinced me that the problem lies not so much in discrimination (although it is part of the equation) but in the enduring nature of dysfunctional communication patterns and the stereotypes that accompany them."

In this chapter we are obviously arguing against the blanket indictment of women's communication patterns as dysfunctional. Instead, we have endeavored to counterbalance such judgments by showing how the communication patterns of women align well with a new order of organizations in a new century, even though those patterns may not have served women well in previous centuries.

SUMMARY OF KEY POINTS

Researchers have observed differences in the ways men and women communicate in business. These differences may help to account for the barriers to leadership roles and promotion experienced by many women in male-dominated organizations. The solutions to exclusion of women from some positions of corporate power lie not so much in teaching women to "talk like men" but instead in valuing women's communication tendencies for what they contribute to emerging organizational cultures.

Discussion Questions

1. Do you agree or disagree with the communication differences discussed in this chapter? What have you observed from your business or academic experience in the ways men and women communicate?
2. If women were to change their communication patterns to match those of men, what would women gain in terms of promotability and other areas of increased responsibility and power? What would they lose?
3. For business purposes, what can men learn from women's communication patterns? What can women learn from men?

Issue to Debate

Should company training programs conduct mandatory sessions that attempt to teach women how to adapt their communication patterns more adequately to a business world dominated by male communication patterns?

The Hiring Dilemma at NKG Securities, Inc.

Case Analysis

NKG Securities, Inc. is a brokerage for a wide range of financial instruments—including stocks, bonds, mutual funds, and real estate investments—for a large clientele of individual and institutional investors. To meet the rapidly growing demand for its services, NKG recently began an aggressive hiring program to attract what the company called "fast-track managers"—highly motivated, well-educated candidates who could be expected to assume leadership positions at NKG within the next few years.

Bob Newman, executive vice president at NKG, attended most of the hiring interviews for these prized candidates. Company interviewers looked to Bob for his approval as a major factor in deciding whether to hire the candidate at hand.

Over a period of weeks, however, it became painfully obvious to company interviewers that Bob rarely gave his approval to any female candidate. In fact, of the last 18 interviews (9 men and 9 women), Bob had given his influential approval to 6 candidates for further screening—and all 6 were men. This apparent imbalance did not escape the attention of Linda Alvarez, director of personnel for the company. She stopped by to talk with Bob in his office.

LINDA: I've noticed, Bob, that we seem to be giving the nod to only male candidates in the hiring process. Aren't there any qualified women? I thought the resumes of several of the women were excellent.

BOB: I thought so too, Linda, until I talked with them in the interview. It's hard to describe, but they just seem ... well, weak when compared to the male candidates. Don't get me wrong. I'm not biased against women.

LINDA: I'm not accusing you of bias. I just want to understand what you find objectionable in the women candidates you've interviewed.

BOB: It's subtle, I guess. You have to listen to how they talk and then imagine how their way of presenting themselves and their ideas will work out in meetings and client contacts. I just have the feeling that they won't be able to hold their own. We're trying to hire tough, hard-chargers who can drive home their points, make decisions quickly, and stick to their guns. The women just seemed kind of timid compared to the men. But I guess we should bring in a few women to avoid legal hassles. ■

Questions

1. Taking the role of Linda, decide how you will continue this conversation with Bob regarding the place of women in the organization.
2. What assumptions is Bob making about communication in company meetings? About communication preferences of company clients?
3. Once you have determined how Linda should proceed in this conversation, decide what arguments Bob probably will use to counter Linda's points. What is your own judgment about who is right in this dispute?

References and Suggested Readings

Aries, E. (1996). *Men and women in interaction.* New York: Harper Collins.

Biagi, S. et al. (1997). *Facing difference: Race, gender, and mass media.* New York: Wadsworth.

Kalbfleisch, P., and Cody, M. J. (Eds.). (1995). *Gender, power, and communication in human relationships.* New York: Erlbaum.

Reardon, K. (1996). *They just don't get it, do they?* Boston: Little, Brown.

Romaine, S. (1998). *Communicating gender.* New York: Erlbaum.

Stewart, L. P., et al. (1995). *Communication and gender.* Englewood Cliff, NJ: Prentice-Hall.

Tannen, D. (1991). *You just don't understand me.* New York: Ballantine.

Tannen, D. (1994). *Gender and discourse.* New York: Oxford University Press.

Tannen, D. (1995). *Talking from 9 to 5.* New York: Avon.

Tingley, J. B. (1994). *Genderflex: Men and women speaking each other's language at work.* New York: AMACOM.

Wood, J. T. (1996). *Gendered lives: Communication, gender, and culture.* New York: Wadsworth.

CHAPTER

Gender and Leadership Style

Dayle M. Smith

Act like an owner, not the hired hand.
> —CRISTINA MORGAN
> *Managing Director, Investment Banking,*
> *Hambrecht & Quist*

*Leadership is about motivating other people; it's more of a team effort approach,
sharing the work and not feeling that I have to do it all. . . . Putting customers first,
getting the message out and recognizing the contributions of other people.*
> —ANN SPECTOR LEIF
> *President and CEO, Spec's Music*

It's easier to ask forgiveness than it is to get permission.
> —REAR ADMIRAL GRACE MURRAY HOPPER

Chapter Overview

Given the small number of senior executive women, we lack thoroughgoing studies analyzing the differences between male and female leaders. However, studies on what constitutes effective leadership abound along with prescriptions for what good leaders do. The overarching question remains: Does gender make a difference in leadership styles? This chapter explores these style differences with an eye toward alternative paradigms for leading and managing in the twenty-first century. Presented here are a number of avenues for women to consider in developing their own leadership style and adapting that style to particular business circumstances.

Learning Objectives

■ To identify different perspectives for leading and managing

■ To understand why women may lead differently

■ To analyze how leadership needs in organizations have changed

■ To consider new approaches to leading in organizations

LEADERSHIP STYLE: DOES GENDER MAKE A DIFFERENCE?

Many women become justly frustrated that a double standard seems to exist for women when it comes to choosing leaders for business. The very same behaviors exhibited by male versus female leaders are often evaluated differently. For example, given the same behavior, men are termed assertive; women, aggressive. Men are flexible; women, wishy-washy. Men wearing wedding bands are stable and dependable; women wearing wedding bands pose the risk of having babies and leaving the organization in the lurch. Men are detail-oriented; women are obsessive. Men are sensitive; women, emotional. And the list goes on. Women who take on male behaviors are labeled unfeminine. When men take on more feminine behaviors, they are labeled good listeners and receptive to change. Underlying this double standard is the tacit recognition that leadership behaviors pull from the strengths of both men and women.

But why do women get the short end of the stick? A recent study conducted by the Center for Creative Leadership reaches a disturbing conclusion: "In order to approach the highest levels, women are expected to have more strengths and fewer faults than their male counterparts" (Morrison, 1992). The executive women surveyed by Catalyst in 1996 reported that "developing a style with which male managers are comfortable" was "critical." Deborah Swiss's 1996 study of 325 women executives demonstrated that a majority of the women (68 percent) believed that they were being held to a higher standard than their male counterparts. Women on the rise in corporate America, therefore, face a crucial choice: Should they strive to "beat men at their own game," or should they instead develop and value alternative leadership styles? This chapter explores the nature and implications of those alternative styles for women who aspire to leadership.

A FEMINIST PERSPECTIVE

Contemporary feminist leadership theory views the nature of leadership differently from more traditional leadership and management theory. First, women come to leadership opportunities shaped by a different background than that of male colleagues. Rosener (1990), in a study of women leaders, found that socialization and career paths explain in large part why women lead differently. Although women are certainly capable of leading in the command-and-control mode that men in organizations often take, women in the study preferred an alternative style. The women interviewees described their leadership style as a set of behaviors that seemed to come naturally to them. Rosener explains

> Although socialization patterns and career paths are changing, the average age of the men and women who responded to the survey is 51—old enough to have had experiences that differed because of gender. Until the 1960s, men and women received different signals about what was expected of them . . . women [as] wives, mothers, volunteers, teacher, nurses. . . . In all of these roles they are supposed to be

cooperative, supportive, understanding, gentle, and to provide service to others. . . . Men have had to appear to be competitive, strong, tough, decisive and in control. . . . This may explain why women today are more likely than men to be interactive leaders. (1990, p. 124)

Women in this study described a leadership style that was succeeding "because of— not in spite of—certain characteristics considered to be 'feminine' and inappropriate in leaders" (Rosener, 1990, p. 120). Feminist leadership theorists have been helpful in explicating the nature of this alternative leadership style. Sally Helgesen, in *The Female Advantage: Women's Ways of Leading* (1990), argued that women have the unique advantage of having "fresh eyes to see what was no longer working and to identify new solutions." She compared traditional masculine styles of leadership with her research findings on female leaders and found significant differences with respect to how women leaders spend their time, identify with the job, and share information.

In a comparison with Mintzberg's (1973) classic research on what managers do, Helgesen concluded that women do in fact lead differently. Rather than working at an unrelenting pace with few breaks, as managers in Mintzberg's study reported, women worked more steadily, scheduling small breaks during the day. Whereas men spared little time for activities that were not job-related, women tended to make time for things not directly related to their work. Mintzberg reported that his male managers had days characterized by interruption, discontinuity, and fragmentation. In Helgesen's study, the women did not define unexpected tasks and encounters as interruptions. The most significant difference was in the way men and women identified with their jobs. Mintzberg's male managers tended to identify themselves with their jobs, whereas Helgesen's executives saw their own identities as complex and multifaceted. Mintzberg's managers tended to have difficulty sharing information whereas the women in Helgesen's study regularly scheduled time for sharing information.

Leading from the Center

Helgesen's (1990) work, along with Carol Gilligan's (1982) research, makes the case that women tend to lead from the center of an organization rather than from atop the command hierarchy. She describes a "web of inclusion" with the intended goal of forming interrelated teams linked by a central leader. In a traditional hierarchy, a leader may be looking out for his or her own best interest. In a web structure, a leader attempts to bring people together. From this perspective, women leaders may tune in to organizational information that male leaders at the top may never hear. Leading from the center enables a leader to obtain information directly as opposed to hearing it only through a series of filters and censors enforced by the chain of command.

Feminist Leadership Characteristics

Carmen Griggs (1989), in a study of university women's centers and women's study programs, articulated the characteristics represented in the alternative leadership style espoused and practiced by the women studied by Rosener and Helgesen. She identified them as feminist leadership characteristics. She asserted that women

- Use consensus decision making.
- View power in relational terms as something to be shared.

- Encourage productive approaches to conflict.
- Build supportive working environments.
- Promote diversity in the workplace.

These characteristics suggest that women are more comfortable in work environments that are not boss-centered but instead allow for a more adaptive leadership style. Rosener describes this style as an interactive, or transformational, style of leadership. By examining each of these characteristics in detail, we can distinguish between male and female ways of leading.

Consensus Decision Making/Participatory Structures

Men have traditionally viewed leadership as a top-down hierarchy of power (Helgesen, 1990; Maier, 1992; Rosener, 1990). Masculine approaches to leadership view labor in a vertical perspective—a pecking order where managers tell subordinates what to do. The leader holds sway by authority with respect to organizational influence and decision making. In contrast to this leadership paradigm is Helgesen's concept of the web, as previously discussed. Helgesen describes women's leadership practices as leading from the center of the organization, whereas males tend to lead from hierarchies. Leadership from the center is similar to the way a spider web is formed, with primary focus on connections rather than hierarchies. The goal of the web leader is to form interrelated teams linked by the central leader. A web brings people together, whereas a hierarchy is related to looking out for one's best interests—protecting and enforcing the power base. By leading from the center, a leader can get information from a variety of sources rather than depending on a chain of command. The leader has more input because the leader is not out of the loop and simultaneously gains more input from teams around her (Helgesen, 1990).

Power

Traditional definitions depict organizational power as zero-sum in nature—the more power one person has, the less another has. Masculine conceptualizations of power view this attribute as an advantage you have over other people, something you control. In analyses of this masculine perspective, power has been seen as a scarcity model—get as much as you can of a limited quantity—based on domination and control of others (Schaef, 1981). Feminists have reframed this definition of power in a way that does not require domination of others. A related view of power suggests that it can be defined as energy and strength rather than domination and control (Carroll, 1984; Hartsock, 1979, Maier, Ferguson, and Shrivastava, 1993; Schaef, 1981). Power is viewed as a source of synergy—something to be taught and shared. Whereas the masculine view might look at power over others, a feminine perspective would see power with others (Maier, Ferguson, and Shrivastava, 1993). Power, from this feminine perspective, is understood not in hierarchical terms, but in relational terms. Talking about power in relational terms suggests a power model with attributes such as cooperation and interdependence rather than a model of competitiveness and dominance (Hartsock, 1979).

Information and Skill Sharing

In organizational life, information and expertise have often been perceived to be a source of power. In French and Raven's classic work on the bases of power, expertise is identified as one of the most significant sources of organizational power. The feminist perspective recognizes the power of expertise but differs from more masculine approaches in its view of how information and expertise get shared in the organization. Feminist leadership tends to be more educational in nature, with leaders making a commitment to share information and expertise so that others can become effective as organizational participants and leaders. A focus on personal self-development (Griggs, 1989; O'Sullivan, 1976) or *self-actualization,* in Maslow's (1970) term, is a significant characteristic of a feminist perspective on leadership. Rosener, in her classic article, "Ways Women Lead," describes what the women leaders she interviewed said about sharing power and information:

> Sharing power and information accomplishes several things. It creates loyalty by signaling to coworkers and subordinates that they are trusted and their ideas respected. It also sets an example for other people and therefore can enhance the general communication flow. And it increases the odds that leaders will hear about problems before they explode. Sharing power and information also gives employees and coworkers the wherewithal to reach conclusions, solve problems and see the justification for decisions. (1990, p. 123)

These women leaders went on to say that one of the advantages of sharing information and encouraging participation among employees is that the employees feel important—their self-worth is enhanced, with inevitable benefit to the organization's image and productivity.

Conflict Management

The masculine view tends to perceive conflict as threatening and negative. Conflict should be suppressed "under the assumption that it poses a problematic threat to the group or organization" (Maier, Ferguson, and Shrivastava, 1993). The feminist perspective views conflict as an important interaction for getting issues out on the table and resolved. Compromise and win-win conclusions are possible. Conflict can be cooperative in nature—a group concern—rather than a confrontational challenge to a single leader. Developing methods to work through conflicts is of primary concern from the feminist leader's perspective. In this view, the process of conflict resolution is just as important as the conflict itself. Feminist theorists point out the importance of conflict environments where trust is present and participants are committed to resolve conflicts in a nonconfrontational way (Griggs, 1989).

Kenneth Thomas's conflict management grid (1976) captures this process as well by articulating different ways of resolving conflict by balancing cooperativeness (attempting to satisfy the other party's concerns) with assertiveness (attempting to satisfy one's own concerns). On the grid five strategies are identified: avoidance, competition, compromise, accommodation, and problem solving. Of these strategies, the feminist leadership perspective emphasizes compromise and problem solving. The heart of the feminist perspective on leadership is captured well in Thomas's definition of problem solving: to seek true satisfaction of everyone's concerns in the conflict by working through differences and developing consensus on how to solve a problem. In this approach, everyone can win.

Supportive Work Environment

Of all the components of feminist leadership style, a supportive work environment matters most for women in management. The feminist perspective argues that leadership practiced from a feminist point of view creates work settings characterized by warmth, understanding, encouragement, support, nurturance, listening, empathy, and mutual trust (Griggs, 1989). Norma Carr-Ruffino, in *The Promotable Woman* (1993), makes the case that women have a significant advantage with this component of leadership skill. They possess, as women, the ability to understand worker needs and, therefore inspire loyalty based on how they, as women, have been socialized. Research on how boys and girls learn and are socialized in classrooms suggests that women have developed supportive, people-oriented skills; women function best in environments that require those skills (Sadker and Sadker, 1994).

Organizations at the dawn of the twenty-first century find themselves moving toward such environments. To compete globally, businesses are finding that they require the type of leadership that builds effective work teams and capitalizes on people skills to meet the challenges of continuing change (Naisbett and Aburdene, 1990). Skills that reflect this feminine perspective can be summarized as more facilitative and consultative in nature. These skills might include empowering others, coaching, inspiring, sharing information, building trust and loyalty, encouraging cooperation and consensus, tuning in to employees' needs and desires, and showing compassion (Carr-Ruffino, 1993; Glaser and Smalley, 1995; Smith, 1997).

Commitment to Diversity

This final component has been a mainstay of the feminist movement since the early nineteenth century. As discussed earlier in this chapter, feminists have taken a stand against oppression related to gender, race, and sexuality. They have, by their different leadership styles, demonstrated that diversity of skill, thought, and management approach is valuable. Women have been instrumental in bringing flexibility and adaptability to the work environment by a number of initiatives including the adoption of work and family balancing strategies, enactment of a parental leave act, and advocacy for alternative work arrangements, with positive implications for employee motivation and increased productivity (see, for example, Smith, 1991).

NEW PARADIGMS FOR EXPLORING LEADERSHIP STYLE

In many ways, the characteristics previously articulated demonstrate how leadership skills drawn from the feminine perspective create access to a new style of leadership for both men and women, with marked advantages for the way businesses are being managed in an era of global competition. Mark Maier (1992), in a study on evolving paradigms of management in organizations, drew from a survey of the literature to provide a useful analysis showing how assumptions about men and women leaders have changed over the years to reach this new style (see Figure 3-1).

Figure 3-1 highlights several benchmarks of perceptions of women in the workplace. Although the basic assumptions about female versus male managers have come full circle (i.e., that men and women are similar), the implications of the current theoretical trend in management styles suggest that men and women can learn from each other's unique leadership traits and incorporate the positive aspects of each into a more androgynous style. This style results in a work environment where "men and women can both be 'like women' and 'like men' " (Maier, 1992, p. 31). The effective leadership style is one that captures the best of both styles of leading.

Evolution of Theoretical Perspectives on Women in Management, 1955–1990

Assumptions about Men and Women	Implications for Managerial Women	Type of Change
I. Essentially Different (1950s–1960s)	Sex-Based Exclusion "A woman's place is in the home"	Maintenance of status quo No individual or structural change
"Masculinism" (Sexism)	Women and men contribute to society in separate, role-differentiated ways	Independence of work and family assumed
II. Essentially Similar (1970s–present)	Role-Based Inclusion Assimilation to masculine role	Individual change (women) No structural change
"Equal Opportunity" (Feminism)	"A woman can manage just as well as a man" Value women's ability to contribute "like a man"	Independence of work and family assumed
III. Essentially Different (1980s–present) "Feminine-ism"	Sex-Based Inclusion Integration-diversity "Vive la difference!" Value women qua women's "unique" contributions	No individual change Some structural change Independence of work and family is still assumed
IV. Essentially Similar (1990s–?) "Transformative Feminism"	Role-Based Inclusion Androgyny-Diversity Men and women can both be "like women" and "like men"	Individual and structural change Interdependence between work and family is acknowledged

FIGURE 3-1 Changes in Assumptions about Men and Women in the Workplace and the Implications for Managerial Women

Source: M. Maier, 1992, "Evolving paradigms of management in organizations: A gendered analysis." *Journal of Management Systems, 4*(1), p. 31. Used with permission.

Glaser and Smalley, in *Swim with the Dolphins* (1995), use a series of linked metaphors to compare workplace behaviors of "sharks, guppies and dolphins." Sharks represent the "command and control" model. Tough, arrogant, ruthless, cold-blooded sharks run the business in hierarchical style; they tend to be very task oriented and aloof. The shark rarely delegates, fosters dependency in subordinates, and prefers to act alone. The guppy metaphor is used to capture the ineffective, weak applications of management. The guppies are uncomfortable with hierarchy and try to be everyone's friend. The guppy likes to be one of the group. The guppy is overly dependent on others' strengths and rarely acts alone. The guppy is uncomfortable with power and often misunderstands it. The guppy is "food for other fish." The dolphin is highly intelligent, excels at communication, and is warm-blooded and friendly. Dolphins, like sharks, are concerned with profitability and the balance sheet but choose an alternative style to maximize an organization's effectiveness. They are task oriented and people oriented; they prefer operating in more of a web style, leading from the center rather than from a hierarchical position. Dolphins foster independence in their subordinates and are comfortable with power, using it to accomplish tasks. They prefer consensus but are able to act alone when necessary. Dolphins share agendas and vision rather than using hidden agendas. They are true leaders, not bosses. Both men and women can be dolphins, yet a woman's style of leadership, influenced by years of socialization in feminine traits, positions her well to take the dolphin role and become an effective leader.

Developing Effective Leadership Skill Sets

If women have these significant advantages as leaders for modern organizations, why haven't they reached the top of corporate America? The Feminist Majority Foundation (1991) reported that, based on how long it has taken women to advance in corporations to date, another 475 years would be required to reach parity with men in the executive ranks. As organizations begin to change and make progress in dealing with the external barriers to the glass ceiling, women must look at their own internal barriers and think through how best to develop an appropriate leadership skill set. Men, too, in changing organizations must consider their internal barriers and look toward the styles most appropriate in changing organizations.

Norma Carr-Ruffino (1993), citing a 1990 Gallup poll, found that traits most admired in men include the abilities to be aggressive, independent, objective, dominant, unemotional, not excitable in a crisis, active, logical, worldly, and competitive. Respondents also associated many of these traits more closely with men than women. Not surprisingly, these traits are also expected of a strong leader. In a discussion of the male and female qualities that androgynous managers should develop, Alice Sargent makes the case that women can learn the skills that are typical male strengths, such as becoming more focused on task and regarding it as just as important as relationships. They can also enhance their more feminine traits, such as the ability to accept task failure and not take it as personal failure. Other strengths that can be developed and/or expanded on are outlined in Figure 3-2 (adapted from Alice Sargent, by Carr-Ruffino, 1993).

The advice presented in Figure 3-2 describes how women might begin to think through developing more masculine-oriented traits and enhancing their feminine-oriented strengths to become more successful managers. These strategies may significantly impact career mobility and advancement opportunities.

Beyond the advice suggested in Figure 3-2, what else can explain how gender may impact leadership? Where can women, with their interactive style of leadership (Rosener, 1990) make great advances? The next section explores one of the significant new paradigms in leadership and provides some strategic directions for women in leadership to pursue.

WOMEN AS LEADERS
IN THE TWENTY-FIRST CENTURY

One significant way to break the ceiling is to analyze how leadership in organizations has changed in recent years and to foresee women's meaningful place in those changes. The most significant leadership challenge facing organizations in the 1990s and beyond is the ability to find leaders equipped to work in an environment made up of self-

FIGURE 3-2 List of Typical Masculine and Feminine Strengths Related to Effective Androgynous Styles of Management

Typical Masculine Strengths Women Can Develop	*Typical Feminine Strengths Women Can Expand*
• Learn how to be powerful and forthright. • Become *entrepreneurial.* • Have a direct, visible impact on others, rather than just functioning behind the scenes. • State your own needs and refuse to back down, even if the immediate response is not acceptance. • Focus on a task and regard it as at least as important as the relationships with the people doing the task. • Build support systems with other women and share competence with them, rather than competing with them. • Build a sense of community among women instead of saying, "I pulled myself up by my bootstraps, so why can't you?" • Intellectualize and generalize from experience. • Behave "impersonally," rather than personalizing experience and denying another's reality because it is different. • Stop turning anger, blame, and pain inward. • Stop accepting feelings of suffering and victimization. • Take the option of being invulnerable to destructive feedback. • Stop being irritable, a "nag," and/or passive-resistant about resentments and anger. • Respond directly with "I" statements, rather than with blaming "you" ones ("*I'm* not comfortable with that" rather than "*you* shouldn't do that"). • Become an effective problem solver by being analytical, systematic, and directive. • Change self-limiting behaviors, such as allowing interruptions or laughing after making a serious statement. • Become a risk-taker (calculating probabilities and making appropriate trade-offs).	• The ability to recognize, accept, and express feelings. • Respect for feelings as a basic and essential part of life, as guides to authenticity and effectiveness, rather than as barriers to achievement. • Accept the vulnerability and imperfections of others. • A belief in the right to work for self-fulfillment as well as for money. • A belief in the value of nonwork roles as well as work identity. • The ability to fail at a task without feeling failure as a person. • The ability to accept and express the need to be nurtured at all times. • The ability to touch and be close to both men and women without necessarily experiencing or suggesting sexual connotations. • Skill at listening empathetically and actively without feeling responsible for solving others' problems. • The ability to share feelings as the most meaningful part of one's contact with others, accepting the risk and vulnerability such sharing implies. • Skill at building support systems with other women, sharing competencies without competition, and feelings and needs with sincerity. • The ability to relate to experiences and people on a personal level rather than assuming that the only valid approach to life and interpersonal contact is an abstract, rational, or strictly objective one. • Acceptance of the emotional, spontaneous, and irrational parts of the self.

Source: Adapted from *The Androgynous Manager* by Alice. G. Sargent (New York: Amacom, 1981); Cited in N. Carr-Ruffino, *The Promotable Woman* (Belmont, CA: Wadsworth, 1993).

directed teams. In the future, the best leaders may be those who make themselves eventually unnecessary or at least relatively invisible for self-directed teams. That paradox—that leading often means giving up power rather than accumulating it—lies at the heart of the leadership challenge for the twenty-first century, and ironically, stems from early feminist thought on what makes an effective organization. This approach to leadership, frankly, has been difficult for traditional male leaders to learn. It's hard for them to imagine that the band may be able to play quite well without the conductor.

The participatory, networking style of women leaders may make them better candidates to lead teams, whereas the leadership skills for traditional, and largely male, team management are essentially directive in nature, including such skills as maintaining control, focusing and directing member activities, accepting responsibility for final decisions, setting and enforcing work and quality standards, distributing rewards and sanctions according to member performance, and motivating team members.

For some business situations and purposes, this set of leadership skills is well suited, at least for attaining short-term organizational goals. It may fail, however, to serve organizations well in the longer term. Traditional leadership approaches to team management exercise the talents of the leader but do little to encourage independent thinking, innovation, team spirit, and accountability among team members. Women leaders have been at the forefront of organizational efforts to reengineer the leadership functions necessary for team-based work.

Delegated Leadership

A small step toward less directive leadership involves the delegation of selected leadership tasks to team members. In this leadership style, the team is hardly self-directed, of course. The leader is still pulling most of the strings under the guise of giving team members a chance to perform as designated leaders-for-a-day.

Let's say, for example, that a leader asks team members John, Alice, Ruth, and Bill to each serve in turn as meeting leaders for weekly team meetings. To some extent, this option does serve to develop these individuals' leadership skills. But the whole arrangement may come to look and feel like a training exercise—preparing *for* independent initiative rather than practicing it. A lockstep rotation of meeting leaders may also tend to defuse any team action agendas. What seemed important in John's meeting may not be important when Alice, Ruth, or Bill take their turns at bat.

Elected Leadership

A supervisor can turn the selection of leaders over to the team itself. This option certainly empowers team members and underlines their responsibility for independent problem solving. Interpersonal relations on the team, however, must be sufficiently developed for consensus selection of leaders. Close votes, with a significant minority left grumbling on the sidelines, can sabotage any elected leader's efforts.

In addition, elective leadership can sometimes lead to the "slaves creating the master." There is no guarantee that a leader elected from the ranks won't quickly fall into the role of a traditional taskmaster. A team empowered to select its own leadership can be disempowered by selecting the wrong leader. This undesirable result is all the more likely if team members have no training or experience in team leadership. Old leadership styles may crop up not because they are preferred by the team but because they are familiar.

Shared Leadership

In the shared leadership approach, the nature of leadership itself undergoes a marked transformation. From the supervisor's point of view, shared leadership means redefining the leader's role in five ways:

- The old leader displays greater knowledge, experience, and wisdom in decision making than that possessed by team members. The new leader shows others how knowledge, experience, and skill in decision making can be acquired.
- The old leader tells team members what to do. The new leader participates in deciding with team members what courses of action to take.
- The old leader talks most of the time. The new leader listens most of the time.
- The old leader discourages risk taking and punishes missteps on the part of team members. The new leader encourages team initiative and accepts risk and occasional failure as part of the learning process.
- The old leader has a relatively low opinion of the intelligence, motivation, and trustworthiness of team members. The new leader respects team members and values their contributions.

Shared leadership, in effect, removes many of the boundaries between the leader and the led. The supervisor given responsibility for the team and its results blends in as a team participant. This approach to leadership resolves the problem of "talent divorce," in which one particularly skilled individual (the supervisor) is summarily excluded from team processes. Empowerment of the team by the supervisor, in other words, does not have to mean walking out of the meeting room and hoping for the best. It does mean climbing down from the traditional leadership pedestal. With the rest of the team, the supervisor exerts developmental leadership using three strategies:

1. The supervisor *gets to know* team members and lets himself or herself be known. All team successes depend directly on the degree of interpersonal trust shared by team members. The supervisor can begin to build that trust by modeling sincere interest in others.
2. The supervisor *raises process questions* without dictating answers. In early meetings, the supervisor can ask the team such questions as
   - What do you think is our purpose as a team?
   - What are our individual roles?
   - What norms or implicit and explicit rules can we agree on for our discussions and to govern our behaviors? [For example, we can agree to welcome divergent opinion and seek consensus whenever possible.]
3. The supervisor *interprets organizational politics.* In their formative meetings, team members understandably have many "what ifs" about their degree of support in the organization, performance expectations from top management, and their vulnerability if results aren't immediately forthcoming. The supervisor needs to be a channel for whatever assurance and support top management is willing to give to the team. It is crucial that a supervisor's words of encour-

agement on the part of top management be sincere and trustworthy. A team quickly can be destroyed by reassurances that turn out to be false.

Leadership at a Distance

This final leadership option is practiced most often with executive teams made up of experienced team players. Once given their charter, these self-directed teams are free to achieve their goals (and often define or refine them along the way) in any way that makes sense to the team as a whole. The leader is available to the team for counsel, access to resources, and other forms of support. But, day to day, the leader's contact with the team is minimal. The team reports its results to the organizational leader. If the results meet or exceed expectations, both the organizational leader and team members are rewarded. If not, the team is put on notice by the leader to "hit the numbers" or face dissolution as a group.

This leadership style downplays the potential contributions of the leader to the team in favor of ultimate empowerment for the team itself. For such empowerment to draw the best from team members, it must be real in the organization. In the words of one director of a Fortune 100 company, "Around here, the authority of our project teams is, at best, ambiguous. We are told 'you can make decisions.' But, in reality, if senior management doesn't like it, it won't fly." In this situation, teams are not really empowered to do their own best thinking and acting, but instead to play an expensive guessing game called "What does the boss want?"

The qualities of the leadership style described in this last section support the points raised by the feminist leadership perspective. That this perspective can readily link with the needs of organizations in the twenty-first century is a compelling argument for embracing a model of androgynous leadership, which is gender blind.

SUMMARY OF KEY POINTS

This chapter explored differences in leadership style, comparing the command/control style of leading to a more participatory structure. Analyzing how leadership styles differ on male and female dimensions, the chapter identified why women may lead differently. The feminist theories of leadership suggest that the way women are socialized and the career paths they take may impact the style they choose. Women tend to lead from the center, value consensus decision making, share information and power, manage conflict through joint problem solving, and embrace diversity. Paradigms on the differences in masculine and feminine styles of leading have evolved over time. Today's organizations aim toward valuing the best characteristics associated with the way both men and women lead. Capturing the best of both styles, and developing and/or enhancing the strengths associated with these characteristics provides a recipe for leadership success. An argument is advanced in the final section of the chapter that, given the move toward teams and team structures within organizations, a place for the feminine, web model of inclusion may be an effective strategy. Women, because of their socialization and comfort level with the characteristics of effective teamwork, may be well situated to excel as leaders in this new paradigm for organizational design.

Discussion Questions

1. Do you agree that men and women lead differently? Why or why not? Which leadership qualities from the different perspectives would you want to develop? Why?
2. What are some of the critical differences between leading from a hierarchy and leading from the center as in "the web of inclusion."

Issue to Debate

Are organizations changing fast enough to value a new way of leading? Will women be able to break through the double standard of what constitutes effective leadership?

Case Analysis
Ana Cortes:
The Challenge of Team Leaders

Ana Cortes worked as a new team leader in a distribution center for a major retailing organization. She was 27 years old with a high school education, an Associate of Arts degree in management from a local community college and approximately 6 years of experience both part time and full time in retail operations (customer service, inventory control, and distribution operations). Her promotion to team leader was in recognition of her motivation, dedication to the organization, and demonstration of management potential. Whereas supervisors managed between 15 and 20 individuals in a variety of distribution operations, the teams were designed to be more specialized and consisted of 5 to 7 team members who were responsible to a team leader.

As the distribution center moved increasingly to a team environment, with less emphasis on traditional supervisor–crew type structures, those individuals promoted to team leaders found themselves facing many challenges. Many members of the teams had been used to having a supervisor and doing the specific jobs out-lined in their job descriptions. They followed the supervisors' directions to the letter with little or no input. In most cases, the supervisors, as well as the workers, tended to be men. Ana was one of three women who had been promoted to the new team leader position. Two additional men were promoted to this role. In addition, several employees who had been supervisors were offered the team leader job as well. All team leaders were considered to be equal in organizational level. One of the supervisors left on hearing of the new arrangement. Two accepted the new job as team leaders. The remaining supervisors were integrated onto the teams as team members. Ana was excited about the new responsibility and motivated to implement the team skills she had learned both on the job and in the company-provided training. She thought that, given her camaraderie with the employees and her bosses prior to the restructuring, the transition would be smooth. It appeared to be just the opposite.

During the transition to teams, Ana found herself frustrated by the lack of respect she garnered in this new position.

Previously, she had considered herself and was treated as one of the guys. Now she was a leader. She perceived that her team members did not trust her and felt that they were being spied on while on the job. Several of the team members were insistent on testing her by stretching the limits of what they could get away with in terms of lower productivity. Ana learned that the other women team leaders were experiencing similar problems. The supervisors who were now team leaders offered little support. Ana, along with one of her peers, set up a meeting with the distribution manager and the vice president of human resources and asked for their support. ■

Questions

1. What leadership skills might Ana employ to turn around team member attitudes?
2. What support does Ana need from other team leaders and the organization?
3. How might Ana become a more "interactive" leader?

References and Suggested Readings

Carr-Ruffino, N. (1993). *The promotable woman: Advancing through leadership skills.* Belmont, CA: Wadsworth.

Carroll, S. (1984). Feminist scholarship on political leadership. In B. Kellerman (Ed.), *Leadership: Multidisciplinary perspectives* (pp. 139–156). Englewood Cliffs, NJ: Prentice Hall.

Catalyst. (1996). *Women in corporate management.* New York: Catalyst.

Feminist Majority Foundation. (1991). *Empowering women in business.* Arlington, VA: FMF.

Gilligan, C. (1982). *In a different voice.* Cambridge, MA: Harvard University Press.

Glaser, C., and Smalley, G. (1995). *Swim with the dolphins: How women can succeed in corporate America on their own terms.* New York: Warner.

Griggs, C. S. (1989). *Exploration of a feminist leadership model at university women's centers and women's studies programs: A descriptive study.* University of Iowa: UMI Dissertation Services.

Hartsock, M. (1979). Feminism, power and change: A theoretical analysis. In B. Cummings and V. Schuck (Eds.), *Women organizing: An anthology* (pp. 2–24). Metuchen, NJ: Scarecrow.

Helgesen, S. (1990). *The female advantage: Women's ways of leading.* Garden City, NY: Doubleday.

Maier, M. (1992). Evolving paradigms of management in organizations. A gendered analysis. *Journal of Management Systems, 4*(1), 29–45.

Maier, M., Ferguson, K., and Shrivastava, P. (1993). Organizational dysfunction as gendered practice: The space shuttle Challenger disaster (working paper).

Maslow, A. (1970). *Motivation and personality* (2nd ed). New York: Harper and Row.

Mintzberg, H. (1973). *The Nature of managerial work.* New York: Harper & Row.

Morrison, Ann. et. al. and the Center for Creative Leadership. (1992). *Breaking the Glass Ceiling: Can women reach the top of America's largest corporations?* Reading, MA.

Naisbett, J., and Aburdene, P. (1990). *Megatrends 2000: Ten new directions for the 1990s.* New York: William Morrow.

O'Sullivan, L. (1976). Organizing for impact. *Quest, 2*(3), 69–80.

Rosener, J. (1990, November/December). Ways women lead. *Harvard Business Review,* 119–125.

Sadker M., and Sadker, D. (1994). *Failing at fairness: How America's schools cheat girls.* New York: Scribner.

Sargent, A. (1981). *The androgynous manager.* New York: American Management Association Communications.

Schaef, A. (1981). *Women's reality: An emerging female system in a white male society.* Minneapolis, MN: Winston Press.

Smith, D. (1997). *Leadership.* Lincolnwood, IL: NTC/Contemporary Publishers.

Smith, D. (1991). *Kincare and the American corporation: Solving the work-family dilemma.* Homewood, IL: Business-One, Irwin.

Swiss, D. (1996). *Women breaking through.* Princeton, NJ: Peterson's.

Thomas, K. (1976). Conflict and conflict management. In M. D. Dunnett (Ed.), *Handbook of industrial and organizational behavior* (pp. 889–935). Chicago: Rand McNally.

PART

Experiences

Part II is organized around a prevalent theme regarding women at work. The research, anecdotal evidence, and collective experiences of women in corporate and public life reveal that there are certain challenges inherent in the working environment that prevent women from moving ahead in their careers or derail them in their attempts at success. Often the challenges women face are referred to by men and women as outright barriers or obstacles and paint a picture of a workplace plagued by perceptions of inequity or unfairness. Yet, the experiences of women at work are both positive and negative. The chapters in part II attempt to capture those experiences outlining the realities faced in the workplace.

Chapter 4, "Gender Roles," underscores the need to explore how gender roles develop and ultimately impact the workplace. From birth through workplace entry, the roles of men and women are often defined by a variety of societal influences, which influence the career experiences of men and women. Chapter 5 takes us beyond the discussion on gender, arguing that the experiences of women of color are both similar and uniquely different. Race, ethnicity, and other related factors impact many of the issues presented in the book and are detailed here. Although issues of race and ethnicity are integrated throughout the text, the author presents a more in-depth treatment of the experiences of women of color in corporate life. Chapter 6 introduces a new concept, dysempowerment, relevant to any discussion on men and women's perceptions of how people become disenfranchised at work. The authors have coined the term *dysempowerment* to capture the experience of how people are treated in the workplace and the ultimate impact of that treatment. Chapter 6 includes an actual case study in which readers can analyze the dysempowerment experience as it unfolds. Finally, chapter 7 depicts the legal environment as it relates to gender issues. A thorough treatment of gender discrimination is presented that outlines how employment law shapes workplace experiences and trends for change.

Before beginning these chapters, read about two leaders thoughts and personal experiences on many of the issues highlighted in part II.

Meet Judy Rose

Judy Rose, Athletic Director, University of North Carolina-Charlotte Charlotte, NC

BACKGROUND

When Judy Rose was named athletic director (AD) at the University of North Carolina (UNC) at Charlotte, she was only the second woman in the country to become an AD for a Division I school. Back then, it was still "a good old boys network," and as Judy indicates, women were treated with skepticism. "I'd go to meetings and the guys would look at me like, "what are you doing here." Today, there are more than 100 women in Divisions I, II and III in leadership positions, but at the time, Judy was breaking the ceiling. She got started when playing basketball at Winthrop College in 1970. After graduating, she wanted to continue her education and matriculated at the University of Tennessee. She attributes her career start to a timing issue. Meeting Pat Summitt who intended to be a basketball coach, she had an opportunity. She and Pat had played against each other in college and were friends. Pat, planning to be a basketball coach, wanted Judy to assist her. Judy remembers, "I wanted to wait—keeping up with school was enough but she kept asking."

Title IX passed about the time Judy had completed a year of graduate school. Many new jobs in coaching were becoming available. Timing was a factor because suddenly there were many opportunities for women. Coaching in a college program presented a major career option. "While the guys graduating got jobs at high schools, the girls were being offered serious coaching jobs at universities and colleges. Title IX was key for us at that time. My first job was as a dorm mother and coach. Then you had to coach volleyball, basketball, and tennis and manage sorority type stuff. To get to coach basketball, you had to do the other things too. Then came the offer from UNC. I would get to work with the coach in basketball. The starting pay at the time was $8,000 per annum. I knew I could make more in public school, but this was a great opportunity."

"Over the years, I progressed." Judy held a number of positions at UNC, coaching everything from tennis to basketball, becoming the coordinator of women athletics and then the assistant athletic director. "The program was growing so fast," she comments, "I needed to make a choice since the program needed a full time administrator. It was a hard decision, because all I ever wanted to do was coach basketball. It was one of the toughest decisions to leave coaching and make the move to administration. The 'highs' from coaching are different than administration." Judy made the decision and was named associate athletic director. In 1990, she was appointed athletic director. Again, Judy attributes this position to timing. "The current men's basketball coach was AD at the time. This was a time of unrest with drug testing and other abuses. The job was too large to be both a head coach and an AD. In North Carolina, a mandate finally came down that you couldn't do both. I was recommended for promotion."

Since that time, Judy Rose has had an extraordinarily successful career as a Division I athletic director for UNC. Although she says that the position "fell in her lap," there is no doubt that skill as a leader has characterized her meteoric rise.

THOUGHTS ON LEADERSHIP

"Leadership is important in my industry. Having quality leadership means the most important ingredient is surrounding yourself with good people. Our coaches and top leaders have the opportunity to influence young lives and mentor them. Imperative to this is to hire the best people to do this."

The other keys to leadership include the following according to Judy. "Don't be afraid to seek help and information; if you don't ask it may not happen. Leaders don't make decisions in a vacuum. Get input and the necessary information. Take the responsibility to make the final decisions but ask for input. If you decide otherwise and don't take the input, be sure to give a reason. Provide opportunities for others.

"Leading by example is the most important. I rarely ask people to do something I wouldn't do myself. One example of the toughest thing I ever had to deal with was working with a coach who was very successful (in terms of wins and losses) but the young people weren't receiving a well-rounded experience. They didn't like how the coach treated them. He was well liked publicly. Now, I'm very competitive. I want to win and represent the university well but not at any cost. I didn't renew this coach's contract. I allowed him to resign and said that I'd help him, but we agreed we wouldn't discuss this with the media. He called a press conference and said he was

forced to resign. The media blasted me. I had issued a press release—it was a personnel issue. I had to abide by the agreement we had even though he had violated our agreement. People were only looking at a 'winning' coach being let go. It was the right decision but a tough one because I couldn't share the truth and go back on my word to speak on the issue. Later . . . a radio announcer [who had been critical of Judy] left me a message. I called him back. He told me, 'Judy—just want to tell you that I know what you did and why. A former student athlete had given me some insider information on the treatment of players. I applaud you and your decision.' Even though his message to me wasn't public, I knew enough of myself that I did the right thing even if no one knew. Not a popular decision but leaders have to look at what is most important. The image for the program is to view UNC and it's athletic program as ethical."

Judy's "lead by example" philosophy is demonstrated in other ways as well. In 1990, the program started an initiative for community service. "Each sports team has to do a community project. The administration does it too. Our athletes are talented and gifted. We need to give back to the community. We have to volunteer. We do Adopt a Grandparent, Habitat for Humanity, blind children races where our track athletes become their eyes, mentoring and tutoring in the schools, and more."

FACING CHALLENGES

"My philosophical approach to the [gender] challenges was a bit different. My attitude became if you can't lick 'em, join 'em! In intercollegiate athletics, you have to prove you deserve to be in their [the majority] company from an employer's perspective. You had to earn respect and prove that you knew what you were doing."

In terms of dealing with gender challenges specifically, Judy was quite open about her feelings regarding the experiences of how to best meet the needs of women and other minorities. "I don't believe in being separated; by that I mean I don't do women's groups because I am opposed to that. I am an AD for both men's and women's programs. I have to do what puts the best light on the university. I can't afford to alienate anyone. So I avoid groups that are all women or being in a group that is perceived as an all-women activity. There's a national collegiate athletic administration for women. I won't join. I've been criticized for this but my peers and colleagues feel joining would be detrimental to the university. Ironically, if men did this—joined organizations that were national associations for just men—women would go crazy! For the same reason, I don't believe in the Black Coaches Association. I am into integration not separation."

Yet, Rose knows what it will take for women to have the necessary experiences to succeed and manage an upwardly spiraling career. "I have been criticized for the fact that my women's basketball coach is male, but he was the best person for the job at that time. It was not my job to train that coach then. I needed a top-notch coach. Two of the assistants are women and hopefully they are getting the experience they need to be head coaches some day. Our young people deserve the best. If I hired a woman and she was not the best candidate for the job, I wouldn't be doing the right thing."

Judy is very realistic about the challenges and experiences of women and minorities, however. Her advice? "Attend and be active in the trade shows and organizations. It's easy for females and minorities to get more involved than white males. They want our involvement. It's a disservice, really, to qualified white males. They may not have the opportunities. It's unfair but we need to catch up to the unfairness over the years. Hopefully the best people [male or female] get the opportunity to serve. You have to help mentor and network with these young people.... In my professional organization, I'm on the board and actively involved. At the tail end of the convention we have continuing education seminars. You have to be involved with what's there and take advantage of opportunities. I have a young woman assistant who I think would make a great AD; I take her with me to meetings. Get your hands into everything, I tell her."

Her approach to career development also demonstrates a reality on what people experience. It's important to mentor the staff regarding their careers. "It's a daily challenge when there's X number of positions and I have 50 staff members. The younger staff has a timetable that they think about in terms of how they want to advance. There are only 300 Division I programs and everyone wants to be the athletic director. I try to guide them and be realistic. I've been here 23 years and at the same place. That's unusual. I didn't have to move to advance. But I need to mentor and guide our young staff and help them be realistic about advancing. I try to give them added responsibility but they are often not satisfied with the progress they want. Try to be honest and give them what they want to know. Direct them but be honest regarding career path. Don't get tied to a job in a particular city or institution. Have a broad focus. Be flexible and know people in the industry."

EXPERIENCES AS A WOMAN MANAGING A CAREER

"Early in your career you have to make choices regarding marriage, family, and career. It's particularly hard when coaching. For example, if I am the basketball coach and my kid has chicken pox and there's an away game. . . . If I go, I'm a rotten mom. If I leave the team, I'm a rotten coach. If I put my career on hold, it doesn't necessarily wait until you are ready to drop back in. I didn't have young children so in that way, I never had to make the choice or have that inner struggle. My spouse is not intimidated by my position; he is supportive and loves sports. If he didn't, we wouldn't have made it."

Regarding sexual harassment and discrimination, Judy has had her share of experiences as well. "I think some of the sexual harassment and discrimination problems are waning a bit. I have a little bit more tolerance. As only the second woman named to a Division I school, I put up with more than most, but I tried to be one of the guys and fit in and not make an issue of it. But now, it is unacceptable. Tolerance [for sexual harassment] is decreasing. We are all more sensitive and think twice before opening our mouths. Also, it's a public job. I should've been more sensitive years ago but had the goal to be successful for my organization."

Although Judy commented a lot about fitting in and being "one of the guys," she tells a story that points to another perspective. "An upcoming meeting was to be held at Amelia Island. The commissioner called to let me know there was a problem with the Amelia meeting. I said, no problem-- I've never been there but I bet it is lovely. He said, we rent condos. I said good, I like condos. He said, but we share--and I was the only woman. I said, each bedroom has its own bathroom, right? What's the problem? He was upset with me that I suggested that. I am not going to sleep with the guys, I said, and I'll have my own bathroom. The family room separates the bedrooms. What's the problem? I don't have a problem, you do.

"Well, we all went down to Amelia Island. I went and had my own three-bedroom condo all to myself. The commissioner opened the door for me and he's apologizing. Anyway, we go out in a van one evening. And when we come back, they park the van near their condo. Rather than asking them to walk me through the dark, very dark, parking lot, I walked off confidently and then started running. It was not well lighted and a bit scary. I called my husband and said to him, honey when you travel, don't ever let a woman walk by herself. . . . He cut me off and replied, 'we don't know how to treat you. You have the responsibility to say, I need you to walk me. If he had assumed this for you, you may have had questions about his intentions.' My husband was right. Our responsibility (as women) is to educate men on what we need. Now, I can do that. Then, I had to prove a point—which is a disservice to all women. I looked at it one way. My husband was a good sounding board. He saw the other perspective."

Meet Cathy Hughes

Cathy Hughes, President and CEO,
Landmark Systems,
Vienna, VA

BACKGROUND

Cathy Hughes got her start after completing high school. She went to work with Blue Cross and Blue Shield Insurance Company in the Washington, DC area. She was promoted to computer operator and soon moved from a trainee to a senior systems programmer after many quick promotions. Along with a co-worker, Cathy designed software that would make their jobs easier and make them more effective at work. As time went on, they thought the software had commercial potential and started thinking about leaving to start a new company. "We negotiated an agreement with Blue Cross to get the rights to the software and they were very helpful. We had to pay a small royalty to them on the first sale of product but then we were able to get the company started up while working at Blue Cross....We left when we figured we had enough money to go for about six months and see if we could make it." Landmark Systems, the company Cathy helped found, now has more than 250 employees; it is a publicly held $50 million company.

THOUGHTS ON LEADERSHIP

"For me, leadership is about a willingness to do things even if you don't know what you are getting into....For example, I was attending a week-long class in Atlanta, and I didn't know the city or the participants very well. At night we would walk to a restaurant. I tended to walk fast and was at the front. I had no idea where we were going—no clue at all. But, people followed. So even if you don't know, pretend you know, walk fast, and people will follow." Cathy's understanding of different leadership styles points to what it takes to be successful. Her mantra or philosophy of leadership is "Lead by example." She professes, "I don't expect people to do what I wouldn't do myself. At my best, I think I am extremely enthusiastic and driven to achieve a goal. You have to know what you want to do and know how you measure success. Then, get people to believe in it. At the end of a project, people have to feel ownership as well—not have them say, 'wow—you got us here.' Make everyone feel it's their project too."

THE CHALLENGES

The primary challenge that Cathy addresses is that sense of being overwhelmed with taking the plunge. She describes what happened. "In the early days, our jobs were technical—systems and programs. Trying to start a business without any finance, sales, and marketing background was tough but we had supreme confidence in the product. We did feel overwhelmed but we knew how to get help. You have to go for it no matter what. You'll either do fine or make a mistake. If you make a mistake, you learn and can redo it. It's the inaction that will kill you. Trying to tackle new things with no experience is challenging, but when in that situation, bring people in who are strong and fill the needs you have. Sometimes they don't work out—so try again."

Gender, as a barrier, isn't something that Cathy herself felt or experienced. "It could have been a barrier," she says, "but I never saw it." She does note that there are very few women in executive roles and those that are tend to be in marketing and sales. Of companies founded and started in the past 15 years, she still feels there are too few women and they are certainly underrepresented on the technical side. She has, however, recognized what her role might be in addressing the glass ceiling and makes a point of being involved in mentoring and helping women in terms of their career development. "Because I am a woman of a $50 million company, I get a lot of opportunities to be on boards, involved in community and political groups, and so on. I probably get more opportunities as a female CEO than a male CEO of a similarly sized company. There are too many opportunities for me to handle and I say no, I want to recommend a woman to take my place. But, I found that I didn't know many. That's a sorry statement about things. So I made the effort to start something. I knew two women and one of those knew another and we started the group two years ago with five women chief executive officers (CEOs). We grew to about 20 with CEOs ranging from small start-ups to companies of our size. We found we had many similar experiences and with this experience and being older, we are trying to mentor and help younger leaders get there faster by finding opportunities for them (i.e., press, public relations, getting them on boards of high-profile organizations). Women are not as good at networking as men seem to be, so we need to do more."

When asked about the challenges of worklife, Cathy shares the classic entrepreneurial truth: "With start-ups, there is no balance at the beginning. It requires a full-time commitment—nothing else can be a higher priority. If you succeed, then the time will come when you can do the balancing; once you are over the hump, then it's OK to take the time to hire more people, delegate, and hire the kind of people who will support you in the organization and at home." Cathy, herself, describes another impact and toll of the business. "I married my cofounder. It was great while we were focused on building a company. When the finances improved, we could afford things and time. What we found out was that we were different. We divorced but stayed business partners."

Another challenge involves office politics and power issues. Cathy explains, "When you start a company, you say, 'my company is never going to be like that . . .' but eventually when you get to a certain size the politics creep in. I've seen it at my company and in others this size. My advice? Ignore it! I have found lots of people who are successful but who waste time and energy discussing politics and gossiping. But if you are not contributing to a specific goal or objective, then it's a waste of time and unproductive."

The greatest challenges in Cathy's view are the tough business crises that face all leaders—men and women. She recounts the history of her start-up and points to the importance of recognizing the different phases a company goes through and the leadership challenges inherent in each. "Our company went through the start-up, growth and expansion, crisis, and IPO [initial public offering] stages. Going public was fun but we were private for 14 years and grew the company during the first 2 stages with little help. Growth and expansion in the 1980s was easy; things were going so well that even though we had little business experience, we assumed things would always be easy. We didn't plan for the future. The market was growing and we had the right product, at the right time and place. Everyone was making money. The crisis phase in the 1990s was a result of the market and economic recessions. The market had come to a halt in the IBM mainframe area when IBM quit selling and our market was saturated. It was difficult with competitors because prior to this time there was enough business for everyone.

"We became unprofitable for the first time and couldn't get financing. We had to reinvent ourselves, look at the future and see what markets were out there. We refocused and developed new strategies. After about five years, we were ultimately successful. The mainframe market came back. But having gone through this difficult period helped us with the IPO. We had been through so much over a 14-year period. The IPO was rough initially because of market conditions and external factors. We had a team of underwriters, and activities were going on to get us ready. Just as we were ready, NASDAQ took a dive. We postponed for a quarter but the underwriters still wanted to wait. We found new underwriters and filed with the SEC [Security Exchange Commission] in September of 1997. Our roadshow was set for October with the first presentation on October 27—the day the market crashed. Scary day for us. We left for London not knowing if people would even see us. The market came back over the next 10 days. We really didn't panic. After being through the hard times of the early 1990s, and the 14 years of this and that the bottom line is you learn to lead through it!"

EXPERIENCE AND ADVICE

What has Cathy learned from her experiences? She talks about the advice she has for other women regarding their experiences in developing their leadership roles. "When asked to give speeches, I talk about six secrets of success:

1. Take risks—don't be afraid to start something new. When I left to start a company, I thought I'd either make it in six months or get another job. For years I thought that's what anyone would do but others saw that as a great risk.

2. Think Big! You gotta really have the biggest dream you can. Whatever you are shooting for, if you get all the way there, then you didn't think big enough.

3. Know your strengths and capitalize on them. Don't waste time trying to improve weaknesses—get other people who have the strengths you don't.

4. Don't give up. Even when you go through the real challenges, what we called the *oh sh*** phase that our company went through, you have to hang in there.

5. Give back. Successful people didn't do it or get there by themselves. In our case, things happened along the way that had nothing to do with me and what I did. We have an obligation to recognize this and help others.

6. And finally, have fun!"

CHAPTER

Gender Roles: From Childhood to Professional Life

How Gender Develops and Impacts the Workplace

Alissa Hauser and Emilie Zaslow

"I heard one of my children's teacher say on the first day of school 'Jenny, what a nice new dress you're wearing, you sure look pretty' then she looked at my son and said 'and Lou, are those new sneakers? I bet you can run really fast!' "
—O. B. SMITH, CEO
Freespirit, Inc.

Chapter Overview

Picture a woman manager in her workplace. What does she look like? Act like? Who are her peers? Many people, when they envision women managers, see them surrounded by men and assume they will either be nurturing and kind, sexy and seductive, or unemotional and "male." Why do these stereotypes develop? Furthermore, why are women's experiences in the workplace often so different from men's?

Studies have shown that women's leadership and management styles are different from men's. This is a result of both upbringing and of the ways in which others perceive women managers. Women's abilities, commitment, style, and skills are often less valuable in the workplace. The stereotypical skill set that men bring to the office is more highly regarded in a business setting than the stereotypical skill set of a female manager. We will examine what these gender-specific skills and capabilities consist of and why American businesses tend to value those typically ascribed to men more than those to women.

Many of the differences between men and women managers took root before birth. Gender roles and gender stereotypes are influenced by the many societal and environmental messages that people receive growing up. As girls and boys grow into professional men and women, they learn from their parents, peers, schools, teachers, and the mass media how they are supposed to act, communicate, learn, think, and look. These messages are prevalent at a very early age, and children carry the lessons learned from observation and imitation with them into adulthood and then into their workplaces.

As a result, gender-specific behaviors are common in today's managers. Rampant stereotypes about how women managers act versus how men managers act create more gender role expectations, assumptions, and even discomfort in talking about gender issues in the workplace. This chapter focuses on the roots of gender stereotypes that affect the way managers are treated by their bosses and peers, how they lead, and how ultimately successful they are in a corporate environment.

Learning Objectives

■ To understand what it means to be a boy or a girl and analyze the difference between "sex" and "gender."

■ To assess whether gender roles are based in biology, sociology, or some combination of these.

■ To explore whether gender determines what toys we should play with, what we look like, what we wear, what we should study in school, how we lead, what kind of job we should get when we grow up, or what role we should play in our families.

■ To determine how women's and men's roles in organizations are valued and understand perceptions of "women's work" versus "men's work."

■ To understand how development of gender roles affect workplace issues such as glass ceilings, dysempowerment, work/family tension, and pay inequity.

GENDER DEVELOPMENT THEORIES

Gender stereotypes start early. For example, between 1989 and 1990, educational gender inequity researchers Myra and David Sadker (1994) asked more than 500 male and female students in 3 southeastern states to write essays about what they would do if they woke up as a member of the opposite sex. Although girls had varying desires to be boys, nearly 45 percent of them saw positive changes that would occur as a result of the change. In general, they felt that as boys they would command greater respect, feel more secure, and be less fearful of being judged. In contrast, very few boys listed positive changes to which they would look forward. Many boys even elaborated on how they would escape the dreadful fate of waking up female—one boy said, "If I woke up tomorrow as a girl, I would stab myself in the heart 50 times with a dull butter knife. If I were still alive, I would run in front of a huge eighteenth gear and have my brains mashed to Jell-O. That would do it."

Gender stereotypes are so well defined in young people that some would even resort to suicide to avoid having to live in a new gender role. The notion that sex essentially seals a young person's fate stems from how vigorously society promotes gender roles for males and females.

Men and women are different. We have different biological traits and different social traits that affect our behavior, our socialization, and our role in society. Gender roles are defined as "sets of norms that communicate what is generally appropriate for each sex" (Eagly, 1997). They develop from a wide range of social forces that teach children their natural role in their culture. Each culture exerts its own ideas and definitions

---
BOX 4.1

Men, Women, and Dreams

Men and women dream differently. Studies have shown that men dream about action, the outdoors, and unfamiliar people and settings, whereas women dream about their homes and workplaces, people they know, and activities that they feel comfortable doing. People in women's dreams often share friendly, nonaggressive interactions. Men dream about conflict, weapons, violence, sports, sexual activity, and achievement. They tend to see more male characters in their dreams, whereas women see more children and family members in their dreams (Bursik, 1998).

---

of what is appropriate behavior for men and women based on the history and values of that culture. Some argue that gender roles are a natural outcome of biological differences; others assert that gender roles form from social pressures and prejudices.

Biological Determinism

Biological determinism argues that distinctions between boys and girls are based in evolutionary science. A child's sex is scientifically determined and shapes and informs a person's role in society from the crib to the grave.

Because girls are born with the ability to bear children, we ascribe to them certain traits and responsibilities. Biological determinists argue that because women carry babies and endure labor and delivery, they are more serious about sex and sexual partners than men. Women are supposedly more likely to look for commitment from mates and are thought to be less promiscuous than men. Conversely, men are biologically necessary only during fertilization and less crucial to the childbirth process. It is argued that this is why men are more focused on the sexual act itself, and less interested in commitment and emotional investment in their relationships with women. Biological determinists further extrapolate that, as childbearers, women are more connected to children, more nurturing, and more caring, thus making them better suited for careers in the social service industry or in nurturing professions like nursing and teaching.

A woman's 4-week menstrual cycle is thought to bring biological changes in behavior, which include swings in mood, self-esteem, energy level, and physical comfort. When a girl enters puberty, not only does she begin a menstrual cycle, her secondary sex characteristics develop. Her body fat increases, her breasts start to grow, and her hips broaden. This biological reality is often linked directly to decreasing self-esteem in adolescent girls (Lough, 1998).

Another important biologically based difference is in the human brain. Scientists have found that the base of the brain, the hypothalamus, is more delicate in women than in men. Because the hypothalamus determines a person's reaction to severe emotional trauma or shock, some scientists hypothesize that women react more strongly to shock and emotional crises than men do because of their more fragile and sensitive hypothalamus.

Furthermore, studies show that the corpus callosum, the connector between the right and left brain hemispheres, is more pronounced in men than in women. Thus the left brain, assumed to be the hemisphere that rules logical, linear thought, and the right brain, which houses creativity, emotion, intuition, and artistry, are more closely connected in women than in men. Some argue that the different corpus callosum size results in men being more left-brain dominant, whereas women use both sides equally, which may explain why some women are less adept at math, science, and other logical pursuits, and some excel in writing, art, and other "soft" and "emotional" endeavors. Men are more logical, linear, and rational and are ruled by their minds more than their hearts (de Lacoste-Utamsing, cited in Rosenor, 1995).

Scientists have also documented that men are typically taller and physically stronger than women. Men's superior physical strength led biological determinists to argue that pure physical strength caused early men to be hunters and defenders of the community and early women to be gatherers and nurturers. As humans evolved, men logically became the leaders of their families, whereas women, with their delicate reproductive role, were often protected and taken care of.[1]

The cornerstone of biological determinism is that differing reproductive systems, body shape and size, brain structure, and capacity for physical exertion and strength cause gender roles to develop logically and naturally based on biological reality. Therefore, traditional gender roles should not and cannot be altered artificially by forcing women into traditionally male roles, such as breadwinner, inventor/scientist, defender, or leader. Some extremists even argue that women are unsuited for leadership and management positions because they are too emotional and erratic in their moods and because they cannot be trusted to make logical, competent decisions.

Social Constructionism

Social constructionists assert that gender is formed by cultural forces that indicate how people should act, play, move, and dream based on their sex. Sex is biological, but gender is an identity shaped through interactions with others.

In response to the biological determinist argument, some researchers have shown that women, with proper social guidance, can achieve as many physical feats as men. Women can grow to be just as tall as men, run just as fast, hit a ball just as hard, and excel in math and science to the same degree. Without negative social messages teaching girls that they cannot accomplish the same physical and intellectual feats as boys, social constructionists believe that girls can do and be everything that boys can.

Albert Bandura developed the social learning theory in 1963 that is still used widely to describe the way children learn. Children, he explains, imitate and model behaviors they observe from their parents, teachers, friends, and the media. As children parrot gender-specific behaviors, they learn about what it is to be male versus female. Gender roles, according to the social learning theory, are generated through an ongoing process of teaching and modeling gender stereotypes from generation to generation.

In 1974, the Bem Sex Role Inventory, still a popular determinant of gender role identification, showed that traits widely associated with nurturing and expressiveness

---

[1]It is important to note that women of color were not treated with such delicacy. Women of color did not have the privilege or social role that would allow them to be protected from hard labor. Often they worked in fields along with their husbands, fathers, sons, and brothers.

were feminine, whereas assertive and directive behavioral traits were considered masculine (Bem, 1996). Gender role stereotypes have changed very little since the early 1970s, and, although women's roles in the workplace and family have changed somewhat, the assumptions about women's abilities have not.

PARENTS

As the most immediate purveyors of culture for their children, parents are critical in determining how children view gender roles at a very early age. Parents are responsible for modeling household roles, buying toys, encouraging play, reading books, choosing video and TV programs, and feeding and clothing their children. All of these activities are integral to children's formulation of men's and women's roles.

With technology that can tell the sex of a fetus before it is born, the influence of parents often starts in the womb and carries strongly into adolescence. Parents who know the sex of their baby before birth talk to the fetus differently depending on its sex. Researchers have discovered that boys are spoken to casually and with full-bodied voices, whereas girls are spoken to in gentle, cooing voices. In fact, women who are expecting girls often rub their stomachs with more frequency than those who are expecting boys (Silverstein and Rashbaum, 1994).

A study by Jeffery Rubin found that parents described their newborn babies using stereotypical language depending on the child's sex. Even though the newborns were the same weight and length, parents described the boys as "firm" and "alert," whereas the girls were "delicate," "soft," and "awkward" (Lindsey, 1990). Girl babies were also handled and held more gently than boy babies, with the assumption that a girl is more fragile than a boy.

Women are assumed to be more emotionally fragile in the workplace, also. Women's feelings are considered more delicate and co-workers expect women to react emotionally to negative information. Consequently, critical feedback is often softened to protect the woman manager's feelings, and she is not able to grow and improve as an employee with the same level of candid and honest feedback that a male manager might receive.

Through childhood, boys' and girls' bedrooms send distinct gendered signals. Boys rooms are often painted in dark colors and have decorations related to action and adventure. Girls' bedrooms are typically decorated in pink, or other soft colors.

Young girls are often encouraged to dress up in their mother's clothes as a way to identify and bond. They become aware of the power of clothing at a very early age with the understanding that clothing brings them closer to their mothers. It is mom's clothing that gives a young girl ideas about how women should look, dress, and smell.

In an office, it is often assumed that women should wear pantyhose, skirts, and makeup. In some workplaces, women who wear pants are thought to be overly aggressive or trying too hard to be like a man. It is important that a woman's physical appearance be appropriate for traditional expectations.

Parental Role Modeling

In the traditional two-parent household, even when both parents work, the mother generally is responsible for feeding and cleaning, and the father takes responsibility for fixing and building.[2] Girls learn that the female role in the family involves cooking, cleaning, shopping, decorating, and caring for children. Boys learn that the male role involves physical labor, planning, manual dexterity, and financial savvy. Boys are more likely to have chores that involve maintenance, such as mowing the lawn. Girls are more likely to have domestic chores, like doing the dishes or cleaning. Men's jobs outside the home are taken more seriously than women's, and the mother is often expected to be more accessible and available to her children. A result of this role modeling is that young children identify gender role appropriateness for various household activities and carry stereotypes about men's and women's work with them as they mature.

In the workplace, women are more frequently expected to plan parties, make coffee, buy presents, and perform other caretaking tasks. Because boys and girls learn that it is the mother's job to nurture and do domestic tasks, it is assumed that women are also better suited to these types of endeavors in a professional environment.

Studies show that when parents create an atmosphere with nonsex-typed messages, children have a stronger sense of personal ability, achievement, self-worth, and self-esteem. For example, mothers who work outside the home teach their children that everyone in the family has a role in the outside world, and that work roles are not gender determined. Interestingly, families that exhibit nongender stereotyped behaviors, such as those with a father who cooks and cleans and a mother who fixes the car, are found to be more supportive of one another and closer than in a traditional family with traditional gender roles (Witt, 1997). We hypothesize that as more and more children are raised in this type of environment, corporate cultures will dictate that nurturing, caretaking work is shared among all employees.

Toys

As children develop their first sense of men's and women's work from watching their parents, they also begin learning social interaction skills as they play with their first toys. Sex segregation in toy marketing and purchasing leads girls and boys to develop different skill sets, knowledge bases, and self-identities. Often girls play with toys related to caretaking, homemaking, and crafts, allowing them to curry their imaginations and creativity, to build relationships, and to develop nurturing skills such as baking, caring, and holding. However, playing with these toys limits girls to identifying with the world of the kitchen and the house, rather than with the world outside. Furthermore, doll play, which involves hair styling and fashion design, encourages girls to focus on beauty and clothing.

Boys typically play with toys involving sports, science, building, and mechanics, encouraging them to develop their skills in problem solving, planning, and physical/spatial relationships. Through mechanical and scientific games, boys learn to see the world

---

[2]The traditional family is not the norm in the United States, although it is a pervasive image on TV and in movies. According to the U.S. Bureau of Census, in the United States, more than 28 percent of families are single-parent households, and single-mother households make up more than three-fourths of these. In single-mother households, mothers serve as role models who do everything. They bear the full responsibility for the financial and emotional care of the family. In such a household, a girl might become extremely self-reliant and look toward her mother for both nurturing and care, and problem-solving and creating.

BOX 4.2

Barbie

When Barbie was released in 1959, she presented a whole new range of options to young girls. As a teenager with no children, Barbie represented a departure from the domestic sphere, a movement toward carefree womanhood. But over the years Barbie's personality has come to mean much more than entrance into the public life, it has meant entrance into the world of adult sexuality, and into the shopping mall, the eating disorder clinic, and the cosmetic surgeon's office.

An American icon whose population nears 800 million, Barbie represents an unattainable femininity. In an anthropometic study that scaled measurements of Barbie's body to that of an average American woman who measures five foot four, researchers found that "Barbie's body differs wildly from anything approximating 'average' female body weight and proportions." Barbie, if she were a living woman, would have bust, waist, hip measurements of 38–16–38. The average model is 33–23–33, 5 feet 9 inches tall and weighs 110 pounds (Urla & Swedlund, 1995; Motz, 1992).

Not only has Mattel, the manufacturer of this plastic woman, been criticized for donning her with a body that could be deemed clinically anorexic, but they have been attacked for giving her unusually large breasts and an unstoppable consumption of clothes, shoes, dream houses, and cars, which have rarely insinuated that Barbie has a place in the paid workforce. Until recently, the company has also received negative attention for its failure to create and market other dolls of color.

---

around them and how it is built. Their involvement in sports also expands their world view, taking them out of the house and into a wider environment with more opportunities for growth. Toys marketed to boys do not often challenge them to think about their relationships with others or about domestic needs. Even the toys that encourage open communication and relationships with others, such as action figures, are almost always based on physical violence, aggression, and warfare.

When we look at how children's play mirrors adult roles for men and women, we note that, as boys are encouraged through their play to consider and navigate in the world outside the home, they learn that as adults they will be expected to and prepared to venture forth into the workplace and into lifelong careers. However, girls are given the option of careers, but also learn that many women have short-lived careers, which they will set aside for family and domestic pursuits. Girls' toys teach them about their future roles as homemakers and caregivers. If boys play with girls' toys, they are chastised and thought to be sissies, effeminate, or gay. They learn that grown men do not do the bulk of the domestic work and that their wives will stay home and take care of the house and children.

However, girls who play with boy toys or engage in typically male activities, like sports, building, or mechanics, are often called tomboys. Although our culture is changing to make room for, and even reward, athletic girls, there still remains a stigma toward girls who do not also learn how to be girls (i.e., how to cook, sew, clean, and caretake).

PEERS

According to Janet Lever's (1978) study of children's play behaviors, a child's peer group has far-reaching effects on girls' ability to communicate and compete. The friends that young people cultivate and the games they play shape how they will interact in their future workplaces (Wolff, 1993). Some of the distinct differences between the play styles of boys and girls include

GIRLS	BOYS
Play inside, in private	Play outside, in public
Have best friends	Have buddies
Play in pairs or triplets	Play in large groups
Take turns and play cooperatively	Engage in competitive, physical, rough-and-tumble games
Complain to adults when boys invade space	Play games for longer periods of time than girls
Play for shorter periods of time, taking breaks if there is a conflict between friends	Control more playground space than girls
	See girls as "polluting" and having "cooties"

From their play, boys learn to participate successfully in competitive situations, develop societally valued organizational and networking skills, feel comfortable in public spaces, and gain independence. Girls do not learn these skills and lessons. Instead, they learn to care for others, build relationships, and share through their play (Lever, 1976).

Friendships between girls are based on sharing thoughts and feelings, whereas boys' friendships are more activity-based (Wolff, 1993). Girls organize themselves into small cliques and their alliances to friends shift regularly. In girls' groups, the leader is chosen based on subjective criteria like clothes, looks, and popularity. In boys' groups, leadership is based on athletic or other well-defined skills and measurable successes (Wolff, 1993). Researchers also found that young women spend more time in conversation with friends than boys do. Girls discussed relationships, people, and personal issues, whereas boys discussed sports and activities.

Carol Gilligan's 1992 study, *Meeting at the Crossroads,* published with colleague Lyn Mikal Brown, tracked 7- to 18-year-old-girls at a private day school in Cleveland, Ohio. With a team of researchers, Brown and Gilligan went into the Laurel School between 1986 and 1990 to observe the process of the mostly white middle- to upper-class girls' social and psychological development. They found a gradually developing recognition by girls that their experiences and feelings are not valued. At seven and eight, the relationships these girls had with one another appeared genuine; although they tried to be pleasant, they were honest about feelings of not always wanting to be nice. Girls challenged authority figures and each other when they felt issues of fairness were at stake. They spoke honestly about friendship and openly about emotional love and pain. These girls had strong relationships and strong voices.

But by 9 and 10, many girls had already come to realize that "it is better not to speak, to pretend things are fine when they are not, to act as if nothing has happened—especially maybe if you are a girl." They had learned to follow the lead of an idealized perfect girl, "the girl who had no bad thoughts or feelings, the kind of person everybody wants to be with, the girl, who in her perfection, is worthy of praise and attention, worthy of inclusion and love." The interviewers found repeatedly that as these girls "come up against a relational impasse that shuts down their experience or shuts down their loud voices," they lose confidence in themselves, begin to feel a growing confusion about their own emotions and desires, find their voices constricting, and lose the ability to articulate their experiences and thoughts.

The researchers also identified girls, who, by age 11, had begun to resist the pressures they felt to silence their voices and to move out of relationships with themselves and other girls and women. Brown and Gilligan admit that in studying the great number of girls who do move toward becoming the "perfect girl," they missed an opportunity to carefully examine the girls they identified as "resisters." Continuing to ponder the ways in which girls find the strength to reject what their peers swallow, the researchers did identify many of the working-class girls and the girls of color as the resisters. They surmised that these girls who "live in the margins, who are so clearly at odds with the dominant models of beauty and perfection [are able to] reveal the cultural hand behind these standards."

Girls clearly interact with peers very differently than their male counterparts. As girls move toward adolescence, their desire to be vocal and honest dissipates in favor of belonging and inclusion. Girls are relationship driven and prefer small, intimate groups of friends. Boys form relationships based more on skill and less on emotion.

When boys grow into adults and enter the workplace, the ability to engage with others based on objective, skill-based criteria is highly valued. Promotions and rewards are often based on criteria such as number of deals closed, revenue generated, number of new clients, lowered expenses, and sometimes results of customer satisfaction surveys. Men learn about these types of evaluation measures early. As boys, they choose leaders based on who runs the fastest, gets the best grades, or scores the most goals.

However, girls' relationship building and emotional connection skills, according to Lever (1976), "have little market value and can even impede their success." Women's leadership styles, which are often based on relationship building and maintenance, are typically undervalued and misunderstood in organizations. Girls pick leaders based on highly subjective criteria—clothing, attitude, physical attractiveness, and popularity among the boys. When they later enter the workplace, they sometimes strive to be popular by not making waves, befriending everybody, and focusing on people more than on objective, quantitative performance measures. The natural instinct to nurture and caretake, which was reinforced throughout childhood through toys, activities, and parental role modeling, are not typically skills that are valued in a workplace unless they contribute very directly to the bottom line.

EDUCATION

Children spend thousands of hours in school and are heavily influenced by teachers, educational content, and the school's social environment. In school, children learn to think and absorb information, build their intellectual self esteem, develop analytical and critical thinking skills, and begin to consider areas of future professional interest.

BOX 4.3

Girls and Sports

Until 1972, it was not illegal in the United States for a school to deny participation and scholarships to young athletes based on sex. Title IX of the Education Amendments Act of 1972 changed that by mandating that all educational institutions receiving federal funding treat males and females the same regarding "any education program or activity," which included sports (Greendorfer, 1993).

Although there is still a great deal of controversy whether or not schools really do practice equal treatment for male and female athletes,[1] Title IX did contribute to increasing girls' participation in sports. Today, more than 2 million young women are active in sports, as compared to only 300,000 before 1972.

The benefits of sports participation are both emotional/mental and physical, especially for young women. Girls who play sports are less likely to develop chronic diseases as they reach adulthood, are less likely to be smokers, and have better body images.[2] Studies show that children ages 9 to 10 who participate in sports are more physically and socially adept than their nonparticipating counterparts. Adolescent females are 40 percent less likely to drop out of high school and 33 percent less likely to become pregnant as a teenager if they play sports. They are also better students and are thought to have a higher likelihood of future success as leaders.[3]

Sports teach young women about their bodies and their physical health. Girls learn to be more action-oriented and active, learn about teamwork and large group dynamics, and are given opportunities to practice leadership roles. The masculine leadership traits of competition, aggression, and achievement-orientation are modeled in sports, and girls who learn how to compete, assert themselves, and value measurable achievements are mastering the traits associated with success in today's workplace.

---

[1]Women college athletes receive less than 24 percent of college sports' operating budgets and less than 18 percent of college recruiting money according to the Web site maintained by the Feminist Majority Foundation, www.feminist.org, "Empowering Women in Sports."

[2]Miller, J. and Levy, G. (1996). Gender role conflict, gender-typed characteristics, self-concepts, and sport socialization in female athletes and nonathletes. *Sex Roles, 35* (1/2), 111–120; Web site maintained by Girls, Inc. at www.girlsinc.org.

[3]This is true across race boundaries. For example, a study of Hispanic girls showed that sports participation was a significant indicator of higher grades and better test results in school according to the Web site maintained by the Feminist Majority Foundation, www.feminist.org, "Empowering Women in Sports."

Teacher–Student Interactions

Young women are particularly influenced by their teachers and often look to these adult role models to develop life plans. Studies show that women who strive for high-level management positions often had strong female role models in college or were intellectually challenged by parents and other adult role models (Golombok, 1994).

Teachers create subtle gendered messages, especially at precollege levels, just in the *way* they teach. For example, several studies have found that teachers, often unwittingly, instruct, talk to, perceive, and praise girls differently than boys in the classroom.

In 1975, psychologists Lisa Serbin and Daniel O'Leary examined gender distinctions in the way early childhood educators explained instructions to boys and girls. Repeatedly they found that teachers took time to offer boys detailed instructions that ultimately enabled the boys to complete the assignment or task on their own, whereas female students were less likely to receive explanations, and instead, teachers completed the tasks for the girls.

Boys receive more consistent and varied responses to their work including praise, encouragement, criticism, and acknowledgment (Sadker, 1994). By giving boys the tools to learn and evaluate, educators ensure that boys are lifelong learners who feel secure in their abilities. However, for girls the system reinforces and builds a lack of confidence and encourages girls not to question mechanics or process.

A study conducted by the American Association of University Women (1995) explained how teachers contribute to girls' loss of self-esteem by showering males with attention and praise despite their lack of adherence to classroom regulations. In school settings where hand raising is a rule, teachers accept answers for and give more praise to boys even though boys break the hand raising rule more often.

As psychologist Barbara Mackoff (1996) writes, "When teachers are calling on boys, they ignore the needs of girls, especially those who may need more 'wait time,' and who are less likely to risk giving the wrong answer. As a result girls get less practice in the lessons of speaking out or learning by trial and error. They learn to let the boys answer."

The equation is not as simple as boys versus girls; race and socioeconomic status also play a significant role in how teachers approach their pupils. Studies indicate that when African American girls and white boys have similar successes in the classroom, the girls are credited for putting a great deal of effort into their work, whereas the boys are chastised for not working up to their potential (Grant, 1984).

From interactions with teachers, girls develop less faith in their intellectual abilities, learn to rely on others to do the thinking for them, and allow boys to express opinions first. In many cases, young women may become so discouraged by their perceived lack of intellectual ability, that they do not reach for the top when it comes to career planning. As they carry these messages with them to work, women are afraid to express their point of view and feel insecure in their ability to form creative, intellectual solutions to problems.

Most business settings encourage men and women managers to actively assert their opinions in order to be heard. A professional who fails to speak up in a workplace can be considered lazy, passive, unambitious, and not committed to the overall success of the company. These people often are passed over for promotions because they do not demonstrate leadership, innovation, or commitment. When women learn that they do not need to speak up in school, they carry this message with them into their professional life, and consequently, are ignored, resented, and/or overlooked for promotions.

Classroom Content

Take this quick test: Name 10 famous women in history. Now name 10 famous women inventors or women scientists. It is very likely that you had trouble. When we look at many history textbooks, we discover that they are based on a history-of-the-heroes

---

BOX 4.4

Classroom Strategies for Teaching to Girls

Researchers and educators have suggested the following strategies for ensuring girls take a more active role in learning, and experience greater success and rewards in the classroom (Pollina, 1995).

1. Connect math, science, and technology to real world.

2. Foster a collaborative learning environment where students learn in small groups and teams.

3. Provide opportunities for girls to act as experts by allowing them to design and critique their own work.

4. Create positive role models for girls by encouraging them to take leadership roles in science labs, computer labs, and sports.

5. Teach girls to use technology as both a tool and a toy. Girls need to learn how computers can help them solve problems and encourage communication.

6. Encourage girls to use their verbal skills, especially in math and science classes. Girls may be less intimidated by math and science if they incorporate words, instead of just numbers, as they learn. For example, Ann Pollina, dean at the Westover School in Connecticut, asks her math students to keep a written journal focusing on their experiences in the math or science class.

7. Use testing that accommodates analytical thinking, experimentation, and real-life examples. Testing that is multiple choice or true/false has been shown to favor boys' detached learning styles. Girls will have greater success if they are able to engage with the testing material.

---

approach. In other words, most of our textbooks focus on the contributions of successful men and ignore successful women.

Because of U.S. women's history as nonvoting, nonvalued citizens, women have been excluded from or hold minimal importance in history books. Although most people know the names Rosa Parks and Susan B. Anthony, a significant number of women in U.S. and world history are overlooked or underdiscussed in textbooks. A study conducted nearly 30 years ago found that two sentences was the typical amount of space subscribed to the 1920 victory of women's right to vote. You might be surprised and disappointed to learn that these patterns have not changed dramatically since the 1970s. In fact, when researchers Myra and David Sadker (1994) examined history textbooks used in 3 states during the 1992 school year, they found that elementary school textbooks had 25 percent more pictures of males than females. One world history textbook mentioned only 11 female names throughout and had only 7 pages related to women.

Science and math textbooks are even worse at including women. Although almost every science text remarks on Marie Curie, most texts do not mention other women inventors and scientists. In math textbooks, boys are used in examples and pictured far more often than girls. Study questions are often based on scenarios more familiar to boys than to girls. For example, math word problems tend to focus on building, transportation, spatial relationships, and sports.

Furthermore, girls do not see as many positive role models in math and science-related fields and are sent the message that girls are not equipped for success in academic pursuits that are typically considered masculine. For example, in the late 1980s,

---

BOX 4.5

The Spice Girls

These authors agree that probably the most disturbing, annoying, and contradictory role models for girls today has been the Spice Girls. We totally disagree on the value of the Spice Girls, and we find many of our friends arguing about whether or not the Spice Girls are positive role models for young women.

"We're freshening up feminism for the nineties," they said in an interview in 1997. "Feminism has become a dirty word. Girl Power is just a nineties way of saying it."[1] Scantily clad in tight, trashy clothing, the Spice Girls very consciously use their sex appeal as a selling point. They simultaneously teach that girls should be assertive and independent but should also use their

---

[1]From Web site maintained by the Feminist Majority Foundation, www.feminist.org, "Empowering Women in Sports" and Miller and Levy, 1996.

sexuality and femininity to find power and voice. Recently, when two of the Spice Girls announced that they were pregnant, adults everywhere worried that these larger-than-life icons of girl power were sending the message that it is "cool" to be young, pregnant, and unmarried.

Their message resonates for young girls: Stand up, speak out, be a good friend to women, embrace your sexuality, take risks, and express your individuality. But adults criticize them endlessly for their questionable beginnings as a profit-driven women's answer to the Beatles, for their tabloid-covered quibbles, and their general trashy appearances. We don't know whether they have done more good than harm for influencing a new generation of feminists, but they do a great job of highlighting some of the conflicts within feminism today.

---

women earned only 21 percent of the doctorates in chemistry, 17 percent in math, 9 percent in physics and 9 percent in engineering (National Science Foundation, 1997–1998).

These seemingly little omissions from the pages of textbooks and the dearth of female role models, especially in math and science, can, over the course of a childhood of schooling seriously affect a girl's perception of herself. As girls study and find that females are voiceless, nameless, and faceless, they begin to question the value of women in the world and assume that the contributions made by women are unimportant.

Educational institutions and practices are widely responsible for shaping self-esteem, especially regarding an individual's perception of his or her own intelligence and future career potential. As young women learn that they are not as mentally capable as boys and are more valuable for their bodies than for their minds, they have less professional drive and motivation. They question their own competence more in a business setting because they were taught as girls that they aren't as smart as boys. Furthermore, their sense of what is possible for their careers is less grandiose and visionary than for boys. Although girls and boys start thinking at an early age that they can do or be anything they want, girls learn both at home and in school that they don't have the ability to excel at everything they attempt.

MEDIA

The most omnipresent influence in the development of gender roles is the mass media. It is virtually impossible for a child to escape the reach of TV, movies, newspapers, magazines, music, and video games. All of these media outlets transmit messages and images that are carefully constructed by public relations firms and advertising agencies to sell ideas or products to certain populations.

Media images invade our everyday lives and heavily impact the way we view ourselves, our families, our friends, and our roles in society. They reflect on and reshape our notions of gender. Daily acts as simple as watching television, reading magazines, or turning on computers can trigger minute changes in the ways we identify ourselves in relation to our gender or can add to the existing boundaries that we create for ourselves. For instance, a young girl might open a teen magazine to any given page and find an advertisement for makeup. It is impossible to say how she will interpret this ad, but the marketers would like her to believe that she is not complete, not mature, not feminine enough without makeup. Through the ad, she is encouraged to spend her money on a certain brand of makeup and to believe this product and the practice of makeup application is essential in her growth process as a woman.

Children are particularly susceptible to framing an understanding of gender roles through the lens of the mass media. They look, watch, and listen to these images without knowing consciously what is happening to them. Children believe that these images reflect who they are supposed to be. Television characters and sports figures become role models.

Most of us dream of having lives similar to the near-perfect existence of our favorite TV family, or believe that beauty is defined by the models in the ads for our favorite brand of clothing. Given the sheer volume of media exposure that children (and adults) receive, it is no surprise that TV, movies, and video games are some of the most influential forces in the socialization and gender role identification of a child. The mass media bears a huge responsibility for informing the attitudes of entire generations of children.

A Neilsen media study in 1993 showed that the average American child watches 23 hours of television per week and the average teenager watches 22 hours. If video movies and video games are included, the teenagers watch up to 55 hours of programming weekly (Strasburger, 1995). Children have seen an average of 360,000 ads by the time they reach age 18 (Harris, 1989).

The more a child watches TV, the more he or she engages in gender stereotyping. Toddlers and preschoolers begin associating gender labels with certain behaviors and stereotypes. Preschoolers imitate cartoon characters that are the same gender as themselves (Durkin and Nugent, 1998), and by kindergarten, children can already identify gender-based activities and occupations from TV (Thompson and Zerbinos, 1995).

When we look at gender-stereotyped images and behaviors the mass media puts forth, it becomes clearer that, as children model these behaviors and aspire to these images, they are developing distinct gender roles that have the potential to carry forward into adolescence, adulthood, and into the workplace.

Content analyses of cartoons, commercials, daytime programming, and prime time TV shows prove again and again that women characters are severely underrepresented as compared to male characters. Women are portrayed in domestic or service-oriented roles, whereas men are represented in a wide range of occupations, mostly white-collar. Women are usually younger than men and are more likely to be married and unemployed. Women are dependent, nurturing, unintelligent, can't make decisions, and are often victimized; men are assertive, smart, quick, objective, authoritative, and need to defend and protect the women in their lives. As young men and women observe these characters, they develop a societally accepted notion of women's work and women's roles in homes and workplaces. They learn that men's work is more versatile, responsibility-laden, and profitable, whereas women's work is domestic and geared toward serving others.

In magazines marketed to girls, endless pages of ads for beauty products and clothing tell young women that their appearance is what will get them noticed and accepted by their peers. Articles on relationships, teen idols, and the latest teen fashion trends overpower the few articles on professional careers, leadership, or sports. As girls read these magazines, they come to believe that their value to society is measured by how they look, act, and who they date and spend their time with. In order to fit in with other girls, they must wear makeup, have blemish-free skin, dress fashionably, have a boyfriend, and watch certain TV programs and movies.

As girls and boys view and absorb mass media images, they learn about how they should act as men and women in society. The definition of what is attractive and desirable in a woman is created by the images on billboards, magazines, TV, and in movies. Consequently, girls grow up believing that women with model-like appearances are considered beautiful and measure themselves against an unhealthy, virtually unattainable definition of beauty. A study published in *Newsweek* found that girls begin discussing weight at age seven and often begin dieting at age nine (Orenstein, 1995). The obsession with unattainable beauty does not stop at adolescence: One recent poll showed that 48 percent of American women are dissatisfied with their appearance as compared to 23 percent in 1972 (Schneider, 1990).

The exclusion of female role models in textbooks, TV shows, movies, and books makes us believe that women are relatively unimportant and have less to contribute to society than men. This media-imposed attitude spills over into the workplace where women struggle for legitimacy as managers and leaders. "Sex role spillover" happens when gender stereotypes that are pervasive in families, schools, peer groups, and the mass media become relevant in the workplace. Even though a woman may enter a workplace under the assumption that her colleagues are professionals, and, therefore, she will be thought of as an individual with specific skills and experience, she may not be able to escape the confines of the culture in which she lives. The workplace is a very natural home for stereotypes and gender-based assumptions that we make as a society and that are fed by the mass media.

WORKPLACE IMPLICATIONS

Given the different ways that boys and girls are socialized, and given the common stereotypes about men and women, it should be no surprise that men and women have gender-distinct experiences in the workplace. This book discusses some of the challenges that women face as they try to climb corporate ladders, earn equal pay, juggle work and family, and change patriarchal, male-dominated corporate cultures. These challenges are deeply rooted in the way we are raised, the lessons we learn growing up, the people we imitate and aspire to be, and the people with whom we surround ourselves.

BOX 4.6

New Feminist Movements

Feminism has taken many twists and turns, from Seneca Falls, New York, to the suffregettes winning a woman's right to vote in the United States, to modern-day feminism. The modern feminist movement has been widely criticized for being too single-minded and narrowly focused on affluent/middle-class white women and the issues facing them. As new feminist movements have taken firm root in the United States and all over the world, one of the most interesting and promising feminist discourse happening today is among Third Wave feminists.

The Third Wave Agenda incorporates some of the typical feminist discussion around beauty, sexual abuse, and power imbalances in the world, but it also makes use of the "pleasure, danger, and defining power of those structures." Third Wave feminists explain, "we are products of all the contradictor definitions of and differences within feminism . . . what oppresses me may not oppress you, that what oppresses you may be something I participate in, and what oppresses me may be something you participate in."[1]

This lively discourse generated by Third Wave feminism has helped shape some of the most current trends for young feminists. For example, the explosion of small press journals and 'zines in the past five years has created a voice for young women to express their anger, rage, ideas, and talk about issues that are important to them. Zines are usually low-budget operations, and the most important aspect of their publication is not sales or revenue but giving voice to young feminists.

---

[1]Third Wave, feminist activist collective mission: Third Wave is a member-driven multiracial, multicultural, multisexuality national nonprofit organization devoted to feminist and youth activism for change. Our goal is to harness the energy of young women and men by creating a community in which members can network, strategize, and ultimately, take action. By using our experiences as a starting point, we can create a diverse community and cultivate a meaningful response. From Heywood, L. and Drake, J., *Third Wave Agenda: Being Feminist, Doing Feminism.* Minneapolis, MI (University of Minnesota Press, 1997).

Some researchers maintain that men and women share similar values and styles in the workplace; corporate culture is the only factor that shapes how women are treated. Others explain that men and women really do lead and manage differently, and that women's styles are undervalued, and consequently, keep them from achieving high-level success in a company. We think it is both.

Furthermore, it is with extreme trepidation that we discuss women's ways of leading and managing versus men's. It would be impossible to say that all male managers are one way and all female managers are another. In fact, as more women reach higher levels of management, they change expectations and stereotypes. When 10 years ago, male managers looked to their one female peer as the voice of all women managers, they now have several female peers who may all have unique styles, skills, and experiences.

It would be ridiculous for us to view the research we reviewed as inclusive of all women. In the same way that women's accomplishments are excluded from entire bodies of knowledge, much of the literature on women in the workplace focuses solely on white women. Unfortunately, the research does not always acknowledge that it centers on the experiences of heterosexual, white women and pretends that women's experiences are universal. Often excluded from women and management research and gender role development literature are women of color, women with disabilities, and lesbians. The experiences of women in all of these groups are not only unique, they are very difficult to learn about. Although there are a few studies of African American women's experiences in the workplace and occasional statistics on young women of color and the developmental struggles that go beyond gender stereotyping, we found no research on lesbian managers and women managers with disabilities. Therefore, we caution readers from believing that this section universally addresses *all* female managers.

Because women have often been raised to be passive, sweet, nurturing, gentle, caring, and concerned with the feelings of others more than their own needs, they are assumed to be the same in the workplace. Throughout their lives, girls learn that they are not good at math, science, or business. They have few role models in these areas, further reinforcing a sense that women are ill-equipped for linear thought. They are supposed to be driven by emotion and not logic and are hard-pressed to fix, build, or engage in physically or spatially oriented tasks. They learn to bend over backward to protect others' feelings.

In her very popular study of women and leadership, Judy Rosener (1990) explains that women tend to lead "interactively." They take feelings and relationships into consideration as they build a team, share power and information, and give positive feedback to staff. Men tend to be "transactional" as they lead. They have a clear-cut exchange with staff: rewards from the boss in exchange for a job well done. The male manager is undeniably the person in charge of the power and information, and he does not let go of it as he conducts "transactions" with his staff.

Other paradigms of leadership include employee-centered versus job-centered, task-oriented versus interpersonal, autocratic versus democratic, participative versus command and control-oriented. All of these popular models are based on gender stereotypes. In every case, it is clear which leadership style is male and which is female.

In a comparison of Henry Mintzberg's study of male managers and Sally Helgesen's study of female managers, Judy Rosener (1990) found that work habits of men and women are different. For example, men tended to work with no breaks in activity and spent little if any time socializing or engaging in nonwork activities. They tended to base their identities on their job, did not like to share information, and spent little time reflecting. Women, however, took small breaks and spent time socializing with co-workers and team members as a way to build community. Their self-concept was more multifaceted than simply their job and included outside activities and family. Women also spent time reflecting on how their decisions affect others and frequently shared information with co-workers and staff.

The concept of power has very different implications for men and women. Most people associate power with the ability to get things done. In her book, *The Promotable Woman,* Norma Carr-Ruffino (1997) explains that men believe that power in the workplace involves how much information and how much expertise over which they can have control. Women consider themselves powerful when they can offer meaningful support to others.

Carr-Ruffino further explains that men are much more assertive about their skills and expertise. They are more likely to be the primary speaker in a meeting and often try to be persuasive by showing how much they know. Women downplay their skills in an effort to fit into a group. Consequently, men are noticed by male superiors, whereas women are bypassed.

Women make up 40 percent of management positions in the United States, but they are often in staff positions, supporting the work of other people. The jobs most frequently held by women, in human resources and communications-oriented departments, mirror the assumptions made about what women are good at. Women are also expected to do certain kinds of work—planning parties, typing, filing, making coffee, recognizing staff birthdays, and coordinating volunteer or fundraising drives for social causes.

Rosabeth Moss Kanter (1992) identified four typical roles for women in the workplace: the mother, the confidante, the seductress, or the pet. As the mother, a female manager is expected to take time to care for, nurture, and dote on her staff. The confidante must listen compassionately and empathetically to the complaints, concerns, and gossip of co-workers. The seductress is seen as a sex object who makes her male co-workers and superiors feel virile and powerful by flirting with them. The pet is the "good girl" who does not act out, disagree, or challenge. When a woman does not fit into any of these roles, she is an outcast to be feared, ostracized, ignored, and/or teased. Co-workers find the outcast unpredictable because she does not conform to a specific well-known stereotype. She becomes either a militant feminist, women's libber, or deviant, and she is not included in the activities of her peers. She is often passed over for promotions and other professional growth opportunities.

We believe that nonwhite, nonheterosexual, and disabled women create a great deal of fear and unpredictability and thus deviate even further from the norm in a workplace. These women almost always fall into the outcast category, just by virtue of skin color, cultural background, sexual orientation, or physical ability.

In a study of female politicians, Celinda Lake (1992) found that voters turned away from female candidates who were ambitious or aggressive but that they valued those traits in male candidates. By deviating from what voters saw as appropriate behavior for female politicians, women lost votes and lost elections. Voters were frightened and confused by women who acted like men.

Also contributing to difficulties that women have as they climb the corporate ladder is the assumption that women are not risk takers and do not have the cutthroat instincts needed to survive in business. Furthermore, male managers disregard women in making promotion decisions because they assume that women are focused primarily on their families, whereas men are focused on their careers.

Several researchers have written about androgynous management styles that fluctuate depending on situations. The androgynous manager is diplomatic, sincere, committed, innovative, reliable, effective, and flexible. He or she is highly capable of being assertive or passive, logical and emotional, direct and gentle. By framing managerial success in gender-neutral terms, men and women stand on more equal footing. They are equally as qualified to meet the workplace definitions of success when success consists of being flexible and adaptive to various situations, innovation, commitment, integrity, and effectiveness.

SUMMARY OF KEY POINTS

Because of the ways in which gender roles are developed and manifested through children's interactions with parents, peers, teachers, and the mass media, we can begin to understand the roots of gender-based prejudices in the workplace. Expectations of men are very different from expectations of women because of stereotypes we have about men's and women's appropriate roles in society. Women face workplace challenges that men never have to face because of attitudes about women's abilities and leadership styles. The rest of this book identifies some of these challenges, and we hope that you can now read about them with the understanding that they begin as early as the day you were born. We can't escape our gender roles, nor can we escape expectations that our workplace places on us. But we can be aware of how gender roles work, and we can participate in shifting corporate and societal cultures that discourage women from leadership roles based on gender-based assumptions.

Discussion Questions

1. Give an example of a job that a woman may be asked to do in the workplace that mirrors a role she plays in her family.
2. Give three examples of lessons women learn growing up that would cause them to fall into a management stereotype that Rosabeth Moss Kanter describes (mother, confidante, seductress, pet, deviant). How would you describe your workplace personality? Is it similar to any of Kanter's descriptions? What makes you comfortable with your role in a workplace? What is uncomfortable about it?
3. Think about this quote:

   Look like them, talk like them, learn their games, and you will succeed in their world. Unfortunately, following those rules brought to women many of the unhappy consequences as well: emotional distance, isolation, loss of connection to other women, devaluing of family responsibilities, and the hollowness of pretending to be someone else for the dream of success. Women did not change the workplace by entering it in this way; they merely sacrificed themselves to it. (Robin Derry, 1990)

   Do you think this is true? Do women give themselves up to succeed in the workplace? What do women give up? What would you be willing to give up in order to succeed in a corporation?

Case Analysis *A Self Study*

Write a case study of yourself by using the following questions as a guide. The end result should be a story of how the gender roles you watched and emulated shaped you into the person you are today.

1. **Media** What TV shows did you watch? What books did you read? Who were your favorite characters? Were they male or female? What did you learn from these TV or literary characters?
2. **Parents** What roles did your parents play in your household? How did your parents or guardians have an effect on who you are today? What were the important things they told or taught you that you still practice today?

3. **Play and peers**   What were your favorite toys? Do you think someone of the opposite gender would like those toys? What was your favorite game? Did you play inside or outside? Who were your best friends growing up? Were they male or female? How did you interact with them? What was your favorite game during recess at school? Who did you play it with?

4. **School**   Have you had any particular role models in school? Which teachers taught you the most? What classes were your favorite during elementary school and junior high? Were there classes that you didn't like? Why didn't you like them?

5. **Who you are today**   Do you think you are a stereotypical male or female? In which ways do you follow traditional gender roles? What aspects of your development have made you a nonstereotypical male/female?   ■

References and Suggested Readings

Bem, S. (1996). The measurement of psychological androgyny. *Journal of Consulting and Clinical Psychology, 42,* 155–162. Cited in K. Lawrance, D. Taylor, and E. S. Byers. Differences in men's and women's global, sexual and ideal-sexual expressiveness and instrumentality, *Sex Roles, 34*(5/6), 338.

Brown, L. and Gilligan, C. (1992). *Meeting the crossroads.* New York: Ballentine Books.

Bursik, K. (1998). Moving beyond gender differences: Gender role comparisons of manifest dream content. *Sex Roles, 38* (3/4), 203–211.

Carr-Ruffino, N. (1997). *The promotable woman: Ten essential skills for the new millennium.* Franklin Lakes, NJ: Career Press.

Davidson, M. J., and C. L. Cooper. (1992). *Shattering the glass ceiling: The woman manager.* London: Paul Chapman.

de Lacoste-Utamsing, C. (1995). In J. Rosener. *America's competitive secret: Women managers.* New York: Oxford University Press.

Durkin, K. and Nugent, B. (1998). Kindergarten children's gender-role expectations for television actors, *Sex Roles, 38* (5/6), 387–402.

Eagly, A. H. (1997). *Sex differences in social behavior: A social-role interpretation,* Hillsdale, NJ: Erlbaum. Cited in A. Konrad

and K. Cannings, The effects of gender role congruence and statistical discrimination on managerial advancement. *Human Relations, 50* (10), 1307.

Golombok, S. (1994). *Gender development.* New York: Cambridge University Press, p. 50.

Grant, L. (1984). Black females' 'place' in desegregated classrooms. *Sociology of Education, 57,* (2), 207.

Greendorfer, S. (1993). Gender role stereotypes and early childhood socialization, *Women in Sports: Issues and Controversies* (pp. 3–13).

Harris, R. J. (1989). *A cognitive psychology of mass communication.* Hillsdale, NJ: Erlbaum.

How schools shortchange girls: The AAUW Report. (1995). AAUW and Wellsley College Center for Research on Women. Washington, D.C., AAUW Educational Foundation 1992.

Lake, C., unpublished report for EMILY's list. In D. W. Cantor, and T. Bernay. *Women in power: The secrets of leadership.* New York: Houghton Mifflin. 1992, p. 27.

Lever, J. (1978). Sex differences in the complexity of childrens play and games. *American Sociological Review, 43,* 47–48.

Lindsey, L. (1990). *Gender roles: A sociological perspective.* Upper Saddle River, NJ: Prentice Hall.

Lough, N. (1988, May/June). Promotion of sports for girls and women: The necessity and the strategy. *Journal of Physical Education, Recreation & Development, 59*(5), 250–286.

Mackoff, B. (1996). *Growing a girl: Seven strategies for raising a strong spirited daughter.* Bantam Doubleday.

Motz, M. F. (1992). "Seen Through Rose-Tinted Glasses: The Barbie Doll in American Society," In J. Nachbar and K. Lause *Popular Culture: An Introductory Text,* (pp. 211–234). Bowling Green, OH: Bowling Green State University Popular Press.

National Science Foundation. (1997, December–1998, January). Breaking the gender barrier in the physical sciences. *Educational Leadership.*

Orenstein, P. (1995). *School girls: Young women, self esteem and the confidence gap.* New York: Doubleday.

Pollina, A. (1995, September). Gender balance: Lessons from girls in science and mathematics. *Educational Leadership,* pp. 30–33.

Rosener, J. (1990). Ways women lead. Reprinted in *Reach for the top: Women and the changing facts of work life.* Cambridge, MA: Harvard Business School Press.

Sadker, M., and Sadker, D. (1994). *Failing at fairness: How America's schools cheat girls.* New York: Macmillian.

Schneider, K. (1996). Mission impossible. *People Weekly, 45*(22), 64.

Serbin, L., and O'Leary D. (1975, July). How nursery schools teach girls to shut up. *Psychology Today,* 56–58, 102–103.

Silverstein, O., and Rashbaum, B. (1994). *The courage to raise good men.* New York: Viking.

Strasburger, V. C. (1995). *Adolescents and the media: Medical and psychological impact.* Beverly Hills, CA: Sage.

Thompson, T., and Zerbinos, E. (1995). Gender roles in animated cartoons: Has the picture changed in 20 years? *Sex Roles, 32*(9/10), 652.

Urla, J., and Swedlund, A. C. (1995). The anthropometry of Barbie: Unsettling ideals of the feminine body in popular culture. In J. Urla and J. Terry (Eds.), *Deviant bodies: Critical perspectives on difference in science and popular culture,* (pp. 277–313). Bloomington, IN: Indiana University Press.

U.S. Bureau of Census. (1998, April). Current Population Reports, pp. 20–509. "Household and Family Characteristics, 3/97" by Ken Bryson & Lynne Casper, Washington DC.

Witt, S. D. (1997, Summer). Parental influence on children's socialization to gender roles. *Adolescence, 32*(126), 253–259.

Wolff, N. (1993). *Fire with fire: The new female power and how it will change the twenty-first century.* New York: Random House.

CHAPTER

Beyond Gender: The Experience of Women of Color

Marilyn Kern-Foxworth

> *To me equality is the important thing. I don't want preference. I don't want to be preferred as a woman. But I want it acknowledged that I am a human being who has the capacity to do what I do, and it doesn't matter whether I was born a man or woman. The work will be done that way.*
>
> —EUGENIA CHARLES
> *First female prime minister in the Caribbean*
> *Commonwealth of Dominica, 1995*

Chapter Overview

At the intersection of race and gender stand women of color, battered, demoralized, and often beaten by the lines of bias that currently divide white from nonwhite in our society, and male from female. The roads these women navigate demand different and often wrenching alliances. As a result, female African, Latino, Asian, and Native American (ALANA) group members face significant obstacles to their full participation in America's profit, nonprofit, private, educational, and corporate sectors of society.

In their professional roles, women of color are expected to meet or exceed performance standards set for the most part by their white male counterparts. Yet their personal lives extract a loyalty to their cultural heritage that is essential to socializing with family and friends. At the same time, they must struggle with their own identity as women in a society where thinking like a woman is still considered questionable activity. At times, they can even experience pressure to choose between their racial identity and their womanhood.

The work experience of women in America is so varied and vast that those histories and experiences cannot be collapsed into one singular historical context. Women's labor force history in America, although divergent, has always and will continue to be interconnected. Researchers Amott and Matthael (1991) reinforce this analysis by stating, "in a very real sense, the lives of any one group of women have been dependent upon the lives of others, just as they have been dependent upon those of men" (p. 3).

Learning Objectives

- To explore information relative to the status of women of color in the workplace

- To examine employment statistics of women of color working

- To identify cultural traditions that make a difference in the work performance of women of color

- To explore suggestions for helping women of color reach upper-level management positions in corporate America

- To identify strategies to help managers integrate women of color into the workforce

VARIED PERSPECTIVES

The chapter title, "Beyond Gender: The Experience of Women of Color," suggests that participation in the workforce can't be lumped into categories of men and women's experiences. Women of color, in fact, face a different set of experiences altogether than that of white women in the workplace. Even grouping women of color into one category is inadequate in addressing the uniqueness of the individual experience. However, a study by the Catalyst Organization (1999) makes a cogent case for separating the experiences and analyzing the personal, perceptual, and professional differences among women of color.

Statistically significant differences among women of color are illustrated in Figure 5-1. An analysis of this data, along with an exploration of other professional and perceptual differences, clearly demonstrates ways in which African American, Asian American, and Hispanic women differ. The study found differences in education, career mobility, compensation, and supervisory and functional responsibilities among all three groups, although compensation for all three groups, based on median salaries was within $3,000 of each other (Catalyst, 1999).

In terms of their perceptions of barriers and success in the organization, the Catalyst study found that women of color report the same factors (high visibility assignments, exceeding performance expectations, influential mentors, and communication skills) contribute to women's success; however, they attribute different priorities to each of these factors than white women. Whereas many white women reported that significantly exceeding expectations would help drive success, women of color felt that "a double standard of performance existed for people of color compared to whites, so that the performance of women of color was systematically devalued when compared to white women, thus this strategy may not be as effective for them" (Catalyst, 1999, p. 10).

Regarding barriers, again women of color agree that the most significant barriers to advancement are "not having an influential mentor or sponsor, lack of informal networking with influential colleagues, lack of company role models who are members of the same racial/ethnic group and lack of high visibility assignments" (Catalyst, 1999, p. 11). But, their perceptions regarding which barriers affect them most significantly differ from white women. The study concluded, for example, that "the incidence of women of color reporting lack of access to mentors as a barrier is considerably higher than that of white women—47 percent vs. 29 percent—suggesting that experientially and/or perceptually,

Professional:	*Personal:*	*Perceptual:*
Asian Americans are more likely to have graduate education and yet less likely to be within three reporting levels of the CEO or to have supervisory responsibilities.	Latinas and African Americans are more likely to have been born in the U.S. Asian Americans and Latinas are more likely to be bilingual. African Americans are more likely to be single.	African Americans are more likely to believe that they must adjust their style to fit their work environment; that stereotypes about them exist in their organizations; and that AA/EEO helped recruit them to their jobs.

→ *Graduate education:*
- African Americans: 52%
- Asian Americans: 59%
- Latinas: 38%

→ *Reporting within three levels of CEO:*
- African Americans: 13%
- Asian Americans: 6%
- Latinas: 12%

→ *Supervisory responsibilities:*
- African Americans: 57%
- Asian Americans: 41%
- Latinas: 58%

→ *Marital status: Single*
- African Americans: 48%
- Asian Americans: 30%
- Latinas: 35%

→ *Foreign-born*
- African Americans: 5%
- Asian Americans: 66%
- Latinas: 27%

→ *Bilingual:*
- African Americans: 13%
- Asian Americans: 77%
- Latinas: 78%

→ *Need to adjust style:*
- African Americans: 36%
- Asian Americans: 25%
- Latinas: 20%

→ *Existence of stereotypes:*
- African Americans: 56%
- Asian Americans: 46%
- Latinas: 37%

→ *AA/EEO helped with recruitment:*
- African Americans: 55%
- Asian Americans: 30%
- Latinas: 43%

FIGURE 5-1 Statistically Significant Differences among Women of Color

Source: Catalyst, 1999.

this is a more salient issue for women of color" (p. 11). Although white women believe that their opportunities in corporate America have improved during the past five years, less than half of the women of color surveyed in the Catalyst study felt there were any changes. The study reports that women of color are "more than twice as likely as white women to believe that there has been no change in advancement opportunities (38 percent vs. 15 percent)" (p. 12).

The perspective of extending a discussion of gender differences to racial and ethnic differences within gender presents organizations and leaders with an opportunity to think about diversity in the broadest way possible. Clearly, individuals share some common experiences, but the differences really can affect policy, strategy, and ultimately, equity.

AFRICAN AMERICAN WOMEN

The women of this world must exercise leadership quality, dedication, concern and commitment which is not going to be shattered by inanities and ignorance and idiots who would view our cause as one that is violative of the American dream of equal rights for everyone.

—Barbara Jordan
International Women's Year Conference
Austin, TX, 1975

The African American female manager faces an extra burden of adjustment that is not required of her Anglo female counterparts. As a black person, she is confronted with racial discrimination. As a woman, she encounters the male, informal, sexist subculture, with its stereotypical and distorted assumptions, which is heavily laden with behavior that is disrespectful toward women. Such an environment may be constrictive to the professional development of black female managers. As one white manager noted, "They [black managers] demonstrated an extremely humanistic outlook—they are keenly aware of the plight of their subordinates."

Inspired by John Howard Griffin's *Black Like Me* (1961), written a full decade earlier, Grace Halsell, a middle-class white woman, decided to turn her own skin black through pills and exposure to the sun so she could document America's racial strife. Her experiences were recorded in *Soul Sister* by Grace Halsell (1969). The journal that she kept began in July 1968 and recounts her experiences as she pretended to be a black woman searching for employment in New York and Mississippi.

The reader walks down the streets of Harlem and Jackson and Clarksdale with Grace Halsell and shares her intimate and often terrifying experiences—with the patronizing white intern in Harlem Hospital's emergency ward who ignores the third-degree burns on her feet because "you people should bathe more often"; with the white employer, a banker, and a member of the White Citizens Council, who assaults her; with the Mississippi police who stop her from using a phone in the white section of the bus station.

In 1940, 60 percent of all black women were employed as domestics. Fewer than 5 percent had white-collar positions. By 1980, only 4.7 percent of black women were employed in domestic work, whereas 50 percent held white-collar jobs. Between 1983 and 1986, the percentage of executives, administrators, and managerial jobs black women held increased from 4.9 percent to 6 percent. In professional areas, black women held 10.7 percent of positions in such areas as medicine, science, teaching, and engineering. During the past decades retail sales workers, nursing aides, secretaries, cashiers, cooks, elementary school teachers, janitors, and cleaners have been the most common jobs for black women—accounting for as much as 33 percent of the group's employment in 1990. African American women compose only 1 percent (142,000) of the 4 million persons employed in the skilled trades (DiMona, 1995). In 1993, there were over 6 million African American women in the workforce. Although diligent, committed, and dedicated employees, they were concentrated in low-paying service and clerical positions in which they earned less than their white peers.

More specifically, in 1993 half of black women were still working in low-paying clerical and service occupations, and more than 6 percent were precision product craft and repair workers. Black women represented 35 percent of all retail and personal service sales workers but only 16 percent of all executives and managers. The largest number of black women in management were in government service, mainly in management-related occupations as opposed to line executives and administrators. The disparaging underrepresentation in corporate management is said to result from the "double whammy" syndrome of being both black and female (Shields, 1993, p. xiv).

One of the women interviewed for this book remembers a time when she had a manager who once told her that the reason she wasn't getting promoted to a sales position in Seattle was because Seattle was a conservative area and she (a black woman) would have a hard time being successful. In another incident, this very successful woman tells the story of how, when interviewed for a job with a large, high-tech company, in the last interview with a vice president she was told that the job was completely different from what had been advertised and told to her recruiter. "This was the one time that I knew in my gut, someone was treating me differently because of my color. . . . It made me mad and it hurt my feelings but I didn't let it keep me from going to the next interview, with another company. I didn't carry that experience any further than the front door of that VP's office. It's as if I refused to let him get to me."

Unlike their black cohorts, in the first few decades of the twentieth century white women had low-workforce participation. A little known fact is that African American women have historically had higher rates of participation in the labor force. In fact, the 1890 high-workforce rates for black women did not reach parity with white women until 1960. Nevertheless, by 1990 the working rates for black and white women had equalized.

Based on an analysis of labor trends, experts project that by 2006 women will comprise 47.4 percent of the workforce. Of this composition, black women in the labor force will grow 35 percent to represent 6.2 percent of this workforce (Bureau of Labor Statistics, 1997). In a comprehensive three-phase study conducted by the Catalyst Organization (1999), the findings, which use national census data analysis, surveys, qualitative studies, and diversity policy analysis at various companies, describe the current status for women of color in the corporate environment as follows:

- Women of color make up 22.6 percent of women in the workforce.
- Among women holding managerial and administrative positions, women of color make up only 14.3 percent of all women represented.
- Women of color are promoted more slowly (averaging 3.6 years between promotions compared to 2.6 years for white women).
- Women of color, along with white women, tend to hold disproportionately more staff positions than line positions.
- Women of color, like white women, earn less than comparable male subgroups.

The job performance of women and people of color is commensurate with that of their white counterparts, according to two Michigan State economists, Harry Holzner and David Neumark. The researchers studied employees of more than 3,200 randomly selected employers in Detroit, Atlanta, Boston, and Los Angeles. They studied the qualifications and job performance of newly hired people of color and women hired as part of affirmative action policy. These employees were then compared to white men in comparable jobs, as well as to workers employed by companies without affirmative action plans.

The researchers observed no substantial difference between the groups relative to performance ratings and other measures of job success. More specifically, African American women generally had performance ratings that were higher than their white male peers, according to their supervisors. The researchers further explained, "The evidence for white females, black males, and Hispanic females also indicates that their performance is not lower than that of white males in similar firms" (Morin, 1997).

Authors of *The Black Manager* (1991), Floyd Dickens, Jr., and Jacqueline B. Dickens, delineated a learning process characteristic of black managers as they evolve through four phases of professional development:

1. **Entry phase.** Having a false sense of security; lacking direction.
2. **Adjusting phase.** Testing the organizational environment, pushing angrily, exhibiting dissatisfaction and frustration.
3. **Planned growth phase.** Using concentrated and strategic plans.
4. **Success phase.** Gaining confidence; reaching milestone goals; planning for the future.

This phase model, designed by Dickens and Dickens (1991), can be utilized by black managers to explain what happens, why it happens, and how individuals can change to reach their highest professional potential and advance to the upper echelons of corporate America. The model is effective because it relates the individual black experience of other blacks who find or have found themselves in similar situations. "It helps explain, in part, what happens to blacks psychologically as they face the difficulties of prejudice and discrimination" (Dickens and Dickens, 1991, p. 39).

The model also can be a tremendous resource for white managers because it offers an explanation of what happens to blacks in predominantly white corporations. Knowledge of the model also will help white managers better facilitate the assimilation of blacks into their organizational culture. Research indicates that white managers can be instrumental in ending institutional racism. One of the ways that this can be achieved is by helping white managers understand cultural nuances that may be germane to the African American heritage. "Taken as a whole, the model gives white managers hope that the interface between a white manager and a black subordinate can be made more effective" (Dickens and Dickens, 1991, p. 39).

> "As a person of color, I expect that some people will treat me differently. I expect that some people will make me prove myself. I expect that some people will never believe that I can do a job as good as a white person. I expect that some people will hate the fact that they have to work with me or for me. I expect that some men will try to come on to me because I am a woman of color. I expect all of these things but I don't look for them and I don't carry a negative in anticipation of what might happen. In the end, I really expect people to treat me fairly and with respect" (Sales Manager, Silicon Valley, CA).

Responses to the model from other people of color in managerial levels indicates that the model is transferable to other multiethnic groups. The assertion is based on the similarities of life experiences encountered by all members of marginalized, multiracial groups.

Historically, Hispanics and blacks have been, and still are, members of an oppressed class of people; to some extent this is also true of Asian and white women. Hispanics and blacks are not an equally accepted part of American society. Discrimination separates nonwhites and women from the mainstream and women from the issues within and between groups of people (Dickens and Dickens, 1991, 39).

Some of these commonalities of experience include the following:

- Oppression
- Exclusion from the mainstream activities of society
- Feelings of being different (in a negative way) from those in a dominant position
- Low self-concept, self-esteem, and self-confidence
- Being barred, and not encouraged to seek a better position and status in society—or in life
- Lack of equal opportunities

The authors further extoll the transmission of the model from one multiethnic group to another by asserting that, "The subordinate position of various minority groups to a dominant group makes the model transferable because minorities tend to display similar attitudes in their subordinate positions" (Dickens and Dickens, 1991, p. 40).

The authors surveyed African American managers and posited the following as the characteristics of top level blacks in managerial positions:

- Have dreams and develop a vision
- Articulate dreams to others
- Commit to a dream, goals, objectives, values, and so on
- Use judgment
- Garner respect (not necessarily love) from people
- Recognize, know, embrace, and effectively use power
- Use creativity and the creativity of others
- Get people to follow them and draw people to them emotionally
- Are intuitive
- Accept responsibility for themselves and others
- Set high standards and feel challenged
- Display high energy, focus, dedication, and purpose
- Display integrity
- Perform well under stress
- Display job knowledge and competence especially at their own level
- Know their people and treat them as valuable resources
- Motivate and reward people
- Develop a success style
- Take ownership for their organizations and set examples for others
- Take charge of and continue their own professional and personal development

Perceptions of African American women in the work environment are exhibited in Figure 5-2. The images in Figure 5-2 not withstanding, the rise of black women in the corporate arena has been consistent and deliberate. Standing on the principles and laurels of Madam C. J. Walker, black women are highly visible in the boardrooms of almost every industry in society. Just as with Walker, who became the first self-made female millionaire in America, the women profiled as the elite in American society have endured their share of disappointments, heartaches, and corporate- inflicted pain. Dr. Dolores E. Cross, president of Morris Brown College and a member of the International Women's Forum (IWF), suggests that there are four strategies

LABEL:	The Corporate Diamond
CHARACTERISTIC:	Professional and extremely polished.
LABEL:	The Bench Warmer
CHARACTERISTIC:	Nonassertive, complacent, and lacks initiative.
LABEL:	Miss Vogue on the Outside, Vague on the Inside
CHARACTERISTIC:	No substance; underneath her exterior, people think there is nothing there.
LABEL:	Sister Christian
CHARACTERISTIC:	A gossip and busybody.
LABEL:	The Queen Bee
CHARACTERISTIC:	Poor interpersonal skills, unapproachable.
LABEL:	The Unpolished Gem
CHARACTERISTIC:	Meek and lacks business maturity.
LABEL:	Soft and Lovely
CHARACTERISTIC:	Pushover, nonassertive, and passive.
LABEL:	The Whiner
CHARACTERISTIC:	Disloyal, uncooperative, and not a team player.
LABEL:	Evilene
CHARACTERISTIC:	Hostile and defensive.
LABEL:	Loud as She Wants to Be
CHARACTERISTIC:	Unprofessional, no discretion or diplomacy, lacks tact.
LABEL:	The Unfashion Bug
CHARACTERISTIC:	Uncomfortable with herself, unpolished.

FIGURE 5-2 Common Images of African American Women in the Workplace

Source: Adapted from Dickens (1993) pp. 101–104.

that contribute significantly to the success of black women and, if executed well, can minimize the pain:

1. Have an agenda in which you have the strongest conviction.
2. Despite what the research shows or indicates, use your own experiences to make choices. Do not be afraid to take risks based upon past experiences.
3. Be prepared to take other people's advice.
4. Gain physical as well as mental strength. Gain a better understanding of black women's health and societal issues.

One woman, a corporate manager for a major Fortune 500 company, summarized her advice:

> There are so many political issues to deal with on a general level and race/gender add another level of complexity. I think that women of color become adept at dealing with all of the issues that their race and gender bring and their behavior reflects this. I know there are things I do unconsciously as a way to survive as a woman of color in the corporate world.

LATINO WOMEN

The good news is that Mexican American women's rates of labor force participation have increased during the past decade. The bad news is that these women have not been able to translate their educational qualifications into higher level jobs and comparable salaries at the same rate their Anglo peers have. In 1986, Mary Romero found that Mexican American women and men still confront stigmas that inhibit their ability to achieve full occupational assimilation.

Unfortunately, they were more heavily concentrated in blue-collar and lower white-collar jobs than were Anglo females. They were particularly excluded from higher status professional and managerial positions. To the dismay of those in these situations, affirmative action legislation has had minimal impact on these occupational patterns. Comparative data for all Hispanic women suggest little had changed by 1990 (Bureau of Labor Statistics, 1991).

Mexican women have lower incomes than almost any group in the United States. Their median earnings in 1990 were $9,286 per year, compared to $10,099 per year for all Latino women and $12,438 per year for non-Latino women; almost half (45.7 percent) of all Mexican, female-headed families were poor. In addition, Mexican women experience higher unemployment rates than their non-Latino counterparts.

Francisco Flores, another leading Chicana feminist, stated

[Chicana] can no longer remain in a subservient role or as auxiliary forces in the [Chicano] movement. They must be included in the frontline of communication, leadership, and organizational responsibility. The issues of equality, freedom and self-determination of the Chicana—like the right of self-determination, equality and liberation of the Mexican [Chicano] community—is not negotiable. Anyone opposing the right of women to organize into their own form of organization has no place in the leadership of the movement (cited in Garcia, 1995, p. 408).

ASIAN AMERICAN WOMEN

As Asian women, like many other women of color, we exist with the added burden of dehumanizing sexual stereotypes and racial/sexual exploitation. As women, we must begin to examine and confront the racist and sexist attitudes which allow any woman to be advertised in our magazines and newspapers as a 'mail-order bride.' In addition, we have to begin, all of us, whether Asian, Asian American, women of color, or white women to recognize that such a racist and sexist system dehumanizes and objectifies each of us.

—Connie Chan
"Asian Women: We're Not for Sale" (1985)

Asian women have worked and raised families in America for more than 150 years. They have accomplished their goals despite the oppression imposed by overt and blatant racism. Emerging from their stereotypical roles as farmworkers, prostitutes, and domestics in earlier decades, today they command respect as they have moved into the higher echelons of corporate America. Their educational, professional, and financial status has given the impetus for the enviable label of "model minority"; among the characteristics of this concept are polite, deferential, hardworking, and achievement oriented. "This climb up 'Gold Mountain,' as Chinese workers called San Francisco, has been arduous and dangerous, calling on the courage and endurance of men and women alike" (Amott and Matthael, 1991, p. 193).

The ascension of Asian women into the higher managerial levels of corporate America must be tempered by historical data, which indicate that over the years Asian females have been outnumbered by males in very significant ratios. Whereas, the ratio of men to women among the Chinese in 1860 was 19 to 1; among the Japanese in 1900, it was 25 to 1; and among the Filipinas/os in 1930, it was 14 to 1. Several factors are attributed to this imbalance: It was easier for unmarried Asian men to get to America, more employers were seeking male Asian workers, and limitations were imposed on immigration numbers.

The eradication of racial desegregation after World War II and a curtailing of tolerance for sexual discrimination in the workplace set the stage for an influx of Asian women to move into nontraditional positions in the labor market. In fact, Chinese women's participation in corporate America grew from 44 percent in 1960 to 58 percent in 1980.

Educational attainment is another factor that has played an increasing part in the ability of Asian women to move into some of the most prestigious professional positions. The ability of Asian women to transform the emphasis of education from males to also include females has been a formidable task, but the effort has paid some very high dividends. In 1980, approximately one-third of Chinese American women held college degrees, and almost one-third of Chinese American women held a managerial, administrative, or professional position. In contrast to the positions of women in other groups, Chinese women have garnered a share of managerial and administrative positions equal to their share of all positions. They are, however, overrepresented in health-diagnosing professions and are also more highly concentrated in engineering than any other racial group.

The most affluent of the Asian groups are the Japanese. Thus, Japanese women are able to capitalize on this financial stability by increasing their visibility and influence on the corporate front. They have traditionally maintained high labor force participation, as well as educational attainment. Despite feeling the effects of discrimination, they continue to have the lowest unemployment rates of all multiracial groups and the lowest poverty rates for female-dominated households. During earlier decades their annual income was 13 percent higher than that for their white female co-workers.

A composite portrait of Asians in 1998 U.S. Census Bureau data shows them to be the most advantaged group of all multiracial groups, having attained more education and higher socioeconomic status than any other population, including whites. The economic success of Asian Americans has been spurred by several factors: (1) immigration of highly educated Asians to America in the past two decades, (2) concentration of Asians in states with high incomes, (3) dual family workers, and (4) very high work ethic.

Asian culture dictates that women be modest and reserved, which is in direct opposition to the gregariousness and assertiveness needed to succeed in corporate America. Asian women have traditionally been absent from feminist issues, but recent conditions have served as an impetus for them to align themselves with women's concerns. Some of these issues include domestic violence, reluctance of Asian males to accept women's independence, and insidious stereotyping of Asian women by the mass media. Similar to African American and Latino feminists, Asians focus more intensely on job- and health-related issues than on political activities.

Focus Group Reports Back

In a roundtable of Asian women speaking about the issues they faced in the workplace, conversations and views of these women were similar to those held by black women in terms of their treatment by white males. Several of these women discussed the reactions of white men to women of color and noted that the reactions depend a great deal on seniority, education, and personal experience. "A globally minded senior manager would welcome a foreign born, educated woman of color. Such white men are enlightened, secure in their own skills and experience, and are likely to view diversity and international experience as an asset to any organization. On the other hand, a man with less education and insecure about his prospects in the job market might find it easy to unleash his frustration on a female co-worker of color." In another comment, "a minority woman might bear the brunt of such an attitude because the man's attitude might go unnoticed or unfortunately play into stereotypes held by the general population. Sometimes such hostility can be cleverly disguised in a number of ways." Examples of this hostility were identified as

- Stealing credit or not giving enough credit where due to a minority woman
- Exclusion from networks—social and professional
- Lower compensation
- Unfairness in performance reviews
- Intimidation by challenging decisions and actions at every step
- Denial of opportunities for new, high-visibility projects.

NATIVE AMERICAN WOMEN

Because of cultural norms, Native American females have not experienced the same occupational inequities with the men in their groups as mainstream and other women of color. According to Native American anthropologist Priscilla Buffalohead (1988), many tribal societies stem from egalitarian cultural traditions that do not concentrate on the equality of the sexes but rather focus on the dignity of individuals and their inherent rights—regardless of gender or age.

For example, some of the Eastern Woodland nation—the Mohawk, Seneca, Cayuga, Oneida, and Onondaga nations—formed an alliance known as the Iroquois Confederacy. Known as the Iroquois Great Law of Peace, the Confederacy's constitution decisions were made by a representative democracy, and the whole tribe, including women, voted on the war captain. The leaders held power through persuasion rather than coercion, and decisions were based on a consensus. Some researchers suggest that this Iroquois example inspired Benjamin Franklin with the idea of a democratic federation of states when the United States of America was formed.

Another tradition of Native American culture was the separation of sex roles (gender) from biological sex. Among certain Plains Native Americans, males who exhibited a desire to emulate the work and lifestyle of women were encouraged to do so; they were known as *berdaches*. Females also were allowed to mirror the roles of men. For example, a young female who wanted to live as a man would submit to a special tribal ritual.

Most Native American women are first- or second-generation urban residents. Over the years, they have been able to leave jobs as maids and domestic workers, but as with African American and Latino women, almost 25 percent are employed in service occupations, performing work outside the home that had formerly been done inside the house. These jobs included food preparation, cleaning, and personal service occupations that were associated with low pay, few fringe benefits, little opportunity for advancement, and job security that fluctuated with the state of the economy. Another 25 percent of Native Americans are employed as administrative support (clerical) workers. Thus, Native American clerical workers are frequently employed by the federal government, which, ironically, has become the largest employer of Native American women. The professional Native American women are most often teachers or nurses, and most Native American female managers are concentrated in lower level positions. They are increasingly underrepresented among top-level executives, and they are noticeably underrepresented in the higher status professions (Freeman, 1995).

Issues such as equal pay for equal work; child health and welfare; and a woman's right to make her own choices regarding contraceptive use, sterilization, and abortion—key issues to the majority women's movement—affect Native American women as well; however, equality per se may have a different meaning for Native American women and men. That difference begins with personal and tribal sovereignty—the right to be legally recognized as people empowered to determine their own destinies. Thus, the Native American women's movement seeks equality in two ways that do not concern mainstream women: (1) On the individual level, Native American women struggle to promote the survival of a social structure whose organizational principles represent notions of family that are different than those of the mainstream, and (2) on the societal level, the people see sovereignty as the key issue in order to maintain a vital, legal, and spiritual connection to the land, in order to survive as a people (Shanley, 1995, p. 416).

The nuclear family has little relevance to Native American women. In fact, in many ways, mainstream feminists now are striving to redefine family and community in a way that Native American women have long known. The American lifestyle from which white, middle-class women cling to themselves, has not taken hold in Native American communities (Shanley, 1995, p. 417).

The other difference between the Native American women's movement and the majority women's movement concerns the importance Native American people place on tribal sovereignty—it is the single most pressing political issue in Native American culture today. For Native American people to survive culturally as well as materially, many battles are fought and won in the courts of law, precisely because it is the legal recognition that enables Native American people to govern themselves according to their own worldview—a worldview that is antithetical to the *wasicu* (or *takers of the fat*) definition of progress. Equality for Native American women within tribal communities, therefore, holds more significance than equality in terms of the general rubric "American" (Shanley, 1995, p. 268).

THE CONCEPT OF PRIVILEGE

Institutional rejection of difference is an absolute necessity in a profit economy that needs outsiders as additional people. As members of such an economy, we all have been programmed to respond to the human differences among us with fear and loathing and to handle those differences in one of three ways: (1) ignore it, and if that is not possible, (2) duplicate it if we think it is dominant, or (3) destroy it if we think it is subordinate (Kesselman et al., 1995, p. 267).

By and large within the women's movement today, white women see their oppression as women and ignore differences of race, sexual preference, class, and age. There is a pretense to a homogeneity of experience covered by the word *sisterhood* that does not in fact exist (Kesselman et al., 1995, p. 268).

As white women ignore their built-in privilege of whiteness and define women in terms of their own experiences, women of color become "other," the outsiders whose experiences and traditions are too alien to comprehend. An example of this is the absence of the experience of women of color as a resource for women's studies courses (Kesselman et al., 1995, p. 269).

This is a very complex issue, but, one of the reasons white women seem to have such difficulty reading black women's work is because of their reluctance to recognize black women as different from themselves. As long as any difference between white women and black women means one is inferior, the recognition of any difference will be fraught with guilt. To allow women of color to step out of stereotypes is too guilt provoking because it threatens the complacency of those women who view oppression only in terms of sex. Refusing to recognize differences makes it possible to see the different problems and pitfalls facing women.

Nevertheless, white women face the pitfall of being seduced into joining white males (the oppressor) under the pretense of sharing power (Kesselman et al., 1995, p. 269). As a mechanism of social control, women have been encouraged to recognize only one area of human difference as legitimate: those differences that exist between women and men (Kesselman et al., 1995, p. 271). Now women must recognize differences among their equals, neither inferior nor superior, and devise ways to use each other's difference to enrich vision and joint struggles (Kesselman et al., 1995, p. 271). Feminism became an incredibly powerful term as it incorporates diversity, not as a superficial, political position, but as a practice (Shanley, 1995, p. 271).

STRATEGIES FOR MAKING THE CORPORATE ENVIRONMENT FAVORABLE FOR WOMEN OF COLOR

The Catalyst study (1999) found that some business environments lend themselves to the inclusion and advancement of women while others are less conducive. In an environment where diversity is devalued, retention of women of color is more difficult, and those types of organizations experience a high turnover of women. Retention of women of color is significantly improved when the environment supports women of color, respect for all cultural backgrounds is apparent, and management is proactively committed to diversity. In other words, policy alone is not enough to demonstrate commitment. Rather, the results must be evident: diverse workforce representation. This study found that women of color "view corporate diversity programs as less than effective at addressing their concerns, despite CEO emphasis on diversity as a business imperative" (Catalyst, 1999, p. 18). Women of color, from this study, see the situation as a "concrete ceiling" characterized by an "accumulation of micro-inequities over the course of women's careers" (p. 18).

At the end of the three-phase study, the Catalyst Organization developed a set of recommendations for the retention and promotion of women of color in corporate America. These recommendations are outlined in Figure 5-3. Many of these recommendations are also valuable in creating a more equitable organization overall, for both men and women of all racial and ethnic backgrounds.

As the workforce becomes more and more diverse, managers must master the skills necessary to facilitate cooperative interactions among people of different

FIGURE 5-3 Recommendations for Implementing or Revitalizing Corporate Initiatives to Advance Women of Color

Though the shape and content of initiatives for women of color will, in many cases, differ from initiatives designed to address gender diversity, critical success factors are the same:

- Demonstrating top-level commitment
- Delineating and articulating the business case
- Establishing benchmarks for change
- Establishing and monitoring accountability
- Communicating
- Measuring results
- Recognizing and rewarding successful managers and organizational best practices

Identify subgroups of women of color in your organization and recognize that they have come to your workplace with different backgrounds and have different needs

→ Learn their perspectives
→ Use surveys, focus groups, and exit interviews to document by subgroup women of color's experiences and perceptions

Benchmark your company's progress with women of color by subgroup against the progress of men and of white women

→ Document recruitment; retention; advancement; placement—functional responsibilities; time in grade; and representation on slates for promotions/key assignments
→ Determine gaps in representation that can be addressed by internal development/promotion vs. external recruitment of advanced hires
→ Where possible, compare your metrics with national data and industry experience

FIGURE 5-3 Recommendations for Implementing or Revitalizing Corporate Initiatives to Advance Women of Color, *continued*

Establish short- and long-term goals

→ Create tracking tools to monitor progress regularly

→ Revise goals as appropriate

Delineate the business case for diversity initiatives

→ Generic—Changing demographics

→ Specific—New product development, marketing including new markets, sales, globalization and other desired growth, costs of turnover; community relations, and shareholder accountability

→ Unique—to your company's business environment

Communicate and demonstrate your company's commitment to women of color

→ Invest financially in women of color management training; executive development programs; inclusion at high visibility events; membership in professional associations; support for corporate networks and networking events

→ Ensure that diversity programs are designed to meet the different needs of subgroups of women of color

→ Support the creation and on-going activities of employee networks for women of color

→ Ensure that women of color have mentoring relationships that foster inclusion in all aspects of the corporate culture

→ Use existing communication tools to announce intentions and record and monitor progress

→ Recognize and reward contributions of high-performing women of color

Identify and reward best practices inside your company

→ Recognize and reward successful approaches

→ Recognize and reward supportive managers

Hold managers accountable for retention and advancement

→ Perform case by case review of reasons for regretted losses

→ Create clearly-articulated plans for the long-term development of women of color and include opportunities for line experience

→ Review managers' performance evaluations by race/gender

→ Ensure representation of women of color on slates for promotions and in high visibility assignments

→ Measure time in grade of women of color

→ Provide financial incentives/disincentives for diversity goals achievement

Integrate diversity initiatives into routine organizational practices

→ Recruitment processes

→ New hire orientation

→ Management training

→ Career development systems

→ Work/life initiatives

→ Succession planning

Source: Catalyst, 1999. Women of Color in Corporate Management: Opportunities and Barriers–The Executive Summary.

cultures, racial heritages, and nationalities. For women of color to reach their fullest potential in corporate America, they must understand the barriers that will block their paths to success. Managers in positions to facilitate the upward mobility of women of color into the boardrooms and traditionally male-dominated professions must be willing to share in the development processes needed for this type of progression. It is essential that all women are groomed to sit at the tables of Fortune 100, Fortune 500, and other companies that have not recognized yet the necessity to employ women in top-level managerial positions. By the year 2005 women will comprise 47 percent of the U.S. workforce. Business leaders have targeted the elevation of women in the labor force as one of their most important imperatives for the twenty-first century (*Catalyst,* 1998).

SUMMARY OF KEY POINTS

Women of color face very different experiences in corporate life. Navigating around the obstacles they face in their professional lives may require a number of unique and demanding strategies. Work experiences are varied. Their obstacles go beyond a consideration of gender alone.

Prejudice, bias, and racial discrimination make difficult the road to professional development and affect equity. Although research provides evidence of comparable qualifications and job performance to that of white men and women, inequity is often the norm with significant and deleterious psychological effects.

Despite uneven playing fields, however, women of color are visible in the boardroom. Strong agendas, risk taking, the use of mentors, and an understanding of related societal issues are all strategies propelling women of color forward.

Improving the corporate environment for women of color comes about as a result of a commitment to the organizational change models that shape a climate emphasizing cultural diversity. Strong leadership, assessment, training, and education, changes in managerial and human resource practices, and clear, consistent follow-up are the processes enabling change. Understanding the barriers and challenges is the first step in women of color reaching their full potential. Managers, throughout organizations, must be willing to facilitate upward mobility and share in the development of organizational culture change necessary to promote fair and equitable work cultures.

Discussion Questions

1. Why should companies be interested in promoting women of color into managerial positions?
2. What program(s) would you implement to make sure women of color in your company achieve their highest professional potential?
3. Select and discuss positive attributes of multiethnic (African, Asian, Latino, and Native American) executive women's heritage that would enhance their job performance.
4. What are similarities and differences in factors that determine success and failure for women of color and their white colleagues?
5. What extra pressures do women of color confront when climbing the corporate ladder?

Issue to Debate

White women should work in a concerted effort to advance the careers of women of color because it will be advantageous to their plight to combat inequality. What do you think? Will this enhance or dilute the quest for equality? Do you think that white women would be proponents of this strategy? Do you think women of color will be open to letting white women serve as advocates on their behalf?

The Best Job for the Person or the Best Person for the Job
Case Analysis

THE NAVA STORY

Nava, Inc., is the fourth largest manufacturer of athletic footwear in the country. Founded in 1947 by Tyrone Martin, Nava has demonstrated a commitment to the sporting apparel industry through its innovative technology (testing and equipment) and aggressive sales and marketing campaigns. The company is headquartered in Atlanta, Georgia, with plants located throughout the United States. Nava's two flagship brands, Performa and EasyFit, provide separate and unique benefits to its customers and are distributed to retailers in 48 states.

For the most part, Nava has survived as the "third fiddle" to what is known in the industry as the Big Three: Nike, Adidas, and Reebok. Its success has been rooted in the trickle-down effect from the others with competitive prices being Nava's main attraction.

NAVA'S PRIMARY CUSTOMERS AND CLIMATE

- Customers are satisfied with products; however, competitors' names are often more familiar to consumers, and they are often unclear about the differences between Nava and its competitors.
- Employees (at corporate headquarters, plants, and in the sales force) have no real attachment to company; they feel left out of management decisions.
- Retailers are uneducated about the benefits of Nava's products but Nava is building strong relationships with them. The ongoing challenge is to ensure that retailers recommend their brands rather than its competitors and to increase retailer distribution.
- A constant challenge involves creating value for shareholders. Nava has experienced pressure recently because of ongoing media coverage of the Big Three.

NAVA CONSUMERS

- Teens, age 12 to 17 (25 percent in ethnic markets)
- Parents of teens
- Men and women, age 18 to 54

NAVA BUSINESS OBJECTIVES

- To increase sales and distribution of products

- To establish Nava's brands as the preferred choice for athletic footwear
- To protect shareholder value
- To promote loyalty and excitement in its work environment
- To initiate ways to improve quality of life in communities where its employees and customers work and live

SITUATION OVERVIEW

In early 1999, Nava executed a multitiered research initiative to determine their status in the industry and how their consumers viewed them. Their approach involved extensive polling of external audiences and an in-depth analysis of its mission, scope of operations, markets, and products.

The research revealed that even though many people were familiar with the various brands, there was no real association with the company name. Basically, the company had no identity. The research also showed that its competitors' success could be attributed to niche marketing that resulted in brand recognition.

In an industry that is heavily driven by comfort, durability, and support, Nava knew it would have to establish an identity for its products and market their

worth. Feedback identified a perceived gap in quality and product development. Respondents felt that the athletic gear was not manufactured to endure.

Capitalizing on this need and its long history of developing quality products through the most advanced technology, Nava adopted technology as a means to establish an identity, unify its brands under one umbrella, and leverage this platform to ultimately help establish market leadership.

With the technology industry being dominated by white males, recent national attention has been focused on why women and minorities are left out of the industry. African Americans and Latinos represented 25 percent of Nava's customers, and women and ALANA groups represented only 17 percent of its workforce (and a lower number for the athletic apparel industry as a whole). Another point of concern is the fact that research has shown that in recent years consumers have begun to shift away from athletic footwear to shoes of different styles (e.g., sport sandals, walking shoes, casual boots, and so on), which has introduced new competitors into their once exclusive market. ∎

Questions

Imagine that you are the executive vice president of human resources for Nava and that you have been given the complex task of finding an executive vice president of operations for Nava—someone who will be responsible for modifying, correcting, implementing, and suggesting programs that will solve some or all of the problems outlined in the case.

Two women, one white and one African American, are the finalists for the position. Both women have creden-

tials that would qualify them to perform well in the position. The African American female has been quite vocal about how she should be given the appointment because she will have the ability to increase the multiethnic customer and employee base.

Your mission is to determine who should get the position. Be very detailed in the explanation of your decision. What would you do to make the correct selection? What questions would you ask prior to making the selection? How do you feel about the attitude of the African American female? What are the positives and negatives of hiring the white female? What are the positives and negatives of hiring the African American female?

References and Suggested Readings

Albrecht, L., and Brewer, R. (1990). *Bridges of power: Women's multicultural alliances.* Philadelphia: New Society Press.

Alexander, K. L. (1990, July 25). Minority women feel racism, sexism are blocking the path to management. The *Wall Street Journal,* p. B1.

Amott, T., and Matthael, J. (1991). *Race, gender and work: A multicultural economic history of women in the United States.* Boston: South End.

Bataille, F. M., and Mullen Sand, K. (1984). *American Indian women, telling their lives.* Lincoln, NE: University of Nebraska Press.

Berdahl, J. L. (1996). Gender and leadership in work groups: Six alternative models. *Leadership Quarterly: Special Issue: Leadership and Diversity,* (Part 1), 7(1), 21–40.

Biagi, S., and Kern-Foxworth, M. L. (1997). *Facing difference: Race, gender, mass media.* Thousand Oaks, CA: Pine Forge Press.

Bonilla-Santiago, G. (1992). *Breaking ground and barriers: Hispanic women developing effective leadership.* San Diego, CA: Marin Publications.

Braddock, J. H., and McPartland, J. M. (1987). How minorities continue to be excluded from equal employment opportunity: Research on labor market and institutional barriers. *Journal of Social Issues, 43,* 5–39.

Buffalohead, P. (1988). *Cherish the children: Parenting skills for Indian mothers with young children.* St. Paul, MN: Minnesota Indian Women's Resource Center.

Buffalohead, P. (1983, Summer). Farmers, warriors, traders: A fresh look at Ojibway women, *Minnesota History, 48,* 236.

Bureau of Labor Statistics, Department of Labor. (http://www.bls.gov/text_only/datahome_text.htm)

Catalyst. (1999). *Women of color in corporate management: Opportunities and barriers.* New York: Catalyst. (Web site: www.info@catalystwomen.org (accessed August 22, 1999.)

Catalyst. (1998). *Advancing women in business: The Catalyst guide of best practices for the corporate leader.* San Francisco: Jossey Bass.

Catalyst. (1997). *Women of color in corporate management: A statistical picture.* New York: Catalyst.

Center for Strategic Urban Community Leadership (http://www.crab.rutgers.edu/camden/CFSUCL/)

Collins, N. W., Gilbert, S. K., and Nycum, S. H. (1988). *Women leading: Making tough choices on the fast track.* Lexington, MA: Stephen Greene Press.

Collins, S. (1989). The marginalization of black executives. *Social Problems, 36,* 317–31.

Collins, S. (1993). Blacks on the bubble: The vulnerability of black executives in white corporations. *Sociological Quarterly, 34,* 429–48.

Cox, T., Jr. (1993). *Cultural diversity in organizations: Theory, research, and practice.* San Francisco: Berrett-Koehler.

Cox, T., Jr., and Beale, R. L. (1997). *Developing competency to manage diversity: Readings, cases and activites.* San Francisco: Berrett-Koehler.

Dickens, F., Jr., and Dickens, J. (1991). *The black manager: Making it in the corporate world.* New York: AMACOM.

DiMona, L. and Herdon, C. (1995). *The 1995 information please women's sourcebook.* Boston, MA: Houghton-Mifflin & Co.

Dobbs, M. F. (1996). Managing diversity: Lessons from the private sector. *Personnel Management, 25*(3), 351–367.

Elain, K., and Otani, J. (1983). *With silk wings: Asian American women at work.* Oakland, CA: Asian Women United of California.

Elashmawi, F., and Harris, P. R. (1993). *Multicultural management: New skills for global success.* Houston: Gulf.

Freeman, J. (Ed.). (1995). *Women: A feminist perspective.* Mountain View, CA: Mayfield.

Fullerton, H. (1991, November). Labor force projections: The baby boom moves on (Table 2). *Monthly Labor Review, 34.*

Garcia, A. (1995). The development of Chicana feminist discourse. In A. Kesselman, L. D. McNair, and N. Schniedewind. *Women: Images and realities.* Mountain View, CA: Mayfield.

Gardenswartz, L., and Rowe, A. (1993). *Managing diversity: A complete desk reference and planning guide.* San Diego, CA: Pfeiffer.

Gentile, M. C. (1993). *Differences that work: Organizational excellence through diversity.* Boston: Harvard Business School Press.

Griffin, J. (1961). *Black like me.* Boston, MA: Houghton, Mifflin & Co.

Halsell, G. (1969). *Soul sister.* New York: World Publishing Co.

Higginbotham, E. (1992). Women never on a pedestal: Women of color continue to struggle with poverty, racism, and sexism. In M. L. Anderson and P. Hill Collins (Eds.), *Race, class, and gender* (pp. 183–90). Belmont, CA: Wadsworth.

Hull, G. T., Scott, P. B., and Smith, B. (Eds.). (1982). *All the women are white, all the blacks are men, but some of us are brave: Black women's studies.* New York: Feminist Press.

Issei, N. (1986). *War bride: Three generations of Japanese American women in domestic service.* Philadelphia: Temple University Press.

Jules, F. (1988). Native Indian leadership. *Canadian Journal of Native Education, 15*(3), 3–23.

Kern-Foxworth, M. L. (1994). *Aunt Jemima, Uncle Ben and Rastus: Blacks in advertising, yesterday, today and tomorrow.* Greenwich, CT: Greenwood.

Kesselman, A., McNair, L. D., and Schniedewind, N. (1995). *Women: Images and realities.* Mountain View, CA: Mayfield.

Kossek, E. E., and Lobel, S. A. (Eds.). (1996). *Managing diversity: Human resource strategies for transforming the workplace.* Cambridge, MA: Blackwell Business.

Kutscher, K. (1991, November). New BLS projections: Findings and implications. *Monthly Labor Review.*

Liswood, L. A. (1995). *Women world leaders: Fifteen great politicans tell their stories.* San Francisco: HarperCollins.

Lorde, A. (1995). Age, race, class, and sex: Women redefining difference. In A. Kesselman, L. D. McNair, and N. Schneidewind. *Women: Images and realities.* Mountain View, CA: Mayfield.

Martinez-Cosio, M. C. (1996). Leadership in communities of color: Elements and sensitivity of a universal model. *Journal of Leadership Studies, 3*(1), 65–77.

Melville, M. (Ed.). (1988). *Mexicana at work in the United States.* Houston, TX: University of Houston Press.

Miller, D. I. (1978). Native American women's leadership images. *Integrated Education, 6*(1), 37–39.

Morin, R. (1997). Affirming affirmative action hires. *Washington Post,* p. D6.

Morrison, A. M., and Crabtree, K. M. (1992). *Developing diversity in organizations: A digest of selected literature.* Greensboro, NC: Center for Creative Leadership.

National Committee on Pay Equity. (1993). Erase the bias: A pay equity guide to eliminating race and sex bias from wage setting systems. Washington, D.C.:

National Community for Latino Leadership ncllpd96@aol.com

National Forum for Black Public Administrators http://www.nfbpa.org

National Hispanic Leadership Institute (http://www.incacorp.com/nhli)

Romero, M. (1986). Twice protected? Assessing the impact of AA on Mexican-American women. *Ethnicity and Public Policy, 5,* pp. 135–56.

Shanley, K. (1995). Thoughts on Indian feminism. In A. Kesselman, L. D. McNair, and N. Schniedewind. *Women: Images and realities.* Mountain View, CA: Mayfield.

Shields, C. & Shields, L. (1993). *Work, sister, work: How black women can get ahead in today's business environment.* New York: Simon & Schuster.

Sokoloff, N. J. (1992). *Black women and white women in the professions.* New York: Routledge.

Stone, A. (1995, February 23). Educated black women make biggest strides. *USA Today,* p. B4.

Tomaskovic-Devery, D. (1993). *Gender and racial inequality at work.* Ithaca: Cornell University Press.

Tsughida, N., Mealey, L., and Thoen, G. (Eds.). (1982). Asian and Pacific American experiences: Women's perspectives. Minneapolis, MN: University of Minnesota.

United National Indian Tribal Youth, Inc. (http://www.unityinc.org)

Urban Leaders majordomo@panix.com

Woody, B. (1992). *Black women in the workplace: Impacts of structural change in the economy.* New York: Greenwood.

Zaloka, N. (1990). *The economic status of black women: An exploratory investigation.* Washington, DC: U.S. Commission on Civil Rights.

CHAPTER 6

Dysempowerment in Organizations

Kathleen Kane
and
Kathleen Montgomery

They just don't get it! How can they expect us to feel "empowered" if they turn around and ignore what we have to say or, worse yet, act impatient and simply trivialize our concerns? I don't know whether they do it on purpose or not, but it sure makes me angry.

—ANONYMOUS

Chapter Overview

Leaders in the twenty-first century will be required to foster workplace environments in which creative and high-performing individuals and teams can flourish. Growing numbers of businesses have enthusiastically embraced the concept of employee empowerment, thus signaling their desire to enhance organizational effectiveness through increased employee involvement, innovation, commitment, and productivity. Nevertheless, research findings, as well as reports from boardrooms to the shop floor, have found the success of such programs to be inconsistent.

We believe that part of the reason for the mixed reviews of empowerment efforts is that another process may be occurring to inhibit or interfere with the desired outcomes of empowerment. We call this process *dysempowerment*. Dysempowerment begins with the perception that a workplace event signals an affront to one's dignity, resulting in a debilitating set of responses with the potential to impair performance. This process can occur between two individuals or at the collective level. When a manager treats an employee with disrespect, not only can the employee interpret the manager's behavior as an affront to her dignity, but those who witness the event can also be affected. At the collective level, an organization's climate can be perceived by its workforce as dysempowering, with a negative impact on the performance of everyone in the organization.

Our research suggests further that there may be individual differences in perception of workplace events, and that these differences may vary systematically by demographic or by social identity groups. As a result, some groups may be more vulnerable than others to dysempowerment. Because dysempowering behavior may be subtle and

101

unrecognized on a conscious level by managers, it is critical that leaders develop an awareness of the potential for dysempowerment and its possible disproportionate effects on employees.

Learning Objectives

- To define the concept and process of dysempowerment

- To understand how the process of dysempowerment occurs

- To analyze a case study on dysempowerment as it unfolds, working through the causes, implications, and strategies for change

A DYSEMPOWERMENT CASE

In this chapter, we present a sequential case study to illustrate how the dysempowerment process can unfold. The setting for the case is ComTek, a six-month-old firm selling telecommunications systems to businesses. The telecommunications systems sales industry is increasingly competitive. As such, ComTek relies on a sales force with sophistication in high technology, marketing knowledge, and sales expertise. To date, ComTek's sales performance has been satisfactory but not outstanding. In order to meet or exceed their first year's income projections and to increase market share, ComTek's top management has decided to offer special training for sales managers in managing and motivating their unique sales force.

Johnson is one of three sales managers, each with a sales team of four individuals. The sales managers' performance evaluations are based on the collective performance of the sales teams, thereby giving the sales managers a strong financial incentive to find ways to increase each team's performance.

Case Part 1: Monday Morning— A New Managerial Approach

It is Monday morning, and Johnson's sales team of Gerry, Tracy, Dale, and Chris have convened for a meeting with Johnson. Johnson has just returned from a week-long training program that emphasized the motivating potential of empowerment. Johnson has thought carefully about how to integrate lessons from the management training course in order to enhance the team's performance and to change previous ways of interacting with the team. For instance, in the past, the manager controlled and coordinated the specific assignments for each team member. Johnson wants to increase the self-determination of team members and, therefore, decides to delegate the scheduling of the week's work to the team itself.

In addition, to give team members a better appreciation of their impact on ComTek's success, Johnson announces that team members will be asked to participate in the development of the strategic marketing plan for the firm during the next few weeks. Johnson is convinced that this opportunity will allow team members to emphasize the aspect of the firm's growth they find most meaningful to them personally.

Finally, Johnson gives the sales team members a convincing pep talk about their competence as salespeople of high-tech telecommunications equipment, especially in comparison to the records of team members of the firm's other sales teams. The team is encouraged to continue to seek ways to develop their expertise and is told that ComTek will consider underwriting the cost of seminars and workshops.

Each of these initiatives seems to energize the sales team, and on this high note, team members leave the meeting with renewed enthusiasm. Johnson feels optimistic that this newly empowered team will respond with fresh ideas and greater motivation to perform at their best. The team is to reconvene on Friday afternoon to report back to Johnson about the week's efforts.

QUESTION: If you were a member of Johnson's sales team, do you believe that this new approach would help your sales performance? Why?

PSYCHOLOGICAL EMPOWERMENT

Empowerment has been conceptualized in a variety of ways ranging from an overarching organizational philosophy to a set of managerial practices. One scholarly approach that has gained prominence is that of *psychological empowerment* (Thomas and Velthouse, 1990; Spreitzer 1995, 1996), which is defined as a type of motivation referred to as "intrinsic task motivation" produced by a set of task assessments arrived at through an individual's subjective interpretations of reality (Thomas and Velthouse, 1990; p. 667). These assessments reflect four "task-related cognitions"—self-determination, impact, meaning, and competence—which constitute an employee's active orientation to his or her work role.

The theory of psychological empowerment states that when people develop these four cognitions—or the way they think about their work—they have a sense that they have some self-determination, or choice, about how they do their work; that what they do has an impact on the organization's overall performance; that the work is meaningful to them and to the organization; and that they are competent to do the work. When people obtain these cognitions, they are empowered in the sense that they are intrinsically motivated to high performance.

QUESTION: In your opinion, did Johnson do a good job of employing these characteristics during the Monday morning meeting? Explain, using the four cognitions.

Case Part 2: Thursday Morning—Missed Connections

It is Thursday morning, and sales team member Tracy calls Johnson to ask about the possibility of attending an upcoming conference on telecommunications marketing. Told that Johnson is on another call, Tracy leaves a message for Johnson to return the call as soon as possible. Tracy is eager for a quick response from Johnson because the conference organizers have limited the number of conference attendees to one per firm. An hour or so later, Johnson still has not returned the call. Knowing that Johnson has a tendency to ignore phone messages for hours at a time, Tracy calls again, but again fails to reach Johnson personally. By the end of the day, Tracy still has not made contact with Johnson, despite placing several more calls and being told each time by the receptionist that Johnson would call back.

The next morning, Tracy sees Chris, another member of the sales team. Chris excitedly tells Tracy of a lunch with Johnson yesterday and of Johnson's offer to sponsor Chris at an upcoming conference. Chris says that they had spent part of the afternoon reviewing the conference brochure and discussing the topics that would be presented.

QUESTIONS: How do you think Tracy felt on hearing the news from Chris that Johnson and Chris had met the day before, when Tracy had been unable to get Johnson to respond by phone? What about the fact that Chris is now being sent to the very conference that Tracy wanted to attend?

This model emphasizes the perceptual nature of psychological empowerment, noting that the objective reality of the work environment is not necessarily aligned with, and may indeed be inconsistent with, the individual's subjective perception of reality. It is important for managers, therefore, to recognize that individuals will differ in their perception of phenomena in the work environment and that these differences in perception will have dissimilar consequences regarding the extent to which individuals achieve the intrinsic motivation of psychological empowerment.

QUESTION: What might be the differences between Johnson's perception of the day's events and Tracy's?

TRIGGERS OF DYSEMPOWERMENT: AFFRONTS TO ONE'S DIGNITY

We have developed an extension of the model of psychological empowerment that goes beyond task-related cognitions to include perceptions of negative events or episodes in the work environment that may also result in differential consequences for individuals and groups (Kane and Montgomery, 1998). We refer to this process as *dysempowerment,* and it is defined as a process whereby a work event or episode is evaluated by an individual as an affront to his or her dignity resulting in a debilitating set of responses with the potential to disrupt the individual's work-related attitudes and behavior. As shown in Figure 6-1, these reactions may include anger, humiliation, indignation, and hostility. Further, such negative emotions may lead to impairments in the individual's task motivation associated with psychological empowerment.

We emphasize that dysempowerment is not the opposite of empowerment and that empowerment and dysempowerment can coexist to varying degrees. The factors

FIGURE 6-1 A Process Model of Dysempowerment

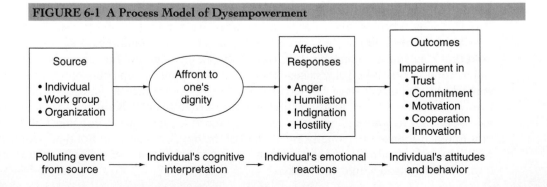

thought to produce psychological empowerment are task-related cognitions (or energizers because of their potential to enhance motivation). In contrast, the factors that trigger dysempowerment are affective responses to events (or polluters because of their potential to impair but not necessarily negate the motivation of empowerment). Thus, dysempowerment should not be confused with concepts such as "disempowerment," which is the lack of empowerment; "powerlessness," which is a feeling of domination by other people and of not being able to reduce or eliminate that control (Blauner, 1964); or "learned helplessness," which is a person's assessment of his or her inability to have influence (Abramson, Seligman, and Teasdale, 1978).

Case Part 3: Friday Afternoon—A Simple Misunderstanding or Dysempowerment?

It is Friday afternoon, and the sales team has reconvened. They have a half hour to meet among themselves before Johnson joins them for a weekly report. Tracy is still steaming over Johnson's failure to return the calls from the previous day. Tracy's anger is compounded by a sense of indignation that Chris has been given an opportunity for growth that now may be unavailable to Tracy. As the team discusses the week's sales activity, Tracy reveals to the other team members yesterday's events. Just then, Johnson arrives, expecting to encounter a highly energized empowered team. Instead, the team members look tense and uneasy.

When Johnson asks what the team had been discussing, there is a long pause. Then Gerry, the team's informal leader, speaks up, "Tracy was telling the team about what occurred between the two of you yesterday." Johnson is dumbfounded, because the two of them had never even spoken yesterday. "What's the problem?" Johnson asks Tracy, who seems reluctant to elaborate. Johnson then turns to Gerry and asks, "Please tell me what's going on." Gerry recounts what Tracy has just told them. Johnson turns to Tracy and says, "Did you get out of bed on the wrong side yesterday? You all know that when I get busy, I don't always return phone calls!"

Tracy protests, "But you managed to find time for Chris! And now Chris is the one you're sending to the conference."

Johnson responds with impatience, "Well, Chris was in the right place at the right time yesterday. I told Chris to bring back copies of all the conference materials to share with the rest of the team, so it's no big deal which one of you gets to go." Then, thinking the issue has been resolved, Johnson quickly says, "Let's move on. . . ."

QUESTIONS: How do you think Tracy feels now? How do you think the other group members feel about the way Johnson responded to Tracy?

RESPONSES TO POLLUTING EVENTS

Respect for the dignity of an individual is an important factor in an employee's work experiences because it has been linked to a perception of fairness (Alexander and Ruderman, 1987; Hosmer, 1995; Korsgaard, Schweiger, and Sapienza, 1995; Mayer, Davis, and Schoorman, 1995). Literature from several perspectives identifies key predictors of the perceptions of fairness. In particular, research on organizational justice (e.g., Greenberg, 1990, 1993a; Lind and Tyler, 1988) indicates that individuals' perceptions of fairness are influenced not only by equity in the distribution of rewards but also by the quality of interpersonal respect for one's status as a member of the work group (Lind and Tyler, 1988). These perceptions facilitate the development of positive attitudes, including trust, emotional involvement, and commitment, which in turn lead to productive work-related behaviors.

Conversely, when polluting events in the form of lack of consideration or respect for one's dignity occur, a perception of unfairness and subjective stress may develop. For example, Greenberg (1990) reports that perceptions of unfairness have been found when individuals believe their treatment did not achieve a level of "ethical appropriateness" associated with treating people with civility and dignity. These perceptions have been found to lead to such negative feelings as anger, hostility, fear, and depression, with subsequent negative behavioral outcomes (Cropanzano and Folger, 1996; Greenberg, 1993a; Kidwell and Bennett, 1995; Motowidlo et al., 1986; O'Leary-Kelly, Griffin, and Glew, 1996; Parasuraman and Alutto, 1984).

QUESTIONS: In what ways might Tracy feel treated unfairly? What do you predict will be Tracy's affective (emotional) responses and the subsequent behavioral outcomes?

Case Part 4: Two Weeks Later— Heading in the Wrong Direction

A couple of weeks pass. Just before the regular Friday afternoon sales meeting, Johnson reviews the team's performance. Uncharacteristically, Tracy's numbers have slipped significantly lower than the numbers for the other team members. Johnson thinks, "I guess empowerment doesn't work for Tracy." Entering the meeting, Johnson is thinking that maybe the old strategy of motivation makes more sense, at least with Tracy. As the team reviews a chart of the month's performance numbers, Johnson points to the column labeled with Tracy's name and says, "Somebody's year-end bonus is taking a nose dive." To Tracy, Johnson adds jokingly, "I guess my new policy of self-scheduling means scheduling yourself into too many afternoons at the club." Tracy says nothing, but looks upset.

QUESTIONS: Do you think there is a connection between Tracy's performance and Johnson's comments and actions toward Tracy? Why?

OUTCOMES OF DYSEMPOWERMENT

As noted previously, perceptions of fairness lead to positive attitudes, including trust, emotional involvement, and commitment. The work-related behavioral outcomes associated with these positive attitudes include interpersonal and motivational effectiveness, group cohesiveness, cooperation, and risk taking in relationships. However, when there are perceptions that one's dignity has been affronted, feelings of anger, humiliation, indignation, and hostility are likely. These negative feelings have been shown to result in impairments in trust, commitment, motivation, cooperation, and innovation as well as subsequent behavioral outcomes such as lack of cooperation and withholding efforts toward goals (Cropanzano and Folger, 1996; Greenberg, 1993b; Kidwell and Bennett, 1995; Motowidlo et al., 1986; O'Leary-Kelly, Griffin, and Glew, 1996; Parasuraman and Alutto, 1984).

QUESTIONS: Do you think Tracy's performance will get better or worse given what we know about dysempowerment? Why?

Case Part 5: Another Week Passes—Trouble Spreads

Another week passes. Tracy's numbers continue to plummet, and much to Johnson's dismay, Dale's figures have started to slip as well. Johnson thinks back over the time since implementing some of the strategies from the sales management training on empowerment. In the beginning, the team seemed excited about the new approach. Johnson vaguely recalls a tense exchange with Tracy at a recent meeting but assumed things had been smoothed out, especially now that Tracy's schedule is being monitored more closely. And Johnson surely can't figure out why Dale isn't responding to this new managerial approach. Johnson ponders, "Whose figures are going to slip next? What's going on? They told me that empowerment had all the answers to motivation and increased performance."

Johnson seeks out Gerry, the informal team leader, to ask advice about what's gone wrong. Gerry has no answers but agrees to talk to the others and get back to Johnson the next day. Gerry invites the team for a drink after work and asks each person to come to the gathering with some ideas about the situation.

Still feeling indignant, Tracy thinks, "There's not much mystery to me about what's gone on. Johnson spouts all this empowerment stuff and then turns around and treats me disrespectfully. How can that be empowering?"

Dale, identifying with Tracy, thinks, "If Johnson's going to treat Tracy so disrespectfully, what's to keep me from being the next target?"

Chris thinks that Tracy and Dale must be in the wrong business.

Gerry remembers the incident about who got to go to the conference but can't imagine that this would be important enough to affect anyone's performance.

QUESTIONS: Why do you think Dales' figures are starting to slip? Do you think the figures of the others will begin to drop too? Why or why not?

DIFFERENCES IN PERCEPTION

Individual differences may affect one's perceptions of inconsiderate treatment. Previous studies have noted that women and men have different interpersonal styles, with women exhibiting greater sensitivity to nuances of the behaviors of others in general (Hall, 1987; Maccoby, 1990; Tannen, 1990). Similar observations have been made regarding the influence of gender on how people react to others' behavior in work settings (Grant, 1988; Gutek, 1985; Konrad and Gutek, 1986; Rosener, 1990).

Vicarious Effects

People learn from observation as well as direct experience (Bandura, 1986). Thus, a witness to the undignified treatment of another, even if he or she is not the intended recipient, may be infected with the same negative feelings of dysempowerment as the individual directly involved in the episode. The initial indication that vicarious dysempowerment may be occurring is a perception that the behavior toward someone other than oneself is disrespectful, rude, impatient, or otherwise lacking in consideration for the dignity of the recipient. If witnesses do not perceive behavior to be inconsiderate, it is unlikely that these witnesses will themselves experience dysempowerment. Conversely, if witnesses do perceive the behavior as objectionable, the potential for vicarious or collective dysempowerment is greatly enhanced.

QUESTION: If Tracy and Dale are both women, and all the other characters are men, would this situation influence the way Tracy and Dale have experienced the events in the case?

Social Identity

The impact of observational or vicarious learning is intensified when witnesses share a social identity with the target because of the tendency to sympathize to a greater degree with the experiences of those with whom one shares salient personal characteristics (Ashforth and Mael, 1989; Brewer and Miller, 1994; Tajfel and Turner, 1985) or with whom one shares a salient work experience such as tokenism (Kanter, 1977). Social identification theory and work on reference groups reveal the importance of deriving an individual identity from certain groups to which one belongs (Brewer and Miller, 1984; Napier and Gershenfeld, 1993; Tajfel and Turner, 1985). Cox (1994) notes the personal affiliation or solidarity one shares with others in the same group and emphasizes the salience of group membership in primary groups that are most physically identifiable—race and sex.

Ashforth and Mael (1989) observe that social identification involves a perception of being psychologically intertwined with the fate of the group with which one identifies. This may imply a tendency to sympathize to a greater degree with the experiences—both the successes and the failures—of those with whom one shares salient personal characteristics than with those who are different. Similarly, the projection hypothesis (Krosnick, 1990) posits that social perception is influenced by one's attitude toward a target, especially when the target is most like oneself.

QUESTION: How might this explain Chris' opinion that Tracy and Dale are "in the wrong business"?

Case Part 6: Johnson Goes for Help

Gerry returns to Johnson with a summary of the conversation and has no ideas for Johnson about how to solve the breakdown in morale and motivation. Johnson decides to consult with the trainer who has given the empowerment workshop. The trainer asks Johnson a few questions about what has occurred and quickly realizes that dysempowerment may have inadvertently occurred within the sales ranks. The trainer explains that even though Johnson may have had good intentions, the behavior was perceived by some team members to be inconsistent with the original goals of empowerment. Johnson realizes that the approach taken with Tracy has been all wrong and repair must be done to improve the trust and perceptions of fairness or Tracy may leave the organization. In addition, Dale may also be at risk. Clearly, the entire team's productivity has been compromised by the recent events.

Based on feedback from the trainer, Johnson resolves to call the team together again on Monday morning, make amends for the previous weeks' actions, and explain to the group how easy it is to dysempower even when one is attempting to empower. Johnson intends to be a better listener and communicator and is now aware that even though the intentions may be good, greater attention needs to be given to the team member's differences in perception and interpretation of events.

QUESTIONS: Do you believe that Johnson's actions will be enough to repair the damage that has been done? Why or why not? What would you do in Johnson's place? What gender have you associated with the characters in the case (Johnson, Gerry, Dale, Chris, Tracy, and the trainer)? Did you notice, while you were reading the case, that no gender had been assigned to the characters? Analyze why you might have assigned a certain gender to each character. How might your perception of the case be different if you had assigned a different gender to the characters?

COLLECTIVE DYSEMPOWERMENT AND ORGANIZATIONAL CLIMATES

To this point, we have primarily treated dysempowerment as an individual-level phenomenon. It is important to recognize that dysempowerment can have collective effects that extend to the group, work unit, or organization level. For example, negative feelings and behaviors resulting from an individual's dysempowerment may spread vicariously to others in the group through interpretive contagion (Barley and Knight, 1992), generating a climate of collective dysempowerment.

Organizational climates can encompass both observable organizational practices and procedures and individual perceptions (Denison, 1996). We have developed a typology, shown in Figure 6-2, to demonstrate the organizational climates that may result from the coexistence of high and low degrees of dysempowering polluters and empowering energizers.

Although the typology suggests four "ideal types" that are unlikely to exist in the real world, it should facilitate the diagnosis of prevailing organizational climates that approach these four types and may thus be useful for potential managerial intervention. In addition, the typology may serve as a useful guide for identifying the type of organizational climate best suited to various organizational activities and goals, as well as to assess person–organization fit.

For example, type A depicts an organization in which there are a relatively low level of negative events associated with dysempowerment but where there also may be little effort to promote psychological empowerment among its workforce. On the dysempowerment dimension, we characterize this organization as hospitable because there may be few, if any, instances of affronts to employees' dignity. At the same time, on the empowerment dimension, we characterize this organization as static because of the low level of task motivation among employees. These combined dimensions generate a hospitable-static climate—neither highly polluted nor highly energized.

	Empowering Energizers	
	Low	High
Low	**Type A** Hospitable static	**Type D** Hospitable dynamic
High	**Type B** Antagonistic static	**Type C** Antagonistic dynamic

Dysempowering Polluters

FIGURE 6-2 A Typology of Organizational Climate

Although this climate may be satisfactory for some types of organizational activity, such as routinized work, it would be inappropriate for many others because a sense of passivity, however benign, may pervade the organization.

A more extreme example of a climate that would be inappropriate, indeed undesirable, for most organizations is that depicted in type B where there is minimal effort to treat employees with respect and dignity and little attention to employee empowerment. This combination of high polluters and low energizers yields an antagonistic-static climate that one might encounter in an organization whose employees feel exploited. Although it is difficult to envision an organization intentionally fostering such a climate, a diagnosis of the relative dysempowerment–empowerment levels may reveal a picture for some organizations that is realistically closer to type B than to the others.

Type C depicts a climate that may appear, at first, anomalous, that is, an organization in which both high polluters and high energizers coexist in a climate that is simultaneously dynamic and antagonistic. However, this climate may be found in some high-pressure sales organizations, which may offer high levels of empowerment in the form of intrinsic task motivation; at the same time, it is not uncommon for the competitive work environment of such organizations to be associated with frequent events that affront one's dignity.

The organizational climate in type D suggests a setting where employees experience low levels of dysempowerment combined with high levels of empowerment. This hospitable-dynamic climate represents the idealized goal of much of the prescriptive teachings of organizational behavior, where organizations aspire to cultivate employees with high levels of intrinsic task motivation, coupled with perceptions that they are treated with dignity and respect.

Understanding more about vicarious and collective dysempowerment is especially important in terms of their far-reaching impact on organizational functioning. This is because witnesses to the disrespectful treatment of someone else may also be affected by their perceptions of the treatment. Therefore, vicarious dysempowerment can be viewed as a "collective" phenomenon with the potential to infect witnesses of, as well as the direct recipient of, undignified treatment.

QUESTIONS: If you had to assess the climate at ComTek, into which category would it fall? Why?

IMPLICATIONS FOR WOMEN IN MANAGEMENT

We mentioned earlier that, whether the dysempowering episodes or events are experienced directly or vicariously, individuals may vary in the meanings and interpretations they place on the episodes, such that inconsiderate behavior may have a more deleterious effect on one employee than on another. In fact, there is evidence that differences in perception about "inappropriate" workplace behavior may vary by demographic or social identity group, as well as by organizational position. For example, researchers have found that men and women, as well as individuals with different amounts of organizational power, differ in their perception of whether or not certain behaviors constitute the "hostile environment" of sexual harassment (Hendrick et al., 1985; Konrad and Gutek, 1986; Murrell and Dietz-Uhler, 1993; Tangri, Burt, and Johnson, 1982; Tata, 1993; Terpstra and Baker, 1986; Thacker and Gohmann, 1993).

In our own research, we have found that women and men do perceive male–female workplace interactions differently and that women are significantly more likely than men to view potentially dysempowering treatment as inappropriate and as constituting affronts to one's dignity (Montgomery, Kane, and Vance, 1997). Not only were there differences in perception when witnessing interactions among others, the women in the study were themselves greatly angered, even though they were not the direct targets of the disrespectful treatment.

Of concern, therefore, is that women may be at greater risk of suffering the effects of dysempowerment than men, even when there is no explicit intent to dysempower. Women may simply be more sensitive to incidents that have the potential to dysempower through a lack of respect for one's dignity, even if this occurs inadvertently. This greater awareness by itself may make women more vulnerable to impairment in their ability to achieve the motivational benefits of psychological empowerment.

Moreover, the unbalanced representation of men and women in organizations may exacerbate this situation. That is, today men are still more likely to hold positions of organizational power than are women. If people in positions of authority are oblivious to the dysempowering potential of episodes like those in this chapter's case study, the likelihood of management intervention to avoid dysempowerment is slim. This is not to say that men will intentionally send dysempowering messages themselves; rather, it suggests that management may unknowingly tolerate such behavior because it is not perceived as objectionable and in need of correction. As a result, workplace inequalities may continue because of the inability of some in lesser positions in the organization to enjoy a workplace free of experiences that may interfere with their psychological empowerment and resulting productivity.

SUMMARY OF KEY POINTS

Although organizations continue to embrace the notion of empowerment, reports from business also indicate an ambivalence on the part of employees. Indeed, in a recent *Harvard Business Review* article, Argyris (1998) observes that, "Despite all the talk and the change programs, empowerment is still mostly an illusion" (p. 98). Our theory suggests that part of the problem results from a lack of recognition of the potential of negative events that pollute the empowering process. Thus, even the most aggressive organizational efforts to enhance empowerment may be compromised in the presence of polluting events. Indeed, dysempowerment may function as a drop of poison in the glass of nectar; one or two drops has the ability to poison the entire glass—whether in an individual or in the entire organization.

Once managers and organizations recognize the potential of dysempowerment to pollute or poison otherwise ambitious efforts to produce empowerment, their leaders may decide to investigate the presence of polluters in advance of formal attempts to promote empowerment, as well as to remain alert to the ongoing potential damage of polluting events. Although an intervention (e.g., politeness training for managers) may be vital to the organization's health, it may also prove to be the most challenging to accomplish because it may require substantive changes in employee and managerial behaviors and, ultimately, a fundamental change in the organizational culture. This will not occur until those in power in organizations understand the necessity for an honest and thorough evaluation of the effects of dysempowerment on all levels of employees in their organizations. Our hope as researchers and authors is that by delineating the dysempowerment process and the potentially polluting and harmful effects of these assaults on dignity, we have contributed something to the well-being and productivity of not only women, but all workers.

Issues to Debate

Point

There should be no difference in how men and women are treated in organizations; everyone should be treated the same.

Counterpoint

Managers must realize men and women may vary in their perception of disrespectful behavior. Respectful behavior includes recognizing the legitimacy of and acting in accordance with these differing perceptions.

Point

Women want to move into positions of organizational power, but they also want to be treated with kid gloves. They can't have it both ways.

Counterpoint

Dysempowerment has no place in an organization regardless of who the target is or what position she aspires to. Respectful treatment from peers and supervisors is an expectation that all employees are entitled to.

Point

Women are now moving into influential managerial positions and can call the shots and change the organizational climate if they want to.

Counterpoint

Climate permeates the organization and can be changed only with large-scale behavior change at all levels.

References and Suggested Readings

Abramson, L. Y., Seligman, M. E. P., and Teasdale, J. D. (1978). Learned helplessness in humans: Critique and reformulation. *Journal of Abnormal Psychology, 87,* 19–74.

Alexander, S., and Ruderman, M. (1987). The role of procedural and distributive justice in organizational behavior. *Social Justice Research, 1,* 117–198.

Argyris, C. (1998, May–June). Empowerment: The emperor's new clothes. *Harvard Business Review,* 98–105.

Ashforth, B., and Mael, F. (1989). Social identity theory and the organization. *Academy of Management Review, 14,* 20–39.

Bandura, A. (1986). *Social foundations of thought and action: A social cognitive view.* Englewood Cliffs, NJ: Prentice-Hall.

Barley, S. R., and Knight, D. B. (1992). Toward a cultural theory of stress complaints. *Research in Organizational Behavior, 14,* 1–48.

Blauner, R. (1964). *Alienation and freedom: The factory worker and his industry.* Chicago: University of Chicago Press.

Brewer, M. B., and Miller, N. (1994). Beyond the contact hypothesis: Theoretical perspectives on desegregation. In N. Miller and M. B. Brewer (Eds.), *Groups in contact* (pp. 281–302). San Diego, CA: Academic.

Cox, T. (1994). *Cultural diversity in organizations.* San Francisco: Berrett-Koehler.

Cropanzano, R., and Folger, R. (1996). Procedural justice and worker motivation. In R. M. Steers, L. W. Porter, and G. A. Bigley (Eds.), *Motivation and leadership at work,* (6th ed., pp. 72–83). New York: McGraw-Hill.

Denison, D. R. (1996). What is the difference between organizational culture and organizational climate? A native's point of view on a decade of paradigm wars. *Academy of Management Review, 21,* 619–654.

Grant, J. (1988). Women as managers: What they can offer organizations. *Organizational Dynamics, 16,* 56–63.

Greenberg, J. (1990). Organizational justice: Yesterday, today, and tomorrow. *Journal of Management, 16,* 399–432.

Greenberg, J. (1993a). Stealing in the name of justice: Informational and interpersonal moderators of theft reactions to underpayment inequity. *Organizational Behavior and Human Decision Processes, 54,* 81–103.

Greenberg, J. (1993b). The social side of fairness. In R. Cropanzano (Ed.), *Justice in the workplace: Approaching fairness in human resource management* (pp. 79–103). Hillsdale, NJ: Lawrence Erlbaum.

Gutek, B. (1985). *Sex and the workplace.* San Francisco: Jossey-Bass.

Hall, J. A. (1987). On explaining gender differences: The case of nonverbal communication. In P. Shaver and C. Hendrick (Eds.), *Sex and gender: Review of personality and social psychology.* Newbury Park, CA: Sage.

Hendrick, S. et al., (1985). Gender differences in sexual attitudes. *Journal of Personality and Social Psychology, 48,* 630–642.

Hosmer, L. T. (1995). Trust: The connecting link between organizational theory and philosophical ethics. *Academy of Management Review, 20,* 379–403.

Kane, K., and Montgomery, K. (1998, Fall/ Winter). A framework for understanding dysempowerment in organizations. *Human Resource Management Journal, 37* (394), pp. 263–275.

Kanter, R. M. (1977) *Men and women of the corporation.* New York: Basic Books.

Kanter, R. M. (1984). Managing transition in organizational culture: The case of participative management at Honeywell. In J. R. Kimberly and R. E. Quinn (Eds.), *Managing organizational transitions* pp. 195–217. Homewood, IL: Irwin.

Kidwell, R. E., and Bennett, N. (1995). Employee propensity to withhold effort: A conceptual model to intersect three avenues of research. *Academy of Management Review, 18,* 429–456.

Konrad, A., and Gutek, B. (1986). Impact of work experiences on attitudes toward sexual harassment. *Administrative Science Quarterly, 31,* 422–438.

Korsgaard, A. A., Schweiger, D. M., and Sapienza, H. J. (1995). Building commitment, attachment, and trust in strategic decision-making teams: The role of procedural justice. *Academy of Management Journal, 38,* 60–84.

Krosnick, J. (1990). Americans' perceptions of presidential candidates: A test of the projection hypothesis. *Journal of Social Issues, 46,* 159–182.

Lind, E. A., and Tyler, T. R. (1988). *The social psychology of procedural justice.* New York: Plenum.

Maccoby, E. E. (1990). Gender relationships: A developmental account. *American Psychologist, 45,* 513–520.

Mayer R. C., Davis, J. H., and Schoorman, F. D. (1995). An integrative model of organizational trust. *Academy of Management Review, 20,* 709–734.

Montgomery, K., Kane, K., and Vance, C. (1997). Vicarious dysempowerment: An empirical test of differences in perception. Presented at the American Sociological Association annual meeting, Toronto.

Motowidlo, S. J., Packard, J. S., and Manning, M. R. (1986). Occupational stress: Its causes and consequences for job performance. *Journal of Applied Psychology, 71,* 618–629.

Murrell, A., and Dietz-Uhler, B. (1993). Gender identity and adversarial sexual beliefs as predictors of attitudes toward sexual harassment. *Psychology of Women Quarterly, 17,* 169–175.

Napier, R., and Gershenfeld, M. (1993). *Groups: Theory and experience* (5th ed.). Dallas: Houghton Mifflin.

O'Leary-Kelly, A. M., Griffin, R. W., and Glew, D. J. (1996). Organization-motivated aggression: A research framework. *Academy of Management Review, 21,* 225–253.

Parasuraman, S., and Alutto, J. A. (1984). Sources and outcomes of stress in organizational settings: Toward the development of a structural model. *Academy of Management Journal, 27,* 330–350.

Rosener, J. (1990). Ways women lead. *Harvard Business Review, 68,* 119–120.

Spreitzer, G. M. (1995). Psychological empowerment in the workplace: Dimensions, measurement, and validation. *Academy of Management Journal, 38,* 1442–1465.

Spreitzer, G. M. (1996). Social structural characteristics of psychological empowerment. *Academy of Management Journal, 39,* 483–504.

Tajfel, H., and Turner, J. (1985). The social identity theory of intergroup behavior. In S. Worchel and W. Austin (Eds.), *Psychology of intergroup relations* (2nd ed., pp. 7–24). Chicago: Nelson-Hall.

Tangri, S., Burt, M. R., and Johnson, L. B. (1982). Sexual harassment at work: Three explanatory models. *Journal of Social Issues, 38,* 33–54.

Tannen, D. (1990). *You just don't understand.* New York: William Morrow.

Tata, J. (1993). The structure and phenomenon of sexual harassment: Impact of category of sexually harassing behavior, gender, and hierarchical level. *Journal of Applied Social Psychology, 23,* 199–211.

Terpstra, D., and Baker, D. (1986). Psychological and demographic correlates of perception of sexual harassment. *Genetic, Social and General Psychology Monographs, 112,* 459–478.

Thacker, R., and Gohmann, S. (1993). Male/female differences in perceptions and effects of hostile environment sexual harassment: "Reasonable" assumptions? *Public Personnel Management, 22,* 462–472.

Thomas, K., and Velthouse, B. (1990). Cognitive elements of empowerment: An "interpretive" model of interpretive task motivation. *Academy of Management Review, 15,* 666–681.

Law and Gender in Management

7

Anne Levy

Nor can I agree with the majority's notion that the effect of pin-up posters and misogynous language in the workplace can only have a minimal effect on female employees . . . when considered in the context of a society that condones and publicly features and commercially exploits open displays of written and pictorial erotica. . . . "Society" in this scenario must primarily refer to the unenlightened; I hardly believe reasonable women condone the pervasive degradation and exploitation of female sexuality perpetuated in American culture. In fact, pervasive societal approval thereof and of other stereotypes stifles female potential and instills the debased sense of self-worth which accompanies stigmatization. . . . [T]he relevant inquiry at hand is what the reasonable woman would find offensive, not society, which at one point also condoned slavery.

—JUDGE DAMON KEITH DISAGREEING WITH THE MAJORITY
OPINION IN *Rabidue* v. *Osceola Refining*

Chapter Overview

Workplace gender discrimination comes in a variety of forms and disguises. It may be overt and easily seen, or it may be so subtle that a woman might wonder whether it has really occurred. Many laws have been passed to help women deal with all of these types of gender discrimination, but, as in the past, eradicating sexist practices that lead to unequal opportunity will not be an easy task. Although the laws are in place, continuing advancement of gender equity in the workplace will take vigilance and courage by women willing to stand up for their own and others' rights and to urge their employers and the courts to continue to advance the cause. Women managers, especially, will be needed, as they are in a unique position to affect business policies and to argue for equal opportunity from their employers. Although it is always hoped that such changes will come about voluntarily and cooperatively, the law does stand ready to force change, when that avenue is necessary. This chapter discusses the ways that employment law has developed in the past 25 years and charts the trends for the future in the area of gender discrimination.

There are a number of laws that protect women and affect decisions regarding their career opportunities. Federally, these include Title VII of the Civil Rights Act of 1964, the Equal Pay Act, and the Family and Medical Leave Act (FMLA). Many states provide their own civil rights acts for challenging workplace discrimination that apply to businesses within that state. Statutes, or laws, like Title VII, are written by some legislative body and provide a variety of "causes of action." A "cause of action" is a "legally recognized reason to sue." Common law causes of action may also be available for victims of discrimination. Common law is law that has been developed over hundreds of years, using court decisions as precedents for dealing with cases in which no statute is applicable to the situation. All causes of action, whether statutorily authorized or recognized under common law, have a variety of bases and principles that must be understood in order to make informed decisions as to when you should turn to the law to resolve workplace problems. Because state laws are unique to each state, this chapter deals mostly with the various facets of federal law, which are often used by the state courts when they have to interpret their own laws.

THE LEGAL SYSTEM AND DISCRIMINATION LAWS

It is the duty of the courts in the American legal system, either through a judge or a jury, to carry out the laws, including deciding which witnesses can be heard, which testimony is the most credible, which side should win, and how much money the losing side should pay. In addition, because even statutory laws are subject to a variety of interpretations, the courts must decide when and how to apply the laws, in other words, interpret the laws. In the area of employment law, interpretation has become very important. For example, such causes of action as hostile environment sexual harassment are not specifically mentioned in Title VII, and it was only through judicial interpretation of Congress' intent in using the term "sex discrimination" that the courts have recognized these types of lawsuits.

Interpretation of the laws begins first with the trial court, or the court in which the lawsuit is first filed. It is here that the witnesses are heard, the evidence is submitted, and the judge or jury makes a decision as to who wins. In the federal system, these are called district courts and there are a number of them throughout the United States.

Once the district court issues an opinion in a lawsuit, any interpretation of the law or other matters decided in the case can be appealed to an appeals court. In the federal system, these are called the circuit courts of appeals. The country is divided into sections or circuits, and appeals from any district court in each section must be taken to the circuit court for that area. A panel of judges in the circuit court of appeals will hear the case and may find that the trial court was correct and uphold the lower court ruling. Conversely, the circuit court may find that the trial court was incorrect and a new trial must be held, the case dismissed, or, in some circumstances, it may change the finding of the trial court. After a circuit court makes a decision, all of the district courts in that region must accept that decision as the rule in the circuit.

A woman could have a cause of action in one circuit but not be allowed to bring a lawsuit under exactly the same circumstances in another circuit. Because this may result in an unjust situation, the legal system provides for a final decider when it comes to legal decision making. In the federal system, this ultimate authority is the U.S. Supreme Court, which generally only hears appeals when it agrees to do so. A party is either granted or denied "leave to appeal" by the Supreme Court after it asks the Court to hear its case. When leave is granted, arguments are heard and a decision is made by the full nine-member Court.

Hostile sexual environment cases presented a conflict in the circuit courts. Some circuits had interpreted Title VII to cover these situations, whereas others had dismissed such cases. The Supreme Court, in a well-known case, *Meritor Savings Bank* v. *Vinson* (1986), decided that Congress had intended Title VII to cover such cases, and since that time, all federal courts have been required to recognize this "cause of action."

It is important to remember that the laws we discuss are not criminal in nature but, rather, are called "civil cases." A civil lawsuit provides an opportunity for one party, the plaintiff, to sue another party, the defendant, for damages that have occurred if the plaintiff can prove that the defendant has failed to live up to some duty imposed by the law. Because these are not criminal proceedings, many constitutional requirements that are imposed in criminal cases are not required, such as the right to an appointed attorney or the right to a speedy trial. In fact, many plaintiffs find that the cases they file take much longer than they had expected. In addition, the standard of proof in discrimination cases is not as high as it is in a criminal case: A prosecutor must prove beyond a reasonable doubt that a defendant committed the crime, whereas a plaintiff in a civil lawsuit need only convince the judge or jury that it is more likely than not that the defendant did not live up to a duty imposed by the law. In most situations, this is called "a preponderance of the evidence."

TITLE VII: GENDER DISCRIMINATION, DISPARATE TREATMENT, SEXUAL HARASSMENT, AFFIRMATIVE ACTION, COMPARABLE WORTH

Fundamentals of Title VII and Gender Discrimination

The employment discrimination section of the Civil Rights Act of 1964 is called Title VII. It is within this section that one finds the prohibition against discrimination on the basis of sex. The alleged story surrounding the inclusion of gender among the prohibited classifications in Title VII is quite interesting. As first introduced as a bill, the Civil Rights Act of 1964 did not include a prohibition against sex discrimination. The major focus of Congress' drive in passing the act was to eliminate discrimination on the basis of race. It is reported that a southern legislator, in an attempt to defeat the act, proposed an amendment that would add sex discrimination to the original list of Title VII classifications (race, color, religion, national origin). According to some sources, he felt that the addition of gender would be sure to defeat the entire act. Interestingly, the amendment and the statute passed and became law. Although there are distinctions made in some fields of study between sex and gender, no such distinction exists in the law and the two terms are used interchangeably.

In 1978, Congress amended Title VII to make clear that discrimination on the basis of pregnancy is prohibited as a type of sex discrimination. In 1993, it was amended again to include, among other changes, the allowance for punitive damages in cases of intentional discrimination.

Title VII specifically prohibits an employer, employment agency, or labor union from refusing to hire, discharging, or otherwise discriminating with regard to compensation, terms, conditions, or privileges of employment, on any prohibited basis. An employer is basically defined as anyone with 15 or more employees. (In this chapter, the term *employer* will be used only.) Although many working women are covered by Title VII, women working for some smaller companies may not enjoy the same protection. Many state statutes also prohibit sex discrimination, however, and they often apply to companies with fewer employees. In Michigan, for example, the state's civil rights act covers anyone with one or more employee.

In order to bring a claim under Title VII, an individual must first file a complaint or claim with the Equal Employment Opportunity Commission (EEOC), the administrative agency created by Congress to administer most of the federal discrimination laws. The time limitations for the filing of a claim are very short and strict, so it is important not to delay when you encounter a potential sex discrimination situation that cannot be comfortably settled within your company. A person who alleges a violation of Title VII must file a claim with the EEOC within 180 days of the alleged discrimination. If there is a state law similar to Title VII, you have 300 days from the filing of a claim with a state agency or the resolution of your state claim, whichever comes first. State laws may provide a longer time period, and some allow the filing of a lawsuit without first filing a complaint with a government agency, but, to protect your rights, it is important to act as quickly as you can when you feel that you have been a victim of discrimination.

Often a number of incidents occur that, in the aggregate, finally lead to a charge of gender discrimination. Some of these may fall within the required statutes of limitations, and some may have occurred many months or even years earlier, but no claim was made at that time, either because the employee was hoping for an internal resolution or was trying to cope individually without involving the law. The law does provide for what is called a "continuing violation." Continuing violation allows admission of evidence of situations, behaviors, or decisions that occurred outside the statute of limitations if they can be tied directly to an event that occurred within the required time. The events must be closely related and generally show a pattern of discrimination. As discussed in more depth later, it is vital to document, continually, carefully, and completely any situations that may later become part of a gender discrimination claim.

Because the face of gender discrimination has been evolving from the "Men Only Need Apply" type of case to those involving more covert discriminatory behavior, the courts have also had to evolve the types of claims allowed under Title VII. These now range from overtly refusing to hire or promote women, to using stereotypical thinking to exclude women from positions of authority, to making the workplace unconducive to women's success. A closer look at how the courts have dealt with a few of these claims will help you understand your rights and those of your fellow workers in this area.

Disparate Treatment Cases under Title VII

Under Title VII an employer cannot intentionally deprive women of any of the benefits of employment because of their gender, including promotions, benefits, perks, and so forth. These cases are called disparate treatment cases because women are treated differently because of their gender.

Express Disparate Treatment

The easiest intentional discrimination to recognize is the type in which employers claim that women cannot do certain jobs because of their gender. These are often called express disparate treatment cases. Although this does not happen often in today's world, Title VII does allow this type of behavior if the employer can prove that there is a bona fide occupational qualification (BFOQ). A BFOQ is allowed as a defense to intentional discrimination only if the employer can prove that *no* woman can do the "essence of the job." Although the BFOQ defense is always viewed as a narrow excep-

---

CASE

Dothard v. *Rawlinson*

The Alabama Board of Corrections excluded women from contact positions in all-male penitentiaries because of concerns about the women's safety and prison security, especially with regard to keeping order among convicted rapists. Dianne Rawlinson challenged the requirement claiming that the BFOQ exception to Title VII, universally understood as a narrow exception, was not applicable here and that stereotypical and false notions of women's abilities were the basis of the Alabama employment restriction. A majority of the U.S. Supreme Court decided that Alabama could prove a BFOQ. As Justice Potter Stewart stated, "A woman's relative ability to maintain order in a male, maximum-security, unclassified penitentiary of the type Alabama now runs could be directly reduced by her womanhood." Justices Thurgood Marshall and William Brennan did not agree with the reasoning of the majority, however, and wrote a strong dissent (a statement written by a justice to ex-

press his or her reasons for disagreement) stating that "common sense, fairness, and mental and emotional stability are the qualities a guard needs to cope with the dangers of the job. Well qualified and properly trained women, no less than men, have these psychological weapons at their disposal." They further noted, in words that have been used by many courts in opinions since *Dothard*

With all respect, this rationale regrettably perpetuates one of the most insidious of the old myths about women—that women, wittingly or not, are seductive sexual objects. The effect of the decision, made I am sure with the best of intentions, is to punish women because their very presence might provoke sexual assaults. It is women who are made to pay the price in lost job opportunities for the threat of depraved conduct by prison inmates. Once again, [t]he pedestal upon which women have been placed has . . . upon closer inspection, been revealed as a cage."

Source: From *Dothard*, 1976.

---

tion, BFOQs are sometimes granted to companies for such reasons as privacy (a female attendant needed in a lingerie department for assistance with trying on items) or psychological ramifications (a female therapist in a rape counseling center, when psychological barriers may exist toward male therapists).

One of the first BFOQ cases to reach the U.S. Supreme Court was *Dothard* v. *Rawlinson* (1976), which is described in the accompanying box. Since the *Dothard* decision, there have been many critics of the rationale used by the Supreme Court majority, and recent decisions appear to show that the Court has advanced in its view of individual career choices. In *United Automobile Workers* v. *Johnson Controls* (1991), for example, the Supreme Court rejected the argument of Johnson Controls that, because of concerns about the health of unborn children, it could legally exclude women from lead-exposure work. The majority opinion, written by Justice Harry Blackmun, decided that

[A]n employer must direct its concerns about a woman's ability to perform her job safely and efficiently to those aspects of the woman's job-related activities that fall within the "essence" of the particular business.

> We have no difficulty concluding that Johnson Controls cannot establish a BFOQ. Fertile women, as far as appears in the record, participate in the manufacture of batteries as efficiently as anyone else. (*Johnson Controls,* 1991, p. 206)

Since the *Johnson Controls* case, the courts have been very reticent to grant a BFOQ for intentional discrimination against women, and few companies now expressly and overtly exclude women from positions.

Implied Disparate Treatment

In today's society, just because people are far less likely to expressly state that they are intentionally keeping women from career opportunities does not mean that it is not still happening. In many cases, the discrimination is hidden behind words such as "You just weren't right for the job," "We found someone more qualified," or "You didn't have the managerial skills we were looking for." Because covert discrimination is difficult to prove and most of the evidence is in the hands of the employer, the courts have created what is termed a *prima facie* case, or a list of required evidence that raises an "inference of discrimination" and allows a lawsuit to proceed without direct evidence of intentional illegal behavior.

1. She or he is in the protected class that forms the basis of the claim.

   This requirement is somewhat redundant as it only means that if you claim that you were denied a workplace opportunity because you were a woman, you indeed are a woman!

2. She or he applied for the workplace opportunity for which the employer was seeking applicants.

   Again, this is usually easy to satisfy. Few people would bring a claim that they were denied a position when they did not apply or there was none open!

3. She or he possessed the minimum qualifications for the opportunity.

   This requirement can be more difficult as employers often use "lack of qualifications" to keep women from positions. The court must decide what the real minimum qualifications should be, not necessarily those that the employer contends are necessary. As an extreme example, a court would not refuse to hear a woman's claim of intentional discrimination because she could not meet the employer's stated qualification for the position that the candidates "be able to grow a beard."

4. She or he was denied the workplace opportunity.

   With this requirement, we are back in the "easy to satisfy" area. If you receive what you applied for, you are hardly likely to claim discrimination!

5. The employer continued to look for someone to receive the opportunity.

   This requirement is not quite so simple. Often, it is hard to determine whether you were rejected before or after someone else was given the position, especially when a pool of applicants is being considered. For purposes of a discrimination claim, most courts presume that all applicants must be rejected before one is chosen. Thus, they are continuing to look for someone after deciding not to hire others in the pool. Often people erroneously believe that someone of the "opposite protected class" must be chosen for a claim to be brought, for example, a man must be given the opportunity for a woman to claim discrimination. This is not true. Although it certainly adds more evidence to the case, it is quite possible for a woman to be discriminated against even though a woman was given the opportunity. Two cases clarifying this possibility will be discussed in more depth shortly.

Once the person bringing the claim has satisfied these requirements, the employer will be required to show evidence of a legitimate, nonillegal reason for the denial of the opportunity. The plaintiff may then show one of the following and still win the case: (1) that the employer's stated reason is a pretext or a false reason given only to cover up illegal discrimination; (2) that there is a mixed motive involved, in other words the reason given by the employer is only part of the story—the other part is illegal discrimination; (3) or that stereotypical thinking has so poisoned the decision making that the stated reason cannot be trusted. There are a number of ways that a plaintiff can show these. Statistics showing a pattern of denying opportunities to women, for example, are often used as evidence, as are statements made by those doing the decision making that reflect bias or expert testimony on gender stereotyping.

Price Waterhouse v. *Hopkins* (1993) and *Lindahl* v. *Air France* (1991) represent two sides of the stereotypical decision making coin. On the one hand, Ann Hopkins claimed that she was denied a promotion because she did not act enough "like a stereotypical woman." Michelle Lindahl, on the other hand, claimed that she was denied a promotion because she acted "too much like a woman" and was thus judged not to have the stereotypical male qualities necessary for supervisory positions.

The *Hopkins* case presented the U.S. Supreme Court with an opportunity to evolve the law of sexual discrimination to handle these emerging types of cases. It is important because the U.S. Supreme Court officially recognized that Title VII was designed to provide opportunities, not just in situations involving overt discrimination, but also in those in which hidden attitudes and views about proper roles for women were involved in workplace decision making. When a woman is required to act in a stereotypically female manner in order to succeed, Title VII is available to protect her. In *Lindahl* v. *Air France* Title VII protects women who are denied opportunities because they *do* act in a manner consistent with traditional views of women.

Both Ann Hopkins and Michele Lindahl found that intentional discrimination can be hidden behind what appears to be neutral criteria. These cases show that it is important for a manager to examine carefully the reasons behind decisions made in the workplace about women employees. They also magnify the importance of bringing the potential for stereotypical and sexist attitudes to light and discussing them with other managers who may be unaware of subconscious biases. In addition, it is vital that all women in the workplace be aware of the possibility that they are being judged differently because of their gender and to question decisions that may be based on covert discrimination.

Disparate Impact Cases under Title VII

In addition to providing remedies for intentional discrimination, Title VII also allows claims when an employer is discriminating unintentionally by using some criterion, test,

CASE

Price Waterhouse v. Hopkins

Ann Hopkins joined Price Waterhouse in 1978 and was nominated for partnership in 1982. Ms. Hopkins was the only woman among 88 candidates nominated for partnership. She had been exceptionally successful in winning important contracts for her firm. The department in which she worked stated, in its appraisal of her candidacy:

> In her five years with the firm, she has demonstrated conclusively that she has the capacity and capability to contribute significantly to the growth and profitability of the firm. Her strong character, independence, and integrity are well received by her clients and peers. Ms. Hopkins has outstanding oral and written communication skills. She has good business sense, and ability to grasp and handle quickly the most complex issues, and strong leadership qualities.

During the nomination process, some partners expressed concern about her apparent difficulties with staff. She was classified as "overly aggressive, unduly harsh, impatient with staff, and very demanding." One person stated that she needed to "take a course at charm school," another noted that she "may have overcompensated for being a woman," and a third agreed that she came across as "macho." As one supporter noted, there was evidence that "[m]any male partners are worse than Ann" but that she was viewed differently because "she is a lady using foul language." Price Waterhouse denied her partnership noting that, although she "had a lot of talent," she needed "social grace." She was advised by a head partner, who was one of her most fervent supporters to "walk more femininely, talk more femininely, dress more femininely, wear makeup, have her hair styled, and wear jewelry" during the year that her candidacy was placed on hold. She was 1 of 20 who were placed on hold. Of those 20, 17 were renominated the following year; Ann Hopkins was not.

Ann Hopkins had no difficulty making out a *prima facie* case of sex discrimination and Price Waterhouse responded by stating that she was denied partnership because of a lack of interpersonal skills. The key to the case then became the issue of whether sexist attitudes and stereotypical thinking had infected the evaluation system. If so, Ann Hopkins could prove, at the least, a mixed motive for denying her partnership.

The U.S. Supreme Court heard the case and decided that Ann Hopkins could bring a case based on evidence that the process was tainted with discriminatory attitudes. If she or any other plaintiff could successfully show this, the defendant would then have to prove that it would have made the same decision, had the discriminatory attitudes not existed.

_____

Source: From *Price Waterhouse*, 1993.

or other decision-making factor that results in unequal employment opportunity. For example, in *Dothard* v. *Rawlinson,* Dianne Rawlinson also brought a claim against the requirement that all correctional counselors, whether or not they were in contact positions in maximum-security prisons, be at least 5 feet 2 inches and 120 pounds. She correctly pointed out that this criterion resulted in far fewer women being able to qualify

---

CASE

Lindahl v. *Air France*

Michele Lindahl worked as a customer promotion agent in Air France's Los Angeles office. In 1982, the agents were told that the company was planning to create a new position of senior customer promotion agent. Ms. Lindahl was told that she was the most qualified for the position and would be given the promotion, but the company decided not to create the position at that time. In 1987, the company announced that it had chosen a male agent, Edward Michels, to fill the newly created position. Ms. Lindahl was told that Michels was chosen because he had the best overall qualifications. After an appeal to the personnel services manager, she was told that the decision was reasonable and that she was not offered the position because of her lack of computer expertise.

The Court of Appeals, which heard the appeal by Ms. Lindahl when her case was dismissed by the trial court before trial, noted that there was evidence in the case that she had been denied a position because of stereotypical views about the abilities of women. Although the company had not made any statements like those in *Hopkins,* the changing reasons given by the company did indicate some possible "cover-up" of discriminatory decision making, as did the fact that computer expertise was not "clearly related to the leadership position" and

"had never been listed as a qualification for the promotion." Finally, the court noted that there were indications of sexist attitudes in at least one reason given for the promotion denial: lack of leadership abilities.

> Moreover, even if Kershaw did make his decision based on leadership abilities, other evidence could suggest that his evaluation of leadership ability was itself sexist. Lindahl points out that Kershaw made statements about the candidates' relative qualifications that reflect male/female stereotypes. Kershaw testified in his deposition that he believed that both female candidates get "nervous" and that the other female candidate "gets easily upset [and] loses control." By contrast, Kershaw described Michel's leadership qualities as "not to back away from a situation, to take hold immediately of the situation, to attack the situation right away, to stay cool through the whole process. . . ." Kershaw apparently saw Michels as aggressive and cool (in addition to being the one who could impose order), while he saw the female candidates as nervous and emotional.

The court went on to note that Ms. Lindahl should have an opportunity to show that the decision was made "on the basis of stereotypical images of men and women, specifically that women do not make good leaders because they are too 'emotional'."

Source: From *Lindahl,* 1991.

for these positions than men; thus, through the use of one of its job requirements, Alabama was unknowingly denying women equal opportunity. These are called disparate impact or disparate impact cases, and if the plaintiff is successful in proving that a disproportionate impact is occurring, the defendant will have to prove that the criterion in question is, in fact, required to do the job—called "business necessity."

CASE

Watson v. Forth Worth Bank & Trust

Clara Watson brought a lawsuit against her employer claiming that Fort Worth Bank & Trust's practice of leaving promotion decisions to the subjective judgment of supervisors was having a disproportionate impact on African Americans. The lower court had not allowed her to use a disparate impact claim, instead stating that she must prove that there was intentional discrimination. The U.S. Supreme Court disagreed and determined that the use of subjective criteria

without discriminatory intent may have effects that are indistinguishable from intentionally discriminatory practice. . . . [E]ven if one assumed that any such discrimination can be adequately policed through disparate impact analysis, the problem of subconscious stereotypes and prejudices would remain.

The Court concluded that "employment practices 'fair in form, but discriminatory in operation,' cannot be tolerated under Title VII. This lesson should not be forgotten simply because the 'fair form' is a subjective one.

———

Source: From *Watson,* 1988.

Generally, these cases are complex ones that involve a number of plaintiffs and extensive statistics. They also usually result, if successful, in changing the challenged criterion, but in very small damage awards for those bringing the lawsuit.

Disparate impact claims have been brought most often in situations involving race discrimination, and some of those that have been brought with regard to gender have not had the kind of results that women might wish. For example, the EEOC brought a disparate impact claim against Sears & Roebuck alleging that the criteria the company was using to choose who would be placed in commission sales positions (which traditionally paid higher wages than noncommission sales positions) was having a disproportionate impact on women (*EEOC* v. *Sears, Roebuck & Co.,* 1988). At Sears, the percentage of men in the commission sales positions was far higher than the percentage of men who applied for sales positions, and the percentage of women in commission sales was far less than the percentage who applied for sales positions. Despite these statistics, the court found that women themselves were in fact "choosing" not to be in commission sales, and Sears was not responsible for their lack of interest. The judge noted that he felt that all of the EEOC's statistics were "virtually meaningless" because they ignored the reality (as explained by Sears experts) that women's nature was to be nurturing, making them unsuited for the vicious competition in the male-dominated world of commission sales.

This does not mean that disparate impact cases cannot be successful in the area of gender discrimination. A 1987 race discrimination case may, in fact, have made it easier to do so. In *Watson* v. *Forth Worth Bank & Trust* (1988), the Supreme Court decided that subjective decision making, which can reflect sexist, as well as racist, attitudes, can be the basis of a disparate impact claim.

It is clear that judging employees on subjective qualities, such as common sense, good judgment, originality, tact, leadership qualities, and ability to handle responsibility opens up the possibility of the use of sexist attitudes and judgment based on how these characteristics are manifested in one's own gender. For example, leadership styles can be quite different for men and women, and the use of subjective decision making might allow differences to be viewed as inadequacies. Managers should always be careful to examine the criteria that might be "screening out" women who would be highly valuable to the company, making sure that "requirements" are really necessary in order to do the job and that all candidates are being judged appropriately. Often there are different ways one can adapt criteria to provide better workplace opportunity for both genders.

Sexual Harassment under Title VII

Perhaps no discrimination claims are more misunderstood than those involving sexual harassment. Many believe that only sexually oriented behavior will violate Title VII; others think that an overt offer of sexual favors for workplace benefit is necessary; and still others make the claim that "you can't even tell someone they look nice without facing a sexual harassment lawsuit." It is vital, therefore, that all managers thoroughly understand the "realities" in this area and that women comprehend their rights fully and take action when it is appropriate.

Sexual harassment is allowed as a claim under Title VII because it is seen to violate the requirement that there be no discrimination on the basis of sex in the "terms or conditions" of employment. This means that sexual harassment is harassment on the basis of gender and, as such, can be any behavior that treats or *effects* women differently than men. Thus, sexual harassment is really gender harassment and need not involve overtly sexual behavior: Anything that belittles or demeans women or takes away the opportunity to succeed equally with men could be viewed as sexual harassment.

The law recognizes two types of sexual harassment: quid pro quo and hostile environment. Recently, in a case called *Burlington Industries* v. *Ellerth* (1998), the U.S. Supreme Court blurred the distinction between the two, and although it is too early to tell what this will mean for sexual harassment cases in the future, it is quite clear that the justices are adamant that the traditional quid pro quo case, in which a supervisor takes tangible employment action against a harassment victim, will be treated as strictly as possible by the law.

Quid Pro Quo Sexual Harassment

Quid pro quo is a Latin term used traditionally in a contract situation. It means "something for something." In a quid pro quo sexual harassment case, the "somethings" are sexual favors for workplace benefits. This may be a direct or an implied threat perpetrated by an individual with authority to provide employment opportunities; it usually involves a supervisor using power to demand some sort of sexual interaction in return for providing preferential treatment or for not punishing with detrimental treatment. "Sleep with me or be fired" is a crude example of the latter, whereas "sleep with me and get the promotion" exemplifies the former.

Quid pro quo harassment is especially problematic for employers because, unlike hostile environment harassment, discussed shortly, the employer will be liable to the affected employee, even if there is a carefully crafted policy procedure in place to resolve these problems, and the victim does not report it to the proper personnel. The EEOC makes the liability so extensive in these situations because the employer is viewed as the one who has chosen this person for a position of authority over the victim and, thus given him or her the ability to misuse this overwhelming power on the other person potentially effecting career opportunities. Once any detrimental action is taken against an employee by the supervisor, the Supreme Court in *Ellerth* strongly stated, Title VII has been violated.

The U.S. Supreme Court has stated in a case decided in 1998 that a situation in which a threat is made but no detrimental action is taken is not quid pro quo but could be, rather, hostile environment.

Because quid pro quo harassment can be so costly for an employer, many now make any relationships between superiors and subordinates a violation of company policy. Others make certain that, if a relationship develops, the person with higher authority is not involved in any way with workplace decisions about the subordinate employee. Usually this requires moving one of the parties, but a change of position for the subordinate employee should be carefully considered for the following reason: Even a relationship that appears consensual could be the basis of a claim of quid pro quo harassment in the future, if the affected employee can prove that the relationship was coerced by the superior's position in the company and was, in essence, unwelcomed by the subordinate. Should that be the case, the move to another position could be viewed as retaliation by the company, a separate violation of Title VII, which could incur even more damages.

Hostile Environment Sexual Harassment

When behavior in the workplace creates an atmosphere that denies one gender equal employment opportunity, a claim may be made for hostile environment sexual harassment. A more accurate term might be *discriminatory environment gender harassment*.

As previously noted, this behavior need not be sexual in nature, but, to be illegal, it must create an environment that is less conducive to the success of one gender than it is to the other. Women, by a very large percentage, are usually the victims of hostile environment harassment, although men can bring this type of claim as well. No matter who brings the claim, in order for the victim to win, several criteria must be met. These have evolved over the years but in 1993 were described by the U.S. Supreme Court *Harris* v. *Forklift Systems* as follows:

The Harassment Must Be on the Basis of Gender   According to the U.S. Supreme Court in a 1998 case, *Oncale* v. *Sundowner Offshore Services,* the alleged victim and the alleged harasser need not be of different genders. Thus, a woman may be found liable for sexually harassing another woman, and a man for harassing a man. There is still a requirement, however, no matter what the gender of the perpetrator(s), that the victim prove that the harassment was directed at her or him *because of* her or his gender or that it created an environment that denied one gender equal employment.

The Harassment Was Unwelcomed by the Victim   The term *unwelcome* is not easy to define, but it is clearly not synonymous with voluntary. A person may tolerate a behavior and still prove that, given a choice, this behavior would not have occurred. The U.S. Supreme Court made this distinction very clear in its first hostile environment case in 1986, *Meritor Savings Bank FSB* v. *Vinson.* Mechelle Vinson had endured a great deal of harassing behavior from her supervisor, including 40 or 50 instances of intercourse, that she had never reported. The Court stated that, although Ms. Vinson may be seen as "voluntarily" going along with the behavior, a judge or jury could still find that, given a choice, she would not have wanted it to happen, thus it would be "unwelcome." By making the distinction between *voluntary* and *unwelcome,* the courts seem to recognize that victims often find it impossible not to "go along" with acts that they perceive as harassment but that they feel incapable of stopping, because of a variety of factors such as minority status in the workplace or having a subordinate position to the harasser(s). This may be true whether the behavior is overtly sexual or otherwise demeaning or belittling.

The Harassment Affects a "Term or Condition of Employment"   Legally speaking, behavior that is defined as "trivial" will not reach the level of legal liability because it will not be severe enough to have affected the working environment to such a degree that the victim has been denied equal opportunity. The behavior need not be so severe as to cause psychological damage before it becomes illegal, but the exact parameters of when behavior becomes severe enough to affect conditions of employment are left to the trial courts to judge on a case-by-case basis, by examining the "totality of the circumstances." The U.S. Supreme Court requires that this determination be made from an objective (it must be severe enough to affect the conditions of employment of a "reasonable" person) and a subjective (it must have affected the conditions of employment of *this* plaintiff) perspective.

In making a determination as to whether a reasonable person would be affected, it is quite clear that it is the effect of the behavior on the victim that will be important, not the intent of the harasser. This is a difficult concept to understand, especially for men. They may not comprehend, for example, why sexual "horseplay," jokes, innuendoes, pictures, and so forth are viewed as harassment because they believe that they do not intend to harass and are not affected adversely themselves by such behavior. Studies show, however, that bringing sexuality into the workplace has quite a different effect on women than it does on men. For women, it places them into a stereotypical sex role: subservient and less competent, both in their own eyes and in the eyes of those around them. One commentator, quoted in several court decisions, has stated:

> Pornography on an employer's wall or desk communicates a message about the way he views women, a view strikingly at odds with the way women wish to be viewed in the workplace. . . . It may communicate that women should be the objects of sexual aggression, that they are submissive slaves to male desires, or that their most salient and desirable attributes are sexual. . . . All of the views to some extent detract from the image most women in the workplace would like to project: that of the professional credible co-worker (Abrams, 1989, p. 118).

It is easy to see why many courts have decided that the "reasonable person" must be gender specific. To a "reasonable man," sexual behavior in the workplace may create no problem, whereas to the "reasonable woman," it could seriously affect her workplace performance and, thus, "conditions of employment." The 1981 case of *Ellison* v. *Brady* was groundbreaking in this area:

Although the U.S. Supreme Court has not specifically addressed whether a gender specific standard is required, it appears to recognize the reality that the effect of certain behavior is different for certain groups. As it stated in *Oncale* v. *Offshore:*

> We have emphasized, moreover, that the objective severity of harassment should be judged from the perspective of a reasonable person in the plaintiff's position. . . .
> In same sex (as in all) harassment cases, that inquiry requires careful consideration of the social context in which particular behavior occurs and is experienced by its target.

CASE

Ellison v. Brady

Kerry Ellison worked for the Internal Revenue Service (IRS) and found herself the object of a co-worker's continuing attention. He wrote notes to her, asked her out continually, pestered her with unnecessary questions during the workday, and generally expressed his affection for her and his desire for a relationship. Ms. Ellison complained to her supervisors, and Sterling Gray was transferred for a period of time, only to return when his grievance was upheld by the arbitrator. Ms. Ellison left the IRS and sued for hostile environment. The trial court felt that the behavior was "trivial" and did not reach the level of legal liability, but the Ninth Circuit Court of Appeals disagreed and required that the courts under its jurisdiction view such behavior through the eyes of the person enduring it—in this case, "the reasonable woman." To do otherwise, said the court, "tends to systematically ignore the experiences of women."

_____

Source: From *Ellison,* 1981.

Once an act of harassment is known to the employer, it is required to respond appropriately. In fact, an inadequate response can elevate a "trivial" situation into a hostile environment. The U.S. Supreme Court reinforced this absolute requirement of appropriate response in the two cases decided together in June of 1998, *Ellerth,* discussed earlier, and *Faragher* v. *Boca Raton* (1998). In the *Faragher* case, a lifeguard was being sexually harassed by two of her supervisors. The Court determined that, even though the victim had not complained to higher management, the employer was vicariously liable, much as it would be in a quid pro quo case. Although it did not really change what had always been a requirement of a policy and an adequate response, the Court clarified that, if a plaintiff can prove the elements of a hostile environment claim involving a supervisor, it is the responsibility of the employer to prove, by a preponderance of the evidence, what is called the "affirmative defense." In the Court's own words, the "defense comprises two necessary elements: (a) that the employer exercised reasonable care to prevent and correct promptly any sexually harassing behavior, and (b) that the plaintiff employee unreasonably failed to take advantage" of the opportunity provided by the employer or to otherwise avoid harm. This defense is not available when a supervisor's harassment culminates in a tangible employment action, such as discharge, demotion, or undesirable reassignment.

The Court reaffirmed that it is vital for companies to adopt policies that "encourage victims to come forward" and to have procedures in place that meet the requirements of the EEOC. This means that the company must deal with all incidents in a confidential, discreet, respectful, speedy, and sympathetic manner. There are many resources available to companies to help them institute these policies and procedures.

If you find that your company does not have such a policy, urge the management to create policy. Explaining that proper handling of complaints through well-written policy and procedures is often a defense to a hostile environment lawsuit might make the project become more important.

If you are a victim of harassment and your company encourages reporting, file a complaint and see that your rights are protected. This includes making certain that the company is keeping material as confidential as possible, that it is monitoring the situation to make sure that no adverse actions are taken against you because of the claim, and that the matter is handled in a respectful and expeditious manner. Anything less will result in your being able to file a claim with the EEOC or through a state discrimination statute. If your company does not encourage internal reports, an immediate claim to the proper government authorities may be your only recourse. No matter which path you choose, it is vital to keep very accurate documentation of everything that is said and done with regard to the incident(s). At a minimum, directly after any meeting, conversation, or incident, you should write down the date and time, what was said or happened, who was in attendance, and any decisions that were made. This can be invaluable if, despite what you may think at the time, you wish to file a claim in the future.

Title VII Issues under Debate

Currently there are two issues that are widely debated in the area of Title VII law. One of these involves whether preferential treatment is ever allowed and, if so, under what circumstances. The second involves the use of the law to require employers to pay the same wages for comparable positions, challenging a system that appears to value traditionally "men's" work higher than traditionally "women's" work.

Affirmative Action

Perhaps no issue in the law is more widely debated or more widely misunderstood than affirmative action. There are many types of affirmative action and many groups that receive the benefit of them. For example, veteran's preferences are a type of affirmative action, although these are rarely challenged as violations of the law.

Affirmative action is a program in which, in trying to undo a perceived past inequality of opportunity, certain groups are given preferences in hiring, promotions, admissions, or any number of benefits. These preferences usually take the form of an additional number of points on an objective evaluation scale, when the applicant is a member of an underrepresented group.

Quotas (a required number of certain group members) are rarely being filled in workplace affirmative action programs, though many believe that this is exactly how they work. In actuality, the only real quotas appear in companies fulfilling government contracts, quite different from workplace affirmative action programs. Companies that wish to acquire a government contract may be required to show that they have a certain percentage of minority or female employees in order to qualify. In fact, most of the widely reported cases of affirmative action programs that have been overturned by the courts have involved these types of programs, which bring up a constitutional question involving equal protection, an issue that is not normally involved when private employers undertake programs to increase workforce diversity.

One of the major cases challenging a gender-based affirmative action program was *Johnson* v. *Transportation Agency, Santa Clara County, California* (1987). It involved a program in which women applying for positions in the skilled craft category had their sex considered as one of the "plus" factors in determining who would get the position. The Supreme Court upheld that program, noting that it was important that gender was but one of numerous factors taken into account in making hiring decisions; there was a significant problem of underrepresentation of women in the skilled craft category; there were no statistical goal requirements to be met regarding the number of women hired; and the plan did not stop men from applying and being hired for the positions. These are largely the criteria that the courts have looked at to determine whether a workplace affirmative action program is legal, and, so far, there has been little change in these requirements.

Comparable Worth

Although many people feel that comparable worth has been rejected by the courts and is not a valid claim, it has never been specifically rejected by the U.S. Supreme Court. It was rejected by the Ninth Circuit Court of Appeals in a well-known case involving the state of Washington, *AFSCME* v. *Washington* (1987). The state was being sued by the union for a violation of Title VII because a study had found that there was a wage disparity of 20 percent, to the disadvantage of employees in jobs held mostly by women, for jobs to be considered of comparable worth. The court found that neither the disparate impact model nor the disparate treatment model fit this situation and rejected the claim.

The phrase *comparable worth* is used to describe what some see as pay discrimination between men and women, based only on the fact that jobs traditionally done by women are not considered as valuable as those done by men, which reflects the stereotypical view of "women's work." Traditionally, for example, the pay for secretarial work, a large majority of which is done by women, is far below the pay for custodial work, which is mostly done by men. Many claim that, in a comparable worth evaluation, both jobs should be paid identically, or discrimination has occurred.

In a comparable worth program, each job is assigned a number of points for each of the following components: the skill and effort required to do the job, the responsibility of the position, and the working conditions under which it is done. Pay scales are then designed to reflect the total scores. Some companies have voluntarily undertaken such programs, believing that judging worth on an equitable basis is the appropriate course of action. So far, however, no suit has been successful in requiring such an undertaking.

EQUAL PAY ACT

There is one act that does help women regarding disparate pay scales; however, it can only be used in a very narrow circumstance. When men are receiving higher pay than women are for basically identical work, the situation can be remedied by the Equal Pay Act of 1963.

The Equal Pay Act requires that no employer shall discriminate on the basis of sex by paying wages to employees of one sex at a rate less than the rate at which it pays wages to employees of the opposite sex for equal work on jobs requiring equal skill, effort, responsibility, and working conditions. Although these may look like the comparable worth criteria, the courts have been very clear in that they will only allow claims when the jobs are substantially identical and when a comparison of differing positions will not be allowed.

There are four exceptions to the Equal Pay Act's provisions. Pay differentials may exist where they are made pursuant to: 1) seniority; 2) a merit system; 3) a system that pays a worker based on quantity or quality of what he or she produces; or 4) where pay differences are based on any other factor other than a worker's gender. The last exception is quite broad and has allowed courts to uphold wage differentials in a variety of situations.

Although not particularly broad in its approach, the Equal Pay Act does offer some remedy when sexist attitudes preclude a woman from being paid the same as her peers. As Justice Marshall noted in *Corning Glass Works* v. *Brennan* (1974):

> Congress' purpose in enacting the Equal Pay Act was to remedy what was perceived to be a serious and endemic problem of employment discrimination in private industry—the fact that the wage structure of "many segments of American industry has been based on an ancient but outmoded belief that a man, because of his role in society, should be paid more than a woman even though his duties are the same." The solution adopted was quite simple in principle: to require that "equal work will be rewarded by equal wages" (p. 569).

FAMILY AND MEDICAL LEAVE ACT

Until the FMLA was passed in 1993, the United States was the only industrialized nation without protection for women who took time off from their positions for bearing or adopting children or taking care of a seriously ill family member. The FMLA now requires that a worker be allowed to take up to 12 weeks of unpaid leave in any 12-month period to give birth or adopt; to care for a child, spouse, or parent with a serious health condition; or to treat one's own serious health condition that makes it impossible to perform a job. On return from the leave, the worker must be offered his or her old job or an equivalent position. While on leave, the employer must continue health benefits.

The problems with the FMLA are extensive. Many claim that the FMLA is grossly inadequate to really protect women, especially because the employer only needs to provide unpaid leaves. A great number of other countries provide longer leaves, leaves with pay, and provisions for nursing mothers when the employee returns to work. Additionally, the FMLA has the following requirements: Only companies with 50 or more employees are covered by the FMLA; leave may be denied to salaried employees within the highest paid 10 percent of its workforce if granting the leave would create "substantial and grievous injury" to the business operations; a woman must have been employed by the company for at least a year and for at least 1,250 hours; and the employer can ask the employee to repay the health care premiums paid during the leave if the employee does not return to work.

Although many women will benefit from the provisions of the FMLA, many more find themselves without protection. To those who cannot afford an unpaid leave, average less than 25 hours of work per week, or occupy the higher management levels, the FMLA offers few, if any, remedies. It has been observed that the FMLA will aid in keeping the glass ceiling firmly in position if women must give up what little protection the law offers for family care in order to advance to the higher levels of management.

Companies are not restricted by the FMLA, however, from offering more benefits to their workers. Many provide paid leave and strive to accommodate all workers who need a leave for childbearing, adoption, or family care. When making decisions in your own workplace and when looking for a company that accommodates you best, it may be important to remember that the law only spells out the minimum that an employer must provide. Enlightened and family-oriented companies are free to offer much more.

SUMMARY OF KEY POINTS

The law has taken many steps forward in protecting the rights of women since the Civil Rights Act was enacted in 1964. The law, however, is not self-effectuating. Women must recognize when discrimination occurs and take the appropriate steps to remedy it. As managers, women are placed in a vital and perfect position to make sure that discrimination, in its many forms, does not occur and that everyone at the company understands these issues thoroughly. Sexual harassment, sexual stereotyping, unequal pay, and unequal opportunity will not disappear on their own. It will take the efforts of all women, working toward a common goal—a workplace that is conducive to the success of both genders and that rewards everyone for their own diverse value to the company and the society.

Discussion Questions

1. It has been claimed by some civil rights groups that the laws against sexual harassment deny people the freedom of speech granted by the Constitution. Do you agree? Why or why not?
2. Do you think that comparable worth lawsuits should be allowed under Title VII?

Issue to Debate

Antiaffirmative action drives in the United States have most often focused on removing racial preferences but have not been as concerned with gender preferences. Discuss the differences between gender-based and race-based affirmative action programs, and debate whether the current society would be more tolerant of one than the other and why.

Case Analysis

Barbara Salinas

Barbara Salinas was the region 5 sales manager for a large automobile part supplier, Lugnut, Inc. She had been doing an excellent job for more than five years, increasing sales and consistently being nominated manager of the year by her subordinates (though she was never chosen by the head office). Her supervisor, Jack Landes, asked her if she would move to region 7 to lead a sales team that was not doing well in sales and needed motivation. Thinking that this would increase her career advancement possibilities, Barbara agreed.

Almost immediately Barbara encountered problems at region 7 headquarters. Most of them stemmed from one worker, Fred Bert, senior salesperson, once the top company performer, and an obvious unofficial leader of the seven-person sales staff. Beginning with her first staff meeting, he constantly harassed her. When she introduced herself, telling them that she wanted them to consider her a member of their team and that their input would be important in her decision making, Fred interrupted her, "Look Barbie—I don't know what you were taught in that MBA program of yours but we know our jobs and don't need someone making decisions for us. We have always operated with a lot of latitude and we don't expect that it will change now."

Barbara was somewhat taken aback but responded that it was not her intention to change things overnight or to be a tyrannical supervisor.

At lunch time, Fred popped his head in her office and stated, "Barbie—we're off to Hooters to meet with a bunch of grocery managers for lunch. Our last boss always wanted to join us at these lunches; want to come?" Barbara declined and suggested that he reconsider his choice of restaurants for a business lunch.

Over the course of the next few weeks, Fred and the other men continued their pattern of disrespectful behavior, and one morning Barbara came in to find a nude Barbie doll on her desk. She removed the doll but the same thing happened the next day and intermittently for the next two weeks. Barbara finally called Jack Landes and asked for his advice. "Get tough," he responded, "They respect a strong hand—they are 'old school guys' who are trying to get to you—don't let them."

The next day when she asked Fred to get her the sales figures for the previous week in his area, he answered, "Barbie, whatever you want—you can have" and then winked at the secretaries who giggled nervously. When he returned with the figures, Barbara told him that she had put up with this behavior long enough. She demanded that he treat her with respect and noted that if any problem occurred again, disciplinary action would be taken. Later that day, Barbara overheard Fred saying to another employee, "Who does that bitch think she is—coming in here and telling me what to do? I have kids older than her—I ought to take

her over my knee and give her a good spanking—she doesn't know who she is dealing with."

The next day the secretaries came forward and told her that they couldn't take any more of Fred's "kidding around." She then called Fred into her office and told him that he would be given two days suspension without pay. Fred protested and then left her office. Within a few moments, Barbara got a call from Jack Landes asking her what was going on, because he just got a call from Fred Bert stating that he was being falsely accused of harassment. Barbara assured him that Fred was not being falsely accused and that he had been warned before the suspension. Jack told her that this was not company policy and that she should only tell him to stop in no uncertain terms because "Fred has a spotless record with the company and only about five years to retirement—lighten up."

Barbara rescinded the suspension but two days later, when one of the secretaries reported to her that Fred had just grabbed and fondled her, Barbara called Fred into her office and repeated to him what she had been told. He refused to respond except to claim that she (Barbara) had been trying to get rid of him ever since she got there because of his age.

Barbara fired Fred who immediately retained an attorney, claiming age discrimination. Within two weeks, Barbara was told that the company has settled with Fred for $500,000 and full retirement benefits. After this settlement, things in the workplace became unbearable. The other men blamed Barbara for firing their long-time friend because of his age and made life miserable.

About six months after Fred Bert left, Barbara was informed that she was being transferred to an assistant regional manager position in region 10 because she had become too emotionally involved with the situation in region 7 and had not been able to make the sales force respect her as a leader.

At region 10, she was an assistant to Arthur Pendragon, one of the company's most respected regional managers, and when he retired Barbara was made the regional manager for region 10. Two years later, when Jack Landes left the company, Barbara decided to apply for his position. After several candidates were interviewed, including Barbara, the position was given to Jack Barnes, who had taken over region 7 after Barbara left. When Barbara asked for an explanation why she didn't get it, she was told that Jack was the better qualified candidate. When she asked for specifics, she was told that he possessed better leadership skills, was more assertive, had a better record of dealing with complex personnel matters, and had more continuous years of upper-level supervisory experience. When she asked for specifics about her lack of managerial abilities, the director of human resources pointed out the company's loss in the Bert case. She was told curtly that "Jack Barnes has turned that area around. Region 7 is now the top performer in the company. He was able to do what you could not. Are you asking us to promote you just because you are a woman?" ■

Questions

1. What possible lawsuits might Barbara have? What would she have to prove? What evidence would help her?

2. What problems would Barbara encounter in a lawsuit?

References

Abrams, K. (1989). Gender discrimination and the transformation of workplace norms, *Vanderbilt Law Review, 42,* 1183.

AFSCME v. *Washington,* 770 F.2d 1401 (9th Cir. 1985), reh'g denied, 813 F.2d 1034 (9th Cir. 1987).

Burlington Industries v. *Ellerth,* 524 U.S. 742 (No. 97–569, June 26, 1998).

Corning Glass Works v. *Brennan,* 417 U.S. 188 (1974).

Dothard v. *Rawlinson,* 433 U.S. 321 (1976).

EEOC v. *Sears, Roebuck & Co.,* 839 F.2d 302 (7th Cir. 1988).

Ellison v. *Brady,* 924 F.2d 892 (1981).

Faragher v. *Boca Raton,* 524 U.S. 775 (No. 97–82, June 26, 1998).

Harris v. *Forklift Systems,* 510 U.S. 17 (1993).

International Union, UAW v. *Johnson Controls,* 499 U.S. 187 (1991).

Johnson v. *Transportation Authority, Santa Clara County, California,* 480 U.S. 616 (1987).

Lindahl v. *Air France,* 930 F.2d 1434 (9th Cir. 1991).

Meritor Savings Bank FSB v. *Vinson,* 447 U.S. 57 (1986).

Oncale v. *Sundowner Offshore Services,* Supreme Court Docket # 96-568, decided March 4, 1998.

Price Waterhouse v. *Hopkins,* 490 U.S. 228 (1993).

Rabidue v. *Osceola Refining,* 805 F.2d 611 (6th Cir. 1986).

Robinson v. *Jacksonville Shipyards,* 760 F. Supp. 1486 (M.D. Fla. 1991).

Watson v. *Fort Worth Bank & Trust,* 487 U.S. 977 (1988).

PART III

Strategies

This third section of the book builds on the workplace experiences of women and introduces a number of strategies for women at work about managing their careers. Focusing on the practical approaches women (and men) can take, these chapters outline how to manage the challenges, barriers, and/or obstacles so relevant in today's workplace. Particularly, the emphasis in part III is on concrete options for success.

Chapter 8 navigates the strategies toward actively managing your career. This chapter outlines the importance of networking and mentoring processes while presenting a specific set of strategies for networking success and making the most out of mentorship. Helping readers understand how to manage their career path is an additional focus of this chapter.

Chapter 9 presents the juggling act of balancing work and family. Recognizing the dilemmas faced in managing worklife, this chapter explores role conflict, the strategies necessary for balancing work and life responsibilities, and a comprehensive discussion of what different businesses and companies are doing with respect to work/life management.

Chapter 10 provides a strategic perspective on how women can effectively manage their careers overseas. Focusing on the expatriate assignment and understanding how to adapt across cultures, this chapter explores the strategies women, in particular, need to use when their career path takes an international perspective.

Chapter 11 addresses one of the most significant trends characterizing women at work, that is, entrepreneurial career paths. Getting off the "fast track" and choosing an entrepreneurial alternative is a strategy for which many men and women have opted. In this chapter, you will gain an appreciation for the trends affecting women entrepreneurs, in particular, and learn the strategies for entrepreneurship success.

We also meet two more leaders who discuss many of the issues outlined in this section of the book.

Meet Joan Fujii

Joan Fujii, Senior Vice President, Human Resources, Cost Plus World Market Inc., Oakland, CA

BACKGROUND

Joan Fujii, senior vice president of human resources at Cost Plus World Market Inc., didn't always know what she wanted to do or be. But somehow she ended up in the right place: in a fast growing company, with a fun and challenging environment, as part of a closely linked senior management team. How did she get there?

As Joan describes, "My daughter always knew what she wanted to do, but when I graduated from college, it wasn't that easy. At that time, many women had careers, but many didn't, and there weren't as many support systems in place for working parents." Her role model when she was growing up was her mother who was active in her children's school activities and was at home when the children came home from school. Her mother had taught preschool, and Joan leaned toward a teaching career. What would she do? As she pondered the possibilities, she found herself in retail. She began in human resources and operations, but at that point, she never thought about a career leading to senior management. Early in her career, however, she had a supporter in Becky Gould, then senior vice president for personnel at Macy's Department Store, who believed in Joan and made her believe she had the talent to do anything to which she set her mind. Joan advanced rapidly at Macy's. She was promoted from manager into administration, and then to vice president. In 1991 she was re-

cruited by Cost Plus to be the director of human resources and oversee all human resources functions at the company. It was a tough decision. She felt a strong loyalty toward Macy's. Macy's talked her into staying and she declined the position at Cost Plus. Six weeks later, she realized she had made the decision for the wrong reasons: "flattery, loyalty and guilt." Cost Plus, in the meantime, had called her back to see how it was going. She knew it was time to pursue other directions in her career and challenge herself in an unfamiliar environment. She had the opportunity to meet again with the leaders of the company, and she decided that moving to a smaller organization would give her an opportunity to be involved in all aspects of the company. Working in human resources (HR) at Cost Plus would be more closely linked to operations and would offer the most opportunities for personal and job growth.

Joan was promoted from director of HR to vice president in three years. Three years later, she was promoted to senior vice president. The company, during that time, went from a turnaround situation to a successful high-growth company. In 1991 Cost Plus was a private company with 35 stores in 5 states and just over $100 million in sales. By 1999 Cost Plus had grown to a successful public company with 85 stores and more growth projected. By January 2000 Cost Plus expects to have more than 100 stores in 17 states with estimated sales of almost $400 million.

In an interview with the current CEO of Cost Plus, Murray Dashe, one gets a snapshot of the extraordinary leadership qualities of Joan Fujii.

"I first encountered Joan when the board of directors, along with the retiring CEO, Ralph Dillon, were seeking a new CEO. . . . Putting Joan in charge of finding a replacement for Ralph—hiring her new boss—speaks volumes about Joan. She was brought in to coordinate all aspects of the search. The board and CEO had lots of confidence in her. In my experiences of 30 years in retail, Joan is one of the finest in her field. She possesses a balance between a contemporary approach to HR issues and the realities of retailing organizations. She understands the limited budgeting and the fact that there is not much room for implementing the kind of HR policies that the multibillion dollar companies can do and yet she realizes there are many ways to keep the company ahead with HR best practices. Joan is able to confront the difficult issues. Fairness is a cornerstone of her viewpoint and approach. She does it in an unemotional way and is very businesslike. She reports directly to me. Her challenge is to support the growth in store count and get the leverage in headquarters from those whom we have in place—20 percent growth in stores per year with 0 to 10 percent growth in headquarter support. Her challenge, in short, is meeting the needs of growing the company without growing internally. Joan does that so well and really understands the profitability issue. The HR organization will grow to support the store base but remain as efficient as it is today. That's the hallmark of Joan's style and what she has accomplished."

STRATEGIES FOR SUCCESS

When asked about gender differences with respect to leadership and advice for women leaders, Joan argues that there are a lot of variables that explain how to be successful—gender may be one of them. However, she believes that the biggest factor is a strong belief in oneself—how secure and confident a person feels. "If your parents were supportive and made you feel you were smart . . . that plays out in what happens at work. If you aren't confident and secure, the more you think you have to prove yourself; this can sometimes produce negative results." Mentors also play a key role in that confidence. "Becky gave me that confidence. She gave me credit for skills I didn't think that I had, but then I lived up to her belief in me. I now try to do that for others. When I see people with potential, I try to build up their self-confidence, and give them support to achieve things they don't know they can achieve. It isn't gender based; men and women respond to it. You also don't have to have a lot of conversations (with mentees), but you must have meaningful ones. With Becky, there weren't many conversations, but a few with real lasting impact."

Joan uses this mentor and confidence building strategy to help people succeed. "We believe in developing and promoting people . . . my greatest job satisfaction comes from seeing an assistant store manager become a store manager and then a district manager; an assistant buyer become a buyer; or a distribution center team member move into management." She points out that, in most cases, they do it themselves. "They sought out mentors, role models; they enjoy what they're doing, and they are willing to take input from people on how to improve performance. They accept constructive criticism positively and learn from it. They focus on how they can do something better."

In terms of work/life balance, Joan speaks frankly about what employees should seek and what organizations can provide. "If you don't have balance, you can't be a successful leader. We have our district managers work with store managers to achieve that balance. This also means we have to provide the organizational support. In retail, that means posting schedules in advance, providing fair rotation for holiday schedules, and being flexible. You can't ignore employees' personal needs." Joan's own experience as part of a dual-career couple with a child suggests other aspects of support as well. "I was lucky. When my daughter was three, I was able to return to work full time because my husband was very supportive. We shared responsibilities and did not care if others disapproved. I went through some guilt, because I couldn't be home for my daughter the way my mother had been home for me. It helped, however, when I learned that Stephanie (my daughter) was bragging about me to her friends and that she was proud of me." Her daughter gives her a hard time about her lack of cooking skills, but she also lets Joan know that the role model she had become is just as important.

Joan emphasizes the importance of networking as well. "It can be learned, but it helps if you are naturally interested in people and keep in touch with people. I've kept in touch with all those I have worked for, and those who have worked for me." This strategy has been contagious for the people Joan comes into contact with—even her daughter. "When Stephanie was 16 and had a temporary job at FAO Schwartz, she would recruit people for me to talk to regarding oppor-

tunities at Macy's" (Joan's employer at the time).

Other strategies for success are best articulated by people who have worked with Joan. In an interview with Cost Plus senior vice president of operations, Gary Weatherford, praise for Joan's leadership is demonstrated in the following remarks:

Some people are able to get things done because they hold a certain title that entitles them to a degree of power and influence. Joan is able to get things done because she consistently drives the process. In essence, she has been a master at keeping the flow of the company focused on the success of the whole versus any singular area. She is a skilled listener who is able to lead an individual or group to the best resolution through effective questions and answers, getting everyone to focus on what the "real" problem is and how to change it. Joan hears the message rather than the politics. She is able to present issues in a way that politics or emotions are given very little value when discussing the solution to a problem. Joan has earned her quick rise within the company by winning the respect of her co-workers. As a co-worker and a peer, I feel that she has chosen to direct her own destiny with that of the company. She understands how to challenge the process and to teach you what you need to learn. She uses questions to keep the process moving forward in order to make the best decision based on the highest quality of information.

I asked Gary to comment on the issues of power, politics, and strategies that Joan uses to be successful. He responded, "Joan's greatest legacy to me is how she instills a total team attitude. She understands that you can't win every battle and that sometimes in losing properly and gracefully, you really win in the long run. She tries to teach people that sometimes when you win you actually lose (winning for self, but not for the company interests) versus sometimes when you lose you actually win." Gary makes the point that it is not up to HR or other leaders to work to assure one individual's best interests. "Joan is great at gathering intelligence, listening to get core information which will help drive the Company and benefit the overall organization. She strives to protect the core values and interests of the company."

Joan Fujii's success can also be attributed to how she manages perceptions. Both the CEO and senior vice president of stores spoke of her incredible fairness and ability to balance tough decisions with fairness to employees. Gary notes, "What drives Joan is her intense effort to protect the company's culture by promoting teamwork, communication, compromise, and resolution of outstanding issues. She's played a significant role, often working behind the scenes, to lay the foundation of this organization. Joan asks the tough questions in order to get to the truth of a matter, regardless of to whom she is talking. She manages up, down, and sideways equally well. Most of all, she is fair."

When asked about gender and its impact, Joan, Murray, and Gary speak the same message. The CEO says, "Gender is a nonissue. We look at demonstrated action—we grow from within and the culture that is in place is a fair one. The best person gets the job, period!" Joan indicates, "At Cost Plus, we don't have a glass ceiling—people who feel that, often do it to themselves by thinking about it, and it can become a self-fulfilling prophecy here (although it may not be that way at other organizations). The only obstacle here is belief in yourself. The culture will treat you fairly."

INTERVIEW WITH A LEADER

Meet Linda Glick

Linda Glick, Chief Information Officer, Levi Strauss & Co., San Francisco, CA

When managers and others at Levi's headquarters in San Francisco reflect on admirable leaders and mentors, the name Linda Glick almost always comes to mind with a mixture of awe, affection, and admiration. Linda has been the passionate coach for scores of successful Levi executives—women and men—who have heeded her advice to push themselves beyond the comfort zone, to take risks, and to grow.

BACKGROUND

Linda's career did not follow a traditional path for a chief information officer (CIO). Her start was an interesting one. "I've spent my career in this company. When I applied for my first position as an analyst/programmer, I was short on preparation but long on motivation. I had foreign travel in my background, two foreign languages, but not the six months technical experience required for the job. Luckily, my resume went directly to a program manager who was not afraid to take risks on the right people. He recognized that I was an intuitive learner, someone good at putting things together. Looking back, I believe he looked beyond the company's 'competency model' to spot skills that could be useful beyond the programming job at hand.

"From programming I went on to develop people-focused skills and problem-solving abilities. My experience with the international group proved especially valuable. We were too small a work unit to get caught up in titles and specialties. Each of us had to understand the whole business—it was cross-training by necessity. I came to think of myself (and still do) as a businessperson first and a technology person second."

As chief information officer, Linda is in charge of a number of areas in the company. When she is asked about expectations from her area, she offers an interesting perspective that captures more than the technology side of the business. "Well, my boss puts it this way: 'You're in charge of making sure the company doesn't make dumb decisions.' In addition, I'm one of the prime movers in building effective work relationships among individuals and work units in the company. Our company culture is moving more and more toward directive leadership, which can only take place if people want to follow a leader and don't feel squelched or pushed around."

PIVOTAL EXPERIENCES

The challenges as a leader are really captured when one reflects on the different job experiences that Linda has had. "At one point I was given charge of a project that everyone considered a hopeless case, impossible to salvage. I vividly recall my total commitment to that project. My team and I were truly driven. We worked like maniacs, sometimes all night long, to get it done. I've never bonded more completely with fellow workers. But just when we began to glimpse the light at the end of the tunnel, my boss pulled me out of the project. 'You can't do this!' I protested. His answer has stuck with me: 'You've done your job. You're needed elsewhere. Your team can finish up the details.' I learned from that experience that 'finishing' isn't my primary job. I'm supposed to use listening, understanding, and creative thinking to move the organization along, to build strength in others so they can complete the task at hand." Although Linda has learned how to lead from experiences like this one, she reveals that the notion of "letting go" and losing control was a strong challenge.

"I'll be the first to admit that I want and need a sense of control. My years with this company, in fact, are calendared inside me as a series of projects over which I had control. I want to feel and exercise that control until I'm confident that the project is going to be successful. Then I'm content to hand it over to others to carry through." Her effective use of teams and the communication skills she uses with others on the job have helped her balance these challenges.

CAREER STRATEGIES FOR SUCCESS

Managing her career and thinking about career paths has been more or less serendipitous for Linda. As she puts it, "To tell the truth, I've never really initiated an application for a promotion. Typically a new area of responsibility emerges in the company and my boss says, 'Apply for the job.' I usually react by saying that I like my present job and don't want the new opportunity. And my boss predictably comes back with, 'Apply for the job.'

"Once into the application process my natural competitive juices take over. I recall an acquired company I took charge of through one of my promotions. My crew in that case had the undeserved reputation of being goons sitting behind terminals in a basement. I viewed them, and got them to view themselves, as incredible people who could make a strong contribution to the company. After two years I left that leadership position, but I left behind a truly superb department that was no longer demotivated and ridiculed."

Linda's boss sees that leadership quality as a distinct plus in moving her forward in her career. Linda notes, "I think it's a combination of things. He knows I have a leadership style that puts others at ease, whether they are my peers or subordinates. I know that some of my subordinates didn't warm up at first to working for a woman. But I tried to put that out of my mind and move ahead with my agenda. I'm able to adjust my leadership approach to the situation without becoming fake or duplicitous. And most of all, I think, my boss knows that I'm not afraid to take risks and face the unknown."

THE INTERNATIONAL EXPERIENCE

Women managing overseas often face unique challenges. Linda had the opportunity to reflect on that experience,

sharing her thoughts on what happened and why. "When I went to Japan, I didn't have the advantage of cultural training. I walked into gender prejudices head on. At my first vendor meeting, for example, everyone thought I was the translator. I had to learn patience. I recall sitting in all day meetings where conversations flowed almost entirely in Japanese, with only an occasional word of English. My approach was to stick passionately to my goal: to get a positive answer and commitment before I left the room. Often this meant asking a question several times and waiting with a show of interest while others talked on and on in a language I didn't understand."

"More than anything else I believe it was my 'high-energy' approach to relationships that pulled me through these intercultural experiences. They sensed that I would not let them out of the room until they had given me an answer."

Linda has broad international experience and spoke of her work and relationships in Mexico as well. "In Japan I had status within the company hierarchy, I understood the business well, and I fit into the Japanese pattern of serious business negotiations, on-time meetings, organized work, and so forth. But in Mexico I was temporarily set back on my heels by the more relaxed, even chaotic, approach to business dealings. I tried hard as a motivated leader not to 'lose it' every time I called a 9 A.M. meeting and people showed up at noon.

"The macho attitudes were also hard to accept. I had to tell myself again and again not to feel insulted, but instead to compartmentalize, to rationalize some interactions as part of the culture. It worked out."

BARRIERS AND ADVICE

In thinking about the obstacles women face on the job, Linda reflected on her own experiences here as well. "I think there are two kinds of barriers I've faced. First, I've been in situations where I've been treated as if I were in a staff function no matter what my business card said. At one meeting I recall, a senior executive said, 'Linda is a wonderful person, but I don't see what she could add to this discussion.' Others wanted to type cast me as a narrow technologist who couldn't keep up with bigger business problems." The second barrier deals with how people are perceived once they are recognized as a line manager. "That kind of experience motivated me to be more aggressive in putting my point of view forward. It isn't my nature to be loud and prominent in conversation, especially if I think I'm saying obvious things that everyone should know. But I found that if I didn't speak up, I would be ignored and undervalued. If women don't want to become invisible in organizations, they have to speak up louder and more often. One of my first mentors said to me, 'You just need to scream to be heard.' While that isn't literally true, the spirit is right—women need to interrupt, to take credit instead of passing it off to others, and to grab opportunities for making contributions to discussion and decision making."

Another obstacle that interferes with effective leadership is office politics and fights for power and influence. Linda commented on this experience as well. "I think office politics disappoint me most often. I grew up in this company with high-energy teams—we yelled and screamed at each other over business issues but could still go out for beers. We didn't have time for backstabbing. As I've acquired a more visible mantle of power in the company, I sometimes find that those who don't know me well feel they have to communicate through rumors and the grapevine. They don't know that they don't have to manipulate me or communicate covertly. They can just come and tell me what's up."

Although these experiences have shaped who she is as a leader and contributor to Levi Strauss & Co., her focus on how to develop other leaders emphasizes the role of mentors and networking. She notes how valuable mentoring has been for her career and how she has tried to model that behavior with others. "No one wore a name tag that said 'Linda's mentor.' In most cases, I didn't realize I was being mentored. I thought I was just sitting down with someone I respected and having a long, thoughtful conversation about my career aspirations. At some points in my career I felt like a pawn or slave to someone else's plans for my future—but those assignments inevitably proved valuable for my eventual path. They gave me skills I never would have sought out on my own. I think that's a large part of true mentoring: helping someone take on risks you know they can handle. That's how growth happens."

In training and coaching others, Linda takes on a number of roles as mentor. "When I mentor someone outside the organization or for transitioning to new responsibility in the company, I try to pose problem situations, then ask probing questions to help them think through alternatives and implications of their actions. I try to push them out of the rut of ordinary, easy thinking. If they're going to become true leaders, they need to think both systematically and imaginatively.

"As for formal training and coaching, we need to be more creative. For example, we could create a system of sabbatical leaves to keep people fresh and motivated. If we want to move minorities, women, and others up in the organization, we need to be serious about their career development, with specific plans that get carried out for their coaching and mentoring."

In terms of networking, this strategy is helpful in a number of ways. "It's really important to know what the competition is doing. I talk to everyone, and usually know things before most people learn about them. I've built a web of people with whom I share information. I can't sit at my desk waiting for valuable information to come to me. I'm on the phone every morning to make sure what's going on. I may have coffee with my chief architect or lunch with the head of Levi's merchandising. I'm in the cafeteria, I'm over in HR. The tendency is for corporate leaders to lose touch as they become more important in the organization. Keeping your ear to the ground doesn't mean responding to each and every problem you encounter. But it certainly helps you see the big picture and to focus your energies accordingly."

FINAL THOUGHTS ABOUT LEADERSHIP AND CHANGE

Linda's philosophy is summarized as follows. "Change is painful and hard. We all gravitate toward the comfortable, familiar, and cozy. We don't know if we have the stamina and resilience to take on change and see it through successfully. So a real change agent has to have enormous credibility in the organization. She must believe totally in her abilities, and others must share that belief. Add to that credibility a relentless will—she has to remain focused on the goal and keep everyone else focused as well. That would be my advice to women who want to lead and to act as change agents. Be willful and fearless, even if those qualities are less than comfortable for you at first. Take your share of the air time in meetings that otherwise will be taken by someone else. But don't go it alone. Learn to find and trust other key players in the organization who are equally confident in your ability. Make them your mentors, and repay their energies spent on you by superb performance."

CHAPTER

Career Paths, Networking, and Mentoring

Ellen A. Fagenson-Eland
and
Gayle Baugh

We want a female schlmeil to get promoted as quickly as a male schlmeil.
—BELLA ABZUG

Chapter Overview

Individuals need to manage their careers in order to succeed. In this chapter we look at the career strategies that have helped women do just that. We examine the factors that prevent women from achieving their career aspirations and compare their career paths with those of men. Women's networking activities and their mentoring relationships are examined as well: how they differ from men's strategies, why they differ, and the consequences of their activities are explored. We also examine the effectiveness of women's career strategies and networking activities and examine how mentoring relationships are formed and thrive. By the end of this chapter you will know how women should plan, manage, and advance their careers and the sacrifices they need to make in order to be successful.

Learning Objectives

■ To understand the factors that influence the shape of women's careers

■ To examine how men and women's careers differ

■ To explore the obstacles women face in their careers

■ To understand women's career development theory

■ To examine the career strategies of successful women

■ To understand the influence of personal networks on women's careers

- To explore the differences between men and women's personal networks

- To investigate the differences in networking benefits obtained by men and women

- To examine the influence of mentoring on career development for men and women

- To explore the potential difficulties for women as proteges and as mentors

- To understand the potential benefits and costs to women in mentoring relationships

CAREER PATHS

Careers

A career is defined as a pattern of work-related experiences (Stroh, Brett, and Reilly, 1992). A successful career is characterized by ever-increasing salaries, levels, promotions, recognition, respect, and freedom (Larwood and Gutek, 1987; Powell and Mainiero, 1992). At least, this is how men define success. Success means something different to women. Women often focus on their life outside of work—their personal relationships and their families—as well as their careers (Powell and Mainiero, 1992). Balancing these worlds may not be as important and not a priority for men. Consequently, women's careers do not resemble men's. Yet, women's careers have been measured against men's, and, not surprisingly, they fall short. Pity the poor woman who tries to emulate successful men! Research shows that even when women managers "do it all" and have "all the right stuff" they do not attain the same level of success (salaries, promotions, and experience) that men attain (Stroh, Brett, and Reilly, 1992).

Women and Children

Until men can have babies the personal dilemmas and career paths of men and women will be very different. Unlike the popular press would have you believe, women do not leave their organizations to start or take care of their families more often than men do (Stroh, Brett, and Reilly, 1992). Unrewarding jobs, slow career progression, limited opportunities, and discriminatory treatment by employers drive many career women to choose having and attending to a family over a career (Larwood and Gutek, 1987; Konek and Kitch, 1994; Morrison, White, and Van Velsor, 1992).

In fact, many high-level women forego family life. Most are single or divorced and choose not to have children or have few children (Schneer and Reitman, 1997a). Still, even when women ignore their biological destiny, they do not receive the same rewards as men do in the workplace (Schneer and Reitman, 1997a).

Most organizations are not family friendly. Consequently, many women need to take time off from their jobs to balance their career and family needs. These career interruptions have negatively affected women's incomes (Olson and Frieze, 1987). In fact, if women take a career break early in their careers they earn 18 percent less than women who do not interrupt their careers, and this income gap continues for nearly 20 years after the interruption occurs (Schneer and Reitman, 1997b).

Women's versus Men's Career Progression

Many factors influence women's career progression, such as leaves of absence, career gaps, dual career responsibilities, pregnancy, motherhood, household chores, and discrimination. Bailyn (1980) found that although some women may attain the same level of success as men, it takes women significantly longer to achieve it.

The career paths of women are less clearly defined than those of men (Powell and Mainiero, 1992). Men's careers are more of a linear progression than women's, and they are less complex and more orderly (Levinson, 1978). The jobs that women are guided into differ and are less secure than those offered to men. Job segregation on the basis of gender occurs when women are recruited, selected, and trained by their organizations (Ragins, 1995). Women's jobs are less likely to have career ladders attached to them and are poorly compensated (Baron, Davis-Blake, and Bielby, 1986). Women are also offered the less powerful staff positions in the organization (Ragins, 1995).

Moreover, women face more organizational barriers in their careers than men do. Women bump their heads against glass ceilings (see chapter 1), are often discriminated against in pay and promotions, and are subject to debilitating sexist stereotypes and actions (Fagenson, 1993). Still, women are more satisfied with their work than men (Schneer and Reitman, 1997a). This may be because of women's low expectations. Any positive attention they receive from their employer is appreciated, even if it is not at the same level as men are getting or that they deserve.

Early versus Midcareer and Organizational Restructuring

How do women's careers differ at their beginning and in the middle from men's careers? How do women fare when organizations undergo reorganization, reengineering, restructuring, and downsizing? Schneer and Reitman investigated these issues in a series of studies (Reitman and Schneer, 1997; Schneer and Reitman, 1994). They found that women were more satisfied earlier in their careers than at the midpoint. They also found that at midcareer the work environment is less supportive of women MBAs than of men MBAs. The women received less income, were more discriminated against, and felt less appreciated by their supervisors than men. How do women fare when their organizations undergo massive changes, as is typical of the 1990s, in comparison to the more stable 1980s? Worse than men. They are less satisfied and are given less responsible jobs (Reitman and Schneer, 1997).

Career Path Obstacles

Women clearly have to overcome more hurdles than men to succeed. In a recent study by Wentling (1995) middle-level women managers from 15 Fortune 500 companies were asked to identify what the biggest obstacles were in their career paths. The number one obstacle that they reported was having bosses who did not guide or encourage their career development. Many stated that their supervisors had difficulty working with women, did not believe in developing women, and did not provide them with helpful feedback. The second biggest obstacle the women reported facing was sex discrimination. The women gave many instances of the types of discrimination they experienced: They were not taken seriously, they received little respect, they had to work harder than men to prove themselves, they did not receive equal pay for equal work, and they were blocked from obtaining jobs traditionally occupied by men. "Lack of political savvy" was the third biggest obstacle mentioned by women. They reported that they could not fit in at their companies and had difficulty conforming to the company's norms and culture. They also remarked that they had little access to the key decision makers at the company. Finally, the women mentioned that failing to have a career strategy hurt them in their pursuit of a high-level job. They noted that family responsibilities made their career plans more difficult to realize, and they were not supported by their colleagues in this regard. In order to overcome these obstacles the women suggested that women should work hard, let their work be known, demonstrate their competence, and gain experience in several areas of the organization.

Working Harder and Smarter?

Given all the barriers women face in their careers one might ask, do women have to work harder and smarter to get ahead? That was the question that Schneer and Reitman investigated in their 1997(b) study of women MBAs. They examined many factors that could account for some women succeeding and others not, such as, working longer hours, giving greater emphasis to work than home, and having higher incomes available to them. Schneer and Reitman found that only one factor could account for women being at the higher- rather than the lower-organizational levels. The women higher up in their companies had no additional children after they attained their MBA degrees, whereas this was not true for lower-level women. This suggests that if women want careers that are successful in the traditional, masculine sense, they need to minimize their family commitments and time the birth of their children carefully.

Women's Career Development Theory

There has been little theory development regarding women's career paths. However, one theory, proposed by Larwood and Gutek (1987) seems to be cited more often than others. According to Larwood and Gutek, women's careers will never mirror the career path of men's. They will always be unique. They contend that this is because of the following reasons:

1. *Career preparation.* Men and women are provided with different information about which jobs are appropriate for them, and this influences which jobs they will prepare for and select.
2. *Marriage.* Women are more willing to move or adapt to their husband's careers than their husbands are willing to adapt to their careers. Given that men are paid more, given more opportunity, and receive more promotions than women this may be the most economical decision for the family.
3. *Parental responsibilities.* Being a mother requires more involvement, more time, and more effort and energy than being a father.
4. *Societal opportunities.* Women are faced with more discrimination and detrimental stereotypes that impede their career advancement in the workplace than men encounter.

Strategies for Career Success

The essence of Larwood and Gutek's career development theory was tested in a comprehensive study that examined what accounts for women's career success (Ragins, Townsend, and Mattis, 1998). In this study, executive women (vice presidential level and above) working in Fortune 1000 companies were surveyed and/or interviewed to determine what they would and would not advise women to do to build a successful career. The women executives were provided with a list of thirteen strategies. They evaluated the importance of each one. In order of those strategies deemed most important to career success, women reported on the following:

1. Consistently exceed performance expectations (77%)
2. Develop a style with which men are comfortable (61%)
3. Seek difficult or high-visibility assignments (50%)
4. Have an influential mentor (37%)
5. Network with influential colleagues (28%)
6. Gain line management experience (25%)
7. Move from one functional area to another (23%)
8. Initiate discussions regarding career aspirations (15%)
9. Be able to relocate (14%)
10. Upgrade educational credentials (12%)
11. Change companies (12%)
12. Develop leadership outside of the office (11%)
13. Gain international experience (5%)

The investigators interviewed the women to determine why they believed the first three strategies were so critical. Several of the women stated they had to "consistently exceed performance expectations" because they felt pressured to discredit the unfounded sexist stereotypes men held about them. The executive women believed that men questioned their credibility simply because they were women. Consequently, they felt they had to work much harder than men in their organizations to overcome these stereotypes (Ragins, Townsend, and Mattis, 1988, p. 30).

When the women were asked why they felt it was critical to "develop a style that men felt comfortable with," many of them commented that they needed to make the men feel more at ease working with them. They believed that acting "like a man" achieved this goal. "Don't be attractive. Don't be too smart. Don't be assertive. Pretend you are not a women. Don't be single. Don't be a mom. Don't be a divorcee," commented one woman who was interviewed by the investigators (Ragins, Townsend, and Mattis, 1998, p. 30). "Do not make waves. Do not disagree and be correct (Kiss of death!). [Working] longer, harder, smarter means nothing if you have a mind of your own and express your own ideas and opinions," commented another woman (Ragins, Townsend, and Mattis, 1998, p. 30). According to these executives, women should not threaten, challenge, or make their male colleagues feel uncomfortable if they want to succeed.

The women also emphasized the importance of seeking difficult or highly visible assignments. The women interviewed believed that this strategy helps women gain access to individuals in positions of power and prepares them for the executive role. The women also noted that they had to request and pursue these types of assignments. These special jobs did not fall into their laps as is the case for men.

Men CEOs from the women's companies were asked to identify factors that hinder women's careers. The CEOs generally disagreed with the answers the women executives gave. More than 80 percent of the men CEOs, compared to almost half of the women executives, felt that women did not progress as quickly as they could because they lacked significant line or general management experience. Nearly half of the men CEOs, compared to almost a third of the women executives, believed that women simply had not been in the business world long enough to be considered for the top-level slots. Little credence was given by the men CEOs to the idea that men's stereotyping and preconceptions about women were obstacles to women's success. Only 25 percent of the men CEOs cited this as a problem for women. In contrast, more than half of the executive women believed that this was an impediment to women's advancement. Only about a fifth of the male CEOs believed that women's careers were hindered by their exclusion from the informal power network. Yet, approximately half of the executive women believed that this was a major obstacle. A mere 18 percent of the CEO men believed that the organizational culture was inhospitable to women. However, more than a third of the executive women believed this to be the case. When asked whether male managers have difficulty being supervised by women, 31 percent of the men CEOs and 41 percent of the women executives believed this to be the case.

In summing up the findings of their study, Ragins, Townsend, and Mattis (1998) asserted that the men CEOs were "in the dark" about the realities of corporate life for women. They recommended that men's consciousness should be raised and that all managers should be held responsible for the career development of women. They also felt that organizations should design programs to help women understand how they could succeed on a nonlevel playing field. They recommended that organizations should adapt flexible work/life policies, encourage mentoring for women, and track women into positions that provide them with line management experience and profit and loss responsibilities. Men CEOs commented that the latter type of experience was critical for women to secure in order to have successful careers.

NETWORKING

Men and women need the help of others to attain their most desired positions. This help is found in a personal "network"—that is, the set of job-related contacts that one has. Networks provide advantages that are important to career advancement, such as advice, feedback, information, referrals, resources, support, and friendship. Being connected to the right people can expand power, provide access to jobs, increase the flow of important information, raise the likelihood and speed of promotions, and, in general, enhance an individual's reputation as an effective performer (Burt, 1992; Ibarra, 1995; Kilduff and Krackhardt, 1994).

Unfortunately, the networks that women belong to often are not as effective as men's networks (Ibarra and Smith-Lovin, 1997; Mehra, Kilduff, and Brass, 1998). As we describe in the next section, gender has a strong influence on the development of career-enhancing networks.

Network Gender Composition

Each person within an organization has a different network. Networks can vary on the basis of a number of characteristics, including the number of men and women participating in them. Within organizations, men develop networks that include mostly other men, whereas women develop networks that include both men and women (Ibarra, 1992).

What can explain these differences in the gender composition of men's and women's networks? According to several scholars the resounding answers are opportunity and status (Ibarra, 1993; Mehra, Kilduff, and Brass, 1998). In general, the most beneficial networks consist of people who hold powerful organizational positions.

These organizational positions are for the most part occupied by men, not women (Fagenson, 1993). This is because of discrimination in the workplace, which often bars women from high-level jobs; and sex segregation of the workforce, which places women in jobs dominated by women and men in jobs dominated by men (Ibarra and Smith-Lovin, 1997). Therefore, when women build their networks, there is less opportunity for them to include upper-level, high-status, influential people in them because they normally do not work or regularly interact with these individuals (Catalyst, 1996).

In addition to status and opportunity, similarity also affects network development. People like to network with people who are similar to themselves (Mehra, Kilduff, and Brass, 1998). Thus, women will network with other women (and men with other men) because they share the same gender. Unfortunately, networking with people of the same gender is a problem for most women because, as noted previously, women have significantly less clout in organizations than men do (Fagenson, 1993). However, women who have been chosen for rapid advancement within the organization ("fast track" women) are able to include more men in their networks. Women not identified as "fast track," in contrast, network mainly with other women (Ibarra, 1997). Interestingly, men tend to participate in networks dominated by other men whether or not they have been identified as "fast track" (Ibarra, 1997).

When they are networking, men depend on other men for both career assistance (career-related information, advice, feedback, referrals, and recommendations) and emotional support (friendship, confirmation, and counseling) (Ibarra, 1992). Women, in general, turn to other women to satisfy these needs (Ibarra, 1992). However, "fast track" women, rely on men for career support more than they do on other women (Ibarra, 1992). Still, "fast track" women have a unique and peculiar situation. They typically work in departments that employ very few women (Ibarra and Smith-Lovin, 1997). Therefore, if "fast track" women are to include other women in their networks, they are often forced to develop relationships with women outside of their unit and sometimes outside of their organizations (Ibarra, 1993; 1995). "Fast track" women, then, have to work twice as hard as other women (and men) to attain the same support.

Exclusion or Preference?

The research presented in the previous section suggests that women who network with men receive more career benefits than women who network with women. It is, therefore, tempting to suggest that women who are interested in career advancement need only develop a network that includes men, and particularly men in high-status and high-prestige positions. Unfortunately, the work situation is not that simple. Women are viewed as less important, less influential, and less valuable within organizations than men are. This is because of gender stereotypes that suggest that women are more concerned about feelings and less concerned about action than men (Baron and Bielby, 1985; Fagenson, 1993). This stereotyped view forces women to spend more time than men with each individual in their network in order to convince contacts that women are worthy of their time, advice, coaching, and counseling. By contrast, men do not have to counteract negative sex role stereotypes, and, as a result, spend much less time with each individual in their network in order to gain the same level of career benefits (Ibarra, 1993; Ibarra and Smith-Lovin, 1997).

Furthermore, even if women tried to network with men more than they currently do, they will face rejection. Men find that networking with women offers them fewer career benefits than networking with men (Ibarra and Smith-Lovin, 1997). Women's lower prestige and less legitimate status, unfortunately, leads men to exclude them from their networks (Ibarra and Smith-Lovin, 1997; Mehra, Kilduff, and Brass, 1998). Therefore, while women may be advised to extend their networks to include men, this may be a very difficult task.

To offset their low status within (or outright exclusion from) powerful men's networks, women can develop their own networks (Ibarra, 1995; Mehra, Kilduff, and Brass, 1998; Thomas and Higgins, 1996). Ironically, to someone who does not know why women include so many women in their networks, it may look like women prefer to network with other women rather than with men. However, women largely network with women because men unapologetically exclude them from their networks (Ibarra, 1993).

Given that women are more likely to be networking with women than men, are there any ways to increase the benefits that can be gained from women's networks? Networking with women is more likely to be a successful career strategy if the network focuses on work issues rather than social interaction and if it has a meaningful function within the organization (Kanter, 1977). If women's networks are not focused on work, they tend to reinforce the stereotype that women are more interested in "talk" than "tasks" (Brass, 1985). Women's networks that remain centered on work activities offer an alternative to joining (unavailable) men's networks, although they will offer fewer career benefits than men's networks offer.

Network Range

As we noted previously, women chosen for rapid advancement in the organization ("fast track" women) tend to develop networks that include a broader range of people in them than men's networks (Ibarra, 1992; Thomas and Higgins, 1996). In addition, "fast track" women tend to develop networks that include women from different departments or units within the organization, in part because of their preference for networking with women and in part because they are excluded from men's networks. Although this diverse set of contacts did not develop totally out of choice, it, nevertheless, provides career advantages for "fast track" women. Wider networks offer a greater variety of resources to their members than less diversified networks (Ibarra, 1993).

Women who have not been identified as "fast track" will find that the strategy of developing a wide range of contacts will not be as effective for them as for "fast track" women. This is because people in less powerful, less secure positions are less likely to be offered resources by their network contacts. Therefore, women not identified as "fast track" receive fewer benefits from their network than women who are so designated (Baron and Bielby, 1985; Ibarra, 1995). Once a woman has been recognized as having high career potential, however, her network will be more helpful to her. The "fast track" designation makes it clear to others that she will be able to return the career assistance that she received some time in the future (Burt, 1992).

Women not characterized as "fast track" find themselves in a paradoxical situation. They need to develop a network of contacts in order to have access to resources that can further their careers, but network contacts will not help them advance in their careers unless they have already been identified as having high career potential (Burt, 1992; Ibarra, 1992). The solution to this paradox may lie in the development of one or more strong relationships (or ties) with powerful individuals in their organizations. These contacts will confer legitimacy and power on women by association (Burt, 1992).

The issue of relationships involving strong ties (mentoring relationships) is explored later in this chapter.

Work and Family Networks

As noted in the earlier section on career paths, women and men's careers differ because decisions regarding marriage and having children affect men and women differently. Women usually make more adjustments in their careers to accommodate family life, especially when they have children (Larwood and Gutek, 1987). Accommodation to family life affects women's networks in two ways.

First, the amount of time women spend on the home and child care reduces the amount of time available to invest in developing and maintaining work-related networks (Smith-Lovin and McPherson, 1993). Second, after getting married and having children, women also need a more extensive network for family support. Women's family support networks include mostly women and relatives, who do not necessarily share the woman's vocation (Smith-Lovin and McPherson, 1993; Sollie and Fisher, 1989). While these individuals can offer a great deal of family support, they cannot offer women the career-specific advice, information, referrals, and help that work contacts can offer. Therefore, women need to develop two types of networks—one for their jobs and one for their families. Men need only invest time and energy in their work networks, because their wives will develop and maintain the family support network for them (Sollie and Fisher, 1989).

MENTORING

A mentoring relationship represents a very strong bond between people. Mentors are generally people with a great deal of experience who occupy high-level organizational positions and who provide support to junior-level people (protégés) to develop their careers. The relationship between a mentor and a protégé is quite rich, involving an exchange in several different areas, including advice, information, feedback, referral, support, and friendship (Levinson, 1978).

Mentoring provides the protégé with many advantages in career development. Protégés receive higher salaries, experience greater career mobility, and are promoted more often than nonprotégés are (Dreher and Ash, 1990; Fagenson, 1989; Scandura, 1992). Mentoring also increases the protégé's self-esteem (Fagenson, 1994) and results in better attitudes toward their work setting, including higher job satisfaction, career satisfaction, and organizational commitment (Baugh, Lankau, and Scandura, 1996; Dreher and Ash, 1990; Fagenson, 1989). In general, protégés seem to enjoy and experience a better work situation than nonprotégés.

Finding a Mentor

While both men and women protégés benefit from engaging in mentoring relationships, women express more interest in finding a mentor than men do (Ragins and Cotton, 1991). This greater desire among women than men for mentoring is not surprising. Mentoring relationships offer women the status and legitimacy in organizations that they lack. Men do not experience these problems and thus do not need to counterbalance these deficits (Burt, 1992; Fagenson, 1993; Kram, 1985).

Are women as likely to develop a relationship with a mentor as men are? According to a great deal of research, the answer is "yes" (Dreher and Ash, 1990; Fagenson, 1989; Kirchmeyer, 1996; O'Neill, Horton, and Crosby, 1998; Turban and Dougherty, 1994). This does not mean that the process is simple, however.

For one, women believe that it is harder for them to find a mentor than it is for their male colleagues (Ragins and Cotton, 1991), and their belief is well founded. Because women are excluded from networks of powerful individuals, they have less opportunity to meet people who qualify to serve as their mentor (Ibarra, 1993). Women also are more concerned than men are about an unwillingness among managers to mentor them. This concern is firmly grounded because women are, in fact, more likely than men to be turned down by potential mentors (Bowen, 1985; Ragins and Cotton, 1991).

In addition, women face some unique problems in forming mentoring relationships that men do not face. Specifically, women are concerned that initiating a mentoring relationship with a male mentor will be seen by the mentor or others as a sexual invitation or advance (Hurley and Fagenson-Eland, 1996). They also fear that others will see the mentoring relationship as providing them with unfair career advantages in exchange for sex (Ragins and Cotton, 1991). Such misinterpretation does occur; research has found that women protégés can be the target of discrediting rumors or sexual innuendoes (Bowen, 1985). Despite these obstacles, women are just as likely as men to seek out prospective mentors (Ragins and Cotton, 1991).

What motivates mentors to develop relationships with female protégés? Research shows that the most desirable quality in a protégé is competence (Olian, Carroll, and Giannantonio, 1993). Thus, mentors select women as protégés because their high level of competence makes up for their low power and status and compensates for the risks associated with pursuing these relationships (O'Neill, Horton, and Crosby, 1998).

Mentor and Protégé Gender

Although women are just as likely as men to have a mentor, women are less likely than men to have a mentor of the same gender (Ragins and Cotton, 1991). This occurs because there simply are not enough women in high-level positions in organizations to mentor all the women who are interested in having a mentor (Ragins and Cotton, 1993a). As a result, women are more likely to be in cross-gender relationships than men are (Ragins and Cotton, 1991). Although cross-gender relationships are common, there are some unique problems between a male mentor and a female protégé. Sexual harassment is one of them. Mentoring relationships developing between individuals of different power levels can present some degree of risk. This situation offers a male mentor the opportunity to exploit or harass a female protégé (Hurley and Fagenson-Eland, 1996; Scandura, 1998). Although sexual harassment of a protégé is quite rare, the potential for damage to the woman involved is extremely high (Scandura, 1998).

Sexual tension and attraction is another problem that can occur in mentoring relationships. Although sexual relationships between mentors and protégés are uncommon (Fitt and Newton, 1981), the belief that mentoring relationships include sexual contact is widespread (Bowen, 1985; Ragins and Cotton, 1993a). Still, both women and men protégés in cross-gender relationships avoid socializing with their mentors after work because they fear that the relationship might be misinterpreted as sexual by others (Ragins and McFarlin, 1990).

Submissiveness is another problem that can occur when women protégés are mentored by men (Ragins and Scandura, 1997). Sex role stereotypes suggesting that women should be less assertive and independent than men may cause women to be even more passive and submissive with a male than a female mentor (Ragins and Cotton, 1993a). Submissiveness can be detrimental in the workplace because workers are rewarded for independent action, and a mentoring relationship that encourages submissiveness will delay the protégé's development of autonomy and independence. If a protégé becomes overly dependent and continually acquiesces to the mentor, self-esteem and other work relationships may in turn be damaged (Scandura, 1998).

To avoid some of the problems that can develop in cross-gender mentoring relationships, some organizations avoid one-on-one relationships and, instead, develop mentoring teams. Others recommend that mentors provide career assistance but not emotional support to the protégé (Catalyst, 1993). Ragins and Cotton (1993b) suggest ways organizations can reduce the problems of cross-gender mentoring. They are

1. Develop a training program for potential protégés. Talk openly about sexual issues and overcoming sex role expectations.
2. Develop a training program for mentors. Let men know about the barriers women face in forming and participating in mentoring relationships. Discuss the rewards for men in mentoring women.
3. Increase the organizationally sponsored opportunities for women to meet and interact with mentors. Mentoring relationships are less likely to be mistaken for sexual relationships if they are clearly work related.
4. Reduce the number of cross-gender mentoring relationships by increasing the number of female mentors. Women may be encouraged to become mentors if mentoring is recognized in salary and performance appraisals.

A female protégé who finds a woman to be her mentor eliminates the problems that occur in cross-gender mentoring relationships. This solution, however, may not be realistic or practical. Women view male mentors as more powerful in the workplace than female mentors and, consequently, have been found to prefer them in some studies (Ragins and Sundstrom, 1989). In addition, female protégés with women mentors are viewed less favorably than female protégés with men mentors (Chao and O'Leary, 1990). Unfortunately, this finding indicates that even women who have reached high levels in organizations have not yet acquired the status that allows them to confer legitimacy on other women. Furthermore, mentoring provided by a woman does not increase a protégé's salary as much as mentoring provided by a man. Dreher and Cox (1996) found that MBAs who had male mentors earned substantially higher salaries than MBAs who had female mentors, which suggests that there are financial advantages for women protégés in cross-gender mentoring relationships.

While having a male mentor confers an advantage in salary, women with male mentors also incur an important disadvantage. Women have difficulty viewing a male mentor as a role model. A male mentor is less able to model successful strategies for coping with gender-based barriers to advancement and work/family conflict than a female mentor (Kram, 1985; Ragins and McFarlin, 1990). As a result, women who are mentored by men must look elsewhere for this kind of role model, whereas men more easily can use their mentor for this purpose.

Ending Mentoring Relationships

Are there differences between men and women in their willingness to end a mentoring relationship? Sex role stereotypes suggest that women are highly dependent and thus would be less likely to terminate mentoring relationships than men, even when those relationships have outlived their usefulness. This tendency may be even more pronounced in relationships with male mentors, where sex role expectations for women to be submissive are more pronounced. Evidence shows, however, that this is not the case. Women are no more hesitant to end mentoring relationships than men, regardless of whether the mentor is a man or a woman (Ragins and Scandura, 1997).

Women as Mentors

Some women will reach a level in the organization and a stage in their careers when they are no longer protégés, but instead have the capability to become mentors. Do these women become mentors as readily as men do? The research so far indicates that they accept the mentor role as frequently as men do (Kirchmeyer, 1996; Ragins and Cotton, 1993a). Moreover, women choose women to be their protégés just as frequently as they choose men. Men, in contrast, serve as mentors for men more frequently than they serve as mentors for women (Ragins and McFarlin, 1990).

While men and women are equally likely to become mentors, women see more drawbacks to the mentoring task than men do (Ragins and Cotton, 1991; 1993a). Women are afraid that becoming a mentor will take too much time away from their own work. They also are concerned that they are not truly qualified to mentor others (Ragins and Cotton, 1993a). Women are also afraid of being perceived negatively if their protégé fails. They are particularly wary about mentoring another woman. The combination of a woman mentor and a woman protégé is uncommon in organizations, and, as a result, the pair will be highly visible. Therefore, if a female protégé fails, it will be more obvious to others than if a male protégé fails, and this will reflect quite poorly on the mentor (Bowen, 1985; Ragins and Cotton, 1991).

SUMMARY OF KEY POINTS

The literature on women's careers suggests that women's career paths will be different from and more troublesome than men's. Women face more obstacles both inside and outside the workplace. If women define success according to the male definition of it, they may never succeed. However, if they define success on their own terms then they will experience its meaning.

Both men and women develop networks at work in order to advance in their careers. In general, men develop networks that include mostly men, whereas women develop networks that include both men and women. Gender differences in work networks are the result of women's preference to network with women and women's exclusion from men's networks. Women have less time available to develop and maintain work networks than men because they have more family responsibilities than men do. Women can receive greater benefits from their work networks if they increase their status and legitimacy in the organization. Developing a mentoring relationship may be a way to do this.

Mentoring provides men and women with equal opportunities, a situation not enjoyed by women without mentors. Despite their concerns, women secure mentors about as often as men do, and they secure male mentors more often than they secure female mentors. However, women may experience more difficulties in mentoring relationships than men because women protégés are involved in cross-gender relationships more often than men are. This is, to some extent, a result of the relatively small number of women available to serve as mentors. Protégés with male mentors experience salary enhancements that are greater than those of protégés with female mentors. Despite concerns expressed by women about becoming a mentor, men and women are equally likely to be mentors.

At every stage of their career development, women face more obstacles than men do. Some of these obstacles can be overcome by networking and forming mentoring relationships with powerful individuals. Mentoring relationships confer legitimacy on women, which helps them gain more career benefits from their networks and from their organizations.

Discussion Questions

1. What could be done to encourage men to take time away from pursuing their career to care for their family as women have done in the past?
2. Explain how women work harder than men for fewer rewards in many aspects of their careers, yet they are more satisfied than men.
3. Are women better at developing and maintaining network relationships than men, or is this just a stereotype?
4. Can organizations help women resolve the "double bind" issue of being recognized as competent before they can enter the networks that would give them such recognition? How can women find their way out of this "double bind"?
5. How can female protégés benefit from having a male mentor and a female mentor at the same time?
6. Can women and men's networks, mentoring patterns, and careers ever be the same? Why or why not? What needs to change to make them more equal?

Issue to Debate

Do you believe that women should work harder than men to get ahead in the corporate world?

Case Analysis — *Cramer Corporation*

Cheryl sighed as she started to get ready to leave her office. It had been a long day in a series of long days. She often felt that she was spending entirely too much time at work. In addition, she couldn't really see how the time and effort that she was expending were helping her advance her career.

She had been very excited when she first took the job with Cramer Corporation. It seemed to hold the promise for learning a great deal about project management and for moving into new areas of management over time. Now she wasn't even sure that she really wanted to move up. How would she handle even more responsibility?

In her first few months on the job, she had really worked at getting to know a lot of people in the company. As a project manager, she had to depend on other people a great deal in order to meet deadlines. She felt she would do better if she was personally acquainted with the people on whom she would have to depend. They would be more likely to help her, and she was certainly willing to help them. Although she had spent a lot of time developing these relationships, the two-way type of assistance that she envisioned hadn't materialized.

One day she had lunch with one of her close friends in the company, and Diana confided to her that she had been working on a project that was held up in the cost control area. She made a personal visit to that manager, and after some discussion, the problem was solved. In fact, Cheryl thought, Diana seemed to be able to solve a number of her problems that way.

Diana did have one relationship that was troubling her. She confided to Cheryl that although her association with Ralph, a manager several levels above both women, had been very helpful in terms of learning about the organization and the people in it, Ralph had become somewhat overprotective and discouraged her from accepting challenging projects. Cheryl didn't have a lot of advice to offer, but she had noticed the same thing.

Cheryl looked at her watch and sighed again. She was going to be late. She and her husband, Dan, had plans to go out with another couple that night. She had made all of the arrangements herself. She thought she had given herself plenty of time. The other couple might understand if she was running behind schedule, but she wasn't sure Dan would. She knew she was late far too often. In addition, she couldn't find much time to spend with Dan or to do the things at home she really wanted to do.

As she left the office, Cheryl wondered if there was something that she could do to manage her career better. ■

Questions

1. What advice would you give Cheryl about how to manage her career?
2. Does family life have more influence on careers for men or women? Why?
3. Is there anything that Cheryl's company could or should do in order to facilitate career management among its employees, and particularly its female employees?

References and Suggested Readings

Bailyn, L. (1980). The slow burn way to the top: Some thoughts of the early years of organizational careers. In C. B. Derr (Ed.), *Work, family and the career: New frontiers in theory and research,* (pp. 94–105). New York: Praeger.

Baron, J. N., and Bielby, W. T. (1985). Organizational barriers to gender equality: Sex segregation of jobs and opportunities. In A. Rossi (Ed.), *Gender and the life course,* (pp. 233–251). New York: Aldine.

Baron, J. N., Davis-Blake, A., and Bielby, W. T. (1986). The structure of opportunity: How promotion ladders vary within and among organizations. *Administrative Science Quarterly, 31,* 258–273.

Baugh, S. G., Lankau, M. J., and Scandura, T. A. (1996). An investigation of the effects of protégé gender on responses to mentoring. *Journal of Vocational Behavior, 49,* 309–323.

Bowen, D. D. (1985). Were men meant to mentor women? *Training and Development Journal, 39,* 31–41.

Brass, D. J. (1985). Being in the right place: A structural analysis of individual influence in an organization. *Administrative Science Quarterly, 29,* 518–539.

Burt, R. S. (1992). *Structural holes.* Cambridge, MA: Harvard University Press.

Catalyst. (1993). *The 1993 Catalyst census of the women board of directors of the Fortune 500.* New York: Catalyst.

Catalyst. (1996). *The 1996 Catalyst census of the women board of directors of the Fortune 500.* New York: Catalyst.

Chao, G. T., and O'Leary, A. M. (1990). How others see same- and cross-gender mentoring. *Mentoring International, 6*(3), 3–12.

Dreher, G. F., and Ash, R. A. (1990). A comparative study of mentoring among men and women in managerial, professional, and technical positions. *Journal of Applied Psychology, 75,* 539–546.

Dreher, G. F., and Cox, T. H. (1996). Race, gender, and opportunity: A study of compensation attainment and the establishment of mentoring relationships. *Journal of Applied Psychology, 81,* 297–308.

Fagenson, E. A. (1989). The mentor advantage: Perceived career/job experiences of protégés versus nonprotégés. *Journal of Organizational Behavior, 10,* 309–320.

Fagenson, E. A. (1993). *Women in management: Trends, issues, and challenges in managerial diversity.* Newbury Park, CA: Sage.

Fagenson, E. A. (1994). Perceptions of protégés versus nonprotégés: Relationships with their peers, superiors, and departments. *Journal of Vocational Behavior, 75,* 55–78.

Fitt, L. W., and Newton, D. A. (1981). When the mentor is a man and the protégé is a woman. *Harvard Business Review, 59*(2), 3–4.

Hurley, A., and Fagenson-Eland, E. A. (1996). Challenges in cross-gender mentoring relationships. Psychological intimacy, myths, rumors, innuendoes, and sexual harassment. *Leadership and Organization Development, 27,* 42–49.

Ibarra, H. (1992). Homophily and differential returns: Sex differences in network structure and access in an advertising firm. *Administrative Science Quarterly, 37,* 422–447.

Ibarra, H. (1993). Personal networks of women and minorities in management: A conceptual framework. *Academy of Management Review, 18,* 56–87.

Ibarra, H. (1995). Race, opportunity, and diversity of social circles in managerial networks. *Academy of Management Journal, 38,* 673–703.

Ibarra, H. (1997). Paving an alternative route: Gender differences in managerial networks. *Social Psychology Quarterly, 60,* 91–102.

Ibarra, H., and Smith-Lovin, L. (1997). New directions in social network research on gender and organizational careers. In C. L. Cooper and S. Jackson (Eds.), *Creating tomorrow's organization: A handbook for future research in organizational behavior* (pp. 359–383). Sussex, England: Wiley.

Kanter, Rosabeth Moss. (1977). *Men and women of the corporation.* New York: Basic Books.

Kilduff, M, and Krackhardt, D. (1994). Bringing the individual back in: A structural analysis of the internal market for reputation in organizations. *Academy of Management Journal, 37,* 87–108.

Kirchmeyer, C. (1996). *Determinants of managerial career success: Evidence and explanation of male/female differences.* Paper presented at the meeting of the Academy of Management, Cincinnati, OH.

Konek, C. W., and Kitch, S. L. (1994). *Women and careers: Issues and challenges.* Thousand Oaks, CA: Sage.

Kram, K. E. (1985). *Mentoring at work.* Glenview, IL: Scott, Foresman.

Larwood, L., and Gutek, B. (1987). Working towards a theory of women's career development. In B. Gutek and L. Larwood (Eds.), *Women's career development* (pp. 170–184). Newbury Park, CA: Sage.

Levinson, D. J. (1978). *The seasons of a man's life.* New York: Knopf.

Mehra, A., Kilduff, M., and Brass, D. J. (1998). At the margins: A distinctiveness approach to the social identity and social networks of underrepresented groups. *Academy of Management Journal, 41,* 441–452.

Morrison, A. M., White, R. P., Van Velsor, E., and The Center for Creative Leadership. (1992). *Breaking the glass ceiling.* Reading, MA: Addison-Wesley.

Olian, J. D., Carroll, S. J., and Giannantonio, C. M. (1993). Mentor reactions to protégés: An experiment with managers. *Journal of Vocational Behavior, 43,* 266–278.

Olson, J. E., and Frieze, I. H. (1987). *Job interruptions and part-time work: Their effect on the later outcome of MBAs.* Paper presented at the meeting of the Academy of Management, New Orleans, LA.

O'Neill, R., Horton, S., and Crosby, F. (1998). Gender issues in developmental relationships. In A. Murrell, F. Crosby, and R. Ely (Eds.), *Mentoring dilemmas: Developmental relationships within multicultural organizations* (pp. 110–144). Hillsdale, NJ: Erlbaum.

Powell, G. N., and Mainiero, L. A. (1992). Cross-currents in the river of time: Conceptualizing the complexities of women's careers. *Journal of Management, 28,* 225–237.

Ragins, B. R. (1995). Diversity, power and mentorship in organizations: A cultural, structural and behavioral perspective. In M. M. Chemers, S. Oskamp, and M. A. Costanzo (Eds.), *Diversity in organizations: New perspectives for a changing workplace* (pp. 91–132). Thousand Oaks, CA: Sage.

Ragins, B. R., and Cotton, J. L. (1991). Easier said than done: Gender differences in perceived barriers to gaining a mentor. *Academy of Management Journal, 34,* 939–951.

Ragins, B. R., and Cotton, J. L. (1993a). Gender and willingness to mentor in organizations. *Journal of Management, 19,* 97–111.

Ragins, B. R., and Cotton, J. L. (1993b). Wanted: Mentors for women. *Personnel Journal, 72*(4), 20.

Ragins, B. R., and McFarlin, D. B. (1990). Perceptions of mentor roles in cross-gender mentoring relationships. *Journal of Vocational Behavior, 37,* 321–329.

Ragins, B. R., and Scandura, T. A. (1997). The way we were: Gender and the termination of mentoring relationships. *Journal of Applied Psychology, 82,* 945–953.

Ragins, B. R., and Sundstrom, E. (1989). Gender and power in organizations: A longitudinal perspective. *Psychological Bulletin, 105,* 51–88.

Ragins, B. R., Townsend, B., and Mattis, M. (1998). Gender gap in the executive suite: CEOs and female executives report on breaking the glass ceiling. *Academy of Management Executive, 12,* 28–42.

Reitman, F., and Schneer, J. A. (1997). *Snapshots of early managerial careers of men and women post- and preorganizational restructuring.* Paper presented at the meeting of the Academy of Management, Cincinnati, OH.

Scandura, T. A. (1992). Mentorship and career mobility: An empirical investigation. *Journal of Organizational Behavior, 13,* 169–179.

Scandura, T. A. (1998). Dysfunctional mentoring relationships and outcomes. *Journal of Management, 24,* 449–467.

Schneer, J. A., and Reitman, F. (1994). The importance of gender in mid-career: A longitudinal study of MBAs. *Journal of Occupational Behavior, 15,* 199–207.

Schneer, J. A., and Reitman, F. (1997a). *Women in the executive suite: Are they different from the good old boys?* Paper presented at the meeting of the Academy of Management, Cincinnati, OH.

Schneer, J. A., and Reitman, F. (1997b). The interrupted managerial career path: A longitudinal study of MBAs. *Journal of Vocational Behavior, 52,* 411–434.

Smith-Lovin, L., and McPherson, M. (1993). You are who you know: A network approach to gender. In P. England (Ed.), *Theory on gender/feminism on theory* (pp. 223–251). New York: Aldine.

Sollie, D. L., and Fisher, J. L. (1989). Career entry influences on social networks of young adults. In E. B. Goldsmith (Ed.), *Work and family: Theory, research and applications* (pp. 205–225). Newbury Park, CA: Sage.

Stroh, L. K., Brett, J. M., and Reilly, A. H. (1992). All the right stuff: A comparison of female and male managers' career progression. *Journal of Applied Psychology, 77,* 251–260.

Thomas, D., and Higgins, M. (1996). Mentoring and the boundaryless career: Lessons from the minority experience. In M. B. Arthur and D. M. Rousseau (Eds.), *Boundaryless career: A new employment principle for a new organizational era* (pp. 269–281). New York: Oxford University Press.

Turban, D. B., and Dougherty, T. W. (1994). Role of protégé personality in receipt of mentoring and career success. *Academy of Management Journal, 37,* 688–702.

Wentling, R. (1995, May). Breaking down barriers to women's success. *HRMagazine, 40,* 79–85.

9

Balancing Work/Life

Cynthia A. Thompson
and
Laura L. Beauvais

I love my life! My husband and I have arranged our work lives so that we can spend as much time as possible with our kids, and still feel like we're making a difference at work.

—JESSICA DeGROOT, FOUNDER, THE THIRD PATH INSTITUTE

It just got to be too much. Monday through Friday I caught the 6:30 train for the city, and didn't return until 6 P.M. I loved my job, the money was good, but there was no flexibility, no possibility for part-time work. And I really missed my kids. My husband was making more than I did and we finally decided we could live on his salary. So I quit.

—LISA CELONA, FORMER NASDAQ EQUITY TRADER, CURRENT AT-HOME MOM

I spent four years working for an insurance company as director of media services. Because my wife was a performer in New York City and had to work evenings, I was the primary caregiver for our two children. That meant I had to leave work earlier than any of the other managers, and that caused a lot of friction and resentment. . . . The tension it created for me at work was instrumental in my eventually having to leave the company.

—MICHAEL KERLEY, PRESIDENT, CREATIVE DIALOGUES

Chapter Overview

This chapter focuses on how women (and, increasingly, men) attempt to balance the multiple competing demands on their time and energy. The authors discuss the types of conflicts that often occur as employees try to meet the needs of their spouses, children, elderly parents, community, and employers. They discuss both the positive, life-enhancing effects of participating in multiple roles, as well as the inevitable stresses and strains associated with life's daily traumas (e.g., the baby is sick and can't go to day care, an elderly mother slips, breaks her hip, and needs immediate help). The authors describe both individual coping strategies as well as organizational policies and programs designed to help employees manage their multiple commitments. They explore barriers that prevent organizations from helping employees achieve work/life balance and ways of overcoming these barriers, emphasizing the importance of a supportive organizational culture. The government's role in enhancing work/life balance is also examined. The chapter concludes by recommending a partnership between employees, organizations, and government to forge a new perspective of work/life balance in the twenty-first century.

Learning Objectives

- ■ To explore work/life balance. Are there any negative consequences associated with juggling work and other commitments (e.g., work/family conflict)? Are there any positive consequences? Can we reframe the discussion away from conflict toward synergy?

- ■ To examine how working parents can cope with multiple roles. What coping strategies are most effective?

- ■ To identify what organizations are doing to help. What barriers do they face when implementing work/life programs? How can these barriers be overcome?

- ■ To discover how important a supportive work/family culture is. What is a supportive work/family culture? Are there any companies that have reached this level of support?

- ■ To examine the role of public policy in helping employees attain work/life balance.

- ■ To understand how employees, organizations, and the government develop a new perspective of work/life balance for the twenty-first century.

CHALLENGE OF MANAGING WORK AND FAMILY LIFE

It seems everyone is talking about work/family or work/life balance these days. Some people think you can have it all, others argue that you have to make choices. For most people, there are no easy answers. Michael Kerley, who loved being the primary parent for his daughters, was torn about what it was doing to his career. Lisa Celona, who is happy in her decision to stay home with her two boys, sometimes misses the excitement of the trading floor. Even Jessica DeGroot, who works 35 to 40 hours a week, shares parenting equally with her husband, and "loves her life," has crazy days when there is too much to do and too little time. As these examples suggest, there are many ways of managing the boundary between work and family. The traditional family, where Ozzie went off to work and Harriet stayed home to manage the homefront and raise the kids, is far from the norm today. In fact, less than 13 percent of all American families fit this mold in 1997. Most married couples are in dual-earner or dual-career marriages, where both husband and wife work outside the home either in pursuit of careers or simply to make a living. The number of single-parent families is growing as well, and many women find they have to provide for *and* take care of the children. The fact that 62 percent of all mothers with children under the age of six are employed, and 75 percent of mothers with children ages 6 to 17 are employed (Department of Labor, 1997), suggests that life has gotten a bit more complicated since the days of Ozzie and Harriet.

Not only are more women working while raising children, they are increasingly caring for aging or elderly parents. As the average age of Americans increases, more employees will be called on to help care for their aging parents. In a recent survey of a nationally representative sample of the U.S. labor force, 13 percent of workers interviewed currently had elder care responsibilities, and 25 percent had had such responsibilities during the previous year. Nearly one in five working parents had both child care and elder care responsibilities at the same time, making 20 percent of the workforce part of the so-called "sandwich generation" (Bond, Galinsky, and Swanberg, 1998).

It is not just parents of small children or employees with aging parents who are struggling with work/life balance. Many single or childless employees are increasingly concerned about leading a balanced life. One newspaper article described an insurance executive who "dropped out of the rat race." After 20 years on the fast track, she quit her job, moved to Vermont, and got a job as a secretary. "No more 16-hour days. There is time for baking cookies, ice skating with her niece, even dating" (Kofodimos, 1993, p. 1). People are redefining success to meet their own expectations rather than the company's. Gail Snow, for example, quit her job as public relations representative and bought a ranch in rural Oregon. Neither she nor her husband had a job lined up, but they were intent on finding a slower paced life (Hordern, 1993).

In addition to the sweeping changes in the makeup of the family and new concerns with work/life balance, today's work environment is dramatically different than it was 20 years ago. With cell phones, fax machines, home computers with E-mail capability, and vacation resort hotels with modem hookups, it is virtually impossible to escape work. We now have 24-hour work days because of the globalization of business, and employees who have survived downsizing work harder than ever to prove their worth to the company (Kofodimos, 1993). This new work environment is very different from traditional ways of working, where organizations supported and encouraged the separation of work and family, and rewarded employees for their singular focus on their careers. According to Rosabeth Moss Kanter (1997), there was a "myth of separate worlds," where men were expected to make their jobs a priority and women were expected to make their families a priority. Men were supposed to "act as though" they had no competing loyalties and were expected to compartmentalize family life so that it did not impinge on their work. As we describe in detail later, organizations were designed with these assumptions in mind; that is, that a man had a wife at home to care for the home and family so that he could focus his attention on the company.

Given these outdated assumptions, many organizations and employees have begun to search for new ways of organizing work and family life. This process involves questioning the ways in which we structure work, manage employees, and define career and family success. This chapter helps clarify the issues involved in this questioning process. We define work/life balance and work/family conflict, and we discuss ways in which individuals, organizations, and communities can work together to create synergy between work and the rest of one's life. Although there are difficulties inherent in trying to pursue a balanced life, we believe it is a worthy and achievable goal.

WORK/LIFE BALANCE

Joan Kofodimos, in her book, *Balancing Act: How Managers Can Integrate Successful Careers and Fulfilling Personal Lives* (1993), defines balance as "a satisfying, healthy, and productive life that includes work, play, and love; that integrates a range of life activities with attention to self and to personal and spiritual development; and that expresses a person's unique wishes, interests, and values" (p. xiii). She describes an unbalanced life as one that is dominated by work, where employees focus on satisfying external demands at the expense of inner development and time for self and family. To put it simply, *balance* can be defined as the ability to manage job and nonjob responsibilities in ways that result in individuals having satisfying and productive work and nonwork lives.

In the early 1980s, balance was perceived by many to be a woman's issue. Women were portrayed in the media as having it all: an exciting career, a handsome husband, and two adorable, well-behaved children. The superwoman myth was that she could (and should) balance it all. In the late 1980s and early 1990s, the media began describing women at the other extreme: stressed out, bedraggled, and bug-eyed from lack of sleep. The reality is somewhere in between and depends on the individual's job and family circumstances and the extent of support from spouse, family, friends, coworkers, and bosses.

To get a sense of how much balance you have in your life, take a minute to answer the questions in the accompanying box. This exercise has been used in management training programs and in university classes to help individuals think about how balanced or unbalanced their lives are. Students and managers who find that they are out of balance often respond that their imbalance is temporary and that balance will return

---

BOX 9.1

Is Your Life out of Balance?

1. Assign percentages according to the *importance* of each of the following areas in your life (they should total 100 percent):

   Work (or school) _____%

   Family (or intimate relationship) _____%

   Leisure _____%

   Community _____%

   Religion _____%

2. Assign percentages according to the amount of *time and energy* you devote to each of the following areas in your life (they should total 100 percent):

   Work (or school) _____%

   Family (or intimate relationship) _____%

   Leisure _____%

   Community _____%

   Religion _____%

3. Compare the two columns. Is there a discrepancy between your values and your behavior? If there is a discrepancy, how comfortable are you with the imbalance it implies? Is it a temporary imbalance? What can you do to improve the balance in your life?

   _____

   Source: Adapted from Kofodimos (1993)

once their careers are on track or once they graduate from college or graduate school or once their company completes its restructuring, and so on. In reality, the more time and energy one devotes to work, the more likely one is to be successful. Success leads to more interesting and challenging work opportunities, which leads to even more time at work. And of course the more time one spends at work, the less time there is available for family, leisure, community, or spiritual renewal (Senge, 1990).

WORK/FAMILY CONFLICT

Many believe that work/family balance is the absence of conflict between work and family roles. But as the description of Jessica DeGroot's life suggests, even when individuals thoughtfully plan how they want to balance their time and energy between work and raising children, "crazy days" will happen. Life is full of unpredictable events: The basement floods, the dishwasher breaks, a child gets sick, there is a crisis at work. The goal for most people is to reduce the number of crazy, overwhelming, out-of-control days to a minimum. Understanding work/family conflict and its causes is part of the process of gaining control of one's work and nonwork life.

Work/family conflict has been defined as a "mutual incompatibility between the demands of the work role and the demands of the family role" (Parasuraman and Greenhaus, 1997a pp. 3–4). When an employee is in a meeting at work, for example, it is physically impossible for her to attend her child's soccer game. Most research on work/family conflict has investigated the extent to which work interferes with family life rather than the extent to which family interferes with work, and in fact, the former appears to be more prevalent among employees (e.g., Gutek, Searle, and Klepa, 1991; Williams and Alliger, 1994). According to Greenhaus and Beutell (1985), there are three types of work/family conflict:

- *Time-based conflict* occurs "when the time demands of one role make it difficult or impossible to participate fully in another role" (Parasuraman and Greenhaus, 1997a, p. 4). For example, the trend toward early breakfast meetings makes it difficult for a single parent to take her children to day care, forcing her not only to rely on others to transport the child, but also to make all the arrangements and trust the neighbor or friend to get the child safely to day care. Similarly, late afternoon meetings make it difficult for some parents to pick up their children from day care on time. Conflict runs in the opposite direction, too. For example, having to take an ill parent to the doctor might cause an employee to miss an important deadline at work.

  Time-based conflict can also occur when pressures from one role cause someone to be preoccupied with that role, even while physically present in another role (Greenhaus and Beutell, 1985). Who hasn't, for example, been physically present at work or school while thinking of other events going on in one's life (e.g., an upcoming wedding, a fight with a significant other)?

- *Strain-based conflict* occurs "when symptoms of psychological strain (e.g., anxiety, fatigue, irritability) generated by the demands of the work or family role intrude or 'spill over' into the other role, making it difficult to fulfill the responsibilities of that role" (Parasuraman and Greenhaus, 1997a, p. 4). For example, a parent anxious about his child's illness may not be able to concentrate fully on his job as copy editor, or an accountant who has been working long hours to meet the April 15th tax deadline may be irritable or too exhausted to respond fully to her family's needs.

- *Behavior-based conflict* occurs "when the behaviors that are expected or appropriate in the family role (e.g., expressiveness, emotional sensitivity) are viewed as inappropriate or dysfunctional when used in the work role" (Parasuraman and Greenhaus, 1997a, p. 4), or when behaviors appropriate for work (e.g., aggressiveness) are dysfunctional at home. For example, a manager in a financial services organization may be expected to be aggressive and hard driving to be accepted and promoted at work. Yet these same behaviors can create conflict and tension at home. Many executives have to make a conscious effort to change their behavior when they walk in the front door of their homes. Malcolm Marsden, president of a small aeronautical service company, finds it difficult to stop issuing orders when he comes home from work. His wife has learned to gently remind him that his children are not his subordinates. Malcolm says, "Sometimes the best thing to do after work is have a dance party with the kids. It loosens all of us up and helps me drop any pretensions or delusions of grandeur!"

Factors Associated with Work/Family Conflict

There are numerous demographic, attitudinal, and workplace characteristics that are associated with work/family conflict. Not surprisingly, employees with young children or with large families are more likely to experience conflict (Frone, Russell, and Cooper, 1992; Greenhaus and Beutell, 1985), as are employees whose aging parents need care. In one study, for example, employees who were caring for elderly dependents were more likely to experience work/family conflict and to have stress and health-related problems (Scharlach and Boyd, 1989). Higgins, Duxbury, and Lee (1994) found that gender and life cycle stage were related to the experience of work/family conflict. For men, work/family conflict decreased as their families went through three stages: stage 1, families with preschool children; stage 2, families with grade school children; and stage 3, families with adolescents. For women, work/family conflict did not decrease until the third stage, when their children were adolescents.

Other research also suggests that women experience more work/family conflict than men (e.g., Gutek, Searle, and Klepa, 1991), which is not surprising given that they are still responsible for the majority of household chores and child care activities (Hochschild and Machung, 1989). One recent large-scale, nationally representative study of the nation's labor force found that on workdays, working mothers reported spending nearly an hour more than fathers caring for and doing things with their children (3.2 versus 2.3 hours). On days off, mothers reported spending nearly two hours more than fathers in child-related activities (8.3 versus 6.4 hours) (Bond, Galinsky, and Swanberg, 1998).

But not all working women experience conflict between their work and family roles, and not all stay-at-home moms are happy hanging out with the kids all day and managing the homefront. In the study previously mentioned, employed mothers who had traditional attitudes about women working (i.e., they believed that everyone is better off if the man earns the money and the woman takes care of the home and children) experienced more work/family conflict than women with less traditional attitudes (Bond et al., 1998). In another study, women who were highly involved in their jobs before deciding to stay at home full time with their new babies tended to be more depressed and irritable, compared to women who were not so involved in their jobs (Pistrang, 1984). In fact, women were least depressed when their decision to work or not work was consistent with their own and their husbands' preferences, and they were most depressed when they were stay-at-home mothers but wanted to be working (Spitze, 1988). Thus, the attitudes women have toward mothers working, the degree to which they are involved in a job or career, and their own comfort level with working (or not working) while raising children appear to play important roles in predicting their well being.

Workplace characteristics can also contribute to higher levels of work/family conflict. Researchers have found that the number of hours worked per week, the amount and frequency of overtime required, an inflexible work schedule, unsupportive supervisors, and an inhospitable organizational culture for balancing work and family all increase the likelihood that employees will experience conflict between their work and family roles (Galinsky, Bond, and Friedman, 1996; Greenhaus and Beutell, 1985; Thompson, Beauvais, and Lyness, 1999). Having an unsympathetic boss or a job that requires heavy amounts of overtime or travel, for example, can make an employee feel stressed and conflicted about the effect her job is having on her family, not to mention the effect on her own mental and physical health. Part of the stress comes from employees feeling they have no control over their worklife, and in fact, many employees tend to adjust their family or personal lives to accommodate work requirements. Some family-friendly policies and practices, described in a later section, are designed to give control back to employees. Supportive practices such as flexible scheduling and supportive supervisors have been shown to have a positive effect on employee perceptions of control, and ultimately, can reduce levels of work/family conflict (Galinsky, Bond, and Friedman, 1996; Thomas and Ganster, 1995).

Finally, certain characteristics of a person's job can affect the level of work/family conflict experienced. In a study of more than 2,900 wage and salaried workers, Galinsky, Bond, and Friedman (1996) found that employed parents experienced less conflict between their worklife and their family/personal life when they had greater autonomy in their jobs, less demanding or hectic jobs, and more job security. Other job characteristics predictive of work/family conflict include nonchallenging, routine, or unimportant tasks, role ambiguity, poor person–job fit, role conflict, stressful events at work, and boundary-spanning activities (see Greenhaus and Beutell, 1985, for a review).

Consequences Associated with Balancing Multiple Life Roles

Although not everyone who attempts to juggle multiple work and nonwork roles experiences conflict, a substantial number of employees do. Researchers have found that trying to balance work and family roles can result in job and family distress, work/family conflict, job and life dissatisfaction, depression, anxiety, anger/hostility, and perceptions of a lower quality of life (e.g., Duxbury and Higgins, 1991; Frone, Russell, and Cooper, 1992; Thomas and Ganster, 1995). There are also unhealthy consequences for the organization, including absenteeism, tardiness, and loss of talented employees (Kossek, 1998). These findings support the scarcity theory of role accumulation, which suggests that the sum of human energy is fixed and that adding more roles creates a greater likelihood of overload, conflict, strain, and other negative consequences for well-being (Marks, 1977).

With the potential for experiencing such negative consequences, one might wonder whether it is worth even trying to balance work and family. The good news is that there are, in fact, positive consequences associated with trying to balance multiple roles. Several studies by Grace Baruch and Rosalind Barnett (1987) found that women who had multiple life roles (e.g., wife, mother, employee) were less depressed, had higher self-esteem, and were more satisfied with their marriages and their jobs compared to women and men who were not married, unemployed, or childless (see Crosby, 1991, for an excellent description of this research). So how do we explain the apparent contradiction?

Baruch and Barnett argue that it is the *quality* of roles rather than the *quantity* of roles that matters. That is, there is a positive association between multiple roles and good mental health when a woman likes her job and likes her home life. The greater the quality of her roles (e.g., an interesting and challenging job, in which she uses her skills and talents), the greater her self-esteem and freedom from depression (Baruch and Barnett, 1987). In addition, according to the enhancement theory of role accumulation, multiple roles may increase one's energy by increasing sources of identity, self-esteem, rewards, and resources available to cope with the multiple demands (Thoits, 1987).

Nevertheless, there are limits. We may successfully juggle our roles as wives, mothers, employees, and daughters. But can we also be social activists, community organizers, and class parents? Can we also be gourmet cooks, school fund-raisers, and great tennis players? Probably not. At least not all at the same time. Even when we limit ourselves to our most important roles, there will be days when we want to throw in the towel and fire our bosses, subordinates, husbands, and/or children. How do successful jugglers do it? The following section describes some coping strategies recommended by the experts in work/family role dynamics.

Individual Balancing Strategies

According to Kofodimos, there is no standard recipe for creating balance; it does not involve devoting equal amounts of time and energy to work, family, and personal life. Instead, bringing work and life into balance is an ongoing process that involves finding the right allocation of time and energy to suit one's needs and values (Kofodimos, 1993; Leibow, 1998). Sometimes work has to take precedence, for example when there is an important deadline to meet, but sometimes family has to take precedence, such as when children are sick or when relatives are visiting from Denmark. The key is for employees to make conscious choices about how they want to live their lives, and then find a spouse and an organization that supports the choices they have made.

Part of this choice process involves thinking about one's life priorities (review the earlier exercise), and part of it involves thinking ahead to the future. For example, students who are parents or who are planning to be parents in the future should think about how they want to combine work and family. The following questions may help individuals and their significant other or spouse think through some key issues (adapted from Schwartz, 1992, p. 282).

- What does parenting mean to each of you?
- What level of involvement will it require from each of you?
- What does career mean to each of you?

- How do each of you prioritize career achievement versus other areas of life?
- How many hours of work per week is it reasonable to work?
- Whose career, if either, will take priority in your marriage or partnership?
- What do each of you want most, and what are you willing to trade off to get it?

Answers to these questions will undoubtedly change throughout the life cycle, and it is important to rethink priorities as circumstances change.

There are several ways that dual-career couples manage their work and family roles (Gilbert, 1993). In the traditional family, the wife is responsible for the parenting and household duties in addition to her job duties. In what Gilbert (1993) calls *participant dual-career families,* parenting is shared but household duties are still primarily the wife's. In *role-sharing relationships,* both wife and husband share responsibility for parenting and household duties while working full time. Marianne O'Hare (1997), a psychologist at Drew University, has found that husbands often believe that they are "role-sharing" when they are actually in "participant" relationships, creating tension between husband and wife. Jessica DeGroot, founder of The Third Path Institute, a not-for-profit organization dedicated to expanding the collective vision of how individuals and organizations successfully integrate work and personal life, advocates a type of *shared care* where both husband and wife scale back their work hours while their children are young. In *role-reversal relationships,* the husband stays home to manage the children and home while the wife works full time. (Hopefully one day this kind of arrangement won't be seen as a reversal of traditional roles but a natural outgrowth of men wanting to spend more time raising their children.)

No matter how a working woman structures her life, there will be times when life feels out of control. Psychologists have identified several strategies for coping with multiple role demands, although some are more effective than others (Greenhaus and Parasuraman, 1986; Hall, 1972). One coping strategy is to *modify the stressful situation* through direct action. That is, the employee must figure out the root cause of the stress, and attempt to change the situation (e.g., others' expectations) that produces the stress. This might involve negotiating with one's boss to reduce the amount of travel required or negotiating with one's spouse to take on more responsibility at home. The key is to confront and modify the source of the stress.

A second type of coping involves *modifying the meaning of the situation* by changing one's personal concept of role requirements or by changing self-expectations for career and family. This might involve establishing priorities (e.g., "I will work hard to establish my career before I have children but will scale back my work hours when my children are young"), overlooking less important role expectations (e.g., "Does it really matter that my home is a mess?"), and keeping things in perspective (e.g., "I may not have a spotless home but my children are happy and healthy").

A third type of coping is referred to as *reactive coping* and involves trying to meet everyone's expectations. Instead of trying to confront the source of the stress or change the meaning of the stressful situation, some individuals try to fit the superwoman image by planning or scheduling better, working harder to meet everyone's expectations and sleeping less, or using no conscious strategy at all. This strategy is not very effective in reducing the stress associated with balancing multiple roles.

Finally, it is helpful to *manage the symptoms* of stress (e.g., by exercising, eating well, getting enough sleep, meditating, listening to music) because these activities help increase an individual's overall health and resilience. However, while this strategy may alleviate stress symptoms, it does nothing to resolve the source of the stress (Latack, 1984). For example, exercising four times a week for at least 30 minutes may improve your health and sense of well-being, help with weight loss, and reduce overall anxiety, but it will not change the fact that you are unprepared for tomorrow's exam or that your boss has given you no instructions for performing your new job. The best approach in these examples is to tackle the problem head on.

One of the most important resources for coping with the stress of balancing multiple roles is support from others (Cohen and Wills, 1985). Support may come from one's spouse, significant other, friends, family, supervisor, co-workers, or others and may come in the form of instrumental or emotional support. *Instrumental support* refers to tangible assistance, such as providing time, skill, advice, or resources to help solve the problem. *Emotional support* refers to caring behaviors such as providing empathy, trust, love, or simply listening. For example, a supportive spouse can help put work problems in perspective, and a supportive boss can help by letting an employee work from home on a snow day so that he or she can watch the children. Research has shown that support in the workplace (e.g., from supervisors and co-workers) can affect an employee's perceptions of her job, her quality of life, and her experience of work/family conflict and stress (Bond, Galinsky, and Swanberg, 1998; Thompson, Beauvais, and Lyness, 1999; Parasuraman, Greenhaus, and Granrose, 1992; Thomas and Ganster, 1995). Another way to cope with the stress of managing multiple roles is to obtain help from the organizations in which we work. The next section discusses what organizations are doing to help employees balance their work and nonwork lives.

ORGANIZATIONAL RESPONSES TO WORK/LIFE BALANCE

> It is more important than ever for business leaders to accept the importance of work/life issues in today's corporate culture, and consider them in their strategic planning. The focus must be on aligning work/family issues with the corporate culture and work processes within the organization. This effort is not about tinkering at the margins of the organization and doing something "nice" for employees. It is about real change that challenges long-held beliefs about the ways of doing business that are out of synch with the needs of workers and the demand of competition.
>
> —DANA FRIEDMAN, director of corporate solutions
> The Resource Group, Corporate Family Solutions

In the previous sections of this chapter, we focused on what individual employees can do to improve the balance between their work and nonwork lives. Now we explore what organizations are doing to help employees lead a balanced life, primarily focusing on family-friendly policies and programs. In addition, we examine the barriers employers face when implementing such policies and programs, and what can be done to overcome these barriers. We highlight companies on the cutting edge of work/life issues and examine the importance of a supportive organizational culture in achieving true work/life balance.

Family-Friendly Organizations

The results of a recent survey by RHI Management Resources, a consulting company that specializes in placing senior-level accounting and financial professionals, indicate that managers are increasingly recognizing the importance of organizational support in helping employees balance work and other aspects of their lives. Of the 1,400 chief financial officers surveyed, 55 percent said it was "very important" and 39 percent said it was "somewhat important" for firms to provide programs to attract and keep valued employees. The most frequently offered benefit was flexible hours (65 percent of CFOs said their companies offered it), followed by part-time work (40 percent), job sharing (27 percent), and telecommuting options (13 percent). The managers in the survey did not believe their companies were being altruistic in their motivation to offer these programs. Rather, they believed that these programs enhanced recruitment and retention efforts while reducing the high costs of turnover ("CFOs See Bottom Line Value," 1998).

Does offering these types of benefits make a company family-friendly? Generally, companies that offer a variety of policies and programs to meet the needs of employees with family commitments might be considered family-friendly (Lewis, 1996). These policies are designed to help employees manage time pressures and/or meet their family responsibilities while on the job (Marshall and Barnett, 1994). More recently, companies have begun using the term *work/life* or *lifecycle,* rather than *work/family* or *family-friendly,* to reflect the wide array of personal issues that affect the workplace and to send the message that these programs are not only for employees with children or elderly parents. Even though families are often the focus of attention, the new terminology is more inclusive of employees who are not adequately described by the term *family* (Minnesota Center for Corporate Responsibility, 1997).

There are four general types of work/life programs offered by companies to support employees (Lobel and Kossek, 1996). ***Time-based strategies*** help employees manage time pressures and include flexible schedules (e.g., flextime, compressed workweeks, permanent part-time work, telecommuting, or job sharing) and various leave programs (e.g., vacation time, sick leave, parental leave, child or elder care leave, phased return to work, and unpaid or personal leaves of absence). Flextime allows employees to decide when to start and end their work days, as long as the required number of hours are worked (e.g., begin at 8:30 rather than 8:00 A.M. and work until 5:00 rather than 4:30 P.M.). Compressed workweeks permit one to work fewer but longer days per week rather than the traditional five days (e.g., one may work four 10-hour days rather than five 8-hour days), which leaves more days for nonwork activities. Permanent part-time work allows the employee to work part-time hours on a more or less permanent basis, with a commensurate reduction in employee pay and benefits. The number of hours considered part time varies according to industry. For example, part-time work for a partner of a law firm may be 35 hours per week, whereas for a health care worker, 20 hours may be considered part time. With telecommuting, an employee works in a different location than the company worksite (usually home) for all or part of his or her work hours. The employee often uses electronic technology to communicate with and transfer work to co-workers and supervisors. In job-sharing two or more people share the same job and divide the salary and benefits accordingly. Parental leave, paid or unpaid, is provided for the birth or adoption of a child, and child or elder care leaves allow time off for the care of a child or elderly relative or friend. Phased return-to-work programs allow an employee to gradually return to work following a leave (e.g., work part time for six weeks).

Information-based strategies are policies and programs that provide information to employees to help them make decisions regarding balancing work and nonwork responsibilities. They include resource and referral programs, support groups, stress and time management seminars, relocation assistance, dependent care provider fairs, preretirement planning, and employee assistance programs. ***Money-based strategies*** are programs that provide financial assistance to employees in managing their responsibilities, such as affordable health or long-term care insurance, flexible spending accounts (i.e., deposits of pretax wage dollars into company accounts designated to reimburse child or elder care expenses), tuition reimbursement, and adoption assistance. Lastly, ***direct services*** include programs provided directly to employees from the company, such as on-site child or elder care, sick child care, emergency child care services, holiday and vacation care programs, and before and after school programs.

Some of the more creative services offered by companies and communities to make life a little more manageable include the following:

- Eddie Bauer allows employees an extra day off, called "Balance Day."
- Mentor Graphics has partnered with the Orchard School District in San Jose to provide a day care and preschool program for employees of Mentor Graphics and the school district.
- Maplewood, New Jersey, offers one of the first community "concierge services"; while waiting for a train, commuters can arrange for many town services, including dry cleaning, car repair pick up, and dinners from local restaurants to be ready on the return commute.
- The St. Paul Companies' mail room will package and ship boxes through UPS for employees.
- Wilton Connor Packaging offers on-site laundry drop off and has a handyman to do home repairs.
- Autodesk in San Rafael invites employees to bring their pets to work because they believe it relieves stress.
- For more examples, check out this Web site: *http://tigger.stthomas.edu/mccr/WL_Rept.htm*

The Families and Work Institute (FWI), a non-profit think tank, surveyed a number of Fortune 500 companies to determine the types of work-family programs and policies offered (Friedman & Johnson, 1996). In addition to disability leaves for new mothers, which are available in all of the companies that were surveyed, the remaining programs and policies can be viewed in three groups. The first group of programs identifies the most prevalent programs and/or policies offered. The second group includes the next most frequently offered programs. The last group includes those programs and policies offered by just a small percentage of the companies surveyed.

The most significant work-family programs—the top ten—found in the Fortune 500 companies surveyed are, in rank order, identified as follows:

1. Part-time schedules
2. Employee assistance programs
3. Personal days
4. Flextime
5. Personal leaves of absence
6. Child care resource and referral
7. Spouse employment assistance

8. Dependent care assistance plans (DCAPs)
9. Job sharing
10. Flexplace (forms of telecommuting)

The next group of frequently-offered programs include the following:

- Family, child care leaves for mothers, fathers, and adoptive parents
- Relocation counselling and assistance
- Work-family seminars
- Cafeteria benefits
- Wellness/health programs
- Elder care consultation and referral
- Adoption benefits
- Child care centers
- Work-family management training
- Work-family support groups

The last third are programs and/or policies found in just a small percentage of the firms surveyed. These programs include:

- Corporate foundation giving
- Family illness days
- Discounts for child care
- Sick child care
- Work-family coordinators
- Work-family handbooks
- Long-term care insurance
- Consortium centers for child care
- On-site caregiver fairs
- Vouchers for child care

Certainly, the programs listed above give an indication of the range and variety of work-family programming. However, offering programs or services such as those described does not guarantee that employees perceive a company as family-friendly. Although these options are undoubtedly helpful, they do not ensure that the company's informal culture supports work and family balance.

To get a more accurate picture of the underlying culture, ask the following questions: Are employees allowed to make and receive personal calls at work? Take time off for short periods and at short notice to deal with personal emergencies? Participate in programs without fear of losing their jobs or damaging their careers? Are these policies and programs available to managers as well as technical, clerical, and manufacturing employees on an equal basis? Are these options offered to contingent or temporary workers hired by the organization? It may be that your company is only as "family friendly" as your immediate supervisor. This may be the case, if you feel that you can't take advantage of company programs and policies because the culture within your department isn't supportive (Smith, 1992). In fact, job candidates are beginning to ask very pointed questions about a company's work/life values.

Even supporters of work/family programs are somewhat guarded in their enthusiasm for options that require employees to accommodate their lives to work. Underlying the accommodation view is the assumption that traditional business practices (e.g., lengthy work hours and total commitment to the firm by employees) are the desired norm and that family-friendly practices are paternalistic corporate welfare benefits that may have no or perhaps even negative effects on the efficiency and profitability of firms. This assumption prevents us from challenging the more fundamental ways in which business strategies are highly unresponsive to families (Friedman and Johnson, 1996; Kingston, 1990).

For example, consider typical relocation policies in most companies. Many promotion decisions at mid- to upper-levels of management are contingent on an employee's willingness to relocate, the assumption being that one must have a variety of experiences in different parts of the organization in order to succeed in these positions. For single-earner families, the psychological and social costs of such relocations are significant, especially if the move brings the family to a foreign country. However, these costs are multiplied for the dual-earner couple who also must consider the spouse's job-related needs. Many companies are "accommodating" these couples' needs by providing job search assistance to the spouse, such as providing airfare to the new city to search for jobs, arranging job interviews, and providing access to a job bank. However, a more fundamental approach to this problem would be to reexamine the need for relocation in the first place. Are there other ways for a manager to gain the necessary experience for the new position? Can one gain experience by remaining in the same area but taking on different responsibilities in that area (Cooper and Lewis, 1994)? The point is that viewing work and family balance as an accommodation process may prevent us from developing more creative solutions to these problems. The next section explores in more detail the various barriers to achieving balanced workplaces.

Barriers to Promoting Balanced Workplaces

> The attention on programs has sounded the clarion call that "all is well" in corporate America, when in reality the bell is sometimes made of tin—it looks impressive to the public eye but is hollow-sounding to the employees, who know the reality only too well.
>
> —Perry Christensen, 1997, p. 29.

There are six major barriers to implementing work/life programs in organizations: (1) ingrained cultural values and assumptions regarding work and nonwork domains; (2) structural difficulties in implementing programs; (3) lack of support from managers and supervisors; (4) the perception that family issues are women's issues; (5) maintaining equity among all employees; and (6) lack of evaluation data on work/life programs. Although these barriers are highly interrelated, each should be discussed separately.

Ingrained Cultural Values and Assumptions Regarding Work and Nonwork Domains

Of all the barriers to implementing work/life programs, values and assumptions regarding work and nonwork domains are probably the most significant because they stem from deeply held beliefs developed during the course of social history in the United States. When the United States was first settled, most people worked on family farms that allowed for the integration of work and family lives. Both men and women engaged in earning money, raising children, and maintaining the household. However, as industrialization grew, the domains of work and family began to split into separate activities. Men went into the factories to work for wages, whereas most women remained at home taking care of the household and child rearing activities. Because families could be supported wholly on men's wages, women did not need to be engaged in the production of goods, either at home or in the factory. The home became the private domain of families where intimate relationships, socialization of children, and relaxation took place. Work became the public sphere where (mostly) men carried out economic activity. In essence work became the masculine domain and home became the feminine domain (Kanter, 1977; Thompson, Thomas, and Maier, 1992).

Today, the separation of the two spheres is still deeply ingrained in how we think about our work and nonwork lives. The reality for most people, however, is that the two domains are intricately linked. Women are in the workforce in greater numbers, and, because of technological innovations in work processes, work is now increasingly performed at home. Family and work lives are not segmented as clearly today as they were even 20 years ago. However, many corporate cultures still operate as if the old model still existed for everyone: that men are the primary wage earners who have wives at home to take care of the children and housework. Particularly with managerial and professional workers, organizations often demand "single-mindedness" from their employees, requiring them to invest excessive time and psychological energy in work. A successful managerial career usually requires these investments just when child rearing is at its most intense, curtailing many women's (and increasingly, men's) ability to advance in an organization designed for industrial age lives. Additionally, common practices and assumptions regarding "face time" abound, employees feel they need to be physically at work for long hours each day to show dedication and commitment to their careers. An example of this mentality is the "parking lot syndrome," where employees leave work only after the boss has gone home. In another example, a compensation consultant was nicknamed "Union" (implying that she worked union hours) because she left every day to catch the 5:18 train home (Christensen, 1997). Apparently it didn't matter that she put in two or three more hours of work after her children were in bed.

Another outcome of the view that work and family are separate spheres is the fact that many organizations place no value on the experience one gains from the family domain. Managers fail to recognize that many valuable work skills and habits (e.g., time management, budgeting, asset management, coaching and training, cooperation and teamwork) are developed and honed in the family sphere. In addition, we often fail to see how employee's home lives may be a source of stability (or instability) for the organization. As Peter Senge (1990) notes, "we cannot build an effective organization on the foundation of broken homes and strained personal relationships" (p. 312). He argues that "organizations must undo the divisive pressures and demands that make balancing work and family so burdensome today" (p. 311). Instead, they should focus on developing synergy between work and family, rather than ignoring the extent to which the two spheres are deeply intertwined.

Structural Difficulties in Implementing Work/Life Programs

Managers often have problems when trying to develop and carry out the procedures associated with work/life programs. Many companies still have rigid, hierarchical systems of organizing work, whereas many work/life programs require flexibility and continuous negotiations among workers and their managers in order to work effectively. Scheduling the appropriate number of employees, managing the increased paperwork, calculating benefits, satisfying client demands, and arranging for special equipment for telecommuters are some of the additional responsibilities managers have in running these programs. Not only do these duties take time and effort away from other activities, but they also may be perceived as diluting the autonomy and control that managers take for granted in managing their subordinates (Parasuraman and Greenhaus, 1997b; Thompson, Thomas, and Maier, 1992).

Lack of Support from Managers and Supervisors

The third barrier is often a consequence of the structural problems previously identified. Supervisors are unlikely to be supportive of policies and programs that increase their workloads. As the ranks of middle management and first-level supervisors continue to decrease due to downsizings, these employees are likely to resist attempts to add more responsibilities to their jobs. In addition, managers may find that they are required to administer policies for which they themselves are not eligible due to their key positions in the organization. Furthermore, managers may find it difficult to choose and prioritize among employees regarding who is able to take advantage of certain programs. For example, is it appropriate to deny single employees flexible schedules in order to accommodate working parents' needs? What happens when two employees in a four-person team ask for parental leave at the same time? In essence, how does one continue to meet business objectives, treat all employees fairly, and help individuals balance work and life demands (Christensen, 1997)? Lastly, managers and supervisors may resist work/life programs because they hold traditional views of the separation of work and nonwork as described earlier. To achieve their current positions of authority and responsibility, managers often sacrifice family life for work, and they may resent providing the flexibility to aspiring leaders that is not given to them. As managers and supervisors play a crucial role in ensuring the development and implementation of work/life policies, their resistance is a key barrier to overcome.

The Perception That Family Issues Are Women's Issues

Separate role expectations for men and women are at the heart of how work and family issues are currently framed (Bailyn, 1993). Consistent with the belief in separate private and public lives previously discussed, successful workers are those who keep a strict separation between work and family, never letting family concerns intrude in the workplace. Given women's traditional gender expectations and "double burden" (i.e., they work both at home and at work), they usually need to use these work/life programs more than men do. Managers begin to see work/life programs as primarily benefiting women with children and fail to regard them as legitimate business strategies that will impact corporate profitability and competitiveness. Furthermore, these programs may result in discrimination against women in the long run (Gonyea and Googins, 1996). That is, if women are perceived as less successful than men in managing the work/family interface, they are less likely to receive the training and promotional opportunities that will advance their careers.

In reality, despite gender role expectations and corporate beliefs, balancing work and family is not just a woman's issue. Joseph Pleck has spent many years studying trends in men's family participation and has found that men's time in family roles has increased over the past 20 years. Although men's participation in child care and household chores is less than that of women's, on average they perform one third of the housework and one in five fathers with an employed wife is the primary child care provider for preschool children (Pleck, 1993). Other research has shown that working fathers as well as women and men without children are just as likely as working mothers to benefit from flexible schedules in terms of greater job satisfaction and reduced work/family conflict (Marshall and Barnett, 1994).

Interestingly, men make use of family supportive policies to a far greater extent than people realize. Working fathers use flexible schedules as well as leaves to spend more time with children. However, men use these options in ways that are not perceived by employers and co-workers as work/family accommodations (e.g., they take informal paternity leave by using vacation and sick days). Consistent with the perception that family issues are women's issues, men fear that more visible use of work/family policies will have negative effects on their careers. The informal leaves they take are short term, involve no loss of pay, and require no formal application and approval. Thus, informal leaves allow men to take time off without publicly admitting that they are trying to balance work and family demands. As a result, men avoid possible negative evaluations from employers and co-workers, such as being uncommitted to one's career, or, worse yet, being unmasculine (Pleck, 1993). Unfortunately, this strategy perpetuates the perception that family issues are mainly women's issues and makes it difficult for both men and women to achieve a reasonable work/family balance.

Maintaining Equity Among All Employees

As indicated earlier, an important barrier to work/life accommodation in organizations is the fear of treating employees differently. Most programs focus on dependent care concerns (i.e., parental leaves and child care). Employees without children may resent that the organization provides such benefits to their co-workers who are parents, but not to them. Researchers at the Families and Work Institute in New York found that 40 percent of workers surveyed were at least somewhat resentful of employers who offered benefits that not all workers could use (Bond, Galinsky, and Swanberg, 1998). Some workers were so disturbed by the proliferation of family-supportive accommodations that they formed The Childfree Network, an organization that seeks to protect the rights of employees who choose not to become parents. Although few employees resent occasional extra work or flexibility to help out a co-worker with personal or family problems, single and childless employees are increasingly resentful of receiving fewer benefits and putting in more time at work than parents, without additional compensation or other reward (Lafayette, 1994).

Lack of Evaluation Data on Work/Life Programs

A final barrier to work/life programs has been the lack of hard evidence that they actually have positive effects on employee attitudes and behaviors, such as satisfaction, commitment, recruitment, retention, absenteeism, and performance (Aldous, 1990). Most reports on their effectiveness have been anecdotal or impressionistic, not based on rigorous cost-benefit analyses. Lacking company-specific evaluation data, some managers are unconvinced that there is a strategic benefit to implementing these programs, especially if a large proportion of their workforce is contract-based labor or low-skilled workers in great supply (e.g., clerks, cashiers, waitresses).

Overcoming Organizational Barriers to Work/Life Balance

By studying companies known for their successful work/life policies and programs, researchers are beginning to discover how the barriers previously discussed can be overcome. Success seems more likely when (1) work/life integration is considered a strategic initiative of the business; (2) research is conducted on the behavioral and organizational effects of work/life policies and programs; and (3) cultural assumptions regarding the link between work and other domains of life are examined and changed.

Work/Life Integration as a Strategic Initiative of the Business

If work/life policies and programs are going to be more than corporate welfare benefits, then managers need to focus attention on making these initiatives an integral part of the strategy of the firm. To do this, firms need to link work/life initiatives to employee recruitment, retention, and work performance; integrate them with programs that value the diversity of all employees, including those with no children; and make these initiatives the foundation of a new social contract of mutual flexibility between employers and employees (Gonyea and Googins, 1996). This new social contract should be based on "principles of trust, independence, and choice" (Christensen, 1997, p. 36). Joint problem-solving around work/life issues needs to occur so that the trust and commitment needed to compete in the global marketplace can be generated. Research has shown that policies and programs that allow employees some autonomy and control over their work schedules reduce work/family conflict and stress and foster responsible attitudes toward the organization. In return, managers gain the confidence that employees are working both conscientiously and efficiently toward business objectives (Thomas and Ganster, 1995).

One company that views work/life issues as a strategic concern is Mentor Graphics, a high-technology firm located in Portland, Oregon. Wally Rhines, CEO and president of the company says, "Work/life is a business issue and a business case can easily be made for it. In the high-tech industry, where the competition for quality engineers is fierce, work/life programs and benefits become a strategic imperative." He believes that Mentor Graphics' work/life programs give them a competitive edge in recruiting and retaining high-quality employees and are critical to their business success.

Research on the Behavioral and Organizational Effects of Work/Life Policies and Programs

One way to break down managerial resistance to work/life programs is to show that they have effects that are important to business success. For example, research is beginning to document the effects of various work/life programs (e.g., flextime, child care support) on recruiting, retention, absenteeism, tardiness, stress, job satisfaction, organizational commitment and loyalty, and performance (Kossek, 1998). The links between individual policies and anticipated organizational effects must be clarified because different policies may have different effects and usefulness for different employees (Raabe, 1990). In addition, this research might show which programs have little return on their investment. Holding work/life programs to the same strict cost-benefit analysis as other business initiatives may encourage more open attitudes toward the programs, reduce the stigma of paternalism associated with them, and pave the way for new and creative solutions for managing work/life dilemmas.

Cultural Assumptions Regarding the Link between Work and Other Domains of Life

There is strong evidence that organizational culture and the managerial attitudes that accompany it influence employee use of family-friendly programs and the repercussions that result from their use (Schwartz, 1992). In a large national study of almost 3,000 workers, it was found that individuals experienced less conflict and stress and developed better coping strategies when they perceived that their supervisors and workplace cultures were supportive. These employees also were willing to work harder to help their companies succeed, were more loyal and committed to their employers, were more satisfied with their jobs, and took more responsibility and initiative on the job than employees who did not experience a supportive work culture. In fact, the way work/family policies are implemented by line management and the legitimization of these policies by the organizational culture may be more important than the actual policies themselves (Galinsky, Bond, and Friedman, 1996). Therefore, to get bottom-line results from work/life policies and programs, both corporate cultures and supervisors' attitudes toward work/life integration need to be considered.

But what is a supportive work/family culture and just how important is it? *Work/family culture* is defined as the shared assumptions, beliefs, and values regarding the extent to which an organization supports and values the integration of employees' work and family lives (Thompson, Beauvais, and Lyness, 1999). In our research, we found that when organizations make work/family benefits available, employees have greater commitment, fewer intentions to leave the organization, and experience less work/family conflict. We also discovered that employees were more likely to use work/family programs when they perceived a more supportive work/family culture. And regardless of program availability, experiencing a supportive culture was related to greater organizational commitment, fewer thoughts about leaving the organization, and less work/family conflict. These findings suggest that an assessment of the organizational culture is a crucial first step in overcoming the barriers to implementing successful work/life programs.

Companies That Have Supportive Work/Life Cultures

In a 1997 survey of work/family strategies in corporate America, in which 12,000 employees from 55 companies responded, MBNA Corporation and First Tennessee Bank ranked highest on family friendliness. In these firms, work/life balance is ingrained in both culture and business strategy. Other companies that rate highly on family friendliness include Computer Associates, Motorola, Merck, Sequent Computer Systems, Mentor Graphics, and Johnson & Johnson. (See the *Working Mother* Web site, whose Web address is listed at the end of the chapter, for their annual list of family-friendly companies.) At Mentor Graphics, for example, CEO Wally Rhines believes that the company's on-site Child Development Center has a significant effect on the company's culture. "For all employees, the Center is a constant reminder of values and our commitment to investing in our employees. Having the children on campus has been a bonus for more than just the parent-employees with children in the program. We all benefit from the perspective their presence gives us."

Organizations are attempting culture change in various ways. Some are revising their mission statements to include statements about their commitment to balance. Johnson & Johnson, for example, revised its 50-year-old Company Credo in 1989 to include, "We must be mindful of ways to help our employees fulfill their family obligations" (Catalyst, 1998, p. 149). Also, since 1990 Johnson & Johnson has required all supervisors to undertake training to be more supportive of their employees and to make the work culture more friendly. In an evaluation of the training two years after its implementation, employees rated their supervisors and the corporate culture as significantly more supportive than before the training (Galinsky, Bond, and Friedman, 1996).

At Baxter Healthcare, employees devised a simple but powerful method to change the work culture. The firm's work/life team, after conducting extensive focus groups and interviews with employees and managers, produced a document that lists concrete behaviors and practices that help support work and life balance (Bankert and Lobel, 1997, p. 187). Some examples include the following:

- Travel on Monday and Friday afternoons should be preferred over weekend travel.
- For all overtime work, 24-hour advance notice should be required.
- Scheduling weekend sales meetings is not appropriate.

Employees at Baxter Healthcare are encouraged to add to the list of behaviors and tailor them to their specific work situations. Managers and employees have responded favorably to this approach to culture change because it gives them a simple tool for discussing and questioning traditional ways of working.

Research at the Families and Work Institute indicates that companies evolve through four stages in developing their work/life strategies (Friedman and Johnson, 1996). In stage 1, firms are focused on child care and women's issues, and are usually satisfied if they implement one or two child care initiatives. In stage 2, managers begin broadening their concerns regarding work and family and adopt an expanded and integrated set of policies and programs. The CEO is more supportive, a "work/family manager" is hired, and flexible work arrangements are introduced. In stage 3, managers begin to realize that culture change surrounding the interaction of work and family is imperative for program effectiveness, and they begin to audit corporate communications for "mixed signals" (e.g., the introduction of flextime at the same time they reward employees for workaholic behavior). Stage 3 companies recognize that the way they value and reward employees sends powerful messages and can either help or hinder work/life efforts. Lastly, in stage 4, the focus shifts to examining work processes and how a work/family perspective can be integrated into the daily operations and strategic concerns of the business. As organizations move through these stages, they begin to recognize that work/life initiatives must improve the quality of life for *all* employees, be integrated in corporate strategy, and promote the view of employees as "whole" human beings.

THE ROLE OF PUBLIC POLICY IN ACHIEVING WORK/LIFE BALANCE

Probably the most significant legislation to help employees balance work and family is the Family and Medical Leave Act of 1993 (FMLA), which states that eligible employees (i.e., those employed for at least 12 months by a given employer) are entitled to 12 unpaid weeks of leave during any 12-month period for (1) birth or adoption of a child; (2) a serious health condition of a spouse, child, or parent; or (3) because of the employee's own serious health condition. An employee returning from a leave must be given the same or equivalent position in terms of pay, benefits, and other conditions of employment. (See *http://www.dol.gov:8002/fmla/wren/vr.htm* for more information about the FMLA.)

The biggest weakness of the law is the fact that the leaves are unpaid. Because men often earn more than women and their families are dependent on this larger income, few men feel they can take advantage of the law without making family welfare more precarious. And because most families are also dependent on the wife's wages, few women can afford to take the unpaid leave. In fact, only 3.6 percent of eligible employees actually took advantage of the FMLA, and the median length of time away from work was 10 days (Repa, 1994). Despite the flaws in the FMLA, it serves as a powerful statement that society recognizes the importance of providing employees with some governmental assistance as they attempt to juggle their roles as employees, parents, daughters and sons of aging parents, and individuals with responsibilities outside of work (Drake, 1997).

ACHIEVING WORK/LIFE BALANCE: A PARTNERSHIP APPROACH

This chapter explored the impact of balancing work and nonwork commitments on women's continuing progress in the workplace. We have discussed personal, organizational, and governmental solutions to the problems faced by women who attempt to have full and rich lives. It should be clear that progress will be achieved only when we examine work/life balance from a synergistic perspective. Such a perspective requires us to reframe the work/life balancing act as an important issue that cuts across workplaces, local communities, the public sector, and citizens (Googins, 1997). As achieving balance has mutually beneficial effects for everyone involved, no one stakeholder should be expected to shoulder the burden of resolving these issues. Therefore, the best solutions will involve partnerships between employers, employees, and government and community organizations. However, these solutions will work only to the extent that we question our fundamental assumptions regarding gender roles, the relationship between the public and private spheres, and the roles of business and government in the lives of individuals.

SUMMARY OF KEY POINTS

Work/life balance can be defined as an employee's ability to manage job and nonjob responsibilities in ways that result in satisfying and productive work and nonwork lives. Balance is often difficult given three types of work/family conflict: time-based, strain-based, and behavior-based conflict. Demographic, attitudinal, and workplace characteristics can exacerbate work/life conflict (e.g., young children, large families, traditional attitudes toward parenting, inflexible work schedules, jobs lacking autonomy, unsupportive bosses, unsupportive organizational cultures). Both positive and negative consequences are associated with balancing multiple roles; the key lies in the *quality* of each role rather than the quantity of roles. There are several ways of coping with work/family conflict, including modifying the stressful situation, changing the meaning of the stressful situation, managing the symptoms of stress, reactive coping ("trying to do it all"), and obtaining support from friends, family, co-workers, and others.

A family-friendly organization is one that offers a variety of policies and programs to meet the needs of employees with family commitments. Four strategies for developing work/family programs include time-based strategies, information-based strategies, money-based strategies, and direct services. Some companies have created additional unique programs to fit the diverse needs of their employees. Unfortunately, six major barriers to implementing work/life programs in organizations make work/life strategy difficult. Barriers include (1) ingrained cultural values and assumptions regarding work and nonwork domains; (2) structural difficulties in implementing programs; (3) lack of support from managers and supervisors; (4) the perception that family issues are women's issues; (5) maintaining equity among all employees; and (6) lack of evaluation data on work/life programs.

Companies that have been successful in overcoming barriers to work/life programs have the following characteristics: (1) work/life integration is considered a strategic initiative of the business; (2) research is conducted on the effectiveness of work/life policies and programs; and (3) cultural assumptions regarding the link between work and other domains of life are being examined and changed. Government has also played a role, the most significant role being helping employees manage work and other life domains through the FMLA.

Attaining work/life balance will require a synergistic approach. Partnerships involving workplaces, local communities, the public sector, and individual citizens, is the approach offering the most tangible hope for success.

Discussion Questions

1. What does work/life balance mean to you? Think of a time when life seemed out of balance. What caused the imbalance? How did you cope?
2. Who provides social support for you? What kinds of support do they provide? Are you comfortable asking for help when you need it?
3. When asked to comment on work and family issues at his company, a management consultant replied that "work/family is not a problem here because there are very few women in this firm." How would you respond to him?
4. You have been asked to devise a strategic plan that focuses on improving work/life balance for all of your employees. What would you include in your plan? Assume your CEO views this as an important aspect of maintaining a competitive advantage over other companies in your industry.
5. What barriers exist to prevent the successful implementation of work/family programs, or more generally, the successful integration of work and family/personal life roles? Do any of these barriers exist at your place of employment? Describe what they are and how they affect work/family or work/life balance.

Issues to Debate

1. In response to recent attempts by organizations to implement family-friendly policies, many employees without children feel resentful because they are not able to participate in these benefits and programs. Many of them argue that work/life policies and programs are not relevant to them because few are applicable to the circumstances of their lives. Further, childless employees are often asked to accommodate the needs of working parents and are treated as if they have no life outside of work. However, family-friendly policies and programs are believed to have positive effects on recruitment, job satisfaction, commitment, and retention of working parents. Debate the merits of each viewpoint in light of organizational attempts to help employees balance work with other life domains while remaining globally competitive.

2. Some business leaders claim that the only family supportive policy that businesses should engage in is tending to business. In other words, by focusing on business initiatives, the enterprise will become more efficient and productive, and thus more jobs for working parents will be created. They claim that businesses should not be engaged in activities that not only cost the organization, but are outside the realm of commerce. Family issues are the individual's responsibility, not the employer's. Debate this laissez-faire view of capitalism with the corporate welfare capitalism of proponents of work/family programs.

3. Many work/life programs in organizations focus much of their effort on child care issues. They offer child care resource and referral programs, on-site child care, sick child care, emergency child care, or contract with local child care businesses to handle their employees' needs. However, there is much controversy regarding the issue of whether nonparental child care is harmful or beneficial to children. What are the arguments for the position that nonparental child care harms children versus the position that it is beneficial for children's development?

Case Analysis
Robin Martin-Jones

Robin Martin-Jones graduated with a business degree in finance from a mid-sized state university. In her last semester of her senior year, Robin began meeting with and interviewing with the college recruiters from a variety of financial service institutions. Although she was most interested in working with a small, more entrepreneurial-type firm, Robin was very impressed with one large Fortune 500 organization. The recruiter shared with her the many advantages of working with his firm. The training programs, future educational opportunities, career development options, and mentoring programs all sounded too good to pass up. When the recruiter mentioned how far women had advanced in his organization, Robin was sold. She accepted the job offering and looked forward to starting with the firm.

As a "fast tracker," Robin joined 15 other men and women in an intense 18-

month training program. These organizational newcomers learned many facets of the business. The best and brightest of these young people were told that 5 of them would be chosen to continue their studies in an MBA program with the firm picking up all the costs. With excellent recommendations from her supervisor, Robin was selected to receive this educational support along with 1 other woman and 3 of the men.

Robin applied and was accepted into a top MBA program and, again, excelled. She worked part-time for the firm and attended classes full-time. Two years later, Robin graduated near the top of her class. She returned to the firm full-time and quickly received a promotion from financial analyst to assistant branch manager. The other MBA graduates received similar opportunities in other locations of the firm. Over the next 2 years, Robin continued to receive strong performance reviews and was given the opportunity to relocate and learn other facets of the business. Although reluctant to leave the branch, she knew that to advance in the company she could not afford to turn down this offer. After a successful stream of different positions, each one building upon the skills of the others, Robin settled into a mid-level management position with responsibility for 10 financial analysts. She enjoyed this position and noted that others who had gone through the same fast-track program were at the same level in the organization and could liaison with her on a number of special projects.

During this time, Robin married and began to balance her career with her family life. When she decided to take advantage of the family leave policy that gave her 6 weeks paid leave after the birth of a child, she congratulated herself on choosing a family-friendly company that accommodated both her family goals and career aspirations. After the birth of her child, she returned to work on an 80 percent flexible work arrangement with full management support from her superiors. Her performance was consistently rated outstanding, and in her last performance review her manager noted that although she worked the 80 percent option, she was accomplishing the objectives of other managers who worked a full-time schedule. Pleased with this track record, Robin began taking notice of the opportunities to advance in the job. Several possibilities emerged, for all of which she was qualified. Her counterparts in other areas assured her that she was just perfect for several of these positions and would recommend her highly for advancement. Robin knew she had the support of her immediate boss as well. She indicated in all of her interviews that she was looking forward to coming back full-time now that her baby was a year old. In three of the promotion opportunities that Robin was up for, she was passed over.

Robin noted that the 3 men with whom she had "fast tracked" were rising steadily in the organization, while management seemed to support her only in the mid-level roles. Her discouragement at being passed over, despite her track record, motivation, commitment, and training, left a bad taste in her mouth. Top management told her that her time would come. After 3 more years of "star" performing and no further advancement in the firm, Robin left to form a start-up with a colleague from graduate school. ■

Source: Written by Dayle M. Smith for use in her Women in Management class, 1997.

Questions

1. In her interviews with college recruiters, are there any other questions that Robin should have asked? How could she have obtained more accurate information?
2. How would you describe the reward system at Robin's firm? How does this reward system affect an employee's ability to balance work and family?
3. Although Robin's firm appears to be family friendly at first glance, what is preventing it from being a truly family-friendly firm?
4. If you were a consultant to the firm, what would you recommend they do to improve retention of women?

References and Suggested Readings

Aldous, J. (1990). Specification and speculation concerning the politics of workplace family policies. *Journal of Family Issues, 11,* 355–367.

Bailyn, L. (1993). *Breaking the mold: Women, men and time in the new corporate world.* New York: Free Press.

Bankert, E. C., and Lobel, S. A. (1997). Visioning the future. In S. Parasuraman and J. H. Greenhaus (Eds.), *Integrating work and family: Challenges for a changing world* (pp. 177–191). Westport, CT: Quorum.

Barnett, R. C., and Rivers, C. (1996). *She works/he works.* San Francisco: Harper.

Baruch, G. K., and Barnett, R. C. (1987). Role quality and psychological well-being. In F. J. Crosby (Ed.), *Spouse, parent, worker: On gender and multiple roles* (pp. 63–73). New Haven, CT: Yale University Press.

Bond, J. T., Galinsky, E., and Swanberg, J. E. (1998). *The 1997 national study of the changing workforce.* New York: Families and Work Institute.

Bright Horizons/Family Solutions: *www.corporatefamily.com/workandfamily. html*

Catalyst. (1998). *Advancing women in business—The Catalyst guide: Best practices from the corporate leaders.* San Francisco: Jossey-Bass.

Christensen, P. M. (1997). Toward a comprehensive work/life strategy. In S. Parasuraman and J. H. Greenhaus (Eds.), *Integrating work and family: Challenges and choices for a changing world* (pp. 25–37). Westport, CT: Quorum.

Cohen, S., and Wills, T. A. (1985). Stress, social support, and the buffering hypothesis. *Psychological Bulletin, 98,* 310–357.

Coontz, S. (1992). *The way we never were: American families and the nostalgia trap.* New York: Basic Books.

Cooper, C. L., and Lewis, S. (1994). *Managing the new work force: The challenge of dual-income families.* San Diego: Pfeiffer.

Crosby, F. J. (1991). *Juggling: The unexpected advantages of balancing career and home for women and their families.* New York: Free Press.

Drake, E. (1997). A legal perspective on work/family issues. In S. Parasuraman and J. H. Greenhaus (Eds.), *Integrating work and family: Challenges and choices for a changing world* (pp. 122–129). Westport, CT: Quorum.

Duxbury, L. E., and Higgins, C. A. (1991). Gender differences in work/family conflict. *Journal of Applied Psychology, 76*(1), 60–74.

Families and Work Institute: (*http://www.familiesandwork.org/*)

Friedman, D. E., and Johnson, A. A. (1996). *Moving from programs to culture change: The next stage for the corporate work/family agenda.* New York: Families and Work Institute.

Frone, M. R., Russell, M., and Cooper, M. L. (1992). Antecedents and outcomes of work/family conflict: Testing a model of the work/family interface. *Journal of Applied Psychology, 77,* 65–78.

Galinsky, E., Bond, J. T., and Friedman, D. E. (1996). The role of employers in addressing the needs of employed parents. *Journal of Social Issues, 52,* 111–136.

Gilbert, L. A. (1993). *Two careers/one family.* Newbury Park, CA: Sage.

Gonyea, J. G., and Googins, B. K. (1996). The restructuring of work and family in the United States: A new challenge for American corporations. In S. Lewis and J. Lewis (Eds.), *The work/family challenge: Rethinking employment* (pp. 63–78). London: Sage.

Googins, B. K. (1997). Shared responsibility for managing work and family relationships: A community perspective. In S. Parasuraman and J. H. Greenhaus (Eds.), *Integrating work and family: Challenges and choices for a changing world* (pp. 220–231). Westport, CT: Quorum.

Greenhaus, J. H., and Beutell, N. J. (1985). Sources of conflict between work and family roles. *Academy of Management Review, 10,* 76–88.

Greenhaus, J. H., and Parasuraman, S. (1986). A work–nonwork interactive perspective of stress and its consequences. *Journal of Organizational Behavior Management, 8,* 37–60.

Gutek, B. A., Searle, S., and Klepa, L. (1991). Rational versus gender role explanations for work/family conflict. *Journal of Applied Psychology, 76,* 560–568.

Hall, D. T. (1972). A model of coping with role conflict: The role behaviors of college educated women. *Administrative Science Quarterly, 1,* 471–486.

Hammonds, K. H. (1997, September 15). Work and family: *Business Week*'s second survey of family-friendly corporate policies. *Business Week,* 96–99, 102–104.

Higgins, C., Duxbury, L., and Lee, C. (1994). Impact of life-cycle stage and gender on the ability to balance work and family responsibilities. *Family Relations, 43,* 144–150.

Hochschild, A., and Machung, A. (1989). *The second shift: Working parents and the revolution at home.* New York: Viking Penguin.

Hordern, B. B. (1993, November). Get a life. *Working Woman,* 53.

Kanter, R. M. (1977). *Men and Women of the Corporation.* New York: Basic Books.

Kanter, R. M. (1977). *Work and family in the United States.* New York: Russell Sage.

Kingston, P. W. (1990). Illusions and ignorance about the family-responsive workplace. *Journal of Family Issues, 11,* 438–454.

Kofodimos, J. (1993). *Balancing act: How managers can integrate successful careers and fulfilling personal lives.* San Francisco: Jossey-Bass.

Kossek, E. E. (1998). Organizational payback from work/life policies. In S. D. Friedman, J. DeGroot, and P. M. Christensen (Eds.), *Integrating work and life: The Wharton resource guide* (pp. 265–277). San Francisco: Jossey-Bass/Pfeiffer.

Kunz Center for the Study of Work and Family: (*http://ucaswww.mcm.uc.edu/sociology/kunzctr/*)

Lafayette, L. (1994, October 16). Fair play for the childless worker. *New York Times,* D3.

Latack, J. (1984). Career transitions within organizations: An exploratory study of work, nonwork, and coping strategies. *Organizational Behavior and Human Performance, 34,* 296–322.

Leibow, C. (1998). Work/life balance: How to become an employer of choice. In S. D. Friedman, J. DeGroot, and P. M. Christensen (Eds.), *Integrating work and life: The Wharton resource guide* (pp. 279–292). San Francisco: Jossey-Bass/Pfeiffer.

Levine, J. A., and Pittinsky, T. L. (1997). *Working fathers: New strategies for balancing work and family.* New York: Addison-Wesley.

Lewis, S. (1996). Rethinking employment: An organizational culture framework. In S. Lewis and J. Lewis (Eds.), *The work/family challenge: Rethinking employment* (pp. 1–19). London: Sage.

Lewis, S., and Lewis J. (1996). *The work/family challenge: Rethinking employment.* London: Sage.

LifeCareNet, a provider of work/life counseling, education, and referral service: (*http://www.dcclifecare.com*) (This site has great links to other work/life resources.)

Lobel, S. A., and Kossek, E. E. (1996). Human resource strategies to support diversity in work and personal lifestyles: Beyond the "family-friendly" organization. In E. E. Kossek and S. A. Lobel (Eds.), *Managing diversity: Human resource strategies for transforming the workplace* (pp. 221–244). Oxford, UK: Blackwell.

Marks, S. R. (1977). Multiple roles and role strain: Some notes on human energy, time and commitment. *American Sociological Review, 42,* 921–936.

Marshall, N. L., and Barnett, R. C. (1994). Family-friendly workplaces, work/family interface, and worker health. In G. P. Keita and J. J. Hurrell (Eds.), *Job stress in a changing workforce* (pp. 253–264). Washington, DC: American Psychological Association.

Minnesota Center for Corporate Responsibility. (1997). *Creating high performance organizations. . . . The bottom line value of work/life strategies.* Minneapolis, MN. (http://tigger. stthomas.edu/mccr)

Mintz, S., and Kellog, S. (1998). *Domestic revolutions: A social history of American family life.* New York: Free Press.

O'Hare, M. (1997). Managing work/family tensions: A counseling perspective. In S. Parasuraman and J. H. Greenhaus (Eds.), *Integrating work and family: Challenges and choices for a changing world* (pp. 57–68). Westport, CT: Quorum.

Parasuraman, S., and Greenhaus, J. H. (1997a). The changing world of work and family. In S. Parasuraman and J. H. Greenhaus (Eds.), *Integrating work and family: Challenges and choices for a changing world* (pp. 3–14). Westport, CT: Quorum.

Parasuraman, S., and Greenhaus, J. H. (1997b). *Integrating work and family: Challenges and choices for a changing world.* Westport, CT: Quorum.

Parasuraman, S., Greenhaus, J. H., and Granrose, C. S. (1992). Role stressors, social support, and well-being among two-career couples. *Journal of Organizational Behavior, 13,* 339–356.

Pistrang, N. (1984). Women's work involvement and experience of new motherhood. *Journal of Marriage and the Family, 46,* 433–447.

Pleck, J. H. (1993). Are "family-supportive" employer policies relevant to men? In J. C. Hood (Ed.), *Men, work, and family* (pp. 217–237). Newbury Park, CA: Sage.

Raabe, P. H. (1990). The organizational effects of workplace family policies: Past weaknesses and recent progress toward improved research. *Journal of Family Issues, 11,* 477–491.

Repa, B. K. (1994). *Your rights in the workplace.* Berkeley, CA: Nolo Press.

Scharlach, A. E., and Boyd, S. L. (1989). Caregiving and employment: Results of an employee survey. *The Gerontologist, 29,* 382–387.

Schwartz, F. N. (1992). *Breaking with tradition: Women and work, the new facts of life.* New York: Warner Books.

Senge, P. M. (1990). *The fifth discipline: The art and practice of the learning organization.* New York: Doubleday Currency.

Skolnick, A. (1991). *The embattled paradise: The American family in an age of uncertainty.* New York: Basic Books.

Smith, D. *Kin Care and the American Corporation: Solving the work/family dilemma.* Lincolnwood, IL, Irwin, 1991.

Smith, D. (1992). Corporate benefits only a start for family friendliness. *Employee Benefit Plan Review, 3,* 46–52.

Spitze, G. (1988). Women's employment and family relations: A review. *Journal of Marriage and the Family, 50,* 595–618.

Text of the Family and Medical Leave Act of 1993. (*http://www.dol.gov/dol/esa/fmla.htm*)

Thoits, P. A. (1987). Negotiating roles. In F. J. Crosby (Ed.), *Spouse, parent, worker* (pp. 11–22). New Haven, CT: Yale University Press.

Thomas, L. T., and Ganster, D. C. (1995). Impact of family-supportive work variables on work/family conflict and strain: A control perspective. *Journal of Applied Psychology, 80,* 6–15.

Thompson, C. A., Beauvais, L. L., and Lyness, K. S. (1999). When work/family benefits are not enough. . . . The influence of work/family culture on benefit utilization, organizational attachment, and work/family conflict. *Journal of Vocational Behavior, 54,* 392–415.

Thompson, C. A., Thomas, C. C., and Maier, M. (1992). Work/family conflict and the bottom line: Reassessing corporate policies and initiatives. In U. Sekaran and F. T. Leong (Eds.), *Womanpower: Managing in times of demographic turbulence* (pp. 59–84). Newbury Park, CA: Sage.

Williams, K. J., and Alliger, G. M. (1994). Role stressors, mood spillover, and perceptions of work/family conflict in employed parents. *Academy of Management Journal, 37,* 837–868.

Womens' Bureau of the Department of Labor. (*http://www.dol.gov/dol/wb/*)

The Work/Family Connection. (*http://www.workfamily.com/*)

Work/Family Directions (WFD, Inc.). (*www.wfd.com*)

Working Mother (*www. working mother.com*)

CHAPTER 10

Women Working Abroad: International Dimensions

Peggy K. Takahashi

In many American business cultures, masculine qualities such as individual achievement, assertiveness, and material success are highly valued. These, however, are not qualities that are universally valued in other cultures.

—D. DRISCOLL AND C. R. GOLDBERG
Members of the Club, 1993, p. 218

Different is different, different is not bad; always respect the differences.

—JAMES MILLER, PRESIDENT
Mazda Motor Corp., first American president of a Japanese company

Chapter Overview

As economies globalize, more and more talented women are entering the workforce. Success in overseas assignments will become a necessity for career advancement. However, in most areas of the world there is a dearth of women executives. How do women succeed in this environment?

Success in this arena depends not only on technical expertise, but also on the ability to understand one's own culture and the ways in which culture affects our assumptions and expectations about human behavior. In many parts of the world, a deal will not be closed based on the attributes of the product, but on whether or not a relationship exists between the individuals.

Learning Objectives

■ To explore why events or situations mean different things to people of different cultures

■ To identify obstacles women face in being selected for and successful in overseas assignments

- To understand key factors for a successful international experience

- To identify key success factors that favor women in overseas assignments

- To explore issues women need to consider before accepting an international assignment

INTERNATIONAL WOMEN MANAGERS: THE TREND

Although change has been slow, American women are securing greater numbers of managerial positions than ever before (Fagenson and Jackson, 1994). This shift is also occurring at slower rates across Western Europe (Davidson and Cooper, 1993) and to a lesser extent in Asia (Adler and Izraeli, 1994). Despite the ever-present glass ceiling, much of the evidence suggests that America is more advanced than other nations in terms of developing and training women managers (Driscoll and Goldberg, 1993).

One reason for this shift is the threat of legal action. As more and more cases of discrimination are found in favor of women plaintiffs, firms are modifying behavior. They simply cannot afford the legal costs and incur the public wrath (in the form of punitive judgments and negative public relations) for discrimination against women.

Another important reason for this shift in the United States is economic. As global competition grows more fierce and as greater numbers of highly qualified women enter the workforce, firms can no longer afford to select their employees from only half of the population.

As greater numbers of highly qualified women enter the workforce, firms that were reluctant to send women on overseas assignments are now sending them abroad. Moreover, women are proving to be successful in their overseas assignments despite initial doubts by corporate headquarters (Adler and Izraeli, 1994). Preparation and flexibility is key to their success. In addition, the anecdotal evidence suggests that women executives may possess a competitive edge over men because of their visibility as women.

WESTERN WOMEN IN ASIA

My academic and professional work, as well as personal experience, has focused on Japan. In 20 years of commuting between cultures, I have noticed a number of subtle changes.

In the 1970s, there were relatively few Westerners in Japan. Westerners were just beginning to study Japan and the Japanese language. As an American of Japanese descent, one lesson I learned then was that it paid to look Western . . . literally. Because of the dearth of native English speakers in the 1970s, American students could earn a good salary teaching English part time to business professionals. Western women in particular were able to earn a premium teaching English. The Japanese were curious about Western women, and the then–Crown Prince Akihito had been educated by an English woman. However, although I was born and educated in America, because I looked Japanese and spoke Japanese, there lurked some doubt about my native English language abilities. As a result, the English-teaching jobs I secured were at lower rates and at less prestigious institutions.

From this experience I realized two things. First, that Western women had an advantage in Japan; their gender was overshadowed by their foreignness. Western women, by virtue of their appearance, had perceived abilities. I learned that to be credible as a professional, I had to establish my identity first as an American, and then as someone who also spoke Japanese and looked Asian.

This distinction is important for Western women because of the traditional role often played by women in Asia. Most women in Hong Kong, Japan, the Philippines, Taiwan, and Singapore have increasing access to higher education. Lack of ability is not what keeps the number of women in managerial positions low. Instead, traditional Asian family values based on Confucianism places societal pressures on women, forcing them to choose between family and career (Adler, 1994).

In addition, although Asian women have authority in decisions about the home and family, they are often perceived by Asian men as emotional and incapable of making decisions at work. Asian women are perceived as lacking the social credibility needed to be accepted in a workplace that is heavily influenced by the creation and maintenance of social networks. As a result, the number of Asian women in managerial positions is very low. However, if Western women are considered foreigners first and women second, they are not expected to fit the traditional roles ascribed to native women.

The fact that Western women are not expected to fit the traditional female role in Asia is an important distinction. It is one that Adler (1987) also found in her research involving 52 women who were successful managers in Asia. "Asians see female expatriates as foreigners who happen to be women, not as women who happen to be foreigners" (Adler, 1987, p. 188).

During my latest visit to Tokyo, I saw more Western women in dark business suits with laptops in tow than ever before. These sightings are encouraging for several reasons. First, it seems that Western firms are dispatching women to Japan on business (probably because of the success of women predecessors), and, second, women are using these opportunities to develop international dimensions in their careers.

WOMEN MANAGERS IN WESTERN CULTURES

The situation in Europe is different than that in Asia because of the greater presence of women in the full-time workforce. However, there are still few European women in decision-making positions in management. Different cultural norms in Europe prevent women from becoming managers. While societal pressures, including child care and family issues, may deter women from reaching high levels of authority, individual choices about entering the competition for career advancement was also a factor (Sedjénian, 1994).

A study of French women managers found that French women chose a unique strategy in their careers. Women undertook traditional roles as staff experts. They assisted men in making decisions, but they were not the ultimate decision makers. Most women managers in the company studied held these positions.

To support their decision to fill these subordinate positions, some of the women maintained they had rejected the traditional 'masculine' game of career competition and search for power and instead advocated what they described as a "feminine morality" based on respect for the individual and on cooperation. (Sedjénian, 1994, pp. 197–98)

In Germany, as in France, there are few women in decision-making roles. As a result, American women managers are seen as an anomaly. This may be an advantage for American women. Susan Duggan, Ph.D., is an American executive who speaks fluent German. She is one of the founders and CEO of the Silicon Valley World Internet Center. Her insights are based on many years of working as a social scientist in Germany. She has worked as a visiting policy and program analyst at the German Foreign Ministry and the Deutscher Akademischer Austauschdienst (DAAD, the German Academic Exchange Service). She was also president for four years of a study-abroad agency where she established and negotiated programs for American university students in Germany, Hungary, Poland, and the Czech Republic. Duggan notes that her encounters with German senior managers is a constant balancing act. "I have to always be conscious about maintaining the interest that comes with being an American female executive and at the same time become an 'insider' in order to establish a working relationship" (Duggan, 1998).

In Germany, Duggan uses a variety of means to make a lasting impression. "I make sure to slip in information about my educational background and degrees. This establishes instant credibility and respect from my German counterparts" (Duggan, 1998). To be effective, name-dropping should be subtle and woven into the conversation. To do this effortlessly means having thought about how to link relevant information about your past in informal and business conversations.

Another tip that will help others remember you is to associate yourself with a particular region. Duggan makes a point of distinguishing herself as a Californian, "California is viewed by Germans in particular and Europeans in general as a place of innovation and good universities" (Duggan, 1998).

Duggan adds that although she dresses conservatively, she is always conscious of adding a piece of jewelry, a belt or a distinctive scarf that will set her apart from German women. Again, her goal is to ensure she is remembered so that later meetings will be productive.

INTERNATIONAL CAREER DIMENSIONS

At this point, some readers may wonder, "Why bother with going abroad?" If adapting to new situations and cultures or dealing with the logistics of spouse and children outweigh the benefits of learning how a different part of the world thinks and behaves, or if creating something in a completely different operating environment is too much of a challenge, then perhaps an international opportunity is not for you.

However, consider this: Employees in many global firms headquartered in the United States believe that international experience is necessary to rise in the corporate world. In fact, most top managers in multinational firms, such as Coca Cola, Colgate-Palmolive, Mazda, and Nestlé, list successful international experiences on their resumés. This trend is likely to continue given the trend toward a global economy.

KEY SUCCESS FACTORS FOR INTERNATIONAL EXPERIENCES

> Successful global managers have demonstrated innate or acquired characteristics that more often resemble female strengths: cultural sensitivity, tolerance for ambiguity and change, flexibility, cross-cultural communication skills, leadership at coalition-building, patience, and persistence. Traditional American management styles often do not work in foreign cultures. Men are perceived as direct, assertive, competing, and controlling, while women are more apt to be accommodating, receptive, and intuitive, bridging to a conclusion that benefits all parties. While generalizations do not apply to all men or all women, they occur often enough to become valid guidelines.
> —D. Driscoll and C. R. Goldberg, 1993, p. 218

It is pointless to make comparisons between men and women. Instead, there are a number of key success factors that work for anyone going abroad.

Sensitivity to Cultural Norms

Being sensitive to cultural norms requires researching your own culture first, and then learning about the cultural norms for a particular country. It is important to realize how our own cultural assumptions influence the way we perceive situations and behavior and to accept other ways of thinking and living.

Culture is very difficult to characterize without falling into broad generalizations and stereotypes. At the same time, without a framework, it would be impossible to explain the variations in behaviors across cultures.

A number of researchers have identified cultural dimensions that, if used as a guideline allowing for individual variations, can provide insights for managers going abroad. The biggest drawback of these studies is that the role of women in management across cultures is not specifically addressed. We can only infer the general role of women in society from how countries compare across each cultural dimension. The following sections briefly outline two notable frameworks. In addition to the dimensions identified by Hofstede (1980) and by Trompenaars (1994), other notable cultural frameworks include the identification of attitudinal dimensions by Ronen and Shenkar (1985) as well as the classification of values and beliefs by Kluckhohn and Stodtbeck (1961).

Hofstede's Four Cultural Dimensions

Geert Hofstede, a Dutch researcher, developed a survey and collected data from IBM subsidiaries around the world between 1967 and 1973 (Hofstede, 1980). The four cultural dimensions Hofstede explored were (1) power distance, (2) uncertainty avoidance, (3) individualism, and (4) masculinity. Each of these dimensions exists on a continuum with high and low degrees of each dimension at each end of the continuum.

Power distance is the extent to which authority is recognized and accepted. High-power distance cultures tend to have centralized decision making with more vertical or pyramid-like organizational structures. Organizations in low-power distance cultures tend to have flatter organizational structures with less skill variation between supervisory and lower level employees.

A manager going from a low-power distance to a higher power distance culture might be expected to exert greater amounts of authority by subordinates. However, because men often are perceived as the decision makers in business, women should be prepared to demonstrate their abilities through reputation, personal achievement, or schooling.

Uncertainty avoidance is the need for individuals in a culture to feel secure and avoid ambiguity. In relatively high uncertainty avoidance cultures, like Japan, the exchange of business cards is important because it establishes the hierarchical relationship between individuals eliminating any ambiguity about how each individual is perceived by the other party.

Individualism represents the degree to which people tend to protect themselves. Individualism is at one end of the continuum, and collectivism is at the other end. Collectivism is the need for people to belong to groups. Group affiliation is recognized through loyalty to the group (Hofstede, 1980). The United States tends to be individualistic; Japan is more collectivist. Affiliation to a school or company is important to the Japanese and lasts for years. University affiliation, for example, not only provides a sense of belonging and even an identity while in school, but it also provides instant networking opportunities throughout the graduate's career.

The **masculinity index** reveals the degree to which cultures exhibit more masculine or feminine behaviors. "Male behavior is associated with autonomy, aggression, exhibition, and dominance; female behavior with nurturance, affiliation, helpfulness, and humility" (Hofstede, 1980, p. 263). For a number of cultures, including Scandinavian cultures, masculine tendencies are not as valued as the quality of life or interdependence.

Trompenaars' Cultural Dimensions

Fons Trompenaars (1994) conducted his study over a 10-year period and focused on dimensions in which people relate to one another based on Parsons' five relational orientations. Trompenaars firmly believes that there is no one best way to manage in a global environment. His contribution involves how culture influences people's assumptions and expectations about behavior.

Trompenaars' study is based on survey data of employees of 30 companies across 50 countries, as well as anecdotal evidence. The five relational orientations are (1) universalism versus particularism, (2) individualism versus collectivism, (3) neutral versus affective, (4) specific versus diffuse, and (5) achievement versus ascription. Trompenaars locates countries along the spectrum of each orientation based on the data collected.

Universalism versus particularism is a dimension that describes the degree to which a culture focuses on formal rules or regulations and on relationships. Universalistic cultures tend to rely on formal rules and contracts rather than on the formation of long-lasting relationships. Particularistic cultures focus on the trust built between individuals. As a result, in particularistic cultures, contracts tend to be flexible and can be modified as the relationship matures.

Trompenaars suggests that managers going from universalistic to particularistic cultures should be prepared for a greater amount of nonbusiness related conversation. A manager who is savvy in overseas business relationships advises not to take these personal conversations lightly. It is a way managers assess whether or not you are someone with whom they want to do business. That particular manager takes the lead from her overseas hosts as to when the conversation turns to business matters.

In contrast, Trompenaars suggests that individuals shifting from particularistic to universalistic cultures should not be surprised to find that meetings focus on business from the beginning, with little time spent on informalities.

The *individualism versus collectivism* orientation has the same basic meaning as that of Hofstede's earlier research: It concerns the degree to which people regard themselves as individuals or as part of a group. However, Trompenaars' research yielded different findings from those of Hofstede's earlier work. Several countries that Hofstede found to be collectivist, Trompenaars found individualistic. This may indicate changes in culture over time as well as changes in culture due to the changing political climate (Hodgetts and Luthans, 1997).

For managers dealing with individualistic and collectivist cultures, patience is key. Individuals in collectivist cultures usually need time to consult with others before reaching a decision. As a result, quick decisions expected by managers from individualistic cultures are often not forthcoming. Managers in collectivist cultures should also realize that opportunities might be lost when organizations cannot reach decisions quickly.

The *neutral versus affective* orientation is characterized by the degree to which there are emotional displays. In neutral cultures, people tend to mask their feelings and remain calm. Both China and Japan have cultures in which emotions are not expressed. In affective cultures, there are more open and natural expressions of emotions. Latin American cultures tend to be more affective (Harris and Moran, 1996).

As global economies bring cultures closer together, managers are becoming sensitive to these cultural differences. For example, I notice that Japanese managers who have been in the United States for an extended period of time tend to smile more and be more outgoing than their counterparts in Japan. However, managers going from affective to neutral cultures should realize that the presence or absence of physical demonstrations of enthusiasm should not be used as a measure of interest.

The *specific versus diffuse* dimension describes the relative personal space of individuals. In specific cultures, such as the United States, individuals allow a large, public space into which others may enter freely, whereas the small, private space is reserved for close friends and family. For example, "In America, a title is a specific label for a specific job in a specific place" (Trompenaars, 1994, p. 80). Whereas, in diffuse cultures a job title, job roles and the like are part of the concept of personal space. In short, one's professional life and personal life are separate in specific cultures.

In diffuse cultures, such as many Asian countries, both public and private spaces are similar in size. As a result, an individual's public and private role become blurred. In diffuse cultures a professional critique can be considered a personal attack or an insult. Trompenaars observed that the comments associated with a "don't take this personally" attitude often backfire in diffuse cultures.

For managers of specific cultures going to a diffuse culture, Trompenaars recommends the continued use of formal titles and formal forms of language. In Germany, for example, professional titles would be used not only in the workplace but in social situations as well. By contrast, in the United States professional titles tend to be used less often in the workplace and rarely in social situations. Managers going to a more diffuse culture should also expect more indirect communications, whereas managers going from diffuse to specific cultures should try to rely on structured agendas in meetings and try not to be insulted at greater levels of informality.

Achievement versus ascription is the dimension that characterizes how status is conferred on individuals. In an achievement culture, an individual's performance level determines respect; it is merit based. In an ascription culture, factors such as age, personal or family connections, or tenure determine the level of respect and status.

Firms sending managers from an achievement to an ascription culture should find out as much as possible about the host country's firm. If overseas hosts and counterparts are senior members of the firm, then equivalent level managers who can make an impression should be sent.

Trompenaars advises that in an ascription culture demonstrations of respect toward those with status are important. In Japan, for example, the exchange of business cards is important because it establishes the relative ranking between two individuals. Based on this rank order, each side is able to show the appropriate level of respect toward the other.

For managers going from an ascription to an achievement culture, technical mastery and the ability to produce data is important. It should be noted, however, that in today's high-tech world, managers belonging to ascription cultures, like those in Japan, expect high levels of technical expertise during meetings.

Using the Frameworks

Trompenaar's frameworks reveal how different aspects of people's behavior in a culture can be perceived and understood. They should not be used to formulate stereotypes about any particular culture. Trompenaars suggests that each culture consists of individuals who represent different norms and expectations. This variety of people can be characterized by an "average" set of behaviors. This "average" differs from culture to culture, and managers need to understand that there is variation among the averages. Some people will not fit the average cultural pattern. However, a basic understanding of these cultural categories helps individuals perceive (or even prevent) some of the dilemmas that arise because of cultural differences in international business.

Other Variables That Differ across Cultures

In addition to the cultural frameworks, there are other variables that we often assume have the same meanings and usage across cultures. In fact, time, relationships, and agreements have different meanings and significance across cultures. Following are a few variables that seem to give Westerners the most difficulty.[1]

In some cultures *time* is often viewed as a finite resource. Meetings start on time. Deadlines tend to be rigid. Tardiness can be viewed as a character flaw. However, in other cultures time is viewed more flexibly. In some cultures personal relationships are key to successful business relationships, and it takes time to develop these relationships. They cannot be built under looming deadlines or through scheduled meetings.

When time is viewed flexibly, waiting is not considered an insult. Therefore, becoming upset because of a delay can often be detrimental to establishing a strong relationship.

In some cultures, like that of Japan, time is elastic, lengthening and shortening depending on the situation. For example, profuse apologies are offered by train conductors if a bullet train is delayed by even a few minutes. Meetings and appointments always start on time. Given this emphasis by the Japanese on time, Westerners believe

---

[1]For more details see Hall, 1960.

that decisions will be made promptly. In reality, Westerners find that the Japanese take far longer to reach decisions than in the West. Part of the reason for the delay concerns group consensus-building. In reaching the decision, all parties affected by the decision have a voice in the decision, and the details for implementation are often considered (Takahashi, 1985). As a result, although reaching the decision may take time, implementation is usually swift. Interestingly, the Japanese complain that Westerners are quick to reach decisions but slow to implement them.

Relationships also tend to have greater significance overseas. In a number of cultures, successful business relations depend on the ability of individuals to form close personal relationships. These relationships tend to be long lasting and include an element of mutual obligation and responsibility. As a result, having a superior product at a low price will not guarantee success overseas (Trompenaars, 1994).

Agreements are often the source of misunderstandings overseas. "One of the greatest difficulties Americans have abroad stems from the fact that we often think we have a commitment when we do not. The second complication on this same topic is the other side of the coin . . . , when others think we have agreed to things that we have not. Our own failure to recognize binding obligations, plus our custom of setting organizational goals ahead of everything else, has put us in hot water far too often" (Hall, 1960, p. 93).

A classic example from Japan is the affirmative nodding of the head. Many Westerners incorrectly interpret this as agreement with what is being said. However, head nodding to the Japanese is merely a sign of polite listening, not agreement.

In addition to these cultural dimensions and variables, there are several other factors that managers should remember when conducting business overseas. These include attentive listening and finding areas of mutual interest to help devise solutions, and they are discussed in the following sections.

Listening Involves More Than Just Hearing

The ability to be sensitive to social cues is very important for conducting business everywhere. It is particularly important in conducting business overseas. Cultural sensitivity reveals evidence of a knowledge of the culture. It can be used to show respect for cultural nuances. Proficiency in these areas will be noted by overseas business colleagues.

Americans tend to be more informal in business settings than people in other cultures. The observance and maintenance of hierarchical relationships are important in other cultures. These distinctions are made in subtle ways, for example, in language that uses formal titles and formal speech or in a reserved demeanor and attitude.

Another example is brainstorming during meetings, which is often done in the United States. However, from a cultural perspective there are many social implications of brainstorming. It suggests that ideas are exchanged openly in an atmosphere of relative social equality. There is little concern for the status of the individuals at the meeting. However, in cultures that tend to be more diffuse and tend toward ascription, brainstorming will often end unsuccessfully because personal opinions, even if they are good ideas, are not expressed in public.

Face and maintaining face is very important in diffuse cultures, in which the loss of face by an individual is tantamount to disgrace. Loss of face occurs in public situations where public is defined as any social situation in which others are present. Loss of face can occur in a variety of ways. A criticism, however slight, made in public can cause the loss of face of the manager in charge of that particular area. In diffuse cultures, think before speaking;

determine whether someone could lose face before making a comment. If the comment must be made, make it in private. A little tact will go a long way toward building trust.

An American woman working for a Japanese company advises, "Remember, you can never compliment enough in Japan. Simple demonstrations that you understand the protocol go a long way, especially on an initial encounter. If you can erase some of the barriers from the very beginning, obviously it will work to your advantage."

Finding Areas of Mutual Interest That Create Solutions

Finding mutually beneficial solutions is important in any business situation, but it is crucial in international business. Americans have been stereotyped overseas as having the tendency to repeat themselves, and the repetition is loud. Unfortunately, this type of behavior leaves little room for finding creative, mutually beneficial solutions.

> In one meeting held with top officials in Mexico, the president of a leading Texas chamber of commerce found himself totally ignored during the negotiations after starting the meeting with a confrontational remark. Most of the remainder of the discussion was directed to the black woman president of another Texas chamber of commerce who began by indicating a desire to work with Mexican officials on common concerns and then proceeded to discuss with them how best to accomplish the set goal.
>
> —Driscoll and Goldberg, 1993, p. 225

Finding mutually beneficial areas is difficult enough to do within one's own culture. In international business it requires the ability not only to see the issues from another company's perspective, but also to see them from another culture's perspective.

FACTORS THAT FAVOR WOMEN

So far this chapter has highlighted the importance and difficulty of an international career. It would be misleading not to discuss a few of the advantages women do have overseas.

Use Visibility to Your Advantage

Ability to Disarm

Overseas business environments are predominantly male. As managers overseas, women can use their visibility to their advantage. Adler (1994) found in her study that women reported their visibility to be a key asset.

To become an American woman manager, most women have had to be very resourceful; some have been very assertive to achieve their success. While resourcefulness is valuable in any culture, women might find that a little charm will achieve better results overseas than assertiveness. This is true especially in cultures that value relationships in their business dealings.

To be successful, women expatriates must first grasp how they fit into the overseas culture and compare it to their own culture. Remember, women are not usually seen as equals in many cultures, which is difficult for American women to accept. Do not display annoyance if questions are directed toward men who might be your assistants. Answer the question yourself. Your overseas associates will eventually get the message.

As one American woman working in Japan observed, "Never kid yourself into thinking that you will ever 'change' anything by yourself—changes can occur, but you have to play by the rules the Japanese have set and do it within the established frameworks—patience is essential."

For example, rather than putting your overseas counterpart on the spot during a meeting, you will get far better results by asking the question in private after the meeting. Doing so allows you to get your question answered without risking the possibility that he could lose face.

If They Sent You, You Must Be Good

Women are not considered viable as managers or decision makers in most overseas cultures. This can be used to a woman's advantage because it is sometimes assumed that for a woman to be dispatched overseas, she must be very talented. Women executives can further bolster that image and enhance their credibility by making sure their overseas hosts get a copy of their resumé or vita listing their educational background and achievements. Furthermore, because age in many countries is respected, being an older woman automatically gains respect.

The burden on women executives is on follow-through. Visibility means women will be remembered, for both positive professional attributes, as well as any mistakes they made. Strive to be excellent in all your undertakings.

UNDERSTANDING THE MYTHS

Despite the need for international experience, women are often not dispatched. Adler (1994), in her study of women expatriates, identified three possible reasons for the lack of women in international assignments. Adler's findings are summarized here along with some practical advice on how to avoid fulfilling these myths.

Myth 1: Women Do Not Want to Be International Managers

Adler (1994) surveyed more than 1,000 MBA graduates and found no significant gender-based difference on pursuing international careers. Women express as much interest as men in pursuing international careers, but both men and women acknowledge that there are fewer international career opportunities for women compared to those for men.

Indeed, Adler found that out of the 13,338 expatriate managers sent abroad by North American multinational firms, only 402 (or, 3 percent) were women. In contrast, Adler found that for these same firms, women held 37 percent of the domestic management positions.

Myth 1 is in fact a myth. Women ARE interested in becoming international managers. However, they are not being dispatched.

- If women truly are interested in an international career, they will either need to make the company understand their interest and make sure the firm acts on it, or find a company that will send them on international assignments.

Myth 2: Companies Refuse to Send Women Abroad

To test this myth, Adler surveyed human resource managers from 60 of the largest North American multinationals. She found that more than half of the companies were disinclined to send women abroad and of these nearly 75 percent reported believing that foreigners were so prejudiced against women that the women managers could not succeed even if sent" (Adler, 1994, p. 28). Another reason given was that dual-career issues made it impossible to send a married woman overseas.

Based on these findings, Myth 2 is reality, not a myth. Firms tend to be unwilling or resistant to sending women abroad.

- If you are confident of your professional and cross-cultural skills, make it clear that you are the right person for the job. Any successful overseas experience in the past gives you an advantage over others.

Myth 3: Foreigners' Prejudice against Women Expatriate Managers

Adler (1994) tested whether or not discrimination of women overseas affected the performance of expatriate women. She surveyed more than 100 women who worked for North American multinational firms on expatriate assignments around the world. Their postings lasted an average of 2.5 years and their titles ranged from junior positions as assistant account managers to senior-level managers.

Based on her survey, Adler reports that 97 percent of these women indicated that their international assignment was successful. In addition to these subjective measures, Adler further found that the women had been able to complete most of their firms' objectives. In fact, based on the success of these women, a majority of the firms sent more women on international assignments in subsequent years.

More significantly, 42 percent of the expatriate women Adler surveyed reported that being a woman mostly had been an advantage and not a disadvantage. Only 20 percent reported that being female was mostly a disadvantage.

BOX 10.1

U.S. Managers Pose Significant Barrier to Placing Women in Expatriate Assignment

Two new studies, presented at the Academy of Management 1999 meeting in Chicago, identify some of the real barriers women face on expatriate assignments. Apparently, the problem is not an inability to adapt to foreign cultures and their bosses on international assignments or the perceived stereotypes of overseas bosses. The real problem appears to be "unfounded bias" of American male managers towards placement of women in overseas assignments. In surveys of 261 women working abroad and 78 supervisors (mostly men) in multinational corporations, researchers Linda K. Stroh and Arup Varma and Stacey J. Valy of Loyola University found that attitudes of foreign nationals were more favorable towards women working overseas than the mostly male bosses of these women. A second study, surveying 323 managers in Germany, Mexico and the U.S. regarding their attitudes on the performance of women expatriates, found that U.S. male managers had more concerns over American women's effectiveness than their female counterparts in the States or men and women managers from Germany and Mexico.

Some of the disadvantages women experienced were not with the overseas business practices, but with their own headquarters. Adler found that women reported a lack of commitment from headquarters in terms of time and that responsibilities were limited thus sending a negative message to her overseas colleagues. These limitations undermine the credibility and authority of women expatriates but are not surprising given the reluctance of firms even to send women on international assignments in the first place.

- Women need to ensure that before they leave, they are given the appropriate title and authority to send a message of commitment to overseas colleagues. Adler (1994) suggests that firms send women on full-term assignments from the beginning rather than only on a temporary assignment. Anything that adds to a woman's credibility will increase effectiveness, and, in the long run, performance.

HOW TO PREPARE

Clearly, an international career is not for everyone. This is equally true for both women and men. The first step is to determine whether or not you have the flexibility required to live abroad successfully. Without the ability to be flexible in both your personal and professional activities, an international assignment will be difficult and may even be unsuccessful. Without flexibility, acceptance of different cultures and perceptions that are different from your own is nearly impossible. As one American woman working abroad for a major multinational company, headquartered in Japan, observed,

> This cultural understanding and acceptance of it is essential since many of the same traditions, beliefs and attitudes will carry over into the workplace. Once you have gleaned an understanding, the next step is to be truly honest with yourself. You must be honest in assessing whether or not you can live by the value system and work ethic to which the society subscribes.
>
> If you are planning to be in the environment long-term, you must be realistic about your own needs. Survival skills can be learned along the way, [including] techniques to help overcome some cultural barriers and achieve easier communication. But if a fundamental difference exists in your value system, achieving real success and maintaining personal happiness becomes more difficult.

Personal Issues

For dual-career families, relocation becomes an issue for the spouse. If the possibility of relocation has been discussed previously, there is less surprise when an opportunity to go overseas arises. Early planning might allow each partner to find a creative solution that will benefit all parties.

Companies should also be flexible in suggesting or generating creative solutions. As the number of dual-career families rises and as globalization increases demand, firms will be sending greater numbers of dual-career families abroad.

Other family members, such as older children, should agree with the move. One of the leading reasons expatriates return early (at great expense to the firm) is because of the family's inability to adjust to living overseas. Aging parents may be a consideration as well.

Some Things to Think about before You Decide

If you have decided to pursue a long-term international assignment, here are a few things to consider before going. This list is by no means comprehensive, but it should provoke thinking about how an international career fits into your personal and professional future.

- **Consider your firm's salary and benefits package when you are overseas.** What is your company's policy regarding overseas benefits? How will retirement accrue? What about health benefits, moving costs, and housing? If you have children, will their schooling overseas be reimbursed? Will your salary be adjusted for the high cost of living in expensive cities such as Tokyo or Paris? These are just a few issues that you will need to consider before deciding on an overseas assignment.
- **Make sure your role and scope of authority are clear both to you and to headquarters.** Do you have a clear set of objectives? If not, it will be difficult for the home office to evaluate your performance. Will you have the appropriate level of authority to achieve these objectives? Make sure you are given enough resources and time to get the job done. Do not let headquarters undermine you or your ability to get the job done.
- **Establish your credibility before you arrive.** Send a current résumé and vita that includes your professional credentials, your educational background, and any awards you have received. Include as much personal information on hobbies or outside interests as you care to share. Ask for similar information on your primary counterparts as well.
- **Determine your role in the firm after repatriation *before* leaving.** Discuss what your role will be after you return from your overseas assignment. Adler (1994) observed that many of the women in her study were promoted or were sent on another overseas assignment on return. A successful assignment will always prevent the "out of sight, out of mind" problem.
- **Study the culture of the country to which you are going.** Most large companies offer training for their outbound executives and their families. Smaller firms may not. If there are no formal training programs offered by your firm, do your own research. If possible, go to a grocery store that specializes in foods of the country to which you will be going. Get used to the sights and smells of the local cuisine. In today's global economy, there are numerous books that deal with "Doing business in . . . ." There is little excuse for not being culturally conscious when you step off the plane.

TIPS FOR ASIAN AMERICAN WOMEN

Asian American women working in Asia are often faced with a double handicap. Not only are they women, but they also look Asian. As a result, it is easy for Asian businessmen to make cultural assumptions and have expectations based on traditional roles of Asian women. Many of the following tips should be observed by both men and women on overseas assignments, but they are especially critical for Asian American women.

Preparation Is Key

If you are going abroad in a decision-making capacity for any length of time, make sure it is clear to your Asian associates, even before you get there, who you are. You might consider having your résumé translated and presented in the appropriate résumé format for the country to which you are traveling. It might be helpful to include a photo on the résumé itself (which is acceptable in a number of Asian countries) so that your Asian associates get used to the idea that an Asian woman can also be an accomplished professional. Have business cards printed in English on one side and in the Asian language on the other. Be sure your title (e.g., vice president of finance) is translated correctly. Include any credentials after your name (e.g., CPA, MBA, JD). All these add to your credibility, and they will be studied in detail by your overseas colleagues.

If there are Western assistants or staff members already overseas, they can help by deferring to your authority. If you are going for a relatively short period with a group consisting of both men and women, make sure the group is aware of potential problems. For example, Asian colleagues might mistake the assistant, a male associate, for the decision maker (the assistant should defer all questions to the manager); the Asian associate might ask an American manager to make copies (managers should sit in the center of the room and assistants should sit close to the door) (Brannen & Wilen, 1993). Decision makers should discuss with staff how to avoid situations that undermine their authority and create situations in which someone could lose face.

Speaking the language is a big advantage. However, because translators tend to be women in Asian countries, be sure to establish that you are not a translator. Also, do not speak the language unless you can do so fluently.

When I am in Japan, I make a point of differentiating myself from Japanese women. My body language is more open; I introduce myself with a firm handshake; I animate my face and I gesture. I begin presentations in English. Most Japanese businesspeople have high levels of English comprehension. In typical Western fashion, I project my voice and I move around. After my presentation is finished, I solicit questions in either English or Japanese. By that time, I have made the point that I am not a Japanese woman, and I can also demonstrate my Japanese language ability.

SUMMARY OF KEY POINTS

Women will have an increasing presence as managers overseas as they enter the workforce in greater numbers. As the economy becomes more global, a successful overseas experience is becoming increasingly a prerequisite for career advancement.

Sensitivity to different cultures requires not only an understanding of different cultures but an understanding of how our own cultural background influences the way we perceive situations and behaviors. The cultural frameworks presented by Hofstede and by Trompenaars offer ways to understand our own culture relative to that of others. These frameworks help explain why there are different ways problems are solved across cultures.

Although women executives are not widely accepted in most other cultures, Western, and, in particular, American, women may have a unique advantage overseas. Visibility and the ability to use that visibility to enhance credibility is important.

For a variety of reasons, many of them invalid, firms are reluctant to send women on extended overseas assignments. For women to develop their international careers, they must express their willingness to go and be prepared both personally and professionally to relocate.

Discussion Questions

1. Are women likely to be accepted in managerial positions worldwide in the near future? Why or why not?
2. If you were an assistant to a woman executive, what steps would you take to ensure that your overseas associates understood her position of authority? Why is credibility so important for women going overseas?
3. If building relationships are an important part of business, what steps can you take to make sure positive relationships are formed? What should you avoid doing?
4. Is "staying out of the rat race" merely an excuse given by women who are not promoted to managerial positions, or is it a valid reason for staying in support positions?

Issue to Debate

If women are to change their status in the global business environment, it is up to Western women to advocate the presence of more local women in managerial positions.

Leadership in Cross-Cultural Meetings

The setting is a meeting of different cultures: American, German, Israeli. The American company (AmCo.) is hosting this meeting. Present are the heads and several staff members of a German company (GCo.), it's local U.S. subsidiary, and an Israeli Co. (IsCo.). GCo. is a major client of AmCo. and IsCo. is a supplier to GCo.

The room is filled with about 20 men including Hans (GCo.'s head of R&D), Tom (the American head of GCo.'s local subsidiary), and IsCo. representatives. There is one last presentation to go.

In walks Diane, the CEO of AmCo. She is very familiar with German culture and is fluent in German. She is confident of her presentation and it shows. She makes a point of greeting the heads of the three companies with a smile and a firm handshake.

As she sits down Hans turns and says in front of the group, "Diane, I have some bad news. I don't think we'll be renewing our contract with your firm." Diane realizes that this does not sound right. Within the first few months of their relationship, her firm had identified and negotiated a significant transfer of technology between a small start-up and GCo. All her instincts told her that GCo. would be foolish to discontinue their relationship.

Diane looked Hans straight in the eye for a full minute and then replied with a smile, "You know Hans, I always have a schnapps before meeting with a room full of men because I know I can't believe anything I hear." To this the whole room burst out laughing. Diane realized that this had been some sort of a test and that she had passed.

Diane's presentation went well as she had expected and she sat back down. Diane noticed that Tom was signaling to her indicating that she should leave. Diane knew that the meeting would be concluding shortly but also realized that if Hans had wanted her to leave, he would have apologized and politely told her that there was additional business that needed to be concluded. After all, Diane's firm had arranged this meeting, so why should she be "signaled" to leave?

Diane also perceived that the meeting was winding down. Diane ignored Tom's motions to her that she should leave and stayed put. She knew she understood more about German business culture than Tom and trusted her instincts. The meeting ended within 15 minutes as Diane had expected. She shook everyone's hand and left the meeting as an equal. ■

Questions

1. Identify at least three specific things that you think Diane did right at the meeting.
2. Do you think she should have left the meeting? Why? Why do you think she could be right in staying?

How would you have responded to the situation and why?
3. How should a woman who is an assistant, not a CEO, handle the situation? Should she handle it the same way or differently? Explain your answer.

References and Suggested Readings

Adler, N. (1987). Pacific Basin managers: A gaijin, not a woman. *Human Resource Management, 26,* 169–191.

Adler, N. J. (1991). *International dimensions of organizational behavior.* Boston: PWS-Kent.

Adler, N. (1994). Competitive frontiers: Women managing across borders. In N. J. Adler and D. N. Izraeli (Eds.), *Competitive frontiers: Women managers in a global economy* (pp. 22–40). Cambridge: Blackwell.

Brannen, C., and Wilen, T. (1993). *Doing business with Japanese men: A woman's handbook.* Berkeley: Stone Bridge Press.

Davidson, M. J., and Cooper, C. L. (Eds.). (1993). *European women in business and management.* London: Chapman.

Driscoll, D., and Goldberg, C. R. (1993). *Members of the club: The coming of age of executive women.* New York: Free Press.

Duggan, S. J. (1998, June 26). Interview. Silicon Valley World Internet Center. Palo Alto, CA.

Evans, P., Doz, Y., and Laurent A. (Eds.). (1989). *Human resource management in international firms: Change, globalization, innovation.* London: Macmillan.

Fagenson, E. A., and Jackson, J. J. (1994). *United States of America.* In N. J. Adler and D. N. Izraeli (Eds.), *Competitive frontiers: Women managers in a global economy* (pp. 388–404). Cambridge: Blackwell.

Hall, E. T. (1960). The silent language in overseas business. *Harvard Business Review, 38,* 87–96.

Hampden-Turner, C., and Trompenaars, F. (1993). *The seven cultures of capitalism.* New York: Double Day Currency.

Harris, P. R., and Moran, R. T. (1996). *Managing cultural differences* (4th ed.). Houston, TX: Gulf Publishing.

Hodgetts, R. M., and Luthans, F. (1997). *International management* (3rd ed.). New York: McGraw-Hill.

Hofstede, G. (1980). *Culture's consequences.* Beverly Hills, CA: Sage.

Karsten, M. F. (1994). *Management and gender.* Westport, CT: Quorum.

Kluckhohn, F. R., and Stodtbeck, F. L. (1961). *Variations in value orientations.* New York: Peterson.

Napier, N. K., and Von Glinow, M. A. (1995). *Western women working in Japan: Breaking corporate barriers.* Westport, CT: Quorum.

Poole, M., and Warner, M. (Eds.). (1998). *The IEBM handbook of human resource management.* London: International Thomson Business Press.

Ronen, S., and Shenkar, O. (1985). Clustering countries on attitudinal dimensions: A review and synthesis. *Academy of Management Review, 10,* 435–454.

Sedjénian, E. (1994). Women managers in France. In N. J. Adler and D. N. Izraeli (Eds.), *Competitive frontiers: Women managers in a global economy* (pp. 190–205). Cambridge: Blackwell.

Takahashi, P. K. (1985). *Japan— Implementation versus decision—An organic approach.* Tokyo: Sophia University Institute of Comparative Culture Business (Series No. 101).

Trompenaars, F. (1994). *Riding the waves of culture: Understanding cultural diversity in business.* Chicago: Irwin.

Tung, R. L. (1988). Career issues in international assignments. *Academy of Management Executive, 2,* 241–244.

Tung, R. L. (Ed.). 1999 (forthcoming). *The IEBM handbook of international business.* London: International Thomson Business Press.

Tung, R. L., and Anderson, A. (1997). *Exploring international assignees' viewpoints: A study of the expatriation/repatriation process.* Chicago: Arthur Anderson Inc.

Whitehill, A. M. (1991). *Japanese management: Tradition and transition.* London: Routledge.

Wilen, T., and Wilen, P. (1995). *Asia for women on business.* Berkeley: Stone Bridge Press.

Yamada, H. (1997). *Different games, different rules: Why Americans and Japanese misunderstand each other.* Oxford: Oxford University Press.

CHAPTER

11

The Entrepreneurial Alternative

Deborah Carr

I am sick of working for other people. I am sick of trying to climb up the corporate ladder. I am sick of doing all this work and getting no recognition and no pay. I want my own business. I don't know how I'm going to do it, but I'm going to do it.

—KATHY TAGGARES, PRESIDENT
K. T. Kitchens, Glendale, CA

Chapter Overview

Taggares is just one of millions of women who abandoned corporate jobs in the 1980s and 1990s to start their own businesses. Educated, ambitious, armed with managerial skills honed in the boardroom or on the shopfloor—and disenchanted with the corporate glass ceiling—these women view entrepreneurship as the pathway to profit, autonomy, and (for some) a family-friendly work schedule. Yet even Taggares would acknowledge that there are steep hurdles along the path to business ownership, including blocked access to start-up capital and government contracts. Why are women forming their own businesses at an unprecedented pace? What are the unique problems confronted by women who start their own businesses? What steps must all women (and men) take to ensure that their dreams of business ownership don't fail? This chapter address some of these issues.

Learning Objectives

■ To describe trends in women's self-employment during the past 25 years

■ To present the classical theories of entrepreneurship and business ownership

Research for this chapter was supported by a seed grant from the Institute for Research on Women and Gender, University of Michigan. Diligent research assistance was provided by Jennifer Malat and Stacey Waxtan. Direct correspondence can be sent to Deborah Carr, Department of Sociology, University of Michigan, 500 S. State St., Ann Arbor, MI 48103-1382, or carrds@umich.edu.

■ To contrast the profiles of "traditional" and "second generation" woman business owners

■ To explore the reasons women start their own businesses

■ To understand the gender gap in the earnings of self-employed women and men

■ To identify the unique problems faced by women entrepreneurs

■ To uncover the five crucial steps for forming a successful business

TRENDS IN SELF-EMPLOYMENT

A minor revolution has occurred in the labor force during the past 25 years. Women are forming their own businesses in record numbers. As recently as 1970, women owned only about 5 percent of all businesses in the United States. In 1996, women owned more than one-third (36 percent) of all businesses. This seemingly meteoric rise has actually occurred very steadily and gradually. The number of woman-owned, nonfarm, sole proprietorships has increased from 702,000 in 1977, to 4.4 million in 1987, to 6.4 million in 1992. By 1996, women owned more than 8 million businesses in the United States, generating $2.3 trillion in revenue in 1996 (U.S. Small Business Administration [SBA], 1988; 1998). The share of women and men who formed their own business during this period has also increased markedly. As Figure 11-1 shows, the proportion of American men who are self-employed rose from 10 percent in 1975 to nearly 13 percent in 1990. While only 4 percent of women worked for themselves in 1975, nearly 7 percent owned their own businesses in 1990.

Women's movement into business ownership has important ramifications for the U.S. economy. Female-owned businesses currently employ about 18.5 million people, or roughly one out of every four company workers in the United States. Business start-ups also play a role in the creation of technical advances and economic innovations, and they often lead the way in terms of research and development of new products. As a recent report of the House Small Business Committee concluded, "women-owned businesses may well provide the cutting edge—and the American advantage—in the worldwide economic competitiveness fast upon us. The loss to the Nation would be incalculable were public policy-makers not to foster this development to the fullest extent possible (Committee on Small Business [CSB,] 1988, p. iii). Policy makers are heeding this call. As we discuss later in this chapter, the U.S. government has implemented programs to increase women's access both to start-up capital and to lucrative government contracts.

But the growth of women's entrepreneurship may also impact the American economy in more subtle ways. Corporations may be forced to become more woman-friendly in response to an exodus of their top female executives who seek self-employment. According to Heidi Miller, chief financial officer of Travelers Group, a part of Salomon Smith Barney, "It is vitally important that large companies understand why women may consider entrepreneurship over corporate careers in order to create an environment within corporate America that is responsive to their needs."

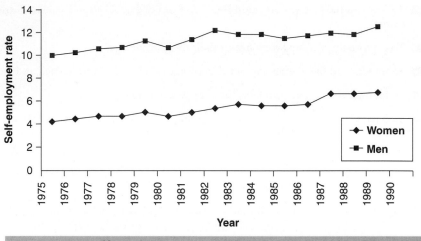

FIGURE 11-1 Self-Employment Rates in the U.S. Non-Agricultural Sector by Sex, 1975–90

Source: Devine, Theresa (1994). Characteristics of self-employed women in the United States. *Monthly Labor Review* (March), 20–34.

WHO BECOMES AN ENTREPRENEUR?

In 1990, 11 percent of all American men and 6 percent of women were self-employed (Devine, 1994). But who exactly becomes an entrepreneur? Do entrepreneurs have unique personality traits, or are they simply responding to economic and social-structural forces? Two classical theories of entrepreneurship provide a framework for examining the characteristics of the self-employed. On one hand, the self-employed can be seen as persons with particular abilities, and self-knowledge of these abilities motivates them to establish their own enterprises (Knight, 1933). This "career" theory would predict that persons with more education, those with specific skills, or those who were socialized by their parents to become entrepreneurs would be most likely to form their own businesses. On the other hand, the contrasting perspective regards self-employment as a "default" option for those facing constraints and frustrations in traditional wage and salary employment. In this view, business ownership is viewed as a potential escape route for frustrated employees.

Neither the "career" nor the "default" theories of entrepreneurship provides us with a thorough understanding of women's experiences, however. First, the theories were developed to explain men's—not women's—labor force behavior. Second, neither theory considers that self-employment decisions might reflect combinations of constraints and unique abilities. For instance, Carr (1996) has shown that women with young children who face the obstacle of blending work and family duties are more likely than other women to be self-employed, yet these women also have particular skills to sell, and often have high levels of educational attainment. Thus, rather than classifying correlates of self-employment as competing "push" and "pull" indicators, the following discussion will focus on factors that impact the diverse pathways to entrepreneurship.

TABLE 11.1 Traditional versus Modern Women Entrepreneurs

	Traditional *1945–1970*	*Modern* *1970–Present*
Orientation	Home and family	Career
Work	Income supplement	Incubator effect
Entry	Segregation in service and retail sector	Male-dominated business and new ventures
Financing	Personal sources	External capital
Credit	Discrimination	Equal Credit Opportunity Act, women's banks
Education	Liberal arts	Technical and business administration, with corporate experience
Type of ownership	Proprietorship, low income	Corporate growth, high income

Source: Moore 1990

Personal Characteristics

Who is the typical woman entrepreneur? At first glance, a statistical portrait shows that she is age 30 to 45, white, has at least 1 year of college, and is married with children. She typically works in a managerial or administrative position (Devine, 1994). She is also likely to be the first-born, college-educated daughter of a self-employed father and has typically gained experience with a large organization. In terms of personality, motivation for starting a business, and personal values, however, she is not much different from the "typical" male entrepreneur (Buttner, 1993). As we delve further into the question "who are the female entrepreneurs?" we will see that there is no simple answer to that question.

Two Types of Women Entrepreneurs?

The traditional theories of entrepreneurship (Schumpeter, 1934; Knight, 1933) are limited in that they focus solely on men, and they neglect the fact that women's roles and opportunities have undergone a major transition in the past three decades. Consequently, rather than talking about a monolithic category of "women entrepreneurs," we may be better served to think of different categories of women-business owners.

Recent scholars argue that there are two types of women entrepreneurs: the "traditionals" and the "second generation" or "moderns" (Gregg, 1985) (See Table 11.1.). These two groups of women not only differ in terms of their human capital characteristics (such as formal education and work experience) but also in terms of the types of businesses they own and their motivations for becoming self-employed. The typical traditional entrepreneur was most likely a woman with a liberal arts background (Stevenson, 1986), and she was unlikely to be guided to start a business in male-dominated industries (Bowen and Hirsch, 1986). She lacked experience with finance, marketing, and routine business operations, and, consequently, faced major problems in obtaining loans (Hirsch and O'Brien, 1981). Her background, domestic orientation, and limited access to capital led her into sole proprietor service businesses that tended to have low income and low equity and to be small and slow growing (U.S. Department of Commerce, Bureau of the Census, 1986).

The new breed of women entrepreneurs who formed their own businesses in the 1970s and beyond are referred to as the "second generation" (Gregg, 1985). Many were women who had left corporations to be their own bosses, to exercise their educational and technical skills, and to earn more money than they had been earning at their corporate jobs (Fried, 1989).

The two groups of women also specialize in different types of occupations. The second-generation entrepreneurs are substantially more likely to work in traditionally male areas such as finance, insurance, manufacturing, and construction. While access to capital is a hurdle for both groups of women, the second-generation women value advanced counseling in communication skills, training programs, and new business opportunities. Moderns heading corporations—more so than the traditional sole proprietors—seek assistance in sophisticated business areas of short- and long-term planning, planning for cash flow, networking, and identifying and expanding into new markets (Moore, 1990).

The prior experiences of these two types of women also differ. The second-generation women had experience in the workplace exercising control and authority. They came to entrepreneurship with more exposure to the business world, were better prepared with technical and planning skills and network contacts, and were more oriented toward making money and creating new markets (Moore, 1990). They averaged 10 to 12 years of experience before starting their businesses and had used their previous corporate and organizational environments as "incubators" (Murphy, 1992).

WHY WOMEN FORM BUSINESSES

What reasons do women entrepreneurs, themselves, give for forming their own businesses? This question was recently addressed in the report from the National Foundation for Women Business Owners (NFWBO),[1] *Paths to Entrepreneurship: New Directions for Women in Business* (NFWBO, 1998), which presents findings from a recent survey conducted by Catalyst, a research organization concerned with gender and work issues; the NFWBO, and The Committee of 200, an organization of businesswomen.

The study sought to uncover why the number of women-owned businesses in the United States has skyrocketed in the past three decades. Interestingly, for both men and women, the most frequently cited reason for forming one's own business reflected personal desires: The majority of male and female business owners said they wanted to pursue their own interests and fulfill their entrepreneurial desires. But women also frequently reported their desire to adapt to barriers in the workplace—particularly those imposed by family constraints, and by sexism and mobility obstacles in their former places of employment. Women's motivations also varied based on their years of experience as business owners (see Figure 11-2).

---

[1]NFWBO is a nonprofit research and leadership foundation affiliated with the National Association of Women Business Owners (NAWBO). NFWBO supports the growth of women business owners and their organizations through gathering and sharing knowledge. The survey was sponsored by Salomon Smith Barney, and is based on a nationally representative survey of 800 women and men business owners. The sampling frame for the survey was the 1994 membership survey of the NAWBO. To ensure adequate representation of larger firms and women-owned firms, the survey was stratified by employment size and gender.

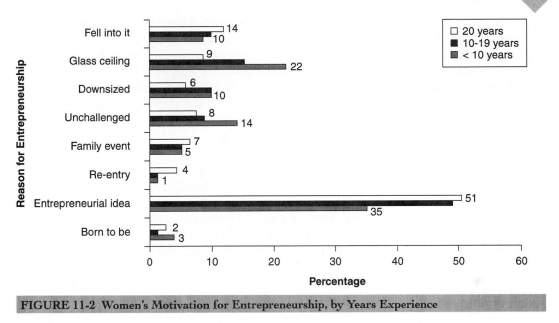

FIGURE 11-2 Women's Motivation for Entrepreneurship, by Years Experience

(Source: 1998 Catalyst/NFWBO Survey)

Blending Work and Family

Numerous sociological studies document that women's work lives are much more in-tertwined with their family lives than are men's. Women are more likely than men to have domestic responsibilities and either interrupt their careers or choose flexible or part-time work options to accommodate these family duties (Presser and Baldwin, 1980) (see also chapter 9).

The need for flexibility was cited by more than half of the female business owners as a major reason for leaving corporate positions, according to the survey by Catalyst and NFWBO. Interviews with women entrepreneurs invariably reveal that flexibility includes spending time with children as well as pursuing a lucrative and challenging ca-reer. A participant in focus groups interviewed by Moore and Buttner (1997) recalls "I was an account and marketing executive, burned out and pregnant. I said 'This is the time to leave,' and so I did. My reason for leaving was primarily to get some balance in my own life and to regroup. I found that the transition at this key time from the cor-porate environment to owning my own business provided the opportunity to balance taking care of my children, spending it with my family, with working and providing flexible hours."

Does self-employment really enable women to have it all? It depends on how one de-fines "having it all." Recent research has shown that 71 percent of all women business own-ers are married, compared to just 60 percent of all women managers, and 52 percent of all high-level women executives who do not work for themselves (Fagenson and Jackson, 1994). Some argue that women entrepreneurs are particularly sensitive to their employees' needs to balance work and family matters, and, in turn, are more likely to adopt policies that are family friendly, including on-site child care and flexible work schedules (Fagenson and Jackson, 1994). Data from the NFWBO (1997) confirms this.

Their survey documents that 54 percent of women-owned firms with 10 or more employees offer flextime or job-sharing arrangements as an employee benefit; only 33 percent of men-owned firms do the same. For example, Cheryl Womack, CEO of VCW, Inc., a Kansas City-based insurance business, provides her employees with an on-site day care center. Says Womack, "[it] was a smart business decision and has paid for itself many times over, by reduced absenteeism, better morale and peace of mind. I am walking, talking proof that a small business just cannot afford *not* to provide this benefit" (U.S. SBA, 1998, p. 14).

Breaking Away from the Glass Ceiling

Women also reported that they formed their own business as a way to circumvent the glass ceiling and other obstacles in the workplace. However, the proportion who felt this way varied widely, based on the number of years of experience a woman had running her own business. More than one-fifth (22 percent) of women in newer companies, or second-generation entrepreneurs, reported that they had hit a barrier, whereas just 4 percent of women in companies more than 10 years old (i.e., traditionalists) cited the glass ceiling problem.

Of those who indicated that the glass ceiling was the primary motivation for starting their own businesses, 44 percent said they felt their contributions were not valued or recognized in the corporation. One-third said they agreed with the statement "you were not taken seriously by your employer or supervisor." In the words of Diahann Lassus: "There didn't seem to be a lot of opportunity for moving up. I felt like the opportunities weren't there anymore." Lassus started her own financial planning firm in New Providence, NJ, after quitting a corporate management position.

Similar views were aired by Merrill Thompson-Hinton, who left her position as special service representative for American Airlines, and formed her own travel agency. In an interview with *Black Enterprise* magazine, Thompson-Hinton recalled witnessing countless incidents where experienced black sales representatives with seniority were passed over for promotions in favor of much younger white sales representatives. She became increasingly frustrated by the slow track she was on and realized that she had little chance of climbing the corporate ladder. "I was making good money, but I knew I wasn't getting the key to the corporate washroom." After 10 years with American Airlines, she invested $90,000 of her own money to form her own travel agency.

CLEARING THE HURDLES OF BUSINESS OWNERSHIP

Women start their own businesses as a step to achieving their goals of economic prosperity, personal challenge, and balance in life. Yet running one's own business is seldom a utopian experience. Female business owners face myriad social and economic hurdles including limited access to professionally relevant social networks, average annual earnings that are substantially lower than their male counterparts, and challenges in obtaining access to capital and government contracts.

Networking

Networking is an integral part of forming and growing a successful business. A personal network consists of all those persons with whom an entrepreneur has a relationship. For entrepreneurs, we can think of business partners, suppliers, customers, venture capitalists, bankers, other creditors, distributors, trade associations, and family members as members of a social network (Aldrich, Reese, and Dubini, 1989). Typically, these are the people entrepreneurs meet face-to-face and from whom they obtain services, information, advice, resources, and moral support. These ties are important not only for the persons directly linked to the entrepreneur, but also because they provide indirect access to people beyond the entrepreneur's immediate contacts (Aldrich and Reese, 1994).

But women entrepreneurs often feel that they are shut out of some important and potentially lucrative business networks. Sociological studies show that the social networks of men and women differ and that these differences are disadvantageous to women both in terms of starting a business and in maintaining profitability. Feminist sociologist Jessie Bernard (1981) has observed that women inhabit a "female world" that only partially overlaps with the "male world." In many important regions of social life, divisions and barriers limit the reach and diversity of women's networks. Because men have historically occupied the central economic positions in society, the networks to which men and women have access and in which they participate are "separate but unequal." Roos and Reskin (1984) argue that because women have traditionally been concentrated in low-level sales and service jobs, they share job information with friends looking for work, thus channeling them into similar jobs.

Professional organizations are an important starting point for women who seek networks and mentors. In 1990 the Small Business Administration launched their Women's Network for Entrepreneurial Training (WNET) program. The program aims to match successful women business owners with newer women business owners to share their experiences and expand their social networks. Other organizations such as NAWBO, the National Association of Female Executives (NAFE), and Business and Professional Women (BPW), as well as industry-specific organizations such as the Association for Real Estate Women (AREW), Association of Professional Insurance Women (APIW), or Association of Women Industrial Designers (AWID) may also provide important resources for women hoping to start their own firms.

Gender Gap in Self-Employment Earnings

One of the most frequently documented findings in the study of entrepreneurship is that women business owners earn substantially less than their male peers, and that this gender gap in earnings is even more pronounced than the discrepancy between male and female wage and salary workers (Devine, 1994). In 1980, the average business receipts of women's sole proprietorships was only 27 percent of the average for men's sole proprietorships. By 1982, receipts generated by women's sole proprietorships represented 35 percent of similar men's receipts (U.S. SBA, 1988). Although women's share of total business receipts has been increasing from year to year, "overall the sales of a typical woman-owned business have not changed drastically" (U.S. SBA, 1988, p. 43). In 1990, for example, a self-employed woman who worked full time had an average annual income of $12,174, compared to $26,087 for a male counterpart. Thus, despite the health of the small-business sector, ownership does not currently provide women with levels of economic success that are comparable to men's.

The gender gap is generally explained by three factors: (1) Women-owned businesses are often smaller than men's because of women's relative lack of managerial experience and access to capital; (2) women business owners are clustered in low-paying, female-dominated industries; and (3) women work fewer hours per week and have fewer years of work experience largely because of their efforts to blend work with family.

Firm Characteristics: Size and Industry

The businesses traditionally owned by women have characteristics that bode poorly for their proprietors' earnings. Women's businesses tend to be smaller than men's, and the majority are concentrated female-dominated industries, such as retail trade and services, where assets and annual earnings are much lower than in male-dominated industries, such as construction or manufacturing (Starr and Yudkin, 1996; U.S. Department of Commerce, 1996).

Firm size is one of the single greatest predictors of income among small-business owners (Aldrich and Weiss, 1981; U.S. SBA, 1984). Liabilities of newness place very young firms at a distinct disadvantage because they lack both an established client or customer base and proven organizational structures (Stinchecombe, 1965). Women's earnings are also lower because they are clustered in women-dominated industries, which are traditionally associated with lower earnings. Sociologists frequently point to gender segregation as an important explanation for women's earnings disadvantage—both among the self-employed and among salaried workers. Across a broad spectrum of industries and occupations, women are segregated into the low-paid, low-prestige positions that men often do not want (Reskin, 1988). This phenomenon may be particularly acute among the self-employed. Research on business ownership emphasizes the strong link between employment field and small-business type; that is, people start businesses in industries that they know. Women, drawing on their experiences in both paid and unpaid "female work," may choose small businesses that draw on female-type skills, and the services and products they offer may be devalued as female-type occupations (Roos and Reskin, 1984).

A related issue is that the early generations of women entrepreneurs lacked access to managerial experience and subsequently either clustered into female-dominated industries or had small and not particularly successful businesses. A landmark study of entrepreneurship concluded that about 90 percent of business failures are because of lack of managerial skill and experience (Dun and Bradstreet, 1967). Because women traditionally are relegated to occupational positions with low-skill and -authority levels (Reskin, 1988), they are likely to bring to ownership fewer business-specific skills than men are (Hirsch and Brush, 1984).

Several studies of women entrepreneurs reveal that women realize that their own lack of adequate financial and managerial skills is a major barrier to their success as business owners (President's Interagency Task Force on Women Business Owners, 1978). Women report frustration with their lack of previous business experience; in particular they feel their marketing deficiencies might be an impediment to success. Given that women have traditionally been underrepresented in managerial positions, they may lack financial expertise in such areas as controlling expenses, cash-flow planning, and forecasting, and raising capital (Humphreys and McClung, 1981). Such skill deficits are particularly problematic during the start-up of a new business. Lack of managerial skill does not stem from a lack of formal education. It results, at least partially, from an educational and occupational system that has traditionally segregated women in nontechnical, nonmanagerial jobs.

The encouraging news is that as women form businesses across a more diverse range of industries, they may eventually achieve earnings equity. Holmquist (1996) has argued that gender differences in the profitability and success of businesses are limited primarily to women's choice of industries in which to operate. In a study of Swedish entrepreneurs, Holmquist (1996) found substantial gender differences in business owners earnings *overall,* but when analyses were limited to specific industries, differences between men and women all but disappeared.

Trading Work Time for Family Time: The Role of Compensating Differentials

According to economic theory, discrimination or sex segregation is seldom invoked as explanations for women's earnings disadvantage. An alternative explanation set forth by economists is the theory of "compensating differentials" (Filer, 1985). According to this theory, individuals are willing to accept lower earnings if they feel they are also receiving positive job attributes. Filer (1985) observes that "men [may] . . . attach more importance to pecuniary rewards (wages and fringe benefits) while women value interpersonal and other nonwage aspects of the job more highly" (p. 427). Thus, women may be willing to accept lower earnings in exchange for agreeable job conditions such as autonomy, creativity, and (perhaps most importantly) a work environment that allows her to balance her work and family responsibilities.

Does "compensating differentials" theory really explain entrepreneurial women's lower earnings? Are women *choosing* to swap profit for job flexibility? There is evidence that women are less concerned than men with material gain. Beutel and Marini (1995) found that between 1977 and 1991 young women were consistently less concerned than young men with materialistic success and much more concerned with finding meaning and purpose in life. However, other studies demonstrate that the majority of women who work part time are not choosing to do so; many would prefer to work full time, yet child care responsibilities prohibit them from doing so (Mason and Kuhlthau, 1992). As more low-cost child care becomes available, and as more husbands participate in domestic duties, perhaps the gender gap in earnings of the self-employed will attenuate.

Despite the current gender gap in business profits, the prognosis for female entrepreneurs' future earnings is quite encouraging. The positive harbingers? Government programs are now in place to ease women's access to capital and lucrative government contracts. Newer generations of women entrepreneurs are slowly leaving the low-paying niches of service and retail businesses (occupied by traditionalists) for more profitable, typically male-dominated industries.

Access to Capital

In May 1996, the first National Women's Economic Summit was run by the National Women's Business Council and Northwestern University's J.L. Kellogg Graduate School of Management. More than 400 women business owners and leaders of government, business, and academia attended the summit. At the close of the two-day session, participants voted on the issues they considered of paramount importance to entrepreneurial women. The consensus was that lack of access to capital was the greatest challenge facing women small-business owners (Lesonsky, 1996). Because banks are reluctant to make loans to small businesses, most entrepreneurs—particularly women clustered in the low-paying sales and service industries—are forced to rely on personal savings and loans from family and friends (Shapero, 1983). The 1993 National Survey of Small Business Finances, conducted by the Federal Reserve, found that 42 percent of all women-owned firms use personal credit cards for short-term financing and 30 percent finance growth through their own savings (U.S. SBA, 1998).

Yet the irony of this pattern is that women have particularly strong records of credit-worthiness and stability. A recent report by the NFWBO and Dun and Bradstreet showed that women-owned firms are actually at a *lower* risk of loan delinquency than firms in general. They are also more likely to endure: Nearly 75 percent of women-owned firms in business in 1991 were still in business three years later—compared to just 67 percent of U.S. firms overall (U.S. SBA, 1998). Then why is access to capital such a stumbling block for women entrepreneurs? And how does access to capital impact women's entrepreneurial experiences?

Women's blocked access to capital has traditionally limited the kinds of businesses that they can open, and this explains, in part, their concentration in the relatively low-paying industries, such as retail trade and personal services, where less start-up capital is needed (Goffee and Scase, 1985). Moreover, women often find that even after they have managed to maintain a successful business, they have difficulty obtaining expansion or investment capital. Their concentration in the service sector proves detrimental: Banks typically lend on the basis of hard assets, such as plants, significant accounts receivable, inventory, or equipment—of which service businesses have few—rather than cash flow. Even women who work in nontraditional industries with higher gross receipts than their counterparts in service and retail industries report difficulty in finding external sources of funding (Hirsch and O'Brien, 1981).

Anecdotal evidence reveals that some lenders believe business ownership is not "socially appropriate" for women, which represents an added obstacle. In testimony before the Banking Subcommittee on Consumer Affairs, a well-established architect reported that she was told that the bank from which she sought funds did not make loans to women. The loan officer told the architect that if she tried to challenge the decision she would find herself completely blocked out from the credit market (CSB, 1988).

Access to capital varies widely by the type of capital sought. To date, venture capital is still the most difficult to obtain: About 1 percent of venture capital each year goes to women. Venture capital firms prefer to fund companies with a strong record; they do not usually invest in new businesses, nor do they fund extensively. For instance, Patricof & Co. Ventures of New York receives roughly 2,000 proposals a year, and of those, it completes 10 business deals (Hiam, 1996). Moreover, many venture capitalists have strong preferences for the types of companies they fund. For instance, New Era Capital Partners invests in information technology and health care. As a rule, venture capital firms want to invest more than a million dollars in companies from which they expect to receive a 30 percent return in 3 to 5 years. This is in sharp contrast with the economic portrait of a "typical" woman-owned business. A study by the Federal Reserve found that 42 percent of women-owned businesses surveyed had assets of less than $25,000, and approximately 1 in 5 had annual sales of less than $25,000 (U.S. SBA, 1998).

Tremendous strides have been made in recent years so that small business owners have access to a greater pool of assets. The Women's Business Ownership Act of 1988 includes a provision to make available to service businesses "mini-loans" (generally defined as $50,000 or less), which are guaranteed by the Small Business Administration. Although these small loans are not earmarked for women per se, they are particularly beneficial to women, many of whom own service firms (requiring only small loans but with few assets as collateral). The 1988 act also amends The Equal Credit Opportunity Act of 1974 to eliminate the exemption for commercial loans. Prior to 1988, the 1974 Act had been broadly but incorrectly interpreted as not applying to business credit (CSB, 1988). Consequently, creditors could use a woman's marital status to determine her loan eligibility (CSB, 1988). Today, banks are no longer permitted to ask the marital status of loan applicants. They must also inform applicants that they have the right to obtain written explanations of the reasons for denial of credit (Nelton, 1989).

Another giant step came with the establishment of the SBA's Women's Prequalification Pilot Loan Program, which helps women looking for loans of less than $250,000 complete their loan applications and presents their bankers with an SBA guarantee of the loan. To be eligible, the business must be at least 51 percent owned, operated, and managed by women; it must have average annual sales for the preceding 3 years that do not exceed $5 million; and, it must employ fewer than 100 people. Since its introduction in June 1994 from 16 pilot sites, the program has helped 574 women receive federally guaranteed loans totaling nearly $59 million. In October 1996, President Clinton expanded the pilot program on a countrywide basis, giving every SBA district director the option of offering the program (Chun, 1997). Clinton proclaimed "I am launching a bold federal initiative to promote the role of women business owners nationwide. Business owned by women constitute one of the fastest growing sectors of the economy. Federal agencies should be committed to the advancement of economic opportunities for women" (U.S. SBA, 1998).

In just two years following the implementation of the 1994 program, the number and value of SBA loans administered to women has skyrocketed. In 1995, one-quarter (more than 13,000) of all SBA loans were made to women, marking an 87 percent increase over SBA's 1994 lending record. The total dollar amount of SBA loans made to women in 1995 topped $1.4 billion.

Access to Contracts

Women business owners have also reported gender inequity in terms of access to government contracts. The U.S. federal government is perhaps the largest business client in the world; it spends nearly $200 billion each year buying goods and services from janitorial functions to jet aircraft. Thus, exactly how the government allocates its purchases has a powerful impact on business owners' success (CSB, 1988). Not surprisingly, small firms receiving government contracts are more likely to grow, enabling them to take advantage of nonfederal market opportunities. Although women business owners have made tremendous strides in gaining federal business over the past decade, their total award values continue to be a very small percentage of the total. Some attribute this to the fact that the Department of Defense (DOD), which is the biggest government spender, contracts to industries in which women are underrepresented. Other studies show that roughly one-third of the DOD's procurement budget is spent exactly on the products and services that women provide, such as the production of uniforms and food service production.

The U.S. government is attempting to increase opportunities for women entrepreneurs to win federal contacts—although progress toward this goal has been slow. In 1994, women-owned small business received 2.8 percent of all federal procurement dollars—a 27 percent increase from the minuscule 2.2 percent they received in 1992.

The Department of Transportation awarded 6.8 percent of its subcontracts to women-owned businesses in 1994—the highest of any federal department. Even within the DOD, strides are being made. The Air Force introduced its "Rule of One" in the mid-1990s. According to this program, at least one woman-owned business must be solicited on all competitive procurements (CSB, 1988).

GETTING STARTED: WHAT WOMEN ENTREPRENEURS MUST KNOW

Business owners agree that starting one's own firm is hard work, but that the path to profitability is made easier by following a set of important guidelines. The following five tips, culled from Small Business Administration (1998; 1996) newsletters, entrepreneurs' handbooks (Naftali, 1997; Stolze, 1989; Maul and Mayfield, 1990), and interviews with business leaders themselves (Enkelis and Olsen, 1995) provide a guide for entrepreneur hopefuls.

1. ***Be emotionally and intellectually prepared.*** Prepare yourself emotionally for the level of work required, and the possibility of failure. According to the Small Business Administration, roughly 24 out of 100 new businesses close within their first 2 years. An additional 27 will fail within 4 years, and more than 60 will fail within 6 years (Hiam 1996). Yet new business owners must also be intellectually prepared; they must know about their business inside and out. The first piece of cautionary advice the Small Business Administration gives to aspiring entrepreneurs is, "You need more than a good idea." Entrepreneurs need a carefully thought-out strategy for turning their ideas into marketable products or services.

    "The most important thing in any business is to understand the business you're in," echoed Dorothy Brunson, president and CEO of Philadelphia-based Brunson Communication. As of 1995, Brunson was the only black woman in the United States to own a television station. She knows the importance of preparation, "You have to know what it takes to get your product into the marketplace. You also have to be very clear about who is going to buy that product and why. It sounds so simple, but it's amazing how many people don't understand this" (Brown, 1996, pp. 63–64).

2. ***Know your networks.*** Social networks are an invaluable tool in starting a business. New entrepreneurs should develop a list of all possible friends, allies, and business associates—both past and present. The first step is to determine who the contacts are who can help you to reach your goal. Make a list both of people you know and those who you would like to meet who could help you. This list should include professional associates, community leaders, friends, and even family. Next, determine what your contacts bring to the table. Evaluate your contacts and determine how much influence and interest they may have in helping you and your business. Once you ascertain this type of information, you can network more selectively and efficiently.

    Assembling a team of business partners with the right mix of skills is often facilitated by social networks. This was the case for Ruth Markowitz Owades, founder and president of Calyx & Corolla, a $15 million flowers-by-direct-mail company. When she started selecting products and creating a catalog for a new product line, she tapped the expertise of a former colleague who previously worked in systems operations at a mail-order business, and another former colleague who had past experience as the president of a premier catalog photo studio. By tapping her social networks, Owades was able to recruit experts in marketing and daily operations for her company (Enkelis and Olsen, 1995).

3. ***Conduct market research.*** As the SBA noted, it takes more than a "great idea" to make a great business. Rather, as a new entrepreneur, you must do market research on your product, your niche, your potential clientele, and your potential competitors. You can use either primary or secondary data in your research. Primary data is information that you obtain on your own through strategies such as making phone calls, or seeking out information about your competitors' pricing, packaging, and promotion and marketing tactics. Secondary data can also be useful, and typically include reports at libraries or analyses of U.S. Census or other survey data.

Conducting solid market research is crucial even for firms that are established. K. T. Kitchens' CEO Kathy Taggares learned the hard way when she tried to develop a new product line without doing any market research. The endeavor, she admits, was a resounding failure. She had decided to create a low-fat salad dressing in response to request letters from customers. She began without conducting taste tests or market research. "A million dollars later the product was dead. I never bothered to find out that when people are on diets, they can't relate to the idea of dipping into thick creamy dressings. To be honest, the stuff tasted terrible too. Next time I try to do a new product, I'll do it right," recalls Taggares (Enkelis and Olsen, 1995, p. 35).

4. ***Determine the legal structure of your business.*** Before starting a business, you must determine the legal structure of your initiative. After a legal structure is established, it must be periodically reexamined and analyzed to ensure the company's viability as it grows. Structure might be altered for a variety of reasons, such as the need to raise additional capital for business expansions or an increase in risk due to additional dealings with creditors, suppliers, or consumers (Sherman, 1997). The primary options include the following:

Sole Proprietorship
The sole proprietorship is the simplest business structure. An individual owns and operates the business, and, as sole proprietor, is taxed as an individual. Thus, the proprietor is liable for business debts and obtains loans based on his or her personal credit.

General Partnership
In a general partnership, an individual owns his/her own business with one or more partners, each of whom is involved in running the business. Each party should know exactly what is expected of them, and duties should be written down. Unless there is an agreement stating otherwise, each partner is liable for any and all business debts.

Limited Partnerships
A limited partnership has managing and limited partners. The managing partner(s) has full control and liability. The limited partner(s) has no day-to-day control of the business, and their personal liability is limited to the amount of their investment in the partnership.

Corporations
Unlike a sole proprietorship or partnership, the corporation is a separate legal entity. If an individual dies, the corporation still lives on. The main reason a person would incorporate is that in most cases, they would have only limited liability for debts or lawsuits against the corporation.

5. ***Develop a Business Plan*** The most difficult, yet crucial, step in forming a business is the development of a business plan (see box 11.1 and 11.2 for business plan development

---

BOX 11.1

What Do Investors Want to Know?

Business Plans attempt to answer seven key questions for potential investors:

- What is the key information that an investor needs to know about your business proposal?

- What products or services will the proposed business produce or provide?

- How will the business market these products and services?

- How will the business be organized and managed?

- What does the financial picture look like currently and in the future?

- What do you want from the potential investor?

———

Source: Adapted from Arthur Bell and Dayle Smith's *Management Communication* (New York: John Wiley & Sons, 1999).

---

hints). The best business plan is not necessarily the longest and most detailed plan. Sophisticated investors often do not have time to review hundreds of pages of text. The plan should be concise and well written, and it should focus on the lender's or investor's principal areas of concern. Overly technical descriptions of the company's products or operations might not be effective. Investors will commit funds on the basis of the quality and clarity of the document—not its bulk.

In one crucial area, however, detail is important: Any budgets, sales projections, company valuations, or related forecasts should be well substantiated with accompanying footnotes, for both legal and business reasons. Unrealistic or unsubstantiated financial projections and budgets reveal to an interested investor inexperience or lack of attention to detail. A realistic approach is also desirable. An honest discussion of the company's problems, along with a reasonable plan for dealing with risks and challenges will have a positive impact on a prospective investor. Investors will feel more comfortable investing in someone who has learned from previous business failures, rather than one who has never managed a company.

Finally, the business plan should emphasize both concept and personnel. "Any experienced venture capitalist will tell you that ultimately they would prefer to invest in a company that has great people and only a good concept, rather than a great concept and a weak management team. Ultimately, the lenders and investors commit funds on the basis of the strength of the management team" (Sherman, 1997, p. 103).

For Kavelle Bajaj, president of I-Net, the computer networking and systems integration firm located in Bethesda, Maryland, the business plan is critical to the success of her multimillion dollar company. "The business plan is your blueprint. It tells you where you are going. . . . Doing your business plan makes you consider all aspects of your business in best-case, worst-case situations so that when things happen, you are prepared for them."

Bajaj acknowledges that the business plan should not be cast in stone. Rather it should be a "living document. . . . We formally revise our business plan once a year, but in practice we do it quarterly. In our quarterly reviews we find out which areas are growing and which are not, which are sucking out more money than they should, and which may be performing better than we expected" (Enkelis and Olsen, 1995, p. 120).

BOX 11.2

Developing a Business Plan

An effective business plan addresses a number of important issues. Specifically, most business plans are divided into sections or categories that provide the potential investor with the necessary information for making investment decisions. Critical sections of the business plan include the following:

1. Executive Summary

    Introduce your business concept, describing the product or service and its market potential. Include a short description of the company and brief analysis of the competition. A summary of financial projections also piques the interest of potential investors.

2. Products and/or Service

    The business concept gets developed here with a full background and justification for your business idea. Describe the nature of the venture and differentiate what you will do from the competition.

3. Market Analysis

    Analyze the competition in this section. Demonstrate your understanding of the market, discussing the strengths and weaknesses of your competitors. Be specific about client and/or customer demand in the marketplace.

4. Market Entry and Growth Strategies

    Outline your approach for entering the market and gaining market share. Discuss pricing strategy, ways of servicing the market, and advertising plans. Tell how you will reach your customers and convince them to buy. Sales projections can be helpful as well.

5. Operations

    Describe facilities and equipment and any information related to research and development, manufacturing process or service activity. An introduction to how the business runs day-to-day may be included.

6. Schedule and Timetable

    Address how and when the business will develop from start-up to ongoing operations. Include a time line to incorporate design and development targets, if appropriate.

    (continued)

Despite the obstacles and challenges facing women entrepreneurs, few would have it any other way. According to the NFWBO/Catalyst survey, only one-quarter of the women said that "high pay" could lure them back to corporate life; a full 58 percent said that "nothing" could entice them to reenter the corporate culture. The opportunities to pursue personal interests, create a unique work environment, face potentially unlimited growth and advancement, blend work and family obligations, and to "be the boss" apparently outweigh the risks for America's eight million women entrepreneurs.

SUMMARY OF KEY POINTS

The number of women business owners has increased dramatically in the past three decades. Women-owned businesses numbered 702,000 in 1977, and topped 8 million in 1996.

BOX 11.2

Developing a Business Plan—*Continued*

7. Financial Information

   Provide the budget for start-up and beginning operations. Projections regarding income, expense and cash flow for a 3–7 year time span should be included. Describe initial capital outlays and how start-up capital will be used.

8. Cost/Benefit Analysis

   Discuss the strengths and weaknesses of your business concept. Be honest when describing the pros and cons. Provide an analysis of how you will address potential problems or barriers and capitalize on opportunity.

9. Management and Organization Structure

   Describe the way the company will be structured and managed. Include an organizational chart if appropriate. Introduce the management of the company by providing brief biographies *(bios)* for each of the key officers or managers. These bios should demonstrate the needed expertise, complementary business skills and overall *know-how* for leading and running the business. Show a strong team of personnel involved in the business.

10. Other Information

   Provide any other information that may be important for an investor to know that is not covered in the earlier sections. Exit strategies such as how investors get bought out, potential for initial public offerings (IPO's), plans for sale of a business, etc. are often described here.

In putting together the final plan, don't forget an attractive cover page, table of contents for easy reference and consider professional style binding, especially if you will be sending out a number of these plans to venture capitalists and other potential investors. Graphs, pictures, use of bullet points, headings and subheadings make a document more persuasive. Remember that this document should sell the investor on your concept. If you can't persuade the reader, you may find it difficult to attract the customer!

Source: Developed by Dayle M. Smith for use in the Global Management Seminars, McLaren School of Business, University of San Francisco, 1999.

When analyzing this business growth, it's helpful to explore the two traditional theories of entrepreneurship including the "career" theory, which says the self-employed have unique skills and attributes to sell; and the "default" theory, which says that business owners face obstacles to success in the wage and salary sector. Traditional theories do not adequately capture change in gender roles and women's unique challenges, such as family responsibilities and sexism in the workplace.

Women entrepreneurs prior to the 1970s had less managerial experience and were often clustered in low-paying, female-dominated industries compared to today's entrepreneurs. The "second generation" of women entrepreneurs are experienced in management and administration and are exiting their corporate jobs in order to maximize both profits and opportunity for personal growth. However, women-owned businesses still earn substantially less than male-owned businesses, primarily because of women's concentration in low-paying service and sales industries, limited managerial experience, and smaller business sizes. Access to start-up capital is also a problem frequently encountered by women business owners, although recent government initiatives are in place to ameliorate this problem.

To be successful, entrepreneur hopefuls should conduct market research, understand their industry, establish a legal structure for their business, and produce a detailed business plan before starting up their new ventures.

Discussion Questions

1. Why do women entrepreneurs still earn substantially less than their male peers? Is it due to sex segregation? Human capital investments? Compensating differentials?
2. What strategies might corporations enact to dissuade women from leaving the corporate ranks for self-employment?
3. What additional reasons can you provide for why women seek to form their own businesses?
4. Do you believe that we will see a plateau in the trend of women entering self-employment over the next 25 years? Do you think entrants will continue at a steady pace? Or do you see a decline?

Issue to Debate

Are Government policies to increase women's access to business loans and contracts only a "band-aid" approach to ensure economic equality between the sexes? Will a major shift in attitudes and gender roles be required to truly ensure gender equality?

Case Analysis *Susan Brown Antiques, Ltd.*

Susan Brown, founder and president of Susan Brown Antiques, Ltd., owns and operates a thriving art and antiques import/export business based in Miami, Florida. Annual sales revenues in 1998 topped $12 million. Her company employs 50 people in Florida and an additional 25 in several Latin and South American countries.

Susan spent most of her youth in Miami and in Argentina sharing her time with each of her parents. With an art history degree from the University of Miami and a love for antiques, she sought a career in which she could use her background to her advantage. She knew she might have to make some sacrifices to ultimately find the position that matched her background, but initially her goal was to surround herself with the things she loved most. She took a job in administrative services for a high-end furniture retailer. After short stints in several departments at the company, she found herself in sales, interacting with customers from around the world. Soon she was promoted to vice president of sales and marketing. Susan stayed in this position for 10 years, happy to be working with buyers of the art she loved but frustrated with her earnings and future potential.

Her motivation to start her own business stemmed from one major factor, "I felt my initiative and efforts were unrewarded; I had the title but was really no more than an administrative assistant who attended lots of corporate meetings." Susan wanted to capitalize on her knowledge of art history and furniture particularly in an international environment. She met with several business brokers hoping to find a company to buy. But her efforts went unrewarded. She felt that the brokers weren't taking her seriously because of her youth, gender, and inexperience. While attending a wholesalers' convention, she learned that a major furniture retailer wanted to spin off its import/export business. The business was profitable; however, it didn't fit in with the company's strategic plan of concentrating in domestic markets and major department stores. Brown quickly got on the phone and, through an attorney friend, sent a proposal to buy this piece of the business.

She knew getting investors interested in a risky venture would be challenging. Raising the necessary capital ($3 million) would prove to be a daunting task but she persevered. "I had no money at all and as a 34-year-old woman, I wasn't sure I was the prototype businessperson an established firm would sell to. It wasn't that I couldn't run a business—I had confidence there; it was my fear that no one would take me seriously and loan me the money." The company wanted $750,000 in cash up front and was willing to carry a note for the $2.25 million. "I needed to come up with the cash and somehow put together the kinds of loans that would allow me to sign the final papers." Susan took some major risks. "I sold my jewelry and several antiques that were gifts from my father. I sold my condo and cashed out my retirement plan, even though it meant a major penalty and payment to the IRS later that year. I ended up with about $350,000. Still short!" Susan took a crash course on how to write a business plan, got some advice from friends, and then "hit the pavement" going from bank to bank trying to find a loan. After a num-

ber of turndowns, she finally found a bank that considered the profitability of the division and reputation of the company. The bank loaned her $300,000. She was close but had no idea where she would come up the last $100,000. Thinking about the assets she would acquire once the company was hers, she realized that she could sell two of the new company's trucks for the amount she needed. Working frantically, she found a buyer. The one sticking point, however, was that she would have to conclude this deal with her buyer before she actually owned the trucks. One day before her deal with the furniture company was to close, the buyer for the trucks found out that they wouldn't get a bill of sale or proof of ownership until close of business the next day. "They were about to back out but I told them the story and how they were the last piece of the puzzle. Although they gave me looks of disbelief, they came through. I closed the deal with the furniture company that next morning and delivered the final bill of sale for the trucks to them at noon. I actually owned my import/export business!"

Ownership papers in hand, Susan then was challenged to begin operations. Most of the employees who had worked for the import/export division had been reassigned or left the company. The most knowledgeable managers were gone. "Those who were left didn't look on me that favorably. They tended to be difficult and wouldn't treat me as the boss." Susan tried hard to build a team and bring in several new people who could help get the operation moving. "What really made the difference was that everyone could see how hard I was trying to make this business successful. I rolled up my shirt sleeves, made runs to the airport with packages and put in the long hours. They saw I wasn't trying to create a new hierarchy—we were all in it together."

Throughout the first year of the start-up, profitability remained constant. She was able to meet payroll, service debt, and increase the client base overseas. Several of her business ideas for new markets went nowhere, but her most recent market concept for e-commerce seems to be taking off. Overseas and domestic customers' ability to view her inventory on-line has increased sales significantly. She realized the importance of this new direction would be critical to her business and hired the right professionals to carry it through. "I am learning everyday how to run and manage this business. I can't be as impul-

sive as I initially was and quite frankly I can't play 'bet the business' on a whim. I now have a number of people working for me here and in Latin America—they are building their careers too and it is an awesome responsibility."

"My success doesn't come from the fact that I know the ins and outs of business or that I am educated in this field. I attribute my success to the fact that I work hard; I took risks, and I wouldn't take no for an answer." ∎

Case developed by Dayle M. Smith, McLaren School of Business, University of San Francisco.

Questions

1. Would Brown be classified as a "traditional" or "second generation" business owner?
2. Brown's business style seems high on risk taking, and low on caution and research. What can young en-

trepreneurs learn from her often unorthodox business practices?
3. How might Brown's profile have been different if she were a man? Do you think her strategies or outcomes would have been different?

References and Suggested Readings

Aldrich, H. and Reese, P. R. (1994). Gender gap, gender myth: Does women's networking behavior differ significantly from men's? Paper presented at the 1994 Global Conference on Entrepreneurship, INSEAD, Fontatainebleau, France.

Aldrich, H., Reese, P. R., and Dubini, P. (1989). Women on the verge of a breakthrough: Networking among entrepreneurs in the United States and Italy. *Entrepreneurship and Regional Development, 1,* 339–356.

Aldrich, H. and Weiss, J. (1981). Differentiation within the United States capitalist class: Workforce size and income differences. *American Sociological Review, 46,* 279–290.

Aronoff, C. E., and Ward, J. L. (1992). *Contemporary entrepreneurs: Profiles of entrepreneurs and the businesses they started, Representing 74 companies in 30 industries including biographical information.* Detroit, MI: Omnigraphics.

Bernard, J. (1981). *The Female World.* New York: Free Press.

Beutel, A. and Marini, M. M. (1995). Gender and values. *American Sociological Review, 60,* 436–448.

Bowen, D. D., and Hirsch, R. D. (1986). The female entrepreneur: A career development perspective. *Academy of Management Review, 11,* (2), 393–407.

Brown, Carolyn M. They've got the power: Black women entrepreneurs, 27, (1996, August): 63–64.

Buttner, E. H. (1993, March–April). Female entrepreneurs: How far have they come? *Business Horizons, 36,* 59–65.

Carr, D. (1996). Two paths to self-employment? Women's and men's self-employment in the United States, 1980. *Work and Occupations, 23*(1), 26–53.

Chun, J. (1997, February). Opportunity knocks: Women's access to capital widens with the help of a new SBA program. *Entrepreneur, 25,* 46.

Committee on Small Business (CSB). (1988). *New economic realities: The rise of women entrepreneurs.* Washington, DC: U.S. Government Printing Office.

Devine, T. J. (1994, March). Characteristics of self-employed women in the United States. *Monthly Labor Review,* 20–34.

Dun and Bradstreet. (1967). *Patterns for success in managing a business.* New York: Dun and Bradstreet.

Enkelis, L., and Olsen, K. with M. Lewenstein. (1995). *On our own terms: Portraits of women business leaders.* San Francisco: Berrett-Koehler.

The facts about how to raise money for a small business. (1996). Washington, DC: U.S. Small Business Administration.

The facts about how to start a small business. (1996). Washington, DC: U.S. Small Business Administration.

Fagenson, E. A., and Jackson, J. J. (1994). The status of women managers in the United States. In N. J. Adler and D. N. Izraelie (Eds.), *Competitive frontiers: Women managers in a global economy* (pp. 387–403). Cambridge, MA: Blackwell.

Filer, R. (1985). Male–female wage differences: The importance of compensating differentials. *Industrial and Labor Relations Review, 38*(3), 426–37.

Fried, L. I. (1989). A new breed of entrepreneur: Women. *Management Review, 78*(12), 18–25.

Goffee, R., and Scase, R. (1985). *Women in charge: The experience of female entrepreneurs.* London: Allen and Unwin.

Gregg, G. (1985, January). Women entrepreneurs: The second generation. *Across the Board,* 10–18.

Hiam, A. (1996). *The entrepreneur's complete source book.* Englewood Cliffs, NJ: Prentice-Hall.

Hirsch, R. D., and Brush, C. G. (1984). The woman entrepreneur: Management skills and business problems. *Journal of Small Business Management, 22,* 30–37.

Hirsch, R. D., and O'Brien, M. (1981). The women entrepreneur from a business and sociological perspective. *Proceedings of the 1981 Conference on Entrepreneurship.* Wellesley, MA: Babson College Press.

Holmquist, C. (1996). The female entrepreneur: Woman and/or entrepreneur. In *Aspects of Women's Entrepreneurship* (pp. 107–108). Stockholm: Swedish National Board for Industrial and Technical Development.

Humphreys, M. A., and McClung, J. (1981). Women entrepreneurs in Oklahoma. *Review of Regional Economics, 6,* 13–21.

Knight, F. H. (1933). *Risk, uncertainty, and profit.* London: London School of Economics and Political Science.

Lesonsky, R. (1996, August). Ready for action. *Entrepreneur, 24,* 38–39.

Lim, Y., and Weissberg, T. (1997). *Pratt's guide to venture capital sources.* New York: Venture Economics Publishers.

Mason, K. O., and Kuhlthau, K. (1992). The perceived impact of child care costs on women's labor supply and fertility. *Demography, 29,* 523–543.

Maul, L. R., and Mayfield, D. C. (1990). *The entrepreneur's road map to business success.* Alexandria, VA: Saxtons River Publication.

Moore, D. P. (1990). An examination of present research on the female entrepreneur: Suggested research strategies for the 1990s. *Journal of Business Ethics, 9,* 275–81.

Moore, D. P., and Buttner, E. H. (1997). *Women entrepreneurs: Moving beyond the glass ceiling.* Thousand Oaks, CA: Sage.

Murphy, A. (1992). The start-up of the 90s. *Inc., 14*(3), 32–40.

Naftali, J. (1997). *Generation E: Do-it-yourself business guide for twenty-somethings and other non-corporate types.* Berkeley, CA: Ten Speed Press.

National Foundation for Women Business Owners (NFWBO). (1998). *Paths to entrepreneurship: New directions for women in business.* Washington, DC: NFWBO.

National Foundation for Women Business Owners (NFWBO). (1997). *Retirement plan trends in the small business market: A survey of women- and men-owned firms.* Washington, DC: NFWBO.

Nelton, S. (1989, May). The age of the woman entrepreneur. *Nation's Business,* 22–30.

President's Interagency Task Force on Women Business Owners. U.S. Department of Commerce. (1978). *The bottom line: Unequal enterprise in America.* Washington, DC: U.S. Government Printing Office.

Presser, H. B., and Baldwin, W. (1980). Child care as a constraint on employment: Prevalence, correlates, and bearing on the work and fertility nexus. *American Journal of Sociology, 85*(5), 1202–1213.

Reskin, B. F. (1988). Bringing the men back in: Sex differentiation and the devaluation of women's work. *Gender and Society, 2*(1), 58–81.

Roos, P. A., and Reskin, B. F. (1984). Institutional factors contributing to sex segregation in the workplace. In B. Reskin and H. Hartman (Eds.), *Women's work, men's work: Sex segregation on the job:* (pp. 245–246). Washington, DC: National Academy Press.

Schumpeter, J. A. (1984). *The theory of economic development: An inquiry into profits, capital, and credit.* Cambridge, MA: Harvard University Press.

Shapero, A. (1983). Pre-venture capital: A critical but neglected issue. *Entrepreneurial Economy, 2,* 3–4.

Sherman, A. J. (1997). *The complete guide to running and growing your own business.* New York: Random House.

The Small Business Administration's Web site provides descriptions of various government programs and resources for small business owners. In addition, it includes a set of answers to the agency's most commonly asked questions, and links to Web sites describing credit programs and state-by-state databases of business resources: www.sbaonline.sba.gov/womeninbusiness

Starr, J., and Yudkin, M. (1996). *Women entrepreneurs: A review of current research.* Wellesley, MA: Wellesley College Center for Research on Women Special Report.

Stevenson, L. (1986). Against all odds: The entrepreneurship of women. *Journal of Small Business Management, 24*(3), 30–36.

Stinchecombe, A. L. (1965). Social structure and organizations. In J. G. March, (Ed.), *Handbook of organizations* (pp. 142–193). New York: Rand McNally.

Stolze, W. J. (1989). *Startup: An entrepreneur's guide to launching and managing a new venture.* New York: Rock Beach Press.

U.S. Department of Commerce. (1996). *1992 economic census: Survey of women-owned businesses.* Washington, DC. U.S. Government Printing Office.

U.S. Department of Commerce, Bureau of the Census. (1986). *Current Population Reports* (Series P-23, No. 1465). Washington, DC: U.S. Government Printing Office.

U.S. Small Business Administration (SBA) (1984). *The state of small business: A report of the president.* Washington, DC: U.S. Government Printing Office.

—. (1988). *Small business in the American economy.* Washington, DC: U.S. Government Printing Office.

—. (1998). *Interagency committee for women's business enterprise newsletter.* Washington, DC: U.S. Government Printing Office.

PART

IV

Future Directions

This last section takes a very broad perspective, pulling together the content of the book as a whole, while recognizing changes that characterize how gender plays out in the work environment. Workplaces are changing—some quickly and others painfully slowly. Attitudes of men and women are changing and new generations of employees are moving into and through the workforce impacting organizational cultures and the political climates within organizations. The two women leaders you meet at the beginning of this section were and are truly change agents in impacting their organizations. They reveal the future direction of organizations' view of gender. The theme of the two chapters in this section is future directions. The two chapters in part IV explore change in organizations and present ideas from a number of leaders about how women in the workforce can become leaders for the twenty-first century.

Chapter 12 explores a new paradigm—tempered radicalism—as a strategy for change. It focuses on how women act as change agents and how they both challenge and change the cultures of their organizations to provide an environment that values the contributions of all. In chapter 13, the lessons learned are summarized. Based on in-depth interviews with a number of women leaders, readers develop a sense of how these women succeeded, how they initiated and/or managed change, and what advice they have for others based on their own experiences. What we know about women, leadership, and change comes alive in these lessons, and new directions for the future are offered. But first, let's meet two change leaders who, in many ways, embody the kind of leadership described in chapter 12.

Meet JoAnn Heffernan Heisen

JoAnn Heffernan Heisen, Vice President and Chief Information Officer, Johnson & Johnson
New Brunswick, NJ

BACKGROUND

JoAnn Heffernan Heisen has had an extraordinary career at one of America's largest and most respected companies. As the first woman officer at Johnson & Johnson (J&J) and the first woman named to the company's ten-person executive committee, JoAnn holds the board-level position of vice president and chief information officer. Her words as a corporate change leader say it all, "Smart companies understand women's issues as business issues."

Growing up in Washington, DC, JoAnn's interest in a corporate career started as a child. Her mother, widowed at 36 with 4 children under the age of 11, raised and educated her family while working as a secretary. That experience crystallized JoAnn's drive and ambition, "I vowed that I would build a career, not just 'have a job,' in order to be self-sufficient and financially independent." From among scholarship offers from several schools, she chose Syracuse University. She majored in economics and was assisted by loans and financial aid. As JoAnn puts it, "I was interested in finance and banking, and I wanted to work in an area where my contributions could be quantified."

"My first real job was at Chase Manhattan Bank. It was a great opportunity, and I was convinced I would retire there after a career in banking." She completed Chase's prestigious management training program and, as her assignments became more visible, the employment recruiters began to call. After five years she moved to Kenmill Textile Corporation as chief financial officer—a position where she could consolidate her financial training and make a difference in a smaller company.

She was recruited to the American Can Company (later to become Primerica) to develop an investor relations function and was promoted to a position overseeing all of corporate communications, including public relations, government affairs, and employee communications. She served on Primerica's executive committee, gaining visibility as she advanced, and the recruiters continued to call—this time to convince her to join Johnson & Johnson.

"I was asked to consider the position of assistant treasurer for investor relations." It was a difficult choice, involving returning to a narrower field of responsibility than the positions she'd held, and it included relocating her family from Connecticut to New Jersey, but it was a career risk she was willing to take. Here was an opportunity to make a significant contribution at one of America's most admired companies.

In 1991, two and a half years after joining J&J, JoAnn was promoted to treasurer, and in 1995 she was appointed corporate controller. In 1997, she was named to the executive committee in the newly created position of vice president and chief information officer (CIO). "Information management is increasingly critical to business success, and the position was elevated to the executive committee. In this role I've had an opportunity to use my people, leadership, and turnaround skills, and the past 18 months have been great."

THOUGHTS ON LEADERSHIP

"Leadership is an art, not a science. But leadership is different than management and knowing that difference is important. Leadership can be taught, and it can be improved. It is the recognition that one person can really make a difference, even within large organizations like Johnson & Johnson. Real leadership is about vision, dedication, and a commitment to making things happen."

That commitment underscores JoAnn's personal challenges as a leader. "Leadership requires stamina. You can't go down with the first arrow. As women, we tend to want to be liked, to take things personally. But there will always be disagreements, and arrows get slung. A leader refuses to go down. Your commitment keeps you standing."

"When you are able to take a challenging assignment and know that a number of people will be naysayers, you must remain convinced that you have the right vision—the vision to deploy the people and utilize the resources and complete the assignment successfully. Leadership is about taking an assignment that looked deadly and knowing you did the right thing."

JoAnn identifies Juanita Kreps, former U.S. secretary of commerce, as a role model in her own leadership development. "She was a professor of economics, involved in business and world economic policy issues, nominated by the president and confirmed by the Senate to a cabinet position. I admired her; she had the credentials; she had the style—she deserved the

job on merit, not because she was a woman."

THE CHANGE AGENT ROLE

As men and women take on more visible jobs, a number of organizational dynamics play out. JoAnn reveals how to handle the barriers from a leadership perspective. "You need a high level of self-confidence. You need to believe that your vision is the right one. Not everyone will share *your* vision, but *everyone* has an equal right to a vision. As a leader, you are not always popular when espousing your ideas. You may have to convince and cajole others to buy in. You have to rise to the occasion—to bring people together, create solutions, and guarantee results." Is it more difficult for women to take on that role? JoAnn considered her own experiences.

TAKING THE INITIATIVE AT J&J

"After joining J&J 10 years ago, I expected to see more women in upper management. After all, J&J is a great place for women to work, with many people encouraging and mentoring others. But not many women could be found in the most senior management ranks. The support for women's progress was very strong at the top, but it was uneven as it trickled down to J&J's 180 decentralized operating companies. We had lots of talented women in the pipeline, but I wanted to help more women develop more quickly. I hoped I could be a catalyst and help make change happen faster. I started by asking for statistics, and then approached a number of senior women during the early 1990s, creating an Executive Women's Forum to help.

"I was the most senior woman at corporate headquarters, with some credibility as the head of investor relations, and was viewed as having made a contribution to our business performance. I believed it would be easier for me to approach senior management about women's issues than some others who were concerned that their involvement might adversely affect their careers. I realized I had a responsibility I could not deny."

The company organized a Women's Leadership Conference, where 325 director-level and above women gathered to discuss their concerns and make recommendations to management about how to address them. The conference was focused on constructive change. As JoAnn said in her welcoming remarks, "Women's advancement is not a social or emotional issue. It's a business issue. The workforce is changing. We are a Fortune 100 company with enormous potential and growth opportunities, but, like other large corporations, we need to focus on what we, as a company, can do better in order to attract and retain women in the upper ranks."

JoAnn's work with the Women's Leadership Conference was noted by many of the women who attended. As one division manager for a J&J company so eloquently put it, "to see corporate support for this kind of conference indicated new cultural hope for the company. I and several of my colleagues saw an inspired leader sharing the demographics and potential new landscape for a J&J that was bringing down the glass ceiling. This was a woman who had reached a board-level position and shared the kind of advice that suggested we, too, could move into the upper ranks, not by

changing who we were as women but by using all of our strengths that brought us success in our jobs. As we looked to the person sitting next to us, and as we networked during the day, we learned so much from JoAnn and from each other. We saw a support network that could serve us as we became partners in the culture."

FAMILY AND WORK

Admittedly, change does not happen overnight. Making a company more family friendly is one example of positive change. Although J&J has some of the most progressive work/life policies, including a statement in the Company Credo, and has received numerous awards, including being recognized as among the 100 best companies in which to work for women and minorities, the road to cultural change is always slow.

Women can help that change, as JoAnn has demonstrated by sharing her own experience. As corporate controller and (then) a single mother of four children, JoAnn had to grapple with family responsibilities along with a demanding job. "Women carry the greatest burden with family responsibilities. Four children want my complete attention when I go home. Perhaps a dad can say 'I need an hour or two in order to finish up some business,' and the wife makes sure the kids respect that—but women rarely have that luxury or support. I was lucky in that I was able to afford extra help at home, but there was still a tremendous amount of work to do and a comparable amount of energy needed for the children and the household.

"In business we must make men comfortable working with us, but we should also make them realize that women have so many balls to juggle. At one point in my career, I would not mention my children in the executive dining room. The guys were talking about sports and weekend entertainment, but I went through a period where I didn't bring up my children unless asked. Yet with time and tenure, it dawned on me that I had a responsibility to other women to help men understand that women still 'have to do it all.' Weekends could be about four soccer games, two hockey games, piano recitals, and so on, and I juggle it. It is important to make men more understanding of the roles that women play so that there are no misconceptions about all that we really do. With this recognition, it becomes OK to walk out at 6:30 P.M. because of a piano recital at 7:00. It's OK to take a child's call. Let's recognize that we have two jobs—work *and* family."

LEADERSHIP ADVICE

JoAnn has been a risk taker, and she advises other women to take professional risks. "Don't always operate in the comfort zone. Forge new paths and go where others have not gone. Developing a comfort level with risk, ambiguity, and conflict are a must. Women tend to back down or lose confidence, whereas men can scrap with their colleagues one day and then be best friends the next. Women need to learn from that."

"Men and women may have different communication styles, and they may lead differently. Women may be more collaborative, more like team players, and less responsive to the command and control model that successful men have used. The key is to be aware of different perspectives and tolerant of different styles and skills."

"Women can succeed by recognizing that there is a 'shared responsibility' to career development. Corporations have a responsibility to develop their people, but an employee needs to take responsibility for her own job growth as well." JoAnn encourages women to credential themselves—take extra courses, earn additional degrees, volunteer for task forces and projects with visibility, publish papers in journals, and so forth. "You can learn new skills in professional and nonprofit organizations—things you could not learn on your 'day job,' especially early in your career. Joining a nonprofit board is an excellent strategy for becoming a winner. You can develop your finance, communication, and board skills—and the organizations benefit from your expertise."

MENTORING

Mentoring is a key factor in helping women as well. "I have had mentors throughout my whole career. The best experiences were when natural relationships developed. Mentors advised me on office politics and other aspects of the organization to help my career. So I try to mentor as many people as I can."

"If mentoring relationships don't develop naturally, then we should structure them more formally. At J&J, at the entry and lower levels, the company will assign mentors. If you are looking for a mentor, do not look to your boss; go one or two levels above you (but not straight up the line and over your boss's head) and express an interest in a 'career development' talk. People feel flattered. But you can't expect the mentor to be responsible for your advancement. You need to understand the boundaries. I have a strong belief in mentoring programs and am continuing to work on this at Johnson & Johnson."

THE GLASS CEILING

Is there a glass ceiling in the corporate world? Absolutely! But JoAnn makes the point the glass ceiling is getting thinner and thinner. "However, it's a pyramid. All of us are vying for the few top positions. This is a reality and can make life difficult for women—but men have to deal with these issues too. The competition is tough for those top few spots."

Women bring to the workplace natural management and leadership skills developed as mothers, home organizers, and community activists. But they must also realize that conflict is a part of the business game—they need to get comfortable with that, and not take it personally.

JoAnn is convinced that women have what it takes to be successful—and fulfilled—in business. If her experience is any indication, women can also be the change agent that helps shape organizational cultures where the competition is fair and the playing field more level.

"Johnson & Johnson is a great company with enormous challenges before us. But we need to work hard to make it stay great—and we are."

INTERVIEW WITH A LEADER

Meet Margot Fraser

Margot Fraser, President and Founder, Birkenstock
 Novato, California

BACKGROUND

Margot Fraser is president and founder of Birkenstock Footprint Sandals, Inc., now in its third decade as the exclusive U.S. distributor of Birkenstock footwear. A native of Bremen, Germany, Margot spent her early years in Berlin. With a background in art and clothing design, she moved to Canada in 1952 and worked as an independent dressmaker until she secured a position as a designer for a clothing manufacturer. Eight years later she married and moved to California.

In 1966, at a health spa in Bavaria during her annual visit to Europe, a fitness trainer suggested Margot try a new German sandal to soothe her chronic foot pain. Inspired by the comfort of Birkenstock's contoured cork footbeds, Margot began purchasing small quantities of the footwear from the German manufacturer and selling them from her home. She soon decided to wholesale the sandals—only to be told by traditional shoe retailers that "women will never wear those shoes!" Margot persisted, and her first turning point came in 1967 at a health food store convention in San Francisco. There she found her first stronghold of customers who cared about the health of their bodies and valued function over fashion.

Since then, Birkenstock's approach to business has been unique in its simplicity: People deserve to be treated fairly, kindly, and with respect. Odd as it may seem, Margot credits much of her success to her lack of formal business training. By not knowing what was "correct" or even "possible," she found her own solutions as she needed them and has been able to accomplish what others would have considered impossible. Her vision for the future of Birkenstock is for it to remain a people-oriented company that values the participation and contribution of each employee. She brings this vision to distributors and stores she works with as well. "We realized more than a decade ago that our essential link to our customer was the independent, often struggling retailer. Especially with their high employee turnover, these retailers needed information from us and strategies on how to best represent our product to customers. We've taken the lead in providing seminars and other forms of product education to these retailers so they can better serve our end customer."

CHALLENGES AS A WOMAN LEADER

"When I started this company, I had a real vision of what I wanted to do and what the company could become. That vision, and my confidence in it, made it easy and natural to invite other people to contribute. I sincerely needed their guidance on how to take things to the next step, and the next. I don't like to talk much about gender differences, but through my experiences over the years I believe there is a difference

and that it stems from our culture. Male managers, I find, sometimes are more eager to find, or be provided with, answers than to work out true solutions. That's a problem for any business, because yesterday's answers may not be relevant as solutions today. I think women have an easier time as problem-solvers, unless they fall into the trap of emulating traditional management behaviors."

STRATEGIES FOR CHANGE

Margot's change-leader behaviors are captured in many of the organizational strategies implemented at Birkenstock. Her extensive use of teams is a classic example. "When we were very small as a company, a handful of people did a little bit of everything to keep us on track. Then as we grew we realized that we needed to establish functional areas of work and responsibility. But soon it became apparent that too many things were falling through the cracks between these rigid areas. The areas needed to connect, and didn't. Therefore, many years ago I started building and rewarding teams that always kept the big picture in mind—how do we serve the larger interests of the company? Otherwise, it's only human to focus on my job, my department, my area of responsibility. It becomes 'us against them.' 'They' made a mistake. I've tried over the years to turn that language from 'us' and 'they' to 'we'— we're all in it together."

Growing leaders within the company is another hallmark of Margot's efforts in the change-leader role. She looks for a variety of qualities. "I look for the qualities of a coach—

someone who can work with people and help them give their very best. The influence of that kind of leader can be stunning. We've had individual employees and some work groups who had a 'go-it-alone' attitude at first. It's truly wonderful to see what a coach/leader can do to bring synergy and relationships to these kinds of employees. Their productivity soars as they learn to trust one another, work well together, talk with one another openly and honestly about their needs and ideas, and help each other out."

FUTURE DIRECTIONS

In growing and developing leaders, Margot pulls from the strategies articulated by the leaders and writers she admires. "My thoughts turn first to people I've read—Dupree, Peter Drucker, Warren Bennis, and others. I urge any rising woman leader to read widely and deeply, and to attend conferences where insightful, inspiring business leaders and professors are speaking. The ideas you bring back to your company from both books and conferences are invaluable."

Professional Women as Change Agents

12

Debra E. Meyerson
and
Kathleen M. Merrill

I have grown weary of those who cry "victim." I believe that there is no sense in wasting energy on that proclamation, but in its stead we should focus on understanding the how and why of where we are. If we want to break the cycle, we need to understand how and why we arrived there, and what needs to change.

As the only female engineer in my immediate group, I am constantly aware of the stereotypical expectations and assumptions, but fortunately I work with very intelligent men whom I see attempting—if nothing else— to understand me. And for my part, I return the favor by being sincere. I do not pretend to be "one of the guys." It is an interesting experiment.
—Participant in workshop on tempered radicalism, May 1998

I know quite a few people who fit this category of tempered radical. Such people are already initiating positive cultural transformation, although in bits and pieces and perhaps with more timidity than they would if they had adequate support. Clearly such people are not alone; however, it is also clear that most are lonely, since it is so hard to find others like themselves. If there were networks for such people, they could get needed support and generate needed coherence for their activities and values.
—Community Organizer, 1995.

Chapter Overview

This chapter presents tempered radicalism as a strategy for women who do not naturally fit into a predominantly white, male, establishmentarian culture to exist, survive, and thrive in an organization.[1] Tempered radicalism is a strategy to remain authentic, true to one's personal values and identities, and at the same time to pursue one's desire to succeed in a traditionally masculine environment.

When women face pressures to fit into predominantly male environments, they can respond in a variety of ways.[2] Some choose to assimilate as much as possible and give up or suppress their personal values and beliefs. Some surrender, suffer in silence, and feel victimized. Others leave their organizations when they feel the pressure to conform has become too great or when they feel that the requirements of the organization compromise their values or identities too extremely. Still others assert, without censoring, their beliefs, antagonistically refusing to pick their battles or compromise their convictions—and typically wind up leaving their organizations.

Tempered radicalism represents an alternative way to respond to conformity pressures: It encourages women to embrace some requirements of conformity and at the same time embrace and assert personal values, beliefs, and identities that challenge the status quo. Countless women have resonated to the concepts of tempered radicalism as they struggled to maintain their legitimacy within traditional contexts, while asserting themselves and their challenges. Tempered radicalism is a strategy that involves maintaining one's sense of self. It is also a strategy of effecting change.

Learning Objectives

◼ To determine how women fit into and succeed within traditionally male organizations while maintaining their values about being a woman

◼ To analyze how women succeed in established institutions, while challenging and trying to change some of the most entrenched norms of those institutions

◼ To examine women who simultaneously pursue commitments and identities that seem at odds with one another and how can this ambivalence can be sustained

◼ To consider the advantages and disadvantages of women acting on their ambivalence

◼ To examine women's personal values and commitments—and a stance of ambivalence—as they relate to a strategy of change

---

[1]The ideas and central concepts of this chapter are applications of an article by D. E. Meyerson and M. A. Scully (1995). Throughout the chapter, we refer to the tempered radical as a woman, and therefore, use the pronouns *she* and *her*. We have chosen this language because this chapter focuses on the professional woman. This language and the focus of this chapter is not intended to reject the idea that men, too, can be tempered radicals.

[2]This chapter discusses women in general, and does not address the responses that will vary with race. For an in-depth exploration of the differences, see E. Bell, et al., 1998.

PROFESSIONAL WOMEN AS TEMPERED RADICALS

> In a variety of studies, female students have . . . expressed lower expectations for occupational success than males. . . . Disparities between traits associated with femininity and traits associated with vocational achievement reinforce gender socialization processes. . . . The aggressiveness, dedication, and emotional detachment traditionally presumed necessary for advancement in the most prestigious and well-paid occupations are incompatible with the traits commonly viewed as attractive in women: deference, sensitivity, and self-sacrifice. . . . Females aspiring to nontraditional or high-status positions remain subject to a familiar double bind. Those conforming to traditional characteristics of femininity are often thought lacking in the requisite assertiveness and initiative, yet those conforming to a masculine model of success may be ostracized in work settings as bitchy, aggressive, and uncooperative (Rhode, 1988).

Deborah L. Rhode, in her article, "Perspectives on Professional Women," (1988), describes the double bind with which so many women students and professionals are all too familiar: the ambition to be successful and to gain legitimacy within an established organization or profession, tempered by the desire to retain some level of commitment to who they are, what they value about being a woman, and for some, what they believe needs to be changed to eradicate inequities.

The dual commitments women embrace—the feelings, beliefs, and ideologies about their identity as a woman, and the need to establish their status and legitimacy in their organizations or professions—often are at odds with one another. Women can believe in their professional institutions and be committed to succeeding within them. At the same time they can feel committed to their own identities as women and, more broadly, to the cause of women and all traditionally disadvantaged groups in their efforts to gain equal social and economic opportunity. The concept of tempered radicalism provides one with the possibility of not having to choose between these desires, between these two facets of self.

In this chapter, we apply and explore the concept of tempered radicalism as a way of surviving, sustaining one's self, and effecting change. For the purposes of illustration, we refer to the work of both tempered and untempered radicals who have in different ways posed challenges to the status quo and the organizations and institutions in which they operate. We draw from examples in business and outside of business to most effectively illustrate the tempered radical's strategies and struggles.

Tempered Radicalism as a Strategy of Authenticity and Change

Meyerson and Scully (1995) define a tempered radical as an individual who identifies with and is committed to her organization and also to a cause, a community, or an ideology that is fundamentally at odds with the dominant culture of that organization. Not only are the *commitments* at odds, the two *identities* of the person with these commitments are at odds as well.

It is probably fair to conclude that most professionals, women and men, want to succeed in their organizations. It is probably also fair to say that many women eventually feel like outsiders within predominantly male organizations. Some of these women feel like outsiders, at odds with the dominant culture, because their identities and beliefs clash with those dominant in the organization. Some of these women embrace a commitment to effect change driven by their identities, values, and beliefs. While some women struggle primarily with their own sense of authenticity in environments that feel alien, others struggle with their desire to challenge the status quo and effect change when such challenges could threaten their legitimacy. All care, at some level, about fitting in and remaining legitimate.

We are suggesting that professional women in male-dominated environments face two types of struggles in their approach to organizational change. First, women who facilitate change *intentionally* face struggles that seem mostly about challenging and changing the status quo. Second, women who facilitate change *unintentionally* face struggles that seem mostly about defining and expressing their identity, or more appropriately, their identities, and protecting their authenticity. Both struggles represent the domain of tempered radicals and both can produce positive change in organizations; both, however, are challenged in ways specific to their approach.

The first group of tempered radicals, the *intentional* facilitators of change, are the women in organizations who see the need to rock the boat, to advocate for inclusion and reform, to speak up, to put their beliefs forward. These are the people who advocate for hiring and promoting more women and people of color. They actively try to mentor people from underrepresented groups. They speak out about pay inequity. They propose programs to help men and women balance work and home responsibilities. They place issues on the agenda. For the intentional tempered radical, *the political is personal.*

To the extent that proposed changes threaten entrenched notions of what is right or fair, or images of who does and does not fit into the culture, these intentional efforts will likely encounter resistance and backlash. Because of the resistance such changes invoke, and because of the risk change agents assume when they pose serious challenges to the status quo, the people engaged in these efforts must learn to "temper" their efforts, or else they seem too radical.

These tempered radicals are only minimally tempered: They may be willing to risk their jobs for what they believe is right and fair. To increase their own effectiveness, they need to recognize and compensate for the inevitable resistance to change and to facilitate change in an unthreatening way that does not undermine their legitimacy or professional reputation.

The second group of tempered radicals, the *unintentional* facilitators of change, are the women who simply assert themselves—their beliefs and their identities—in the form of everyday resistance and self-assertions. These are the women who resist seemingly mundane tests of "fit," when they stand up to pressures to act "like one of the guys," or when they challenge a standard definition of "acceptable" behavior, such as inappropriate joking behavior. In effect, they openly question traditional male norms. Their challenges are often undertaken cautiously and selectively, so they are only rarely seen for what they are—challenges to the established culture. For the unintentional tempered radical, *the personal is political.*

Unfortunately, these unintentional tempered radicals, especially those who are white women, tend to experience pressures of conformity as personal affronts (Bell et al., 1998). These tests of conformity can feel demeaning. They threaten women's confidence and sense of self. They can hurt. The individual experiences these pressures as personal, not political, and they miss the broader issues implicated in these subtle (and sometimes not so subtle) tests. As a result, their responses to the pressures are incomplete and without consideration of the effect their efforts will have on the organization as a whole.

These women may be no more aware of their impact in the organization than butterflies in Beijing are aware of how the flapping of their wings affects weather patterns a week later in San Francisco. They are often quick to deny that they are change agents or even that they care about making change. Some explain that they just do what it takes to "keep their souls." Yet in this process, these women must sustain their dual commitments and identities and, in doing so, become tempered radicals, even if unintentionally.

These women are only minimally, inadvertently radical: They are willing to protect and to assert themselves as individuals but not to actively advocate change on an organizational level. Because these efforts are based on personal assertions of self, rather than on an agenda of change, they may not appropriately reflect consideration of the organizational implications of individual action. In the course of challenging established expectations and pressures to fit in, these women redefine organizational images, communication rules, roles, norms of behavior, and definitions of professionalism—they become role models and agents of change, however unintentionally. To increase their own effectiveness, both for themselves as individuals and as a part of the whole, these women must learn to appreciate the broader effects of these assertions and to consider them in constructing their approach.

Even though the specifics may vary, tempered radicals all face challenges related to the maintenance of their identity and the management of change. The tactics a woman chooses to employ will be influenced by whether she most immediately experiences the challenges of identity or the challenges of change. We have seen, however, that the challenges of identity and change are in fact closely linked: In the course of advancing small, local changes, or forming alliances that have the potential to affect change, people sustain their values and identities. When identities and beliefs do not neatly fit within the traditional ideal, people affect change by asserting who they are and advancing what they believe. Both types of tempered radicals struggle to sustain their dual identities and to maintain their ambivalence.

Tempered Radicalism and Ambivalence

Because tempered radicals embrace dual identities simultaneously, they face the difficult task of embracing their ambivalence, which involves listening and giving voice to both of their "selves" at the same time. While this ambivalence can be utilized as a source of strength, it can also create unique challenges for the tempered radical.

Ambivalence as a Source of Strength

Ambivalence is often associated with hesitation and uncertainty, with a stance that begs for resolution and compromise. For the tempered radical, however, ambivalence is not about compromise or finding a middle ground that blurs her dual identities. The tempered radical's *purposeful* ambivalence is about expressing dual identities simultaneously, with varying degrees of intensity. Though stressful and difficult to sustain, this purposeful ambivalence can serve as the basis for three sources of strength for the tempered radical in promoting organizational change.[3]

---

[3]This section is a direct application of Meyerson and Scully (1995).

First, the tempered radical's ambivalence enables her to act as "outsider within." Ambivalence allows her to be a part of an organization, and to gain knowledge, insight, and legitimate power but at the same time facilitates the tempered radical's critical review of that organization's dominant culture. As an outsider, she is able to recognize the need for change; as an insider, she has the opportunities to make change.

For example, Bernadine Healy, M.D., former director of the National Institute of Health, existed there as an "outsider within." Healy was, and still is, a well-respected member of the established medical community; however, she took issue with the traditional beliefs and assumptions necessary to continue focusing health care on a male norm. As an outsider, Healy was able to identify the inequities and scientific inaccuracies in these assumptions; as an insider, she had the position and power to successfully address, challenge, and eventually dismantle these assumptions. Healy used her ambivalence as a source of strength and in the process made meaningful change within the medical community.

Second, the ambivalent tempered radical is both an honest critic of the status quo and a skeptic of untempered radical change. She is able to break away from the status quo, the accepted norms, and at the same time appreciate that a radical approach to change might alienate more moderate followers. Such alienation would undermine the established basis of power within the organization and, thereby, minimize the potential effectiveness of the tempered radical.

For example, Frances Kissling, president of Catholics for a Free Choice, has created a position from which she can criticize both the Catholic Church and untempered, radical advocates for abortion rights. Kissling criticizes the Catholic establishment for their dogmatic, unquestioning, established positions. At the same time, Kissling criticizes the traditional cessation of moral arguments by the more radical abortion-rights supporters: "We cede the moral territory—you know, the antiabortionists have morals and we have rights. Well, we have morals and we have rights. The bringing of new life into the world is a profoundly moral question" (Stan, 1995). By virtue of her unique ambivalence between Catholicism and an arguably contradictory prochoice ideology, Kissling adds value to the conversation with her criticisms of both.

Third, and on the flip side of the coin, the ambivalent tempered radical is an advocate for both the status quo and radical change. As an advocate of the status quo, the tempered radical reaps organizational benefits as a source of power to then advocate for change within the system. Without such advocacy, the tempered radical would lose her fulcrum for change and sacrifice her ability to make meaningful, radical intraorganizational change.

For example, Francine Moyer,[4] a partner in a management consulting firm, successfully embraced her ambivalence to be both an advocate for the firm and an advocate for change. Moyer arranged for the firm to sponsor a monthly luncheon for the women consultants in the office, believing that both the firm and the consultants would benefit from a tighter, more formalized, women's network. In so doing, she simultaneously reaffirmed her belief in the existing organization of the firm and advocated change in the established power structure.

---

[4]Name has been changed to respect the privacy of the individual.

The Challenges of Ambivalence

Embracing ambivalence can be a source of strength, but sustaining it can also create specific types of challenges for the tempered radical.[5] First, the tempered radical's ambivalence may potentially be construed as hypocrisy. The tempered radical has two polar constituencies: the establishmentarian institution, to which the tempered radical may be seen as too radical, and the more radical "outsider" community, to which the tempered radical may be seen as too conservative. Her perceived inconsistency and lack of ideological commitment threatens her credibility among both groups. In addition, and perhaps even more threatening, the tempered radical herself may begin to think of *herself* as a hypocrite. This can create discomfort, dissonance, threaten her self-esteem, and, in the process, destroy her effectiveness.

For example, Kissling has been rejected by the Catholic Church as not a "true Catholic," and at the same time, rejected by the more radical abortion-rights activists as not a "true feminist." Adopting the middle ground, Kissling has inevitably alienated the establishment of both sides to some degree.

Second, ambivalence often leaves the tempered radical without a natural home—she becomes isolated from both the organization to which she is committed and the cause, community, or ideology in which she believes. The seeming contradiction between these dual identities poses the greatest problem for the tempered radical, as this contradiction threatens her personal identity and integrity. The tempered radical's simultaneous commitment to two institutions or belief systems leaves her without an obvious single home. To survive, to remain authentic to both of her equally legitimate identities, the tempered radical must create her own home.

Kissling, for example, has created such a home—enabling herself to sustain two identities simultaneously that are, arguably, the epitome of contradiction: a simultaneous commitment to both the Catholic faith and the abortion-rights movement. She recognized that, in addition to her fundamental commitment to abortion rights, "[w]ho I am comes from everything that is a part of my Catholic history. . . . It would be denying everything that made me who I am, not being a Catholic."

As a result of this recognition, Kissling has integrated her two commitments, her two identities, in a way that preserves her authenticity. Kissling has reshaped the context of the abortion debate and created a home not just for herself, but also for others committed to the seemingly contradictory prochoice and Catholic identities.

Third, the tempered radical is at high risk of co-optation by the organization—she may become an ordinary insider and eventually reject, or at least distance herself from, the belief system with which she once identified. This co-optation is facilitated by three compromises often made by the tempered radical: compromises of language, timing, and emotional expression.

Compromises of language facilitate co-optation where the tempered radical uses insider language to encourage or to "sell" change. This compromise is tempting as an argument for family leave policies, diversity in recruiting, or untraditional work arrangements that are easily translated into cost-benefit, bottom-line, corporate language. The

---

[5]This section is a direct application of Meyerson and Scully (1995).

problem with adopting the "acceptable" language of insiders for the expression of radical agendas and ideologies is that the continued use of this language could threaten one's "outsider" identity and beliefs. While the means of advocacy may justify the ends of successful organizational change, the true, authentic voice of the woman may evolve into the voice of the status quo. As a result, she may become less fluent in the language of her external belief system, and progressively surrender the dual identity that once enabled her to encourage fundamental change within the organization.

For example, liberal professionals who are committed to affirmative action based on the principles of social justice regularly find themselves justifying affirmative action in terms of economic value-added, return on investment and other traditional bottom-line financial language. Although supporting radical arguments in the language of one's audience increases the chance that one will be heard, *speaking* in establishmentarian terms brings the speaker one short step away from *thinking* in establishmentarian terms—language and thought soon become inseparable. Soon, the language of truth, fairness, and justice becomes secondary, in other words, an afterthought.

Compromises of timing make more likely co-optation because the tempered radical postpones the use of her voice until she has the insider power and legitimacy she perceives are needed to encourage change. A young manager may understand the desperate need for revision of the traditional career track but may feel she needs the legitimacy of a senior title (e.g., vice president) to give her the security and power to fight for such change. In the process, the woman may forego the voice that she needs to sustain her own values and beliefs. In addition, the postponement process, once begun, is easier and easier to accept and continue. The deadline evolves from "when I make vice president" to "when I am on the executive committee" to "when I am named CEO." The power needed to encourage change, even to push in small ways, may have existed all along within the heart and soul of the individual. The suppression of that power only minimizes its potential.

In addition, as her legitimacy and success within the organization compounds, she has more to lose from failing or threatening her success. Only by continually asserting her voice, by pushing the boundaries of what is acceptable and making suggestions for change, can a professional woman gain a more realistic conception of the organization's capacity for the outsider's perspective and ideas.

For example, Elsa Jackson,[6] a marketing executive for a large cosmetics company, had been worried about her company's advertising campaigns. As a Jamaican-born woman, Jackson saw that the company, which sells skin care products, was alienating Caribbean women in its portrayal of them as housekeepers and nannies in the ads. She recognized her own sensitivities and did not want to make a big deal of it, but at the same time, she was offended by this stereotypical portrait. Eventually, she found some trusted colleagues in the right department with which she could voice her concerns and test how they would be heard. Jackson was surprised at how much her colleagues welcomed her comments. From then on, she found it less and less difficult to reveal her voice on all sorts of issues. Had Jackson not compromised on the timing of her objections, had she not remained silent, she might have effectively challenged the racist depictions much earlier and maximized her own potential to make other meaningful changes.

---

[6]Name has been changed to respect the privacy of the individual.

Compromises of expression also facilitate co-optation where the tempered radical silences the expression of her perspective, values, and belief system that deviate from the organization's. Expression of values, beliefs, and emotions are fundamental to the integrity of the tempered radical: Her commitment to the organization is expressed by her hard work and dedication . . . to remain authentic, she must similarly give voice to the basis of her outsider values and beliefs—her heart and her soul.

For example, Moyer waited until she had been awarded a partnership at her consulting firm before she began making active change for the women associates with whom she worked. In the process, Moyer herself was unable to personally take advantage of this change and was less in touch with the kinds of changes that the junior women needed to help them succeed. Moyer demonstrated that the tempered radical can successfully preserve her dual-identities until she possesses the power to facilitate change. Her waiting, however, put her at higher risk for co-optation and caused her to lose touch with the values she once had held that fueled her desire to make changes and champion her agenda.

Fourth, in maintaining the contradiction in beliefs and identities, the tempered radical sustains a significant emotional burden. The tempered radical is saddled with the guilt and self-doubt associated with her inability to live up to her own ideals: She is neither the selfless, ideal employee, nor is she the unquestioning servant of the cause that she espouses. The tempered radical is neither, and both, at the same time. The conflict and ambiguity of how to reconcile these two identities, and the stress they produce, threatens burnout, isolation, and sometimes, self-contempt. However, adopting the voice of the majority is tempting because it seems appropriate, easier, and comes with obvious professional and material rewards.

For example, Rita Coolick,[7] a senior vice president of a large commercial bank, had been increasingly co-opted as she moved up the ranks. Her attempts to fit in rewarded her with professional success, but it took its toll on her sense of self. Coolick did not want to make waves, but once she became the only woman on the executive floor in a Fortune 500 financial services company, Coolick began to recognize the obstacles before her.

This company was the perennial "all boys club", and by virtue of her title, she became a member. The higher she rose in the ranks, however, the more difficult it was for her to fit in—she no longer was surrounded by the female support network she had come to rely on early in her career. By the time Coolick actively recognized the organization needed to change, she had much more at stake, and she felt she could no longer afford to risk her status as "one of the guys" by challenging the status quo.

Coolick knew, however, that she had become part of the "problem." Not only was she not making changes on behalf of other women, she was reinforcing the male norms and codes of behavior and making it more difficult for others to make change. She found she could not throw away all that she worked so hard to achieve, even though she was beginning to no longer recognize herself or even *like* herself. Coolick eventually realized she was willing to pay this price for her success, but many women are not. Despite the strength that ambivalence can provide, the challenges it introduces are sometimes overwhelming.

---

[7]Name has been changed to respect the privacy of the individual.

Ambivalence as a Way of Being and Surviving: A Prescription for Sustained Authenticity and Change

Once an individual accepts her ambiguous relationships with her organization and her beliefs, and possibly identifies herself as a tempered radical, she is in the position to adopt some suggested strategies for the preservation of her true voice. Change efforts reinforce one's values and identities, and in turn, one's values and identities can encourage change. Meyerson and Scully suggest four strategies tempered radicals use to maintain the ambivalence necessary to sustain their identities and, at the same time, assert change.[8]

First, the tempered radical should recognize the significance of "small wins." Karl F. Weick (1984), a psychologist promoting the idea of small wins, explained

> A small win is a concrete, complete, implemented outcome of moderate importance. By itself, one small win may seem unimportant. A series of wins at small but significant tasks, however, reveals a pattern that may attract allies, deter opponents, and lower resistance to subsequent proposals. Small wins are controllable opportunities that produce visible results (p. 45).

Resisting the temptation to minimize these small wins and recognizing them for what they are—successes—establishes the basis for *confidence.* Success breeds confidence, and confidence, in turn, breeds more success and more small wins. The resulting series of small wins can help identify and define existing boundaries, the organization's limits and its capacities for change, and in aggregate, they can begin to trigger fundamental change.

Once again, for example, Moyer, in the earlier example, did not revolutionize her consulting firm's hiring policies or establish cutting-edge parental leave policies. Instead, she achieved a small win by creating a network in which these ideas could be discussed. This discussion forum enabled Moyer to form an alliance of sympathetic colleagues, and it helped her place her ideas in the context of existing organizational boundaries. By bringing revolutionary *ideas* into the organizational conscience, rather than demanding radical, instantaneous organizational *change,* Moyer pushed the boundaries and in so doing helped redefine them.

Second, the tempered radical should accept the importance of "local, spontaneous, authentic action" (Meyerson and Scully, 1995). Although these actions are generally less strategic than small wins, the direct expressions of beliefs, feelings, and identities can counter the pressures of co-optation and help the tempered radical sustain her ambivalence. In short, spontaneous action enables the tempered radical to express her anger, the fuel of her dissent, and channel the expressions of her values and beliefs. These actions enable her to sustain her sense of self, and also serve as the seeds of change by pushing outward the boundaries of what is normal, expected, and appropriate.

Patricia Donaldson,[9] senior manager of a technical division of a fast-growing software company, had been steadily promoted up through the ranks. Donaldson was the only woman at this level of management, and she stood out. Because her male peers,

---

[8]This section is a direct application of Meyerson and Scully (1995).
[9]Name has been changed to respect the privacy of the individual.

particularly the most influential ones, were loud and aggressive, meetings with them were like shouting contests.

At one meeting, one of the more senior executives asked Donaldson for her opinion. After she began to speak, the men interrupted and argued among themselves. Patricia stepped in this time, and said, "Excuse me, if we want to get some work done we can start to listen to each other, else I'm not going to waste my time here."

Silence followed this statement and Donaldson proceeded to calmly outline her thoughts on the topic. Afterward, the president thanked her for her courage and convictions and promised that from now on the meetings would be different. He would take personal responsibility for running the meetings and enforcing new norms of behavior. To her surprise, many of the other men at the meeting thanked her and admitted that they too hated these shouting matches, found them to be a waste of time, and, in the words of one man were just about "the bullshit of testosterone."

Donaldson's steady refusal to participate, her diligent preparation, and her carefully chosen statement reflected who she was, but they also were asserted in a way that allowed people to reflect on the implications of how they were behaving. In so doing, she created a wedge, an opening that begged for new ways of doing things.

Third, the tempered radical should actively construct, maintain, and nurture relationships with a spectrum of people. Different, even conflicting, communities can support a tempered radical and serve as a touchstone for each of her identities. Affiliations with organizational insiders, including more established insiders, can be extraordinarily important. These insiders forge other connections and provide access to resources: They can also help her judge just how far she can push and just how much she must temper herself to both be heard and remain legitimate. Determining the boundaries of what is possible can be a great challenge, and established organizational insiders can provide valuable information to inform these judgments.

At the same time, affiliations with outsiders—either those who represent the more radical side of one's identity or those who represent one's race, ethnicity, sexual orientation, or gender—are also crucial. These affiliations nurture the tempered radical's soul. They serve as the touchstone of her identity as an outsider. The greater the forces of co-optation, the more important it is for tempered radicals to hold strong to these relationships. Organizations may pressure the tempered radical to let go of these relationships and affiliations, but the stronger the pressure, the greater her need to hold on to them. In general, affiliations with both insiders *and* outsiders are important both to maintain one's ambivalent identification and also to sustain one's radical change agenda.

Fourth, professional women can approach conflicts and affronts to their authenticity—even small conflicts and affronts that are apparent only to the tempered radical—as opportunities for negotiation (Meyerson, forthcoming). A negotiation perspective, in which the tempered radical depersonalizes seemingly personal threats, enables her to work with her feelings rather than being controlled by them. This perspective presumes that different interests and perspectives exist in contest with one another. Although some of differences are explicit in a negotiation, many are implicit and hidden, even to those engaged in the negotiation.

By viewing everyday struggles and personal tests of conformity and fit as topics for negotiation, the tempered radical introduces a new set of questions and opens up possibilities for action. Instead of wasting her energy taking the conflict personally, she begins to ask productive questions: "What is negotiable and what is nonnegotiable to me?" "What is my desired end-state?" "What concessions can I make, and what should I expect in return?" "What are the interests and needs of the other party, and how can they be satisfied in ways that don't threaten my integrity and authenticity?"

These four strategies are strategies to maintain one's authenticity, and they are strategies of asserting change. They are not radical approaches. They are approaches designed for the professional woman who wants to remain engaged and successful in her organization without compromising her sense of self, her beliefs, and even her hopes for change.

THE CHANGE AGENT CHALLENGE

Women who work in predominantly male professional environments are regularly faced with situations that seem to impose a choice about fitting in and belonging or sticking up for one's own values and perspectives and becoming a deviant outsider. This is not a pleasant choice. Consequently, many women opt out, and move on from traditional organizations, looking for a situation where the compromises to their sense of self are not so large.

We have suggested the choice needn't be so "either-or" and that women can find a way to work and succeed within traditional male cultures *and* express their values and beliefs. Some women can even effect change as they challenge the status quo.

We are not suggesting that the challenges confronted by tempered radicals are easy ones. The challenges of sustaining an ambivalent stance towards one's employing organization—being both insider and outsider—can be daunting. Yet the women who do manage to find ways to sustain their dual identities, whether through the strategies we have suggested or through their own, have found a place for themselves in organizations where they can be themselves and be effective. Intentionally or not, these tempered radicals have become important agents of change in their organizations.

SUMMARY OF KEY POINTS

The tempered radical is an individual who identifies with and is committed to her organization and also a cause, community, or ideology that is fundamentally at odds with the dominant culture of that organization.

Tempered radicalism is a strategy to remain authentic, true to one's personal values and identities, and at the same time pursue one's desire to succeed within a traditionally masculine environment.

Ambivalence is not a source of hesitation and uncertainty for the tempered radical; instead it is a source of strength that allows the expression of her dual identities simultaneously. Ambivalence does produce certain challenges, however, which must be recognized and addressed for the ambivalence to be sustained.

Four strategies exist for the tempered radical to maintain her ambivalence and assert change: (1) recognize the importance of small wins; (2) accept the importance of local, spontaneous, authentic action; (3) affiliate with a spectrum of people who reflect both parts of her identity; and (4) approach conflicts to her authenticity as opportunities for negotiation.

Discussion Questions

1. Does a woman have to be a tempered radical to succeed within established organizations? What are the costs and benefits of being an untempered radical? What

are the costs and benefits of accepting the status quo?

2. Has the increasing number of women professionals in the workplace made it easier for other women professionals to advocate for change, more tempting to accept the status quo, or both?

3. What role do nontraditional, alternative work arrangements and environments play in the life of the tempered radical? Do they advance the interests of women or not? In what ways?

Issues to Debate

Should we be teaching young women to become tempered radicals? Should men, too, pursue these strategies?

Case Analysis — *The "Tournament"*

Lisa was hired to run the software group of the XYZ division. Her background is impeccable—two electrical engineering degrees from MIT, experience in basic research, and managerial experience running a group at the Department of Defense (DOD). Soon after she began to consider making a move from the DOD, she had several attractive offers lined up. Boeing was lucky to recruit her.

Lisa has risen quickly to a management position and now the game is a bit different. Although her engineering skills are still important, what seems to matter is her willingness and ability to act like a manager, as her boss recently told her. She hates to attend staff meetings or department retreats. These meetings seem to her like tournaments where her peers, almost all of whom are men, compete for who can talk the most and the loudest. In addition, she has always tried hard to give credit and exposure to her subordinates and is uncomfortable self-promoting. Yet, this is clearly not the way to get ahead in this organization. She wonders whether she will make it here. ■

Questions

1. Give examples of advantages in a fitting-in strategy for Lisa; for Lisa's company? What are the disadvantages for Lisa; for Lisa's company?

2. Give examples of tempered radical strategies (these need not be limited to strategies described in chapter). Describe some advantages for Lisa and for Lisa's company. What are some disadvantages for Lisa; for Lisa's company?

References and Suggested Readings

Bateson, M. C. (1990) *Composing a life: Life as a work in progress.* New York: Penguin.

Bell, E. L. (1990). The bi-cultural life experiences of career oriented black women. *Journal of Organization Behavior, 11,* 459–477.

Bell, E. L., Meyerson, D., Nkomo, S. M., and Scully, M. (1998). Tempered radicalism revisited: Making sense of black women's enactment and white women's silences. Working Paper. Center for Gender and Organizations. Simmons Graduate School of Management, Boston, MA.

Bell E. L., and Nkomo, S. M. (1998). *Our separate ways: Black and white women's success in corporate America.* Unpublished manuscript.

Conway, J. K. (1998). *When memory speaks: Reflections on autobiography.* New York: Knopf.

Fowlkes, D. (1992). *White political women: Paths from privilege to empowerment.* Knoxville, TN: University of Tennessee Press.

Lorde, A. (1984). *Sister outsider.* Trumansburg, NY: The Crossing Press.

Martin, J., and Meyerson, D. E. (1998). Women and power: Conformity, resistance, and disorganized coaction. In R. Kramer and M. Neale (Eds.), *Power and influence in organizations: Structures and processes* (pp. 311–348). Thousand Oaks, CA: Sage.

Martin, J., and Meyerson, D. E. (1997). Executive women at link.com. Harvard Business School Case Publishing.

Meyerson, D. (forthcoming). *Standing out and standing up in organizations: Tempered radicalism as a way to survive, thrive, and make change in organizations.* Harvard Business School Press, Cambridge, MA.

Meyerson, D. E., and Scully, M. A. (1995). Tempered radicalism and the politics of ambivalence and change. *Organization Science, 6* (5): 585–600.

Rhode, D. L. (1988). Perspectives on professional women. *Stanford Law Review, 40,* 1163.

Sheehy, G. (1995). *New Passages: Mapping Your Life Across Time.* New York, Random House.

Stan, A. M. (1995, September/October). Frances Kissling: Making the Vatican Sweat. *Ms.,* 40–43.

Weick, K. (1984). Small wins: Redefining the scale of social problems. *American Psychologist, 39,* 40–49.

CHAPTER

Lessons from the Trenches

13

Dayle M. Smith

Chapter Overview

Here's a perplexing question: Given the continuing disparity in women's pay versus men's as well as women's organizational power versus men's, why have so many women remained on the sidelines of issues of equality and fairness? Would men be similarly unengaged if the gender roles were reversed?

I believe that many, perhaps most, women remain casual spectators from a distance because they feel no personal identification with or allegiance to the current "teams" on the playing field of these great social and economic issues. The popular press (including women's magazines) and academic publishers regularly advance oversimplified, single-minded versions of what women experience in business life. The resulting tussle of rhetoric provides good copy but poor verisimilitude to day-to-day workplace experiences.

In effect, a typical single-position publication or TV/radio "documentary" carefully excludes any woman's voice that contradicts its overriding thesis. A book asserting the biasing influence in companies of the "good old boys' club" makes no room for the woman executive who pays sincere tribute to one or more male mentors who helped her achieve her leadership goals. An article on a woman's rightful expectation of balanced work and family responsibilities neatly excises the unapologetic testimony of some women leaders who say that children and partners would have hindered their rise to corporate power. A TV report describing the glass ceiling (that invisible barrier that apparently unperceptive women and other minorities keep bumping up against) excludes the perspective of shrewd women adept at reading the politics of their organizations and responding strategically.

Women do not and should not trust this "Cliff's Notes" version of their business experience. Certainly the dozens of women leaders interviewed for this book do not speak with one voice or from one perspective. They proclaim, above all, that the modern woman's experience in the business world is complex. And it is that very complexity that summary-seekers want to deny. Eager for the headline, they are impatient with the full story.

To deal with the actual complexity of women at work, we must first welcome it in our discourse. Therefore, this chapter like preceding chapters gives voice and example not only to mainstream, familiar perspectives but also to heresies—those whispered admissions of prominent women in their most casual moments. Whatever our political or social agendas, it is important to attend to both what we want and don't want to hear. For example, the woman leader who doesn't confirm our preferred hypothesis should not be dismissed as a gender traitor or anomaly but instead should be included as part of the total picture of women in the workplace.

Next, we should learn from the full range of experiences we uncover. The woman leader who has made the most of male mentorship has valuable lessons to teach, as does the "lone woman leader" (sometimes mischaracterized as a sister-killing Queen Bee) in a male-dominated company. If we have made one central miscalculation in the past decade of literature about and often by women in business, it is the mistake of making *victimhood* the press pass that leads to credibility and an open public microphone. Even granting a business world replete with bias, anyone after Darwin must concede that *survivors* have important experiences to share.

Finally, we must integrate competing and often conflicting versions of women's rise to business leadership into a model that reflects complex truth rather than simplistic propaganda. Only then will real women in the workplace find their own experiences fairly represented, along with alternative paths they may want to explore. In these pages women should be able to find themselves in relation to the experiences of other women. To encourage that process, consider several final summary questions, as addressed by prominent women leaders:

Learning Objectives

■ To gain personal and strategic advice from a broad spectrum of women leaders

■ To address a number of questions regarding the often conflicting advice from leaders and the choices they have made

■ To integrate leadership strategy with your own personal values in determining the career path you ultimately pursue

CAN WOMEN LEADERS HAVE IT ALL?

Ann Spector Lief, Spec's Music

Ann Spector Lief was CEO of Spec's Music, a specialty music retailer in Florida and Puerto Rico, with more than 55 stores, which merged in 1998 with Camelot Music Holdings, Inc., the nation's third largest mall-based music retailer and a publicly held company. Following the merger, Ann stayed on as a consultant to the business in which she literally grew up, which was founded by her father in 1948. "Since I was twelve years old," she says, "I've worked in this family business atmosphere."

She reflects not only on her own experience, but also on that of the Committee of 200, a group of women CEOs of companies exceeding $10 million in valuation. Contrary to the popular notion that work/life balance somehow comes with "the package" for talented women leaders, Ann comments that "you can't have it all. You're working on a balance between work and the rest of your life all the time. As a CEO, my work came first, my daughter second, and my husband third. Sometimes you don't feel very good about that. But you do the best you can. I was personally fortunate because everyone in my family was incredibly supportive of my efforts."

Her husband is a vice president in the company, and they have been married 23 years. She observes of the Committee of 200 that "members are either divorced or have very supportive husbands," among whom she includes her own husband. When she looks back over the past 24 years, she says she would not trade what she has for a less challenging lifestyle. "I hope talented women in organizations don't back off from the challenge of leadership. They have to keep in mind that they have much to offer." Besides, she points out, "interesting parents make interesting kids. A sometimes hectic life doesn't mean that you're a poor parent." One of her most important tools for trying to achieve work/life balance, says Ann, was "control of my own calendar."

She has advice for rising leaders. "Telling the truth, not promising more than you can deliver, is extremely important. It takes a lifetime to build a reputation, but only 10 seconds to lose it." A leader's strength and resiliency comes from "surviving the tough times. People respect the fact that you've gone through adversity. You're a more valuable leader because you've faced difficult challenges." Her own most trying period of adversity came during the severe slowdown experienced across the music industry, until the release of *Titanic* brought customers flooding back to their music stores. Another difficult time was literally surviving Hurricane Andrew in the Florida area. "We saw we could be losing everything and we learned to reach out to each other."

With specific reference to women leaders, she advises against being too egocentric in always claiming personal credit for performance. "What matters is that the job gets done. Who gets credit is often irrelevant. You can't be ego-involved in every act. It's vital to put the business first, and be perceived that way by others."

What does leadership itself mean to Ann? "It's about motivating other people. It's a team-effort approach, sharing the work, and not feeling that I somehow do it all. It means putting customers first, getting the message out, and recognizing the contributions of other people. My own management team at Spec's is full of women—it just turned out that way. When I am leading I am more apt to give women a chance, but it is unconscious on my part."

Ann places high value in maintaining strong ethics as a leader. "There's a perceived lack of ethics in the music industry generally. Within Spec's, our management has consistently high ethical standards. We were attractive to Camelot [the acquiring firm] for merger in part for that quality."

WHAT DOES IT TAKE TO BE SUCCESSFUL?

Kim Polese, Marimba, Inc.

Kim Polese is CEO of Marimba, one of the leading software companies in Silicon Valley. As a child she was fascinated with biophysics and computer science and entered science fairs regularly. Educated at the University of California, Berkeley, and the University of Washington, she brings a strong technology background to her work. When she graduated from college, she was attracted to the fast-paced and creative atmosphere of Silicon Valley because, as she says, "I wanted to do cool stuff." She was able to move easily from company to company because of her skills with object-oriented technology.

When the "hot area" of artificial intelligence took a plunge for most companies in the late 1980s, Kim saw the effects of intellectual enthusiasm that wasn't supported by solid business expertise. "I learned from that experience that 'cool stuff' was not enough without the business side." She learned that business side at Sun Microsystems, where she was able to blend the technical aspects with product development and marketing. She worked with industry trends, clients, and package branding. She says she thrived in this environment because she was able to use her creativity and imagination to "bring complex technology to exciting people."

Her single best stroke of fortune was being selected at Sun as a member of the product development team for the computer language, Java. "It took off like wildfire and caught the imagination of the industry." By the end of 1995 she says, "I had exceeded all my challenges. I had been challenged beyond my wildest imagination and I was ready for something new outside of Sun." So she and three other engineers used the Java platform to start Marimba, a billion-dollar company with 130 employees, which she continues to lead.

"We were basically at the right place at the right time working on a great product. We were lucky we had an incredibly talented team. People who shared our values and commitment joined us."

At the same time Marimba did much to create its own luck. "We always tried to stay just a couple of steps ahead of the market. Internally, we lived the concept of 'team.' We were an exciting place to be and had a sense of creating the future." The company's growth, and her growth as a leader, was not uniformly smooth. "Things happened organically," Kim says. "It's about learning and stumbling and building confidence all at once—taking on different roles and different kinds of jobs. Even if you don't use that experience directly, it becomes part of your brain as a leader and it helps you understand other team members' perspectives."

Kim reflects on what she learned during the rapid growth of Marimba. "First," she says, "we hired people who shared our values. We screened out what I call 'the cowboys,' men or women who care more about their ego satisfaction than reaching company goals." In addition, she believes that a leader "must have interaction one-on-one with everyone in the company, not just with your team of executive vice presidents." As the company grew, she realized she no longer knew all her employees. She started a program called Lunch with Kim, inviting employees from all levels of the company to listen to their perceptions of "where we are and where we're going as a company." She continues that theme of communication throughout the company with her Roundtable Lunches, where a dozen or so people get together to talk about the company and especially its "burning issues." "Everyone needs to know the company direction, the trend, and the market at every level of the company."

Women leaders, Kim points out, are not necessarily "consensus decision makers at all times. You have to be comfortable steering the ship. Balance is key between consensus-building versus taking decisive action."

In her industry, Kim says, "you have to keep putting your head out there to gather perspective on the marketplace, search out and synthesize information that helps you anticipate trends and drive the company. I do this by having regular lunches and dinners with well-connected, smart people in the industry. I have my notebook right at hand."

"My own personal breakthrough as a leader is recognizing that everyone is making it up as they go along and continuously learning. You have to have your antenna up, your notebook open to jot down ideas. You're asking questions, always learning, listening, and staying one step ahead. You have to not be afraid of what you don't know. Go ahead and learn. Talk with smart people, read, take your best guess, and take a chance."

Looking back, she didn't realize how important public speaking skills would become for her in her role as company leader. Whether in talking to customers, industry gatherings, or the media, "I represent the company and my 'must-haves' are depth, substance, and credibility."

Concerning the role of gender in leadership and interpersonal relations, she shares, "it just doesn't register with me. I don't think about it. I'm topically focused. You can't ignore, of course, the fact that one of the few leaders around the table happens to be a women. Gender may be the cause of some additional attention, but it isn't the reason for sustained attention." She recognizes that stereotypes about women exist in business but feels that "they are based on ignorance. When I encounter stereotypes, I keep my head down and execute. I built a great company and a team to deliver and hope the comments fade away. Gender issues have not held me back, but neither have they propelled me forward."

HOW DO YOU MANAGE YOUR OWN CAREER DEVELOPMENT?

Gail Omahana, Landau, Omahana & Tucker

Gail Omahana is senior partner and founder of Landau, Omahana & Tucker, a major law firm based in Chicago with 86 attorneys and 11 offices. She is married to Byron Landau, also a senior partner. "Byron became my husband and partner and we blended children into our life. I had worked with him earlier and admired his tenacity. Clients admired his magnetism and rapport. We have rarely agreed on management issues. We came to a philosophy. I usually take the counterposition because I like to throw in alternatives. I demonstrate my independence in the firm and express it. As a result, others think of us as separate individuals, not clones."

Boundaries are necessary to separate worklife from personal life. "Over the past 10 years we've had a rule we operate by. At a certain time we stop talking about business and turn it off. We really like each other and are friends first. Occasionally we can violate the rule and, in our firm, it can be a benefit. We can travel together, coordinating business travel. Working together can be enriching for the marriage."

Gail says that she "has never felt any special challenges as a woman. I work as hard as anyone else and have not experienced harassment. Some older judges call you 'honey' or 'sweetheart' but you dismiss it as not demeaning, but as a cultural stereotype that's their problem, not yours. In fact, in my business and specialty area, being a woman has been an enormous advantage. There's been a demand for diversity and many of my jobs come from hospital boards, minorities, and women clients."

The glass ceiling is not an issue in her firm. "We're a young firm and have demonstrated that we want women in the firm. You can earn as much as in other firms and be fully accepted. That's the orientation of the firm." She recognizes, however, that glass ceilings are an issue in other firms lacking that perspective.

Gail has an unusual approach to career development. "Sometimes you need to take your focus off your career to truly develop it and yourself. Once you accept you're on track and doing what you want to do, just do it. Look to your support channels, then concentrate on what's important in life: marriage, community, kids, pro bono work, networking, fundraising, and the rest. When your focus is off the day-to-day stresses of business, you just naturally become the best developed person you can be. As I look back over the last 17 years of my career, those are the things that have counted. To be frank, I didn't always feel this way. But I've changed my view as I have changed and my environment has changed."

She sees others in the process of similar change and redirection. "Last week a young female partner who is adamantly pro-career just announced she would stay at home. It did bother me a bit because she had so much potential. Yet I realized that younger women are not on a time treadmill. They can step off the merry-go-around and the career will still be there if they have the confidence to come back. That would have been foolish early in my career, but to their credit they can take braver steps now, thanks to societal changes."

As for differences between male and female leaders, Gail has found that women "can be more savvy at organization and detail, while men may overlook detail just to finish the job. But these different styles are symbiotic. We need synergy between both styles."

Technology plays an important role in Gail's company as a leadership tool. "Our department of MIS is phenomenal and has been instrumental in helping us practice law and achieve high levels of success." An example of how technology aids Gail's team is "the flexibility we can offer. A young woman attorney with three young children may not have to sit at a desk from 8 to 6 so long as we can network by computer."

HOW DO WOMEN COPE WITH FAMILY STRESSES?

Bettye Martin Musham, Gear Holdings

Bettye Martin Musham is CEO of Gear Holdings, a $400 million company with 60 employees in the retail home fashion industry located in New York City. Gear's employee family is almost entirely made up of women except for the chairman of the board and a maintenance man. As such, the company is a particularly good environment to observe how women deal with family stresses that impinge on worklife—and, just as important, how women leaders define the boundaries between family concerns and work issues.

Bettye has strong feelings about the line between work responsibilities and home responsibilities. "Women sometimes think they have a right to play 'home' at work. They need to separate home, work, and family. Things happen in people's lives. Some good managers just can't handle personal life and it gets in the way of their work performance. Balance is hard. It's one of the biggest issues for women. They get the majority of home responsibilities put on their shoulders, and understandably single moms in particular are torn between what they owe to family and what [they owe] to work."

"Women have the financial odds stacked against them. They're on the short end of the earnings spectrum, yet they must spend a lot of money for quality day care. And that's a necessity. If you work, you have to be able to depend on quality day care and be willing to pay for it."

"There certainly is a glass ceiling," says Bettye, "and I don't know how to get around it until women take responsibility for their own selves and their careers. You fight to get around the glass ceiling, you co-opt it. For example, it's not a matter of being polite; you need to be a leader. Being aggressive may be necessary. Stay alert and know where to pick your spots."

"Networking is essential for women and you have to know how to share your success as well as your problems. Be generous with your time and help pull up other women."

Bettye's leadership philosophy is straightforward, "Not everyone has to be a leader; you don't have to be a leader to be successful. If you choose to be a leader, you have to have a passion for it and spend a lot of time doing it—often to the exclusion of other things you could be doing outside work. You have to know yourself and what you really want to do. The biggest challenge for a leader is motivating other people and keeping them on track. Tell people what's expected, and if they don't do it, replace them."

Her general advice for leaders includes "being visionary, looking ahead to see what's needed to create opportunity. Also see what's not there, what's missing that you may be able to provide. Stay focused, take risks, and be disciplined. You can speed your own development by gravitating to people who are or are going to be winners. Those are the people you can learn from. Identify who's going to teach you something. Life isn't a team experience. You need to make your own way and manage the new boundaries that emerge."

ARE THERE HOLES IN THE GLASS CEILING?

Christina Morgan, Hambrecht & Quist

Christina Morgan is managing director at Investment Banking, Hambrecht & Quist (HQ). With a technical background from Memorex and Intel, she "took a personal risk" by starting as a financial analyst in investment banking and was quickly promoted to a senior research analyst specializing in software. She knew that the best investment bankers know the entire industry they serve, and because she had good relationships with CEOs in software companies, she focused on that area and, in the process, became a corporate finance person at Hambrecht & Quist. "HQ likes to throw you in the water and see if you swim," she says, "and that has been a great benefit to my career path."

For Christina, the glass ceiling hasn't been a factor. "In investment banking, the concern is with one thing: success. If you bring revenues in the doors—color, race, and gender don't matter. If you bring in the dollars, you can decide what you want to do next."

"The fact that I'm a female may give me an unfair advantage due to my 'scarcity' value. The redhead may be far more memorable than a zillion investment bankers who all look alike. Genetic dice just works that way. It's up to me not to screw it up."

"My experience is the antithesis to the glass ceiling in many industries. I know that women in many other industries seem to want to have their careers on their own terms. In investment banking, I work all the time—no children, no hobbies. It's all I do, but it's a fun industry. I don't feel a sense of loss. It's a single-dimension existence, but I don't feel deprived. I don't see balance as an issue. You do what you can do, and having a family is often not consistent with investment banking unless you have a partner who knows that 90 percent of your time will be spent on business. Players work their asses off."

"In many industries, you hear that expertise leads and knowledge is everything. But in my business everyone is incredibly smart. My clients are smart, dynamic, and creative. I literally hang out with those who are changing the world. You have to be fast, quick, smart, and lucky and manage people who know that. In my business, leadership development happens by apprenticeship: come along, watch me do it, then you can do it. That's how leadership works."

Her advice for others? "Don't be afraid of things that lead to unconstructive behavior. Stop worrying about others. Focus on being constructive—what can be done to move the ball down the field. Act like an owner, not the hired hand. If you help the project, people see you as a contributer and you get rewarded for that. Don't see the company as your enemy. Your competitors are your enemy. If you ever start to see your own company as your enemy, quit, and start your own company."

IS THERE A PLACE FOR THE HEART IN LEADERSHIP?

Dale Halton, Pepsi Cola Bottlers

Dale Halton is president and CEO of the first PepsiCo bottling company in the United States, which is based in Charlotte, North Carolina, and has more than 325 employees. She took the helm of the 92-year-old company in 1981, a transition she calls "an accident of birth." As the only grandchild, she inherited the job and the business. "Grandfather wanted the business to stay in the family," she explains.

The company was on the brink of bankruptcy when Dale took control. The company has since then experienced a rebirth, with profits up a cumulative 400 percent and case volume increasing 250 percent. Dale is quick to share that success. She says, "The right stuff to run this business was already in place. I was able to persuade a dear friend to stay on as top manager, and he oversees the day-to-day operations."

Halton knew that her first task as CEO was to see the company through its crisis to profitability. But the more profitable the company became the more she wanted to give back to the employees. "They make you what you are," she says, "and they deserve rewards for that." The company has a standing in the community that reflects its commitment to employees. Executive vice president Darrell Holland says that strong employee commitment has evolved into the company's three major goals, "(1) run a company that is fair and considerate of its employees' needs; (2) run a company that produces a product that meets the public's needs; and (3) take some of those profits and apply them back into our people and the community. And that is what we do every day."

The company has established a foundation through which 10 percent of profits are donated to charity. Halton says, "It's really nice to be able to give monetarily in amounts that can do something. We do a lot with the arts also, but I would say the largest percentage goes to women, children, and education."

Halton has forged her career in a region where women's progress has been slow. "It wasn't until 1981 that Charlotte, North Carolina, realized women could be more than teachers and nurses," she notes humorously. "Only two other women in Charlotte ran major businesses, and the boards in town were looking for women. I was green, but learned to punt. At first when I showed up at board meetings, I got the feeling people were saying, 'The secretary's not supposed to be here' or 'Get me coffee.' It wasn't easy to get accepted, but that's the South. Wives of other board members were not accepting, but that's not my problem."

"There weren't a lot of women around in 1981 for me to talk with. I have spoken with many young women since then and it bugs me that they feel that they have to dress like men. They should be proud to be women and feel comfortable in that. My advice is not to act and look like a man in order to succeed. We women think more humanely and from the heart. We have a lot to bring to the table with these sensitivities."

"The heart of leadership is to be fair and honest with others and with yourself. Things can be done with concern for the person, being gentle and not demeaning to others in the workplace. Everyone in the company knows they can come to me if they wish, but I respect other people's jobs and I try to send people in the right direction."

"As for attitudes toward women, I vividly remember attending a national softdrink meeting. We'd stop at a booth and they would talk to my husband, not me. I would look at the equipment and my husband would say, 'I'm not the bottler. Talk to my wife.' They had a tendency to be pushy and arrogant, so I would drop my business card in their bowl and walk away. Later they would see that the woman was the president."

"The glass ceiling is not an issue in my company. We have quite a few women leaders in the business: controller, corporate secretary, vice president of human resources, the head of our fountain department, and so on. Color or gender is just not an issue. There are certain areas where women are best for the job, and they get it."

WHAT'S THE RIGHT RECIPE FOR LEADERSHIP?

Pamela Lopkar, QAD, Inc.

Pamela Lopkar is CEO of QAD, a southern California software development firm. She is married, with two children, 12 and 14 years old. Beginning with a technical background, she saw an opportunity to develop a unique product and started her company around it. Venture capital was scarce, so she rolled up her sleeves, maxed out her credit cards, and mortgaged her home to the hilt. She gave herself a two-year time frame to try to make a success of her venture.

"My role models for leadership are not particular people. Rather, I look toward companies as my role models. For example, Hewlett Packard is excellent at creating excellent products. IBM can market and sell. These are the qualities I try to understand and imitate."

"There are always going to be barriers and challenges in any business," she says, "and you have to be prepared to make tough choices. Knowledge and capability is everything. The technical area is such a melting pot because, with expertise being so much in demand, you can't afford to hire on the basis of race or gender."

"My biggest contribution to leadership in my company is vision. When something excites me, I can communicate that vision, articulate it down to the employees clearly and concisely, and get them excited. But leadership is really about multiple-person participation, where you need four components: entrepreneurial vision, people, administration (including finance), and project management/operations. Few people have all four of these—maybe you have one or two—and you have to have a team to ensure all four."

Her advice for rising women leaders: "Find the easiest route. Some women feel that 'looking at me as a woman' isn't fair. Forget that garbage and go someplace where you feel successful. It's not worth fighting the 'didn't I get the job because I'm a woman?' battle. Find firms where the focus is on the business."

As for work/life balance, it has been Pamela's experience that "work, career, self, and community all require careful balancing. Folks who ignore three of these to focus just on career cannot be as good at work. It's important to keep in tune with yourself and family as well as to be involved in your community. Balancing these factors promotes employee satisfaction, company hiring, and a sense of belonging. My own personal goal is to keep these four aspects fresh in my attention throughout the year."

"In balancing our work/family life, my husband and I have guidelines we adhere to. One of us is always home for dinner by 6:30. We coordinate schedules. We have actively planned family Sundays, and we take a two-week vacation together each year. It works for the kids and it works for us if we tell them the rules and we follow it. If there's a change we tell them in advance. We don't let ourselves make up last minute excuses."

"Because of my own experience relying on others to fill out my leadership abilities, the entire company has come to emphasize the multiple-person model of leadership, especially at the project level. The load is never entirely on one person's shoulders."

Reflecting on differences in style between men and women in her company, Pamela observes that "women's styles tend to be more people oriented and consensus seeking, whereas some men are entrenched in the old style of being more authoritative. We need to have a blend of both. Sometimes you have to put a stake in the ground and make a decision. You have to learn to set aside your ego to trust cross-functional teams to get the work done."

WHAT IS THE RIGHT STUFF FOR LEADERSHIP?

Marcy Syms, Syms, Inc.

Marcy Syms is CEO of Syms Corporation in Secaucus, New Jersey. The company, with more than 3,000 employees and $360 million in sales in 1998, operates a chain of 41 off-price designer and brand-name apparel stores located throughout the Northeastern and Middle Atlantic regions, the Midwest, Southeast, and Southwest. Their 5-year plan includes opening 19 new stores by 2001. The business was started by her father in 1959. Growing up in the business, Marcy saw what it would take to be a successful business leader—14 to 16 hours per day, 7 days a week. She wasn't sure she wanted that workload, so she explored various career options. With a bachelor's in English literature and a master's in communication and public relations, she tried radio and television work as well as media sales. She returned to New York to work full time for her father, eventually becoming one of the youngest female presidents of a NYSE-listed company when the company went public in 1983. She is the author of *Mind Your Own Business—And Keep It in the Family* (MasterMedia, Ltd., 1992).

"For me, it is all consuming to be a leader during major growth," says Marcy, "especially when going from a small to a midsized company. Leadership can include being mother, teacher, coach, and dictator—and modulating all aspects according to the needs of the business at that moment." Underlying that philosophy are Marcy's three necessities for leadership success: "First, a leader needs stamina. Without that, you don't have energy to bring to the business. Second, you need to know where you are going, in other words, have vision or passion. It doesn't have to be fancy, but it does have to be clear. Finally, you must make the vision understood to everyone you want to carry along with you on the venture."

Her biggest challenge as a leader and the point she emphasizes most is "recognizing how important it is to be understood. Communicating clearly is not easy. You think you know what you are saying, but that's not necessarily what's being heard. You must elicit responses from people to determine that they really understand."

Marcy admits the presence of a glass ceiling, which is evident not only in companies "but in Congress as well. In the boardroom there's a wonderful journey ahead with work to do for women." But Marcy does not see networking and mentoring as useful ways to break the glass ceiling. "Those are natural parts of being successful. It will make the career more pleasant, but is no guarantee that you can break through glass ceilings. For that to happen, culture and society have to have a broader perspective and adapt to women's status." In her business experience, "expertise and experience translate as power, and in the long run they win the day."

Early in her career she felt the demands of motherhood would interfere with her work goals. She put motherhood on hold. "Some women can do it, but I recognized that I couldn't, at least then. Now I have an 12-year-old son. My advice would be, 'Know thyself.' You can achieve your personal goals in stages. Timing is all."

As an entrepreneur, her most important lesson learned is "check your ego by the door. Sharing accomplishments and credit is far more powerful than collecting trophies."

ARE WOMEN THEIR OWN WORST ENEMY?

Gail Koff, Jacoby & Meyers

Gail Koff joined Jacoby & Meyers, now a nationwide law firm, as a founding partner when they went from a small firm to national prominence. Building the firm, she says, "was a real roller coaster. You have to have a vision to keep the business going, but financing the business can be tricky because in a law firm you can't have outside investors. Vision should be from the heart. You need to believe in what you are doing and care about it. Find really good people, know your strengths, and fill in with other people because you do not know everything. Then motivate people toward that common vision."

"One of the things I've learned about myself," says Gail, "is that we can be harder on ourselves as women than men can be." She recalls an article in *Fortune* about Schick testing razors: "When a man cuts himself, he throws away the razor. When a women cuts herself, she blames herself." "We can be our own worst enemies. For example, when we were first expanding the firm, I thought we were making a lot of mistakes. But the two guys, Jacoby & Meyers, thought we were doing just fine."

"Here's an example of personal lack of confidence. For years I would be in a meeting and get interrupted and let that happen. But I've been through a lot now. When Jacoby died a few years ago, we were in a tough situation and I had to save the firm. This gave me the confidence I should have had earlier, before I got talked out of many things. Now I am clearer about stating my position. I am open to others' points of view, but I am not afraid to say what I think. The most significant challenge I got over was the 'please-like-me' syndrome."

In terms of work-family balance, Koff describes her experiences. "As the mother of three children, there wasn't a day I left home when I didn't feel torn. It's definitely major role conflict. Because it's my own business I can create flexibility. But many women can't."

As for the glass ceiling, "it just doesn't exist at Jacoby & Meyers. Three out of our top five managers are women and some of our best attorneys are women. This environment has been supported not just during my leadership but by the two partners before me. But we were the entrepreneurs—the maverick law firm. We were the first to advertise (even on America OnLine now). We did things in the public's interest as opposed to the old stodgy firms trapped in the old culture."

"Mentoring isn't a conscious choice or duty for me—it's just what I do, a part of my management style." Gail sponsors young women's efforts in high school and college and works with the mentoring program within the Committee of 200.

Office politics are a reality everywhere, Gail admits, "but I just won't play. I probably wouldn't survive a corporate environment. I have much more inclusive concerns. My natural style is about building leaders."

Finally, Gail urges rising women leaders "to have different experiences, to see what interests you, then see what touches your heart. Try to do that consistently in all aspects of your life—with your business, your children, your friends. The way to be successful and happy in life requires speaking and acting from the heart."

SUMMARY OF KEY POINTS

In summary, these and the other women's voices from previous chapters make a number of salient points:

- Women lead differently.
- Women face unique challenges and barriers as they rise to leadership.
- Women leaders rely on networks, partnering, and mentoring.
- Women leaders often pay a large personal price for career advancement.
- Women leaders recognize that their styles of management tend to differ from styles used by male leaders.
- Women leaders admit the existence of a glass ceiling generally but have experienced it individually in widely differing ways.
- Women leaders tend to value a team approach to data gathering and decision making at the highest organizational levels.
- Women leaders make it a point to know one another; they draw strength and insight from one another's experience.
- Women leaders do not need to be loved in their organizations to be effective and professionally fulfilled.
- Women feel no intrinsic deficits or disadvantages because of their gender. Many women leaders feel that their gender has proven to be a career advantage.
- When compared to their male counterparts, women leaders do not take advantage of the perks of leadership and maintain the appearance of working longer, harder, and more visibly.
- Many women leaders resist being showcased for their gender as role models and prefer instead to "get back to work."
- Women leaders do not perceive their career success primarily as a financial achievement.
- Women leaders perceive no unique difficulty because of their gender in making tough business decisions, managing in times of crisis, and defending their organizations against threats.

These points outlined above capture the lessons to be learned from the leaders interviewed for this book. Clearly, the advice is varied and, often times, even contradictory. The insights and perspectives these leaders share, however, demonstrate one thing certainly—women can lead effectively. Looking toward the future, we can expect to continue the steady move away from the rhetoric of "women's issues" toward the reality of women's place, both in numbers and influence, at the highest levels of organizational leadership.

Index